Shakespearian Production

Wilson Knight as Timon. *Photo:* C. Sauerbrei

SHAKESPEARIAN PRODUCTION

with especial reference
to the Tragedies

by

G. WILSON KNIGHT

NORTHWESTERN UNIVERSITY PRESS

1964

First published in mcmlxiv
by Faber and Faber Limited
24 Russell Square, London, W.C.1
Printed in Great Britain

Published in the U.S.A. by Northwestern University Press

The early chapters originally published under the title *Principles of Shakespearian Production* by Messrs. Faber & Faber Ltd. in 1936 and re-issued by Penguin Books Ltd. in 1949.

To
the memory of
HERBERT BEERBOHM TREE
producer actor and writer
and of
his disciple
in the art of acting
LESLIE HARRIS

Contents

9

Contents

Illustrations

Preface to the Third Edition [1963]

For this republication in a third edition of my *Principles of Shakespearian Production* I have again added material, so that the present volume entitled '*Shakespearian Production*' is composed of layers reflecting a wide span of variously settled and changing opinion. Chapters I to V made the original book. Chapter VI and the first part of IX under the title 'The Professional Stage' were in the second, Penguin, edition published in 1949. Chapters VII, VIII, X and the Appendixes are new. I do not reprint the essay 'Drama and the University' from my Penguin Appendix (first published in *The University of Leeds Review*, June 1949), but some quotations from it are included in Chapter VIII. The extent and nature of these additions appear to justify the new and more comprehensive title.

I have tidied up details of faulty expression in my old text, and made some deletions, but where new sections or thoughts are added to old material they are dated. I did not include my account of *Timon of Athens*, here presented in Chapter VII, in the Penguin edition mainly, so far as I recall, because I still at that time had hopes of being given the opportunity of repeating it on a larger and more public scale.

Following the productions recorded in my original preface (pp. 21–4 below) my Toronto work included *The Winter's Tale* in 1936, *Antony and Cleopatra* in 1937 and *Timon of Athens* in the early part of 1940, together with revivals of *Hamlet*, for which I was joint-producer with Miss Frances Tolhurst, in 1938 and *Romeo and Juliet* in 1939; also *The Tempest* in 1938, directed by Miss Josephine Koenig (see p. 274 below); the two revivals presented by, and the others in association with, the Shakespeare Society of Toronto. These various presentations, though performed in the University area and relying largely on the University

13

for their audiences, were not in themselves university productions, nor was Hart House a University theatre, though both staff and students often took part. We drew widely on the acting strength of the city.

I am happy to hear from time to time good news from Mr. Raymond Card of the Shakespeare Society's activities, so recalling to memory my many friends in the Society, and their goodness to me. Among my Canadian correspondents I record my gratitude to Mr. and Mrs. Stafford Johnston, Miss Josephine Koenig and Mr. Leonard Parker for sending to me particulars of the new Festival Theatre at Stratford, Ontario.

My war-time composite of Shakespearian excerpts and lecture-commentary, given first in 1940 in collaboration with Miss Nancy Price at the Tavistock Theatre, London, was repeated at various centres about England, at one of which Cyril Maude was chairman, and culminated in a week at the Westminster Theatre in the summer of 1941, under the title *This Sceptred Isle*. For this production, though I had no acting support beyond off-stage voices, the late Henry Ainley returned from retirement to read some of my commentaries, as indeed I had heard him read the commentary of Hardy's *Dynasts* in Granville Barker's production at the Kingsway Theatre in 1914. At one performance we had the additional honour of a contribution by Sir John Martin Harvey. Among the most appreciative of those who attended were Sir Nigel and Lady Playfair, whose son Lyon was the Osric of my 1935 London *Hamlet*; and also Violet Vanbrugh, whom I had so admired (p. 51) as Lady Macbeth with Tree in 1911. The support of my mother and my brother did much to ease the anxieties of this ambitious and difficult year.

A facsimile of my programme of *This Sceptred Isle* is given on p. 315, but since the matter lies outside its range it is not covered by my present study. An outline has been given in *The Sovereign Flower* (264–5) and full particulars may be seen among my 'Dramatic Papers', the collection of programmes, pictures and press notices so excellently compiled by The Shakespeare Memorial Library of the Reference Library at Birmingham. At both the British Museum and the Birmingham Reference Library I have also lodged, under the title *A Royal Propaganda*, a typescript account of my difficulties in arranging this Westminster Theatre production, wherein I pay my tribute to the help and encouragement of Miss Margot Davies, without which the endeavour could scarcely have seen fruition. To the Librarian Mr. V. H. Woods, and to the staff of the Birmingham Reference Library, I am very grateful.

Owing to the war I was unable to return to the University of Toronto. At Stowe, where I taught from 1941 until 1946, I had the opportunity of producing *Macbeth* and playing the parts of the Madman in Masefield's *Good Friday* and the Inquisitor in Shaw's *Saint Joan* in productions by Mr. A. A. Dams. For the first the setting was the School Chapel, admirable for the purpose; and the speaking and acting of the Madman's central speech I look back upon as among the most rewarding of my stage experiences.[1]

At the University of Leeds, after being appointed there in 1946 at the instigation of Professor Bonamy Dobrée to inaugurate a course on World Drama and take an active interest in the Leeds University Union Theatre Group, I have been peculiarly fortunate. I remain deeply indebted to the Theatre Group, under whose auspices I produced Louis MacNeice's translation of the *Agamemnon* of Aeschylus in 1946 and Professor Kenneth Muir's translation of Racine's *Athalie* in 1947;[2] repeated *Timon of Athens* in 1948; and had the privilege of playing in *Othello* and *The Merchant of Venice*, produced respectively by Mr. Arthur Creedy and Mr. Frederick May, in 1955 and 1960. I am also indebted to the Staff Dramatic Society of the University, whose *King Lear*, presented in collaboration with the Theatre Group and produced by Mr. John Boorman in 1951, was an event with which I feel it an honour to have been associated. Of the forbearance, sympathy and encouragement of these three producers I am deeply sensible.

I record my gratitude for their gracious welcome of my attempts to the late Hon. and Revd. Canon H. J. Cody as University President and to the Revd. Canon F. H. Cosgrave as Provost of Trinity College, in the University of Toronto; and to Sir Charles Morris as Vice-Chancellor of the University of Leeds, and to Lady Morris; and to Professor Dobrée; and to all, Staff and Students, at both universities—and perhaps especially to so

---

[1] For my tribute to the Shakespearian quality, under performance, of this speech, see *The Golden Labyrinth*, 335.

[2] Subsequently included with other strongly dramatic translations in his *Jean Racine, Five Plays* (U.S.A., Mermaid Dramabook; London, MacGibbon & Kee).

authoritative a Shakespearian as Prof. R. S. Knox of Toronto —who have accepted my histrionic inadequacies and encouraged my pretensions; among them the many students of the Leeds University Union Theatre Group of which for a number of years I had the honour to be President. I remember words of sympathy and kindness, when they were much needed, from the staff of Hart House Theatre, and from Miss Ruth Playter. I recognize the lift given to my stage activities by the dramatic critics of the Toronto press and of Leeds; and also by the critic of *The Times*, Mr. Ivor Brown of *The Observer*, and Mr. C. B. Purdom, all of whom lent me confidence during the run of *This Sceptred Isle*; and by the two distinguished Patrons of that adventure; and by Mr. Richard Courtney, Mr. Frederick May, Mr. Robin Skelton, Mr. Roy Walker and Mr. Kenneth Young, who have written generously of my stage work. I have been grateful for the authoritative encouragement, as from stage artists, of Mr. Edward Roberts and Miss Elise Bernard, now Mrs. Haldane, and of Mrs. Dora Mavor Moore; and for that, as from a poet, of Mr. Francis Berry; and as from a poetess, of Miss Dallas Kenmare; and also of Mr. Arnold Freeman, who has himself over a number of years achieved wonders of Shakespearian and other classical productions on the tiny stage of the Sheffield Educational Establishment, demonstrating how much may be accomplished by integrity of purpose when material resources are slight.

I remember, especially, what I owe to the late Margaret Lucas, who first suggested that I should put on a production of my own and became in 1932 my first Juliet; and also to the sympathy and insight of Mr. James Bridges, at that time. At Leeds the dramatic perception and daily care of Mrs. Olive Hewetson were continual supports. My deepest debt remains to the late Leslie Harris, once of Tree's company, who on the art of acting spoke with authority; and I am happy to include his name in my dedication.

My emphases here and in the following pages on my experiences as an actor may seem out of place in a book on production. But they form part of a necessary insistence that the driving force behind my stage adventures has been the instinct less of a scholar or even of a producer than, despite a host of deficiencies, of an actor. Now that the story is over, I wish to establish the record.

The extent to which my academic and stage theories have, during the last thirty years, affected our professional productions is discussed briefly in Chapter IX (pp. 258–9). Probably little theatres have been more widely affected than the professionals, and I should like to record that my 'ideal' *Macbeth* was honoured by being closely followed in a school production by Mr. Linden Huddlestone at Ecclesfield Grammar School in 1958. When in 1942 I myself produced *Macbeth* at Stowe School I was not able to engage in any elaborations, though the picking out of the three Apparitions by varied lights (pp. 143–4 below) may be regarded as a successful, if only provisional, expedient.

My pictures have been selected as illustrations of the facts or principles handled in my text. They are intended to suggest the whole dramatic person or, if a group, the whole scene, together with the relevances of either to the plays concerned.

It may seem that I should apologize for using so many pictures drawn from my own work, and I have avoided the repetition of my name in the captions. For many weeks I was planning and collecting a selection of possible pictures of well-known actors and productions, trying to wrench them to the service of my book; but somehow it would not come right. This is, after all, a personal study made largely from personal adventures, and the pictures used, constituting as they do visible records of the performances described in the text, give the book a dimension and a reality otherwise unattainable. Certainly I could wish that I had a higher proportion of group-scenes good enough for inclusion; but these, except under professional or school conditions where company, stage-space and photographer can be commandeered for two or three hours during or after a production's run, are usually impossible to arrange; when they were attempted, the attempts were often hurried and the results untidy. I am really fortunate to have found so many groups not unworthy of inclusion, though I regret that more of my stage associates at Toronto, whose kindnesses live in my memory, are not represented. I am fortunate in having been able to present among my captions the names of W. Lyndon Smith, who as Mercutio, Polonius, the Gravedigger, Iago, Kent and Enobarbus so empowered my productions; the late Robin Godfrey, whose sister Patricia was the Queen in my 1935 *Hamlet*, in London; and Miss Patricia Murphy.

For these pictures, various acknowledgments are due. First, I record my gratitude to Mr. A. J. Nathan for allowing me to use Buchel's portrait of Tree as Othello, which is possessed by Messrs.

L. and H. Nathan, on whose premises it can be seen. Mr. Nathan allows me to say that he has a fair amount of documentary material relating to Tree and his productions. For the copying of the portrait I am indebted to Mr. George W. Nash of the Victoria and Albert Museum; and I have to thank Mr. Hesketh Pearson for lending me the photograph of Tree's Forum scene in *Julius Caesar*. For other pictures, acknowledgments are due to the following photographic artists: for 2, 7, 8, 16, E. Mackintosh, Toronto; 9, 10, Ashley & Crippen, Toronto (9 copied by the late Alan Dredge, Photo-General, Leeds); 28, Mr. Bashur-ud-Din; 29, 30, *The Yorkshire Post*. Since some of my pictures bear no stamp, I am unable to state their source. For Picture 31 I thank Dr. Devendra P. Varma who has directed notable Shakespeare productions at universities in Kathmandu (Nepal), Damascus and Cairo. I have for long been grateful to the Revd. Claude Sauerbrei for having in 1940 taken the Timon photograph used as my frontispiece, which, though probably beyond my merits, I have come to regard as a visual symbol of my life-work. Since my approach to *Timon of Athens* is my main contribution to the staging of Shakespeare I have accorded it emphasis in my selection of pictures.[1]

I have to thank Mr. Edward Gordon Craig and Messrs. William Heinemann Ltd. for being allowed to quote from *On the Art of the Theatre*; and the Executors of the late Louis MacNeice for the use of MacNeice's Epilogue to the *Agamemnon*, composed on the occasion of our Leeds production.

An invitation by Mr. Werner Burmeister of the Department of Extramural Studies in the University of London to speak on Beerbohm Tree in a recent course of lectures arranged by Mr. W. A. Armstrong of King's College led to an expansion of my section on Tree's artistry. To Mr. Armstrong I am indebted for help in the collection of information, also to Mr. Frank Cox, Mr. Laurence Kitchin, Professor W. Moelwyn Merchant, Mr. Hesketh Pearson and Mr. C. B. Purdom. I am grateful to Mr. Patrick Saul of the British Institute of Recorded Sound for playing for me records of Tree and Forbes-Robertson; to the National Film Archive for arranging a presentation of the 1913 film of

---

[1] The importance of *Timon of Athens* in our dramatic history is discussed in my 'Timon of Athens and its Dramatic Descendants', *A Review of English Literature*, II, 4; Oct., 1961.

Preface to the Third Edition [1963]

Forbes-Robertson's *Hamlet*; and to the British Broadcasting Corporation, and especially to Mr. George MacBeth, for my own broadcast of Shakespearian speeches (p. 278). Some of my impressions have been checked by Mr. Richard Courtney, Mr. Hans de Groot and Mr. Robert Speaight. Dr. Patricia M. Ball has once again helped me with my index.

With some exceptions the nature and ordering of my analyses makes the use of line-references superfluous. Where they are given they apply to the Oxford Shakespeare. I am distressed to find so many inaccuracies in my old quotations, for which I must sometimes have relied simply on memories of performance. For Tree's theatre, I vary the title 'Her Majesty's' and 'His Majesty's' according to the occasion being referred to. I follow his biographer, Mr. C. B. Purdom, in printing Granville Barker's name without a hyphen. I likewise preserve the old style, forced by some of my references, in 'J. Martin Harvey' and 'W. Bridges Adams', without hyphens.

In giving cross-references to my present volume I use the letter 'p'. For page-references to all other books, numerals only.

G.W.K.

Exeter, 1963.

Preface to the First Edition [1936]

In putting forward my views on Shakespearian production I am conscious of deep and various obligations. This book is the result of long attention to a subject which has been my main interest since childhood and which antedates by many years any of my writings. Therefore I first express gratitude for each and every performance I have witnessed. My criticisms in the following pages are levelled not against producers, but points of production. Especially I acknowledge the grounding and stimulus towards understanding received from frequent visits as a boy to His Majesty's Theatre under Sir Herbert Beerbohm Tree. If today we differ from his principles, we have nevertheless scrapped one great tradition without properly creating another. Tree was an artist and a great one. The richness and dignity which the Shakespearian play, especially Shakespearian tragedy, demands in presentation died with him. For at His Majesty's you attended always something beyond entertainment, of ceremonial grandeur and noble if extravagant artistry. I well remember Tree's marvellous make-up as Othello; and the Weird Sisters floating through smoky clouds at the opening of *Macbeth*; and—how appropriate this a symbol of his whole approach—the incense filling the theatre from the Forum scene of *Julius Caesar*. I had the privilege of seeing, and above all of hearing, Sir Johnston Forbes-Robertson in Shakespeare during his farewell season at Drury Lane in 1913; and *The Passing of the Third Floor Back* still lingers in my memory as the occasion for the most exquisite vocal cadences I am ever likely to hear. To these pre-war experiences I must add another of great importance: Mr. Granville Barker's delightful productions of *The Winter's Tale*, *Twelfth Night*, and *A Midsummer Night's Dream*. To them I owe my earliest insight into the possibilities of solidity and permanence in stage-properties and scenic

21

effects, and the freedom of invention attending a non-realistic interpretation. *Twelfth Night* was the best. Especially I recall the formal kneeling of Dennis Neilson-Terry as Sebastian before Olivia, and his lovely speaking of the lines 'If it be thus to dream . . .'; and the exquisite singing of Feste's final song by Mr. Hayden Coffin. The whole production dwells in my mind still as a single unique quality, indissoluble and unanalysable as the pungent sweetness of an aroma. I assume that my readers are acquainted with Mr. Granville Barker's notable *Prefaces*, to which I would refer any reader who is not. I remember, too, an admirable and somewhat similar arrangement of *The Taming of the Shrew*, with Martin Harvey as Petruchio, by Mr. William Poel.[1] Those were comparatively modernistic productions: but there were also indirect links with the more remote past. I paid a flying visit to Stratford, in 1914 or thereabouts, to see H. B. Irving in *Hamlet*, and I never nowadays sail up the Gulf of St. Lawrence without recalling the death of his brother Laurence Irving, whom I saw as Iago, with Tree, and in *Typhoon*, and felt at that time to be potentially the greatest of living actors. There was a glamour haloing the Irvings, for in all my theatre-going adventures the figure of their father, partly through descriptions and imitations of him by my own, loomed as a felt presence, a kind of god-like and numinous force, its influence over the London stage not yet dissolved.[2] Such are my early obligations. Above all, I owe a debt of lasting gratitude to my own parents, who catered so continuously for a child's hobby of so unorthodox and expensive a variety.

Since the war my most profitable theatre-going has mainly concerned itself with the Shakespeare Festival Company under Mr. W. Bridges Adams. From this company I can hardly overemphasize the advantages I have received. When I first saw the Shakespeare Festival Company I thought their performances almost perfect; nowadays I grow more critical. I conclude that they have themselves been training my faculties. Especially I admire the example set of almost military smartness, and feel that what knowledge I have of the possibilities of significant grouping owes

[1] That is my recollection, but I cannot find Poel's collaboration noted in either Maurice Willson Disher's *The Last Romantic* or Robert Speaight's *William Poel*. [1963]

[2] My father's theatre-going reminiscences were a continual enrichment to my awaking passion for the stage. [1963]

much to Mr. Bridges Adams' productions.[1] I regret not knowing more of the Old Vic., which is nearly always closed when I am in London; or of Mr. Nugent Monck's important work at the Maddermarket Theatre, Norwich.

My own experience of acting and producing dates from the year 1926. During my six years at Dean Close School, Cheltenham, I acted annually in the Cheltenham Branch of the British Empire Shakespeare Society's productions; and I am grateful for having been allowed to do so. At the school I was fortunate in being able to start regular work in Shakespeare production, first with junior forms and later with the Speech Day play.[2] During the last four years this experience has been greatly extended at Toronto.[3] My own productions have been: *Romeo and Juliet*, 1932; *Hamlet*, 1933; *Othello*, 1934; *King Lear*, 1935;[4] also *Henry VIII*, for the Shakespeare Society of Toronto, 1934; together with abbreviated versions, for the Shakespeare Society, of *Richard II* and *Richard III*. In these, with the exception of *Henry VIII*, where I played Buckingham and the Porter's assistant, I gained the additional valuable experience of acting the name-parts. I am indebted to the Shakespeare Society of Toronto for what experience I have gained under their auspices; and also to Mr. Brownlow Card, of Toronto, for experience under his. Toronto, and especially the University, is most fortunate in the location within the University of Hart House Theatre. My recent production of *Hamlet* at the Rudolf Steiner Hall, London, was an interesting and enjoyable experiment. I was particularly pleased with a letter received from such an authority as Mr. C. B. Purdom, whose writing I had admired, from which I have permission to quote this passage: 'I appreciate

[1] An appreciation of Mr. Bridges Adams' work at Stratford is given by Mr. A. K. Chesterton in the section 'Bridges Adams: Master of the Stage-Picture' in his history (1934) of the Shakespeare Memorial Theatre entitled *Brave Enterprise*.

[2] I had earlier produced *As You Like It* in collaboration with Mr. C. A. P. Tuckwell, who has done so much to give the school a Shakespearian tradition. In my subsequent (two) Speech Day productions Mr. Alan Bromly laid the foundation of his stage career with notable performances of Puck and Feste. He also played Rosencrantz in my 1935 London *Hamlet*. Two other old Decanians took part in it: Mr. Francis Berry and Mr. Roscoe Railton. Yet another Old Decanian, Mr. Leonard Jayne, gave me valued advice and encouragement during *This Sceptred Isle* in 1941. [1963]

[3] It was my good fortune to be appointed to the Staff of Trinity College in the University in 1931.

[4] Produced after this preface was written, though I included a short description in my book (p. 121 below). I now make this insertion in my original preface. [1963]

the difficulties under which you were working, but your performance of *Hamlet* certainly gave me an entirely new impression. You unfolded a spiritual significance revealed in no other production I have ever seen'.

To Madame Irving, of the Irving Academy, Cheltenham, and to Mr. B. A. Pittar, whom I first met during a delightful and profitable fortnight at Citizen House, Bath, I am grateful for valuable instruction and encouragement. To all who have in various ways made my Toronto productions possible I record my thanks. But my greatest debt by far is owed to Mr. Leslie Harris of Toronto, whose wide experience, skilful teaching, and continual encouragement have gone far to remedy the worst of my numerous faults in acting, and more than once recharged my attempts with confidence when that was most needed.

G.W.K.

Toronto and Cheltenham, 1935.

PART I

[1936]

CHAPTER I

The Shakespearian Play

I

I have for some time been contending that a Shakespearian play is not purely and only a good story with entertainment and dramatic value linked to profound analysis of character[1] and a heart-thrilling rhetoric; but that, over and above all this, it presents a close mesh of imaginative and intellectual suggestion demanding a more exact study and sensitive appreciation than it has so far received. The persons in the play are vital and human, none more so; but the interaction of those persons within the dramatic texture of the whole, and that texture itself, the action, movement and purpose of the whole artistic pattern, must at each instant be kept in mind. From such a comprehension many old difficulties are quickly resolved: what was inexplicable is found necessary; what suspected as spurious, seen as crucial. The Grave-yard scene in *Hamlet* has been called irrelevant; and modern scholarship still repudiates the Vision in *Cymbeline*—regularly omitted from stage productions—and considers *Henry VIII* a chaotic play of doubtful authorship. There is no longer need or excuse for such confusion: for the powerfully dramatic Vision fits as perfectly into the pattern of *Cymbeline* as the Graveyard scene into that of *Hamlet*; and *Henry VIII* is a carefully constructed and fine play whose pattern I have elsewhere analysed.

Whereas from the old and limited understanding there was

[1] My previous animadversions as to 'character' come under two distinct headings: (i) a refusal to analyse any person in the drama in isolation from the whole play and its various actions and effects; (ii) an antipathy to the term 'character' in the sense of 'fictional person' because of certain dangerous ethical associations. It is not always understood that neither of these objections precludes intense concern with the subtle psychology and richly human action of which the plays are made.

27

slight justification for the long and still living tradition of Shakespearian idolatry, from the new and comprehensive sight novel splendours of the intellect and themes of profundity and universal grandeur continually and pleasingly emerge. We ought not at all to be surprised at this; still less should we be offended. We are used to regarding great poetry as of universal importance, its meanings not limited to the partial and the ephemeral. Shakespeare has somehow stood alone, and for too long, as a solitary figure of irrelevant magnitude. True, we cannot interpret the whole of Shakespeare; nor of Dante; nor Byron.[1] But because we can never exhaust the meanings in a great poet, that gives us no authority to neglect what meanings patently are there. Faced with a plenitude of meanings, we have asserted none: it is an easy way out. We must no longer deny to Shakespeare a quality common to great literature: the quality of universal meanings in the particular event. Shakespeare has something to say to us not only about human life, but about death; not only about England, or Venice, but about the universe. Poetry is metaphoric, its essential purpose being to blend the human and the divine. So those poets who aim primarily to speak of God, do so in terms of man; and Shakespeare, speaking with the accents and intricacies of great poetry of man, speaks accordingly of God.

The Shakespearian play shows a texture of personal thinking close-inwoven with some objective and pre-existent story. Philosophy is entwined with action and event. Shakespeare's philosophy is infinitely variable, not static, as Dante's: *King Lear* may be Senecan, but *Macbeth* is Christian. His philosophy may vary within one play. We cannot find by abstraction Shakespeare's 'own' philosophy of life: his massed statement includes many philosophies, but is subject to none. *Macbeth* is a solid of which the length may be a Holinshed story but the height a Christian philosophy of grace and evil, and the breadth Shakespeare's own emotional experience. Criticism, aware of the two-dimensional nature of the philosophic intelligence, often asserts that such imaginative solids are uninterpretable. This is nevertheless an error, since a Shakespearian play, though it may be complex, is yet far less so than life itself, which the philosophic intelligence has invariably considered a fair quarry. To apply intelligence to the whole art-form is not the same as abstracting from it those

[1] Here Shelley in the first edition was replaced by Byron in my 1949 text.

elements only that seem intelligible. There is no excuse for mental inaction. What happened was really this: criticism came to an impasse. Those elements in Shakespeare it was accustomed to analyse were, certainly, all but exhausted by analysis: as when tunnel-makers come to a nasty piece of rock. A little dynamite, however, may open out new progress. So, by attending as well to imagery and symbolism as to thought and action, to the rhythmic curves of poetry as well as to 'character', we touch the richer dimensional quality of the Shakespearian creation. That does not mean that we now attend only to those elements passed over before; rather that we attend afresh to the whole pattern. I have not, in my own interpretations, neglected to analyse persons or events: but I have taken them together with, and in terms of, the whole.

From such interpretations we become aware of the dominating Shakespearian themes; of love and hate, warriorship, kingship; ideas of state-order, conflicts of life-forces and death-forces; patterns of romance-fulfilment and the tragic sacrifice, and difficult visions that go farther yet. My two most important results I take to be: (i) the discovery of tempests and music as dominant contrasted symbolic impressions throughout the whole, or nearly the whole, of Shakespeare; and (ii) my reading of the Final Plays as visions of immortality crowning Shakespeare's work and to be given as serious attention in their peculiar quality as *Macbeth* and *King Lear* in theirs. Though general acceptance of my contentions is not as yet apparent, it will come; if not soon, then late. Critics are sometimes, quite naturally, alienated by novelty and tend to read into vividness of statement a rigidity and schematism which are not necessarily implicit. To safeguard my essay from misunderstanding I next shortly outline what I take to be the nature of a Shakespearian play, using a succession of simple headings: What it is; What it does; and How it does it. These are chosen to prepare the way directly for my ideas on production. The formulation of scientific stage principles follows logically from any understanding of Shakespeare's positive and challenging significance.

2. WHAT IT IS

A Shakespeare play is primarily an aural time-sequence, like music: a sequence of impressions, thoughts and images, carried across mainly by audible words allotted to various fictional persons.

To these we must add sound-effects such as alarums, trumpets, thunder and music. Visual details concerning the action are not emphasized, as a rule, by stage-direction, except in the latest group of plays; and then only with moderation. It is true that the text is often itself richly descriptive; but these are pictures within the spoken word. That which builds the essential *Macbeth*, which persists common to various readings and stage-performances, is outwardly at least aural, not visual; though the aural can be received by the ear of imagination in silent reading.

But through this medium a varied content is delivered. There are conceptual thoughts, ideas. There are also mind-pictures. Shakespeare is crammed with visual impressions, a chain of them, blending one into another. We do not visualize them at all clearly at a first performance or a first reading, but they are there nevertheless at the back of the words, semi-consciously received. From this flux of ideas and images emerge greater units: the developing persons of the drama, the action and general movement, the marshalling of forces of one sort or another. The play is expressly dynamic, not static. This is true of all Shakespeare's plays, but of his tragedies especially. Compared with a drama of more classical tradition the Shakespearian tragedy is simply crammed with action. You get from it a sense of intense life in conflict, development, and movement. Whatever Shakespeare is doing, one thing is clear: he does it largely through the medium of action. If we grant that Shakespeare expresses profundities, then we must be prepared to see those profundities expressed in terms of intense dramatic activity. Each play is an onslaught on the mind. And action implies conflict. We watch fierce contestants, men or principles. The 'principles' of the middle scenes usually become opposing armies towards the end; the inner psychological disturbance tends to objectify itself as the play unfurls into open military opposition. Observe how often armies are brought on the stage, sometimes actually fighting; and how individual combats may be crucial to the plot, as in *Romeo and Juliet* and *Hamlet*. These are surface symptoms of what is always embedded deep in Shakespeare: the play's significant action.

The Shakespearian movement, whether of a whole play, or a scene, or a speech, undulates: it shows a rhythmic rise and fall. There are vast waves of action, and, within each, subtler minute crests and cusps, a ceaseless rippling variation.

We may have a sense of speed-waves. The middle action of
Hamlet starts with a long scene of ordinary conversation. The
player's speech whips up the action for a while; then it falls back,
but not right back, towards the poignant intensity of Hamlet's
meeting with Ophelia. Then we have Hamlet's address to the
players, working up shortly to the play-scene. From now on the
speed increases rapidly. The King flies, Hamlet's answers snap
back at Rosencrantz and Guildenstern; the King's agonized prayer
swiftly follows, and Hamlet's entry; and Hamlet's interview with
his mother. This interview starts with a rapid dialogue leading to
Polonius' death. There is a pause, Hamlet settles down to his
purpose, the movement is deliberate, but quickly gains speed as
Hamlet loses control; he grows more wild and volleys abuse,
the action gathers, rises to a climax; and the Ghost enters. The
Ghost's appearance checks the whole movement that started with
the Play scene. Hamlet is now limp, his bolt shot, the Queen
too: the whole action is limp. The scene drags on like a wounded
snake, with repetitions: an intentional anti-climax. Shakespeare's
art functions in terms of rising action followed by a fall. He never
fears an anti-climax. It is all done with curves, like a line of undulating hills. After a fall there is continuation: he never cuts off
his action at a precipice.

The tragedies often rise to a crest of action about Act III, then,
with variations, descend. Or so it seems to us today, but the
military conflicts that the modern producer and audience find it
so hard to take seriously were probably far more important to a
contemporary, and as nerve-racking as the sound effects in
Sherriff's *Journey's End* to us. *Julius Caesar*, *Macbeth*, *King Lear* and
Timon of Athens show this central crest. *Othello*, *Coriolanus* and
Antony and Cleopatra rise to a later climax but do not close till the
action is completed and rounded off. We might contrast Marlowe's technique in *Doctor Faustus* where, except for the very short
epilogue, the play is cut off abruptly at a violent climax: Marlowe
is mainly interested in his heroes as individuals, Shakespeare in the
hero's relation to life in general. We have a pattern of the turning
wheel of events, the rhythm and leverage of life swinging over.
We find it in individual speeches at a high moment; the words
gather power, rise, maintain their height, then, wavering, sough
back, as in the King's sleep-speech in *2 Henry IV* (III. i. 18–25),
where the surges pile up steadily to the word 'clouds', and then fall

back for the line following. This is a typical unit. So is Macbeth's 'If it were done . . .' soliloquy (I. vii. I) which rises to a climax and sinks for the last four lines. We may remember that grand moment in *Richard II* when lyrical Richard, brought before Bolingbroke, starts humbly, then grows swiftly in spiritual stature, takes on the tragic purple of dethroned kingship, and sears his enemies with white-hot speech.

The play's whole development repays attention. Richard is first weak, spoilt, careless and cruel, like Marlowe's Edward II. But this, almost the whole of Marlowe's protagonist, is the merest beginning of Shakespeare's. Returning from Ireland he addresses the earth of England in words that recapture some of our sympathy and, above all, create in us a new sense of Richard's sacred office. His confidence in that blackens Bolingbroke with a single phrase. When disaster closes on him his tragic despair is so developed that he becomes before our eyes unearthly, prince of a new world, a saint in sorrow. And still he is England's king; never more so. His words to Northumberland pile phrase on damning phrase that leave his enemies spiritually crushed before they start to win. Then again he reverts to saintly meditation. They go to London. But watch what is happening: he is not falling, but rising. Step by step he climbs his miniature Calvary. At last he is to resign his crown. He does so, humbly. Northumberland would next have him read a record of his misdeeds. Now watch how the words gather strength:

> K. RICHARD: Must I do so? and must I ravel out
> My weav'd-up follies? Gentle Northumberland,
> If thy offences were upon record
> Would it not shame thee in so fair a troop
> To read a lecture of them? If thou would'st,
> There should'st thou find one heinous article
> Containing the deposing of a king
> And cracking the strong warrant of an oath,
> Mark'd with a blot, damn'd in the book of Heaven!
> Nay, all of you that stand and look upon me,
> Whilst that my wretchedness doth bait myself,
> Though some of you with Pilate wash your hands
> Showing an outward pity, yet you Pilates
> Have here deliver'd me to my sour cross,
> And water cannot wash away your sin.
>
> (IV. i. 228)

Observe the references to Christ. Richard towers over them all in spiritual stature, king yet, the elected of God. The scene rises to a climax at 'Containing the deposing . . .' down to 'damned in the book of Heaven'; and then drops, but with a returning and only slightly lesser crest, soon after. It is all done by varied modulation, waves, curves. And after this scene we have Richard's parting with his wife, deep in the luxuriating sunset of sorrow; his meditative listening to music in prison; his death. The climax comes well before the end and the movement curves over.

This spiritual rise under tragic stress we find often: as in Romeo, Hamlet, Lear, and Cleopatra. Shakespeare continually surprises: not by remarkable events alone, but by revealing a continual and growing power in his persons. Each is conceived according to the principle of growth; each tragedy is a rise. Marlowe's Edward satisfies your expectation; Shakespeare's Richard shatters it, revealing strength where we expected weakness. Marlowe's tragedy gives us a study of a failure; Shakespeare's a revelation of grandeur. Even the conclusion to *Faustus* presents rather a sublime wriggling than a sacrificial suffering. Marlowe's tragic heroes are all ambitious materialists, and when they crash they end. Shakespeare's are purgatorial pilgrims. Shakespeare is fundamentally Christian, Marlowe pagan. So a Shakespearian tragedy has always direction and a positive thrust. In developing his persons, in constructing a play, in writing a speech, Shakespeare is master of the seventh wave; crash follows crash, and when we expect exhaustion, and fear, after so much expense of power, a comparatively limp conclusion, the seventh wave towers up, something we had never guessed yet recognize as inevitable, and not till then the return, the vast retraction, and silence.

That Shakespeare's two dominant symbols are aural effects is not therefore strange. As I have shown in *The Shakespearian Tempest*, the Shakespearian universe turns about the axis of tempests and music. True, many of the tempests are given visual though verbal description; but many, too, are presented in stage-directions of thunder. A Shakespearian tragedy is 'full of sound and fury': the action demands flourishes, trumpets, drums, alarums, cannon, sounds which bridge the two opposites of music and thunder. In terms of music and tempest we can discover a certain recurrent pattern in tragedy: some sort of music near the beginning, suggesting peace; followed by the thunder of disrupting action and conflict about Act III; a falling back to a dark serenity and melodious pathos, with often more music, usually in some way a broken music, in Act IV or thereabouts; and then the final tragic impact, usually after an armed conflict, perhaps with stately martial sounds, as in *Hamlet, Timon of Athens* and *Coriolanus*, blending the powers of music and tempest-thunder.[1]

All these are merest samples. There is much more that might be said. To different minds different rhythmic variations will be apparent. I have left unnoticed the romantic comedies, where the persons are on the whole more static and a musical and harmonious resolution is played out with some sort of tempest and division in the background; and also the Final Plays, which start with tragedy and end with a reversal towards union and peace. Plays may often be considered as three—or four—vast waves of action, with intervals between. The usual act and scene divisions are of little use; we must discover rhythms independently. It is a good plan to think of the play as a cinematograph sequence: short scenes are not technically weak in Shakespeare. We may get a flashed view of one army, then of the other, then again the first, giving a sense of speed and action. But the order may be most important: fine effects are gained by juxtaposition, as when Buckingham's execution follows Wolsey's feast and the King's merry-making. There are a myriad subtleties in all this. There is no looseness in the interlinked sequence: and each link in the chain is the more massive for each and all that precede it. The play gathers power as it moves. It is more than an addition. It increases like compound interest. Tragedy becomes a massive and ever-swelling river thundering into a serene and peaceful sea. Shakespeare, remember, does not fear an anti-climax. And the temporal sequences in Shakespeare build a reality beyond the temporal; their crashing and mighty rhythms raise an architecture surpassing speech; for, though the play be 'full of sound and fury', it is very far from 'signifying nothing'.

---

[1] This pattern characterizes Shakespeare's work as a whole, from the early romances, through tragedy and the mysticism of the Final Plays, to *Henry VIII*; Shakespeare's last play corresponding to the ritualistic conclusions of *Hamlet* and *Timon of Athens*. [1949]

The Shakespearian Play

3. WHAT IT DOES

So it will not follow that we are excused from exact analysis of imagery, symbol, and thought. Though a speech be a sound-sequence, it will not sound well unless the speaker has some degree of understanding. Similarly a whole play will not move well unless the producer realizes more than the general rhythmic succession of big sounds. We have stressed the importance of varied movement and rhythmic undulations; but this very variety and rhythm depend ultimately on meaning of various kinds, and the meanings, once you start on them, are most subtle and comprehensive.

The plays were meant to be acted, and even an ideal spectator can at any one performance receive only a general sense of story and grand action. Yet that general sense may be taken to include an awareness of every word that has been spoken during the performance in its interrelation with everything else. That is why one experience of a great work is not enough; we must grow to know it. Shakespeare, like the Greek dramatists, preferred plots not entirely new to his audience, for the early scenes should gain power from some knowledge of what is to come. Ideally the whole play should be semi-consciously in the mind at every moment. The final result will be a massed area of the mind rather spatial than temporal with a spatiality which includes the power and rhythms of a sequence. It is therefore both spatial and temporal.

As our knowledge of a Shakespearian play increases we become more and more intensely aware of a certain quality peculiar to it. This can be held in the mind after the events which help to build it are forgotten; indeed, the ability to leave such an impression is the distinguishing mark of high imaginative literature. This quality, though mental, is to the inward eye partly at least visual, spatial, an expanse. The action of *Macbeth* leaves us with a sense of certain imaginative areas. We see darkness and colour. There is gold of kingship, crowns of sovereignty, ingots of world-power: the poetry emphasizes them, the events build them. Red blood streams, sticks on the hand. Nature's innocence is in the martlet's nest, the tree borne by the crowned child, Birnam wood. Images of divine grace flash out. Night-birds wing the air. Thunder crashes and lightning's scimitars gash the darkness. Feasting, first to honour Duncan and later when interrupted by Banquo's Ghost,

35

or as suggested negatively in the horror of the Weird Sisters' cauldron-stew of filth, is powerful. Varied impressions may be allowed to group themselves into a new kind of *dramatis personae* of symbolic suggestion. Those we have noticed tend to divide into two camps of life-forces and death-forces. This is how we may approach the more universal meanings of a Shakespearian play in terms of certain sense-suggestions thrown up and built in the mind by the story, its persons, and their words.

I have been criticized for selecting cross-sections of imaginative correspondence such as the kingship, crown and sceptre references in *Macbeth* without close reference at every instant to their peculiar contexts and order of sequence in the play. But we are analysing the final effect of the whole play in an ideal recipient's mind, or that which may be attained by anyone after continual study. In this whole result every part is co-existent; though built of a sequence it is a sequence whose nature and end is to accumulate itself swiftly into that whole. Every effect has a simultaneous reference to its own context and to the whole. To attempt to work along the time-surface of particular context with each minute correspondence, showing how this in its context throws back to that and forward to something else in theirs, and to continue doing this, may involve subtleties and intricacies of doubtful value; and even of doubtful honesty, since we should never be able to start doing this on any wide scale without an already formed knowledge of the massed existence of such references without implications of sequence.

We can thus start to know the whole play, action and atmosphere, time-sequence and symbols, as a single almost visual quality built equally of action and sense-suggestions. The main action is often crystallized into some symbolic solidity, such as the three Apparitions in *Macbeth*, the handkerchief in *Othello*, the caskets in *The Merchant of Venice*. It is as though the aim and purpose of the play's movement were to solidify itself. The whole result is weighty, held in the mind as, to use a phrase from *Measure for Measure* (III. ii. 298), 'ponderous and substantial'; it is still, though made of action; solid, though built of flux; or, to use Shakespeare's favourite symbols, it is music created of thunderous and tempestuous conflict. Passive, it radiates power; and, existing subject to neither time nor space, it seems composed of both.

A major poet's resolution of conflicts makes an objective art-form of quiescent yet potent quality. Whatever personal distresses and contemporary conflicts he bodies forth, the resulting stillness makes a significant wedge into life exposing light for other generations with other conflicts; though in Shakespeare the conflicts are generally universal enough, having direct significances for the modern world.

Many of our difficulties—the matter of significant relations independent of order, the mystery of a seeming stillness made of movement, the paradox of a passive activity—are illuminated by our recognizing that the germ of composition is an intuitive perception of a certain stillness, an idea or quality. Such an intuition will condition creation. It will not necessarily come before the work is started, but we must suppose there to be always a moment of conception during the early stages of composition when the essential nature of the work to be is first properly apparent. This becomes the nucleus, preliminary drafts or ideas are re-coloured to tone with it, action and imagery clothe it, grow from it, cluster round it. Or perhaps it is better to say that all actions, events and images that clash with the central intuition are rejected: it comes to the same thing. No doubt such a process may be repeated more than once, as the work grows under writing and revision, under a developing conception. But we need not here multiply our troubles; artistic creation, like any other type of creation, is a mystery. So we shall assume a single central though dynamic stillness at the back of the process, a hub of the turning wheel. From this central principle we can begin to understand the work in its wholeness. That is why, in interpreting a play's intellectual meaning, you cannot or must not work from the surface. However careful and subtle your elucidation of details and correspondences along the surface, you cannot give a dynamic interpretation without some sense of a whole; either the whole play, or the whole of one aspect. To do this we must intuitively recognize a central principle of some kind and call on quotations only as evidence. For example, I feel a mass of references to crowns, sceptres, and regal pomp in *Macbeth*: and in evidence I write down quotations irrespective of their order, since each relates primarily not to others but to a certain centrality that gives them all meaning: here a certain sense-perception of the glories of kingship. At the centre of creation and understanding alike there remains a stillness, the hub of the wheel.

The completed result shares this quality of stillness, as the rim of a whirling wheel is still, or appears so. From the action and movement is thrown up a spiritual edifice, a solid of the mind, a cinematograph roll: every unrolling of it in performance or reading rolls it into a new solid in the recipient's imagination. A performance is therefore not simply a sequence but architectonic, and makes a mind-building. In *Abt Vogler* Robert Browning imagines an organist making of great music a mystic building and in Coleridge's *Kubla Khan* the paradisal dome could be 'built in air' by 'symphony and song'. In describing fine architecture we might say that it seems to be creating itself instant by instant, for such is its expressly dynamic, rhythmic and vital quality; and we may give a corresponding emphasis to the more solid attributes of great poetry.[1] All great art forces the mind to understand the paradox of a pulsing solidity, blending spatial and temporal conceptions. It introduces us directly to that which is built of both and beyond both; space-time or eternity. This is how Dante's great poem, explicitly projecting events in their eternal quality, has an exact, implicit, analogy throughout Shakespeare.

4. HOW IT DOES IT

This peculiar fluid-solid nature of the literary art-form is created by its limiting itself at some point. The end stops the narrative accumulation, and that stoppage turns the river into a reservoir. We must on no account allow a leakage. In terms of an art-form we can get a certain revelation, but only if we respect its limits.

The conventions of poetic drama forbid our complaining at the technical compression by which the loving Othello's mistrust is raised within a half-hour's scene, or our wondering how a man of Iago's peculiar tendencies has lived in freedom until the play's opening. We must confine our attention within certain limits; we must receive the whole play, neither more nor less. Consider the two main types of play: romance and tragedy. These express two primary rhythms, the love-quest and the death-quest; and the relief they instil is a relaxing of tensions, that of unsatisfied love and that of unsatisfied life. But we must not ask too far. We must not inquire as to what sort of a husband Bassanio will

[1] For an extended discussion of such 'musical buildings' see my *Laureate of Peace*, III.

make. The sublimity of *King Lear* depends on our not trying to
work out immortality doctrines from it: the tragic sacrifice is
performed, and, even though *King Lear* itself makes us believe in
some kind of immortality, while watching *King Lear* we must feel
death to be in some sense the conclusion, or we miss the very
impact on which our belief depends. In the Final Plays, where I
argue that the quality of immortality is expanded in significant
designs of resurrection and reunion, we must again not question
beyond the framework. The play's design is our only whole. That
design depends on its limits, and only by respecting those limits
can we focus its quality. To argue that Leontes and Hermione
must anyhow die after the action is irrelevant: they do not exist
after the action. We have witnessed a supposed death and reunion
whose patterned rhythm can awake knowledge of a difficult truth,
like a parable of Jesus. We cannot appreciate a picture's design
if we expand the view on our own beyond the frame. We must
not say: 'That's all very pretty, but I happen to know that piece
of country and there's an ugly factory a little farther on, that ruins
the conception.' This may be true, but it is irrelevant, at all events
until we have got the utmost which we are capable of receiving
from the art-form itself. So the interior action of a Shakespearian
play draws significance from the play's conventional limits: and
this thought helps us again to see how the whole is at once
dynamic and static. There is an interplay of solidity and movement. Later we shall find an important analogy on the plane of
stage-representation.

Not only do conventions bar our consciousness from certain
dangerous directions; they ask us to give positive assent to
strange occurrences. We have to accept people who speak poetry,
but our reward is a richer understanding than normal language
can induce. Consider Cleopatra's speech in *Antony and Cleopatra*:

> My desolation does begin to make
> A better life. 'Tis paltry to be Caesar;
> Not being Fortune, he's but Fortune's knave,
> A minister of her will: and it is great
> To do that thing that ends all other deeds;
> Which shackles accidents and bolts up change;
> Which sleeps and never palates more the dung—
> The beggar's nurse and Caesar's.   (v. ii. 1)

An intuitive perception of a difficult thought, that of death's positive and victorious significance, is expanded; the one white beam split into spectroscopic tints, and displayed for analysis and inspection; so building into us a full understanding of a difficult intuition. This is one instance of what is always happening in Shakespeare. Compare Richard III's soliloquy after the ghosts disappear. Richard analyses at length the workings of his own conscience by which he paradoxically is forced to condemn himself. This baffling intuition of a divided mind conscious of its own division is cleverly presented. Richard questions his own identity. The King's fine prayer in *Hamlet* is analogous. Poetic drama, if we accept its conventions, becomes more substantial than our normal life-view.

Similarly, the play's wider action may present most unusual incidents. Shakespeare relates his hero to society in general and state-order; moreover, he sees that society as part of nature widening out to the whole universe. Logically, therefore, Macbeth's crime eclipses the sun. In order to see any act in its wholeness we must not limit our context at any point. Great literature is at work to interweave temporal and transient subtleties with eternal verities: the swing of the seasons, storm-wrack, sun, stars, comets; and with universal principles, of life, death, resurrection. That is why a Shakespearian play or the New Testament, or any great work of literature, superficially falsifying life's appearances, is to a final judgement the only realism. What we usually call fact is a miserable abstraction, torn from its context, uprooted and dead. Poetic art gives us not the factual, which is dead, but the actual, which lives. It aims to reintegrate our abstractions into their only proper context in the whole of life. The cramming of unlimited significances into one self-limited work necessarily forces statements and symbols at first sight hard to accept. The play's limits force the creation of miraculous events which in turn are to be understood in terms of those limits. The problem of the New Testament is closely related.[1] Such strange events, we had better say, are true in their context and as part of the whole: certainly, they are always most important for our understanding. If we refuse them what Coleridge called our 'willing suspension of disbelief' we mutilate that whole and its meaning; but if we focus the whole pattern, no less and no more, infinite vistas are opened.

---

[1] The more miraculous events in the New Testament are discussed in *The Christian Renaissance* (enlarged, 1962).

This is particularly to be remembered in reading the Final Plays. In *Pericles* we must give the same kind of assent to the miraculous resurrection of Thaisa as we should to the raising of Lazarus in the New Testament.

Poetic drama is both more difficult and more important than the realistic plays of today, but it can address the mind only through conventions. The conclusion to *Measure for Measure* can be understood only from a formal acceptance of the peculiar quality of the whole. Finally, every play demands a different kind of acceptance: so that the peculiar convention of a work of art is that work of art itself. Hence the importance of pure acceptance as the condition of understanding, as when you the more easily do a complicated calculation in mathematics by agreeing that a letter shall stand for a number, and by so doing work out an answer true for all values of your letter: that is, an answer of universal quality.

To sum up: The Shakespearian play is a creation of intellectual and imagistic complexity demanding and exhausting all our powers of analysis. It is primarily an aural time-sequence with rhythmic modulations, but nevertheless creates in the mind a result that may be imaged as spatial, solid, and rich in sense-suggestion. Since this spatial result is wound into the mind along a time-sequence we must call it a 'space-time' creation, tuning our minds to awareness of the space-time dimension. This, its particularly universal and eternal quality, is closely related to the proper use of conventions.

From these considerations I shall now construct some general principles of stage production. I shall concentrate mainly on the Tragedies, which raise most clearly the crucial problems. However, what I have to say applies with equal force to all except the more farcical elements in the Comedies.

CHAPTER II

The Theory of Production

I

The producer should be aware of the play's metaphysical core; that is, of its wholeness. He must not consider *Hamlet* and *Macbeth* as merely good stories with occasional 'dramatic situations'; no modern producer would blunder like that with a Galsworthy play. Close intellectual interpretation must come first, and interpretation involves numerous subtleties.[1] But the closest attention to details, unless also vitalized by a sense of some unifying idea, will prove fruitless. *Macbeth* must be seen first as a conflict of life-forces and death-forces; and not until this, or some other general principle of similar status, is grasped, can surface details find their proper places. I have heard *Othello* called a poetic melodrama without modern meaning or any universal reference. That is the current academic view of it; certainly it is usually produced as such. But it is utterly wrong. The theme of *Othello* is as human and universal as can be. Desdemona is the eternal principle of romantic value; Iago, the insistent demon of denial. Othello, like each of us, is caught between these. Iago is devilishly clever, Desdemona, divinely beautiful. Not only is Othello's story not irrelevant to us: we slay Desdemona half a dozen times most days of our life. Within the human action of any great play eternal conflicts are displayed.

[1] For example at *Macbeth*, IV. iii. 186, Ross addresses Macduff:
> Your eye in Scotland
> Would *create* soldiers, make our *women* fight . . .
It is his way of breaking the news while simultaneously preparing revenge-thoughts as an antidote. 'Create' and 'women' refer respectively to Macduff's children and wife. His eye fixes Macduff as he speaks, meaningfully. The obvious mistake is to speak these lines to Malcolm.

The producer must not deduce his business from the play's surface. He must make a leap to the inward meaning and use the play's surface as expression; we must not start where Shakespeare left off, but rather start with Shakespeare and go with him. Though seemingly irrational, this is a process of universal application. My own interpretations aim to obey this law. They are, in a sense, re-creations, not translations; and they are this because they uncover some central and unifying idea, giving it next a new structure in interpretation. Interpretation will always be a development in a new medium of some central idea of wholeness in the original, grasp of that central idea forcing a vital re-creation. It is the same with production. You must make a leap into the abstract in order to realize the concrete; that unwinding from one roll into another to which I have before referred is not so simple as it at first appears. There is something about the human mind that necessitates this zigzag leap in all endeavour. We must abstract. In our attention to the widest issues of life, we always abstract. Science, philosophy, history—all are abstractions. Abstraction conditions all conscious action. The best way to regain full concrete perception of particulars is the religious way; to make the one grand abstraction and leap of intuition and name it 'God' before seeing everything as expressions of God. That is why the religious attitude is finally more concrete than others, why it touches the actual as they do not; why the account of the creation in Genesis, by putting it all on to God, is the best account of creation that we have. Enlightened abstraction is half-way to concrete understanding. So the producer who hopes for any solid and concrete result shirks at his peril the effort of intellectual abstraction.

He has to get the play from the text on to the living stage. It is rather like moving a delicate piece of furniture or machinery. Carry it bodily across and bits will be broken. It must be carefully taken to pieces and rebuilt. The producer should be able to hold the play in jig-saw bits in his mind, to sort them all out, to build with them and re-create the whole from understanding of its nature. Such understanding gives him full powers to cut, adapt, even on rare occasions transpose, according to circumstances; he has to consider his stage, his company, his audience. The feeling that cutting is sacrilegious derives from a false reasoning. The producer's business is not translation but re-creation. It is however true that nothing more swiftly and irrevocably gives a producer away than unenlightened cutting or iniquitous transpositions and additions. You must by thought and intimate acquaintance acquire the right to do these things. I have seen a production where Ophelia's description of Hamlet's mysterious insanity and newly-dishevelled appearance was cut, presumably so that the hero might, as in every Hamlet I have seen, walk about in a particularly spruce and attractive black suit during the middle action. *The Merchant of Venice* often starts with merry-making, despite Shakespeare's contrast of Venice with Belmont in point of tragedy and the emphasized melancholy of Antonio's first speech.

We cannot properly produce a play without some sense of it as a whole. But we often find actor or producer saying: 'That is a good and profound idea, but it is not dramatic': whereas a good idea concerning a great play must be dramatic; otherwise it is a bad idea and not a good one. Probably the good idea relates to the play as a whole, and may thus be incompatible with some easy but irrelevant dramatic thrill. The immediate and transient dramatic effect is not everything. I have known an actor very naturally proud of gaining a round of applause after a long speech within a scene, but had the action been truly holding its audience applause would have been impossible. To conclude a scene on a powerful climax may miss a subtler and more Shakespearian effect of anti-climax. Getting applause is a psychological trick; certain gestures, certain climaxes, certain ways of drawing the curtains to tempt fresh claps from a desultory audience, all call it down. But let the producer beware lest, like Samson at Gaza, he pull the whole palace of art crashing to destruction on his own and his company's heads. A touring company used to bring down the curtain on the murder scene in *Macbeth* with a crowd of actors waving swords and shouting, 'Well contented!' There was great applause. Then up came the curtain, the swords of the encouraged company waved and flashed again, and renewed volumes rolled out, 'Well contented! We-ell con-ten-ted!' Thunderous applause. Then all over again, as long as the audience would clap. I suppose this must be called a successful dramatic climax. But anything farther from the play's meaning at this point could scarcely be imagined. You would think that they were all pleased, Macduff included, at Duncan's murder. What was called for was, of course, a sullen murmur from a few, and only a few, of the crowd. Or if this makes an undesirable conclusion, then let the producer cut the final speech, and finish with Banquo's words, and the crowd's 'So all!' This is, I fear, an example of what the theatre too often means by the word 'dramatic'.

Thinking not of individual moments but of the whole play, the producer will study to make the grouping and action continually reflect, not the passing incident only, but its relation to the whole. The whole play should often seem implicit in the particular moment. Such a technique may be almost forced, as at the first entry of Antony and Cleopatra, but even this is sometimes distorted, with no play of pageantry or dignified centrality for the two protagonists. The quality of the significant moment, continual in Shakespeare, can often be greatly forwarded by careful arrangement. We must also look to bring out implicit significances where the text at first sight gives us little help. Usually we find fertile instances in the text deliberately killed in production. Romeo's 'O, I am fortune's fool' has been given no particular emphasis and drowned in other noises; and Macduff's 'Wherefore did you so?' spoken without challenge in either position or utterance. At every moment the production itself should seem to be aware of the whole play.[1]

Production should embody the quality of the text in other ways also. Shakespeare's writing varies widely from pure colloquialism to poetic dignity. *Othello* provides an excellent example. Othello's meeting with Desdemona at Cyprus is a moment of high romantic fervour and the poetry swells out with symbolic suggestions of a particular kind. The use of guns here is most important. We see the happy warrior, victorious over man and tempestuous seas, stepping from hard warrior-triumph to the peace of a radiant love. This follows a dialogue of pure colloquialism between Iago and Desdemona. A change must be apparent. Othello's entry will be rich in glamour, probably central and raised, the general effect a tableau. Nevertheless in a recent London production Othello and Desdemona met in what looked like an interior, with no implied suggestion in the action of any war-like excitement or thunderous triumph, no thought of battlements frowning over a tempestuous

[1]This quality my pictures are intended, in *photographic* terms, to project. The reservation is needed since some Pictures (1, 9, 29, 30) do not correspond to any actual stage moment.

sea. There was no crowd pageantry—which we can get with quite a few actors—and no interpretation of the peculiar quality of the scene. The protagonists met as two lovers might meet anywhere. Nor was there anything particularly striking in Othello's dress to suggest the magnificent warrior. In *King Lear* the middle scenes are highly fantastic. How often do we find this madness extravaganza given sensitive projection in grouping, action, and speech? This, the heart of the play, is a world rocking at its foundations. Naked Tom must not sit up to a table with Kent, the Fool, and Lear as though they were all having a comfortable evening meal.

Today we have two main varieties of failure. We have the production that gives Shakespeare as strong melodrama, unfortunately over-cumbered with archaic poeticisms but nevertheless with enough story and interesting situations to make it worth doing. This type gives us no sense of any extra levels of meaning, and we receive no feeling of the art-form as an organic whole. Recently I saw such a production of *Romeo and Juliet*. It was highly praised. Its technique was slick and finished and perfectly timed. The acting was good. But there were no undercurrents of significance. It was smooth melodrama, not poetic tragedy. We had no suggestion of tableaux in the meetings of the Houses; the fights were random sword-clinkings drowning words, street-brawls, no more; music for some reason inappropriately blurred Mercutio's descriptions of Tybalt; the Prince, representative of civic authority, wore a helmet; the Apothecary scene was given hurriedly as no more than a necessary action link; and the final scene was arranged incorrectly with the tombs down-stage. Almost every scene ended in a black-out. What complaints I have against all this will be clearer later. For the moment, I suggest merely that this was a typical modern production, excellent, professional, and mechanical. The sets were a succession of separately pleasing and tasteful scenes, not over-realistic, but bound together by no permanence. The time-stream of event was given with smart unvaried pace; but no deeper suggestions, no spatialized and spiritual architecture, took shape before the inward eye[1]. In the whole production I detected only one really creative stroke. I was

---

[1] Perhaps unjust: the soft colours created an *atmospheric* unity that stands the test of memory [1949]. Yes; and certainly the swift treatment suited so *narrative* a drama. My comments were one-sided. [1963]

told by a friend, Professor Gilbert Norwood, that one performance was exquisite, but he left me to discover which. I selected the one he meant. Tybalt I found impressive, original, significant, though I could not tell why. Professor Norwood had the reason: the part was performed (by Mr. Orson Welles) with deliberate feline suggestion in make-up and action. The result was remarkable. Observe (i) that this was gained by developing something already in Shakespeare, the association of the name Tybalt with cats being pointed in the text; and (ii) that such significances can, as Mr. T. S. Eliot has said of poetry, communicate before they are understood. I did not myself get the point, but recognized, and in some sense appreciated, the significance. Similarly, in my own productions, I do not expect an audience to be conscious of all the issues raised in my own mind during rehearsal. All one asks of an audience is imaginative receptivity; but we must ask more of our producers—the producer must have ideas.

Must have ideas. And yet these too can be disastrous. Which brings us to the second type of failure: the would-be 'symbolical' production, which saddles Shakespeare with elaborations that do not properly relate to the play. I have heard of the Weird Sisters being brought on at the end of *Macbeth*, or maybe only flashed in silhouette on the scene. This is quite wrong. The poetic atmosphere of *Macbeth* changes towards the close. Murk, nightmare and confusion are replaced by daylight, purpose and colour. Macbeth has woken up. The prophecies are revealed as having natural fulfilments. The supernatural has melted: Macbeth has supped full with horrors and direness no more frights him. There is here no place for the Weird Sisters. Recently I saw a well-acted and skilfully produced *Hamlet*. The whole was melodious and enjoyable, harmonious to ear and eye alike. Visually I received impressions of an almost Oriental splendour. The lighting was subtle and subdued, a Celtic twilight brooding over the action, quite alien to the stark intellectual quality of the play. There was some cleverly disciplined crowd-work: the company was especially good at circular crowd-swirls, interthreading into a vortex and unwinding very prettily. But all this was not very useful for *Hamlet*. After the play had unsettled the King, the courtiers and ladies circled for a while like the blessed spirits in Dante's Paradise; ladies clustered over the dead Queen at the finish like Dante's ecclesiastical Rose; and the King died on a glorious pirouette.

Such circlings are scarcely suited to *Hamlet*, which expresses something more angular, enigmatic, out of joint like a broken arm.

I have known *The Merchant of Venice* seriously mishandled. It was a very 'original' production. That, today, means, I fear, that all sorts of queer and wrong things happened that bore no relation to the text. The caskets, which should be dominating and solid, were painted on an arras falling down the side of a higher stage-level. Not distinguishing them, one felt hot during Morocco's speech, suspecting a mistake. Finally he produced the caskets' contents from the wall: I still don't know how. When Bassanio's turn came there was not even the wall. He stood fingering the keys and speaking. 'This time', I thought, 'something *has* gone wrong.' But the higher level slowly rose during his speech, and by the time Bassanio was ready the caskets, or pictures of them, were in place. None of this illuminates the text and much of it will distract and often conflict with words spoken. During Bassanio's speech in the first scene describing Portia to Antonio the stage behind the speakers slowly opened, and Portia was supposed to rise—actually the machinery went wrong—sitting on Belmont: the words did not need that sort of pointing. But here is something we can accept: the Cauldron scene in *Macbeth* has been done with voices off and Macbeth tossing restlessly on a couch. That is far from an ideal arrangement, but it at least preserves the spirit of the play and relates to the numerous nightmare references in the text.

I follow these preliminary and general remarks with more exact argument. This I present under certain separate headings related to the thoughts of my first chapter.

2. MAINLY TEMPORAL AND AURAL

The Shakespearian play is composed of a time-sequence of sounds. The sounds—words and additional effects—are, as it were, given. The producer has to make them live, express them in human action and stage-arrangements and machinery of various kinds, and give them an appropriate setting. Nevertheless, it is well to remember that the sounds come first. Nothing must smother or distort them.

Shakespearian speech demands close and subtle attention, and its satisfactory rendering is so difficult that we may safely call it, on the whole, impossible. That need not prevent us from doing our best. The main principle already laid down for production applies to speaking in particular. We must capture the underlying experience of the words and then, living in the thought and emotion, let the words give them poetic expression. An actor with a good voice may well think that he has only to give varied vocal embodiment to fine rhetoric, side-tracking the intellectual content. He may think that the poet has done all that for him, and that all he has to do is to build from the poetic result. But it will not do. He must get at the experience behind the words, suffer each swift change of thought, actually see, or aim at seeing, the phantasmagoria of imagery, till each phrase is variously and delicately tinted from within by the blood-essence of a felt significance. A beautiful and melodious voice may become a danger; each note and curve, however exquisite, unless closely related to and disciplined by the inward significances, may result in a collection of graceful corpses, perfumed with death.

Often today we hear a stagey ring. If analysed, we shall probably find that this staginess reduces to a series of emphases out of accord with the meaning; especially a tendency to strike a ringing anvil-blow on some not particularly emphatic monosyllable at a line's end, a fault which often seems to attack actors with exceptionally beautiful voices.

I offer some examples of the subtlety Shakespearian verse demands of an actor. In a mood of despair Hamlet thinks how he

> . . . can say nothing. No, not for a king
> Upon whose property and most dear life
> A damn'd defeat was made.   (II. ii. 604)

I suggest that he speaks in a black mood, but rising out from it comes the thought of his father, and the quality of the phrase 'most dear life' should be reflected in the light of the eye, the flicker of a smile, for a fraction of time before the mood recloses on 'damned'. If this were ordinary talk, such a physical change would within one mood be impossible, but the poetry reveals qualities of thought, not tricks of behaviour. It is highly complex, exposing hidden dimensions of human experience. But we must never get too far from the appearances of ordinary speech. Consider Hamlet's lines to his mother:

D

> Look here, upon this picture and on this,
> The counterfeit presentment of two brothers.
> See, what a grace was seated on this brow:
> Hyperion's curls, the front of Jove himself,
> An eye like Mars to threaten and command,
> A station like the herald Mercury
> New-lighted on a heaven-kissing hill.
> A combination and a form indeed
> Where every god did seem to set his seal
> To give the world assurance of a man.   (III. iv. 53)

This is my reading. The first line is colloquial; the second meditative. The third rises to a more rhetorical timbre. Next the specific quality of each god is vocally reflected: glory for Hyperion, awe for Jupiter, militaristic resonance for Mars with reverberations on the word 'command', and then a pure lyricism, a trilling ascent, for the next line's imagistic grace and thin vowels—'like', 'Mercury', 'lighted', 'kissing', 'hill', and the numerous 'e' sounds.[1] It does no harm to dwell on the 'kissing' for an instant, poised there in mid-flight. Then we drop back to matter-of-fact colloquialism for the last lines. The little unit has a poetic rise, meridian, and fall. We must aim vocally to capture these rhythms already deep-bedded in the meaning and embodied in the poetic expression.

All this demands intellectual study. We cannot get a speech properly across without understanding and living it. And yet unfortunately the understanding it and living it will not necessarily get it across. There is the hard physical technique of clear utterance, breath-control, and so on; and in concentrating on these we may lose all the rest.

A stagey ring is bad and an academic sing-song worse. The wrong sort of colloquialism is perhaps worst of all: some people who have no sense of metre split up the verse unforgivably; or

---

[1] Compare Vernon's speech in *1 Henry IV*, IV. i. 97–110. Observe its 'bird' and 'Mercury' images, and the way lightness of action is conveyed by light vowel sounds: *estridges, wind, glittering, images, spirit, cuisses, thighs*, etc. Contrast with this these lines from Hotspur's answer:

> Come, let me taste my horse,
> Who is to bear me like a thunderbolt
> Against the bosom of the Prince of Wales:
> Harry to Harry shall, hot horse to horse,
> Meet and ne'er part till one drop down a corse.

The difference between the 'characters' of Hotspur and Prince Hal is here a matter of vowel-sounds.

point the meaning of each simplest word as if talking to a child or a foreigner. I have also heard an actress whose diction was so perfect and voice so clear that I became conscious only of diction and clarity, forgetting the play; just as a too melodious voice, unless rigidly controlled by meaning, acts as a soporific. We must avoid too much of any good thing. The safest investment is constant and significant variation, *using deeper notes for the appropriate thoughts and images*. Shakespeare's temporal sequences, whether of speech or scenes or the fortunes of his people, continually move in waves. These waves of voice must be closely related to colloquial variation and meaning; and yet again there are times when a single intensity on one pitch gives more power than any degree of colloquialism. I seem to remember Violet Vanbrugh getting some such effect in Lady Macbeth's invocation to evil in Beerbohm Tree's production in 1911, and I have never heard it done so well since. Incidentally, the Weird Sisters almost always fail by using too raucous and naturalistically varied an utterance, whereas surely they do better with a wailing note like the whining of a wintry wind.

Possibilities are legion. Sudden colloquialism may be a stab of lightning across poetic sublimity; or *vice versa*. Each outlines, vitalizes, the other. There is variation in pace to be considered. Today speed is the danger. The modern actor often skips through the verse with a deadly facility. One feels he is not living the experiences behind the words.

I think one should sometimes definitely pause on a grand and glowing phrase, as though to cauterize the minds of the audience with its white-hot iron. In Othello's jealousy the lines are too often given as any old stream of fury to express a psychological state of ungoverned savagery. Rather the implied psychological state is there as rough scaffolding on which to erect the carven edifice of great poetry. Living the supposed actual experience is not enough: you must live the poetic experience. It is clear that poetry does not just express psychological behaviour. See how illogically Cleopatra keeps pouring blank verse at the messenger whilst impatient for his news: dramatic poetry is mainly concerned with expression of deep and complicated inward—or outward—experiences in terms of a most subtle intellectual technique. So, though the actor must, according to his conception, himself in part live Othello's supposed fury, he is to make of it a result very different. His technique is to be as subtle and assured as the poetry. We have all seen Othello look like a big black man in a rage and Macbeth at his play's conclusion like a wild and haggard criminal run to earth. Just what they are: and yet, are not. The actor should feel something of that, but not look it, or sound it. There is a repose and dignity necessary to the essential meaning of all art: 'In the very torrent, tempest, and, as I may say, whirl-wind of passion, you must acquire and beget a temperance that may give it smoothness.' The emotional limits of pure naturalism are quickly reached, and we get shouts and ranting that signify nothing, whereas a close artistic control from the first with defi-nite self-imposed limits has an infinite reserve of power. This is a principle of universal truth and applies to any art; and, for that matter, to life itself. And then again in any art there is a control and dignity and classic grace that is the primrose way to death: which is also true of life in general. The ideal producer will know all this, and have actors, if he is lucky, who can put it into practice.

What the actor has to do is somehow to get the blood-pulse and rhythmic beat of the living lines, and also the wider wave-lengths of each verse paragraph, each surging and dying move-ment; (see pp. 276–82); or the play's gathering to one great moment of tragic dignity, such as that crest which we have noticed in the story of Richard II; and then the cadences, the solemnity, the aftermaths of peace. The necessary control we are considering is one with the point we made in discussing Richard. Shakespeare's tragic protagonists are not to be regarded as weak failures curiously gifted with oratorical power. Rather they are voices giving outward show to a more inward quality; expressing the victory that is always bursting defeat like a bird from an egg-shell; revealing that greater world, that unruffled peace built of turbulence, the extra-dimensional music.

We cannot do full vocal justice to Shakespearian verse, but we can avoid crass blunders. This infinitely subtle correspondence to each fleeting thought and delicate emotion need hardly ever be accompanied by gasps, groans, and sobs. I have seen a six-foot Romeo lie on the stage making awful sob-sounds:

> Wert thou as young as I, Juliet thy love,
> An hour but married, Tybalt murderèd,
> Doting like me, and like me banishèd,

Then might'st thou speak, then might'st thou tear thy hair,
And fall upon the ground, as I do now,
Taking the measure of an unmade grave.   (III. iii. 64)

The maximum of rhetorical power should be put into the fling and abandon of such a speech, but never for an instant should emotion overspill the cup of poetic control. Too often we find simultaneously a fear of rhetorical abandon and a desire for crude expression in sobs and gasps. Romeo should not be a big baby here, but a terrific poetic force. Let the torrential flow gather up and crash over musically. The bodily fall should be itself melodious, matching the fall of the line, while the voice correspondingly descends the scale; and after the grand swaying cadences of the last two lines Romeo must lie still and silent. The emotion should come through the words and action, not in extempore animal sounds of the actor's invention.

In stabbing himself Antony need not gasp or grunt: it makes you think that something has gone wrong and he is really hurt.

Beside and beyond the words we must consider off-stage sound-effects. These are frequent and of great importance: their neglect or slurring is probably the most outstanding defect in modern Shakespearian production. I refer to trumpets, alarums, drums, cannon, tolling bells, and, above all, the thunder-tempests and music. On these two latter, as I have argued at length, the Shakespearian world revolves: they, and all kindred effects, must be employed exactly and powerfully. Nothing must take precedence over them. If no other reasons existed, elaborate and detailed realistic sets would have to be ruled out for their rival and hostile appeal. Off-stage sounds have a valuable quality of mystery and universality that certain types of visual realism will hopelessly mar. They work most powerfully from a restrained and simplified setting.

Too often we find no intelligent emphasis on these sounds. Often they are wrongly used. Over the radio I have heard the Ghost's entry in *Hamlet* accompanied by music. This is seriously un-Shakespearian. Music in Shakespeare is always optimistically charged and deliberately contrasted with such civic and cosmic disorders as Horatio compares the Ghost to. The Ghost, you may suggest, should then enter to thunder, like the Weird Sisters. Yet Shakespeare gives no hint of this. The elemental setting is neither one thing nor the other. It is a cloudy night, 'bitter cold', with stars but only 'glimpses of the moon'. Indeed, we never know quite how to take this Ghost: is he a spirit blessed or goblin damned? It is the problem of the play. The portentous figure is morally and aesthetically enigmatic: hence his enigmatic elemental setting. If we want a sound-effect here we must devise, or search in the text for, something in between, such as wind or surf.

This may all seem super-subtle. Besides, you can perhaps argue that this radio-music was evilly toned, like that barbaric music to which the torture-procession passes in Flecker's *Hassan*. In *Hassan* however the sensuously pleasing is throughout blended with the horrible after a fashion quite un-Shakespearian. Shakespeare, unlike Marlowe and Ben Jonson, refuses to allow sensuous delight to associate directly with evil: his negations are conflicts, never —or hardly ever—harmonies. They thus have appropriate effects of battle-alarums and thunder.

I have heard Juliet's potion speech ruined by the introduction of intermittent thunder. Shakespeare, one feels, would have directed thunder had he wanted it. However, it is a correct Shakespearian effect. Why is thunder here fatal?

Thunder does not accompany purely individual and personal psychic conflicts. Such are often enough compared in simile and metaphor to tempests and thunder; but that is all. In *Julius Caesar* and *Macbeth* the thunder accompanies a wholesale disorder, a vision of almost cosmic, certainly of civil, conflict. Though this may be related, as I have shown elsewhere, directly to the protagonist's own inward disorder, yet that disorder is not, on the stage, accompanied by audible thunder. Brutus meditates in his orchard, Macbeth and his wife murder Duncan, in silence: the poetry speaks of whizzing exhalations or tells us that the night has been unruly, but there are no stage sounds. The quality of these two scenes is pre-eminently one of hushed tensity. Lear certainly stands alone, or almost alone, addressing an actual thunder-tempest, and thunder previously blends with his determination to go mad rather than weep, and intermittently accompanies the cracking of his reason later. But, first, Lear and his setting are peculiarly blended and both peculiarly cosmic: the tempest relates to Goneril, Regan and Cornwall and their cruelty also; indeed, to the whole conception of conflict within creation on a wide scale. And, second, the outstanding and memorable effect of these moments is due to their exceptional daring: it is probably this that does most to make us feel Lear himself as a cosmic force. Fearful supernatural beings, the minatory Jupiter in *Cymbeline*, Ariel and his 'ministers of fate' in *The Tempest*, the Weird Sisters and their Apparitions in *Macbeth*, all may have thunder. But a ghost never does. A ghost is to be considered less than a human being, but a divine or wholly supernatural figure is by way of being a universal force. So thunder is never domestic. Even for Othello's jealousy it would be grossly out of place; the nearest approach is the wind heard by Desdemona in her willow-song scene; for Juliet's mental conflict in extreme and pathetic loneliness it is quite impossible. You cannot help feeling that Lady Capulet ought to hear it and come to see what Juliet is thinking about so to upset Verona's summer weather. It is easy to see why thunder is never used in *Hamlet*, so eminently a psychological play, and why the use of ear-splitting cracks, together with a black-out, at the entrance of the Ghost in the Closet scene, where Hamlet alone sees it, may be particularly distressing. We feel sure that the Queen must have noticed something. The question of an audience's acceptance of a stage person's apparent insensitivity was curiously raised when I did *Hamlet* in Toronto. Hamlet with drawn sword soliloquizes over the praying King. The sheathing of my sword was audible, and it seemed that the King should have heard it. No one worried about the words. The convention of soliloquy and asides is embedded in theatrical tradition, but we have far less latitude with non-verbal sounds, with the occasional exception of music.

Actual stage thunder is always cosmic, and has dramatically communal rather than psychological and domestic reverberations. Besides, thunder is from above, a ghost from below.

The opposing Shakespearian effect of music is, on the contrary, more closely related to individual persons. Often enough music significantly accompanies a general social harmony: as at the first entrance of Caesar, the Danish March in *Hamlet*, the music at the feasting of Duncan, though there is none at the later feast attended by Banquo's Ghost; the feasts given by Timon, and that in *Antony and Cleopatra*. But the subtler music incidents in Shakespeare are more inwardly conceived. At the end of *Richard II*, in the Welsh scene in *1 Henry IV* and the tavern-scene in *2 Henry IV*, the Brutus and Lucius incident in *Julius Caesar*, Ophelia's and Desdemona's songs, Lear's reunion with Cordelia, the mysterious 'hautboys' in *Antony and Cleopatra*, and the recurrent reunions after resurrection in the Final Plays, music suggests either some spiritual harmony related to an individual or the love of two individuals; or some universal and mystic peace touched by the protagonist, such as 'the music of the spheres' in *Pericles* and the solemn music of Queen Katharine's paradise-vision in *Henry VIII*. Hermione is resurrected to music in *The Winter's Tale*. Continually elsewhere music is directly related to love, as in *The Merchant of Venice* and *Twelfth Night*. Certainly it may tend to fill the whole action of the earlier Romances at times; but that is because these are saturated with romantic love, and may be considered dream-projections of inward longing. The Final Plays, including *The Tempest* and Ariel's music, are more realistically conceived, more authentic records of spiritual victory; and their resurrection music demands careful elaboration.[1]

Our continual disregard of Shakespeare's technique in this matter is seen in the persistent ignoring of stage-directions in the *Macbeth* Cauldron scene. The three Apparitions form a precise miniature of the whole play's dramatic conflict. Appropriately, they rise from the cauldron to thunder. They are followed shortly by the line of kings. These, being creative and harmonious visions hostile to the evil, the Weird Sisters are loth to show. Macbeth insists. The cauldron vanishes and the kings, who do not rise from the cauldron, pass to the music of hautboys, like the hautboys of the mystic music in *Antony and Cleopatra*. Modern productions hardly ever leave us clear as to what is happening in this scene.

I cannot over-stress the importance of all these and other kindred sounds. The bell that invites Macbeth to crime, let it not tinkle, but ring ominously. The knocking at the gate too often suggests rather an irritable postman than a fateful summons. The effects in *Hamlet* of kettle-drums, trumpets, and cannon are most important. They come first shortly before the Ghost's entry; then once at Hamlet's first hit in the duel; and again at the close. At both the beginning and the end of the play they are associated with the King's drinking to Hamlet. The main action is framed by these sounds. The trumpets in *Measure for Measure* and *King Lear* should sound a universal judgement call. As for fights and alarums

---

[1] Useful technical information on Shakespeare's music is given by Miss Cécile de Banke, *Shakespearean Stage Production* (1954).

and shouts—as in *Coriolanus*—they all need careful attention and elaborate orchestration. A Shakespearian tragedy normally ends with fighting. The inward conflict finds expression and resolution in militaristic and open opposition. Much of the producer's difficulty here, due to swords being no longer associated in the communal mind with actual danger, can be surmounted by careful sound-effects. A not too closely-defined suggestion of modern warfare might help.

All sound-effects must be carefully interspaced and orchestrated with the words. Neither must interrupt the other: without a pure sequence, you get no waves, no rhythms; and without rhythms, no variation and definition. Stage thunder is usually either pitifully weak or, if strong, it drowns the speeches. There is no reason why the tempest in *King Lear* (III. ii) should not be positively thunderous. The kind of thing I mean you may hear excellently done in musical oratorios which are often far more dramatic than the average Shakespearian production. You should feel that the theatre is coming down. Then let it dwindle, and over it rise Lear's words:

> Blow, winds, and crack your cheeks! rage! blow!
> You cataracts and hurricanoes, spout
> Till you have drench'd our steeples, drown'd the cocks!

More peals of thunder,[1] again curving down as Lear continues:

> You sulphurous and thought-executing fires . . .

Especially we need fine reverberations before 'Rumble thy bellyful . . .'[2]. The thunder is an actor in the play, and the thundermaster must know his cues. Where we have given only a stage-

---

[1] I doubt if I was following the exact *sequence* of wind, lightning and thunder correctly here: see p. 279 below. The general principle is not affected. [1963]

[2] Observe the harsh guttural consonants in Lear's first speech: *crack your cheeks, cataracts and hurricanoes, thought-executing, vaunt-couriers to oak-cleaving thunderbolts, thick rotundity, ingrateful man*. There is a subtle contrast in the sounds of his second speech, striking a more reserved note of pathos. There is a succession of long vowels in Hamlet's 'to be or not to be' soliloquy: *Sleep, heartache, dream, pause*. The thought interrupts them for a while. Then again: *weary life, bourn, returns*. Here is a compact contrast within two lines:

> When Richard, with his eye brimful of tears,
> Then check'd and rated by Northumberland . . .
>
> (*2 Henry IV*, III. i. 67)

The speaking should follow hints such as these as far as possible.

direction at the start, the producer must work out appropriate moments in the dialogue for himself and they must be properly planned. A usual fallacy supposes that words are effectively spoken through sounds such as thunder, shouts as at Laertes' rebellious entry in *Hamlet*, or music. A far finer effect is gained by interweaving, the one dying away as the other comes over; comes over, not through; so that we have rhythmic waves, significant undulations. A highly lyrical passage of spoken verse is not improved by music. Where music accompanies dialogue, as in *Twelfth Night* and *The Merchant of Venice*, great care is needed that no words be lost. The music can die away almost inaudibly, then rise and hold the stage alone, leading up to, shall we say, Orsino's: 'How dost thou like this tune?' In *King Lear* the continual directions of 'storm still'[1] hint at such a technique of intermittent sounds. We need not wait always for actual directions: we can follow their spirit without limiting ourselves to the letter. But the speeches must get across. However loud the hurly-burly, as in the street brawl in *Romeo and Juliet*, we need never drown the words.

The producer should not allow conflicting centres of interest to hold the stage simultaneously. In *2 Henry IV* the subtle comedy of Shallow's words has been ruined by the ragamuffin recruits searching their tatters for fleas. How could subtlety get a hearing with fleas as a rival attraction? I have seen the Gravedigger fidget with his grave and skulls during Hamlet's Yorick speech: such an important, almost formal, speech should rather be deliberately worked up to, and given every chance to get over. Stage business should always either help the words or be given an interspaced opportunity on its own. A Shakespearian play is a temporal sequence rising and falling; let one centre of interest subside and another come up elsewhere, one melt into the other, like waves. We want gentle, continuous variation and undulation, rather than a bubbling saucepan.

The play must flow continuously. A Shakespearian play is crammed with significant action and continual movement, and these must be allowed to express themselves unhampered. Waits between scenes hurt the sequence and disrupt the curves. Scenes

[1] Such sound-directions will be found in the Folio, and are to be distinguished from the scene-directions added by later commentators. Original directions will generally be either (i) aural or (ii) ceremonial; later additions generally scenic.

are not necessarily units at all. Often we can run two together; drawing a traverse behind actors moving down-stage may facilitate progress. But do not end scenes with a black-out. A black-out has no curves of nature about it and is utterly non-significant. A Shakespearian play moves in waves of sound and rhythmic surges. We want nothing too sudden. A black-out decapitates rather than rounds off the action, whereas slow or fast curtains, or a steady lowering of lights, have gradation and significance. The general method will resolve itself into some kind of a permanent set for big scenes played alternately with short front-scenes that allow for the moving of furniture behind. Shakespeare obviously wrote the plays on such a plan: they fall naturally into this arrangement. Do not let the act divisions, which may well be un-Shakespearian, hamper your plans; nor the scene descriptions 'Before Gloucester's castle' or 'Another part of the street': these are late additions. We must not regard the front-scenes as less important than the others. Usually they are most important. Alternate *short* flashes of opposing armies are often best done as front-scenes. There is no looseness of construction in these. The battle-scenes in *Antony and Cleopatra* are no faultier technically than similar short views on a film and to our film-trained eyes they should be strongly dramatic. The whole play should, like a film, move smartly, but not without variation, significant pauses, tableau effects. All the wider movements should rise and fall rhythmically, especially the play's close.

Intervals are necessary. Two usually work well. But they should be chosen to divide the play into significant movements, waves of action: see the divisions of *Henry VIII*, *Othello* and *Hamlet* in the productions described below. *King Lear* might be divided so that the tempest-scenes constitute a central unit. In tragedy we find that our central scenes tend to present conflict, followed by a temporary insecurity and lack of power in the protagonist, whereas the final movement rises to the tragic sacrifice with more assurance and dignity.

One last point. If the play is to be divided into three movements, what use of music, if any, is proper before each? Music as an overture risks clashing with music, or the significant absence of music, during the action. There can be no final rule. *Twelfth Night* or *A Midsummer Night's Dream* clearly allow us more musical latitude than *Hamlet*. I think that most Shakespearian tragedies are far better with a reserved use of trumpets or a low roll of drums, at the beginning and end of any one division. Sound-effects being so delicately and precisely used in Shakespeare, we must beware of introducing any that do not tone with the whole; or thinking that we can easily fill up an ugly gap in the continuity of the action with music or sounds that are not helpful, when a little thought or rearrangement might obviate the necessity altogether.

3. MAINLY VISUAL AND SPATIAL

The time-sequence of a Shakespearian play generates a mental area; its motion creates mass; from the flux and rhythm is built solidity. This I have called the play's 'spatial' nature, meaning its massed unity of imagery, symbols, persons, its colour. All these in any work of great poetry will have a solidity and richness beyond that given by lesser sorts of writing. The mind feels the play both as a time-sequence and as a spatial mass. There is however a difference. In actual fact the play *is* a time-sequence every time you read it, but its spatial quality is only mental or metaphoric. The time-sequence is as temporal as any sequence can be, but the spatial quality is not spatial in the sense that a garden is spatial. Moreover, this spatial quality depends on and varies according to the recipient's receptivity: the sequence, as a sequence, does not. Now the production of a play gives it the spatial and visual actuality that before was indecisive. From which I deduce this most important principle: *the visual and spatial effects of production should primarily subserve the play's emotional quality and poetic colour.* They will solidify the spiritual, make real that dimension of profound and solid significance that great poetry possesses. Thus the visual side of production will be concerned with the play's more significant, universal, and poetic qualities. It will be characterized by dignity, solidity, and permanence.

We proceed to apply this principle in turn to costumes; properties; lighting; and stage-settings.

Wherever possible costumes should illustrate and point the play's meanings. I have seen the Prince's entry in *Romeo and Juliet* after the fight in the middle action spoilt seriously by his standing bare-headed when all the others wore hats. I have also seen the part ruined by the wearing of an Homeric horse-hair helmet. The

Prince symbolizes a very simple quality: civic dignity and civic power. He is most unwarlike, not any too good even in his own office as a disciplinarian, and utterly opposed to all armed wranglings. He wields the power of civil authority. To make him walk the streets in a military helmet is as bad as sending him out hatless. Indeed, far worse. This is a very simple instance of how part of an elaborate production can fail through inattention to meaning. I feel sure that the costumes were all perfect as to period: our care is too often misplaced. In *Romeo and Juliet* the opposing houses should wear distinct liveries; and the Greeks and Trojans in *Troilus and Cressida* should be distinguished with regard to the differing qualities of the two parties. Once in a production of *Antony and Cleopatra* Cleopatra and her two girls wore Renaissance costumes and the rest, Egyptians and Romans alike, proper period dress of the ancient world. Whatever the reason and authority for this there is a damning objection. Cleopatra and her world should suggest the sensuous as opposed to Octavia's chastity: Octavia must therefore be heavily robed, but Cleopatra, her girls and her slaves will contrast in sinuous part-nakedness even with the Roman men, still more with Octavia. To have Cleopatra muffled up and the Romans bare-armed and bare-legged gets the contrast utterly wrong. Dress is always important. Watch the elaborate care with which Cleopatra calls for her regal robe when dressing herself for death; and let this grand and supernal chastity— 'Husband, I come'—contrast with her earlier appearance. See Pericles, reunited with Marina, how he calls for new clothes after his long night of despair. Where some violent effect of nakedness is needed, as for Edgar and Timon, it must be significant. I have twice seen a neat slip of a loin-cloth on a spotless body make Edgar look exactly like a young man going for a swim. Timon's prophetic rags, slight though they be, should fall with Hebraic and minatory implications. The worst and most ubiquitous error in production occurs in *Hamlet*. During the middle action he should look disintegrated, mad, pathetic and fearful all at once, or in turns (Pictures 3–6). Usually there is no change to speak of from his first appearance, in spite of Ophelia's words, thus adding distortion to complexity.

Considerations of period should normally give way to considerations of significance. The ideal will be a blend of some appropriate period—*Much Ado about Nothing* might go well in eighteenth-century dress—and interpretative meaning. We must be suspicious of any attempt to 'get back to the Elizabethans': the ideal production today will be essentially a modern production. If we feel that modern dress is not, except as an interesting and fertile experiment, finally suitable, that will be because Shakespearian costuming must be at some remove from the ordinary to help realize universal significances that are not outwardly apparent in modern life. Shakespeare usually removes his action from England; he is to be contrasted with such a realist as the Ben Jonson of *Bartholomew Fair*. Costumes should assist the heroic quality of poetic drama. They may be right in terms of some reasonable period and yet fail disastrously. I have watched a young actor in the final scene of Marlowe's *Faustus* struggling against an impossible Elizabethan costume: a short cloak pushed out behind by the sword he was unnecessarily wearing: a costume with none of the lines of dignity needed for so tremendous and difficult a scene. Indeed, I have never felt quite happy about Elizabethan clothes for Shakespearian tragedy: most earlier periods of fashion appear to me preferable. A blend of modernistic freedom and correct period would often be, perhaps, best, since Shakespeare usually touches the geographic and historic quality of the period he writes of: in *Macbeth, Romeo and Juliet*, the Roman plays. The question of dignity raises that of richness. Costuming should be 'rich, not gaudy': not solely because Shakespeare's poetic people are lords and kings, but because the quality of their feelings and actions is rich and grand, and our visual effects are to body forth this essential poetry. Of course, Shakespeare's choice of aristocratic persons is closely related to his sense of poetic sublimity: this however raises questions which we must put aside for the present.[1]

If dresses must be rich and dignified, it is equally important that all stage objects should appear weighty and solid. As far as possible they should always *be* what they represent. They should look important, and any not vitally involved in the action should as a rule be avoided. A throne on a dais, state chairs, tables, divans are all easy. But sometimes smaller objects do not receive proper attention. The three caskets in *The Merchant of Venice* are of rooted

[1] In *The Tempest* careful attention should be given to Prospero's mantle and, in contrast, to his ducal robes. His appearance towards the close as prince, indicating the assumption of temporal rule by wisdom, must be suitably striking. [1963]

significance and should be dominating and solid-looking. The quality of importance conveyed by a stage object varies according to its apparent solidity and weight. Any smaller properties, such as the present or presents Ophelia returns to Hamlet, should be used significantly. Hamlet can look at them as he says, 'I did love you once'. That makes them seem rich and important. Just as apparent richness and weight has spiritual force, so any spiritual impregnation loads an object with visual richness. The action should be continually impregnating stage objects with significance. Crowns in Shakespeare are often important: Lear's crown of flowers, Cassius' wreath, Cleopatra's diadem, Queen Katharine's garland of immortality, all have variously toned symbolic power, and must look worthy of it. Everything and every person about the stage should look important, real, and solid; we must be able to weigh them with the eye. We shall argue presently that this demands a fairly simple and preferably dark background.

Many producers love scenic alterations. Their aim however must be wrong, since the continually and subtly changing quality of the Shakespearian stream of event and emotion could never be given a correspondingly appropriate succession of changes in set. You may suggest that modern methods of lighting provide exactly such an infinitely variable means to atmospheric effect: which brings us to my peculiar *bête noire*.[1]

Modern lighting is wonderful, but I oppose the electrician's claim to be properly more than a minor assistance to Shakespearian production. Today elaborate lighting tends to replace elaborate settings, and the one heresy is as dangerous as the other. The old-style realism reduced poetic drama to the level of our normal waking consciousness; modern lighting drags it lower to a sub-human world of twilit dream.

When I first was able to use a proper theatre for my productions I was amazed to find with what ease glorious effects could be obtained. A word to the electrician and the sky-sheet looks mystic and fearsome and any figure in front becomes a grim silhouette; another, and you have a blazing June day; another, and a blushing sunset. All admirable. Better than poetry, easier, immediate, faultless. But why do Shakespeare at all? Listen to Horatio's words:

[1] For Mr. Edward Gordon Craig's claim to have devised a satisfactory method of kaleidoscopic changes, see p. 218 below.

But look, the morn in russet mantle clad
Walks o'er the dew of yon high eastern hill.
(Hamlet, 1. i. 166)

What is the point of it all? Surely this: to have certain significances
driven into the mind through the poetic and verbal intelligence.
That, we must suppose, is our aim and hope in attending to
Shakespeare; and presumably it does us good. Now, whatever
be the truth of a stage sunset, one thing is clear: any producer
can have it switched on, and any audience can appreciate it,
whereas not one actor in a hundred can with full vocal intelligence and richness and perfect accompanying gesture speak those
two simple lines exactly as we want them spoken, and not one
spectator in a thousand can fully appreciate them. Surely its facility
outlines the frivolity of too much reliance on lighting. Nor can
we have rich light-appeals together with other more concrete
effects. The moment we begin to rely on lighting as a primary aid
to significance, the actors begin to dissolve, gesture and facial
expression lose value, words are blurred: and, if all this were not
so, the human mind, incorrigibly flirtatious in matters of visual
appeal, would swiftly prostitute its attention. I once saw the
moonlight and music scene of *The Merchant of Venice* beautifully
arranged with cardboard marbled fountains and silhouette trees
and a delicate play of moonlight on Lorenzo and Jessica. It was
exquisite; I was visually intoxicated. But I did not listen to the
actors. Why, in any case, attempt to spoil these exquisite sonatas of
coloured light with Shakespeare's heavy and laborious language?
Let us have separate shows.

The light-expert paradoxically deals largely in darkness. He
prefers a darkened stage, where he may the more effectively drop
his pools of brilliance. You see a figure walking in twilight suddenly catch a steely ray from the wings, 'stick fiery off indeed' as
he says an important speech, then turn, and with a couple of steps
he is blacked-out, dissolved. Recently in the scene where Othello
comes before the Duke I watched him stand in half-darkness
saying quite important lines that accordingly lost power. Before
the Duke's table was a pool of light. I thought, 'When the time
for his big speech comes he will have to walk up those steps and
get into that light'; and he did. Nowadays instead of a level blend
and diffusion we often have harshly distinct colours from the
wings. We see Polixenes in *The Winter's Tale* take a warm red

from one wing, turn and catch a green from the other. It is a pretty dream-world. The dawn blushes in *Hamlet* and *Romeo and Juliet*, or trees in *A Midsummer Night's Dream* shiver against a moonlight that all but shames the moon.

We buy it all at a price. The actors become dream figures, invisibility clouds expression. Grouping becomes meaningless: if we clearly see only the chief figures, their positional relation to the rest is blurred or lost; and also the relation of every one to the stage itself, especially its centre. The sides of the stage become negative, with no clear-cut conventional limits. Solidity melts into fantasy, reality into dream. Nor is lighting so capable of subtlety as is usually supposed. It can certainly tint areas prettily; but Shakespeare's finer subtleties involve the interplay of persons. Lighting is crassly mechanical compared with the finesse of vocal or facial expression, the lift of an eyebrow, a touch of sarcasm in the voice, the twitching of a finger. Can a mechanical beam single out for emphasis minute significances comparable to these? Often a subsidiary person should register in such ways. While the light expert rules production, the actor can take things easy, and usually does.

Even if we wish to express darkness and mystery it should be done mainly in terms of visual positives. Ghost scenes are no exceptions. What makes the Ghost in *Hamlet* dramatically convincing? A green light? Or the expression on Marcellus' face, the gesture of Bernardo, Horatio's words:

> What art thou that usurp'st this time of night,
> Together with that fair and warlike form
> In which the majesty of buried Denmark
> Did sometimes march? By heaven, I charge thee, speak!
>
> (I. i. 46)

I have never yet seen a performance of *Hamlet* where the actors facing the Ghost were properly visible. The Ghost himself I have known to wear an electric light in his helmet, which he switches off under his cloak when he is to vanish; I have seen him appear as a floating phosphorescence in mid-air, over an otherwise darkened stage; or stalk as a silhouette against a violet sky. Every time the trickery was pretty enough. Every time the chief actors had to speak in darkness. It got across satisfactorily, as such things always do. But did Shakespeare get across? Did the art of the actor stand any chance of showing the possibility of a greater effect which has power not just to please with a transient titillation, but rather to transfix the listener and crucify him to an unforgettable experience? It may be hard to reach that; it is not impossible.

Light variations can be unobtrusively used and then they may be most helpful. But they must remain subordinate. For a night scene just a very little lowering of the lights and a slight dimming towards the wings gives all the hint you want. Or you can always start with the lights down and bring them up gradually before the first words are spoken. You can always quite easily play on your blues and greens for night-time, use your contrasts of amber and steel, warm up with reds when necessary, while keeping a properly diffused light, without ever blurring the expression of an actor's face, and the full stage normally quite visible, without allowing the audience to think about the lighting at all. All this is easy and effective: there is no technical difficulty. The error is this: the modern light-expert is regarding poetic drama as a dream-like fantasy instead of as a revelation of an extra dimension of waking life. He is aiming at the wrong thing.[1]

And now for the settings. The actors and all stage objects must not be dissolved into their background; they should rather stand out firmly. Action is often most powerful in front of a plain black curtain: black always shows up costumes and the actors' faces to fine effect. However, a fairly dark neutral colour that takes various lights with differing results is possibly best for general purposes. Imitation white stone or plaster, often used, does not throw out the face and figure so well: clearly the face, which is of primary importance, cannot contrast with it. The street-scenes in *Romeo and Juliet* often suffer in this way. Too much stage sky is bad, and should not normally form a background for any lengthy and important speech: Antony's funeral oration can be seriously weakened by having the speaker's head melted into a bright sky. The actor's face and figure must stand out powerfully and significantly: too often he, and any objects about the stage, are weighed in the eye's balances and found wanting. The sense of richness given by heavy curtains is often valuable. Once at a performance

---

[1] Later experience has tempted me to adventure farther into spectacular lighting for certain scenes; especially broad effects of whitish light and shadow from the wings. My objection to any emphatic use of blues and greens remains. [1949]

of *King Lear* I received no sense of solidity until the actors took their calls at the end in front of a plain heavy curtain. The costumes leapt up into a rich and lively significance. It was the most real moment in the play.

The setting can be simple, provided that it looks rich and dignified. It need not be definitely localized; and yet few people can totally disillusion their minds of nineteenth-century realism. Antony's speech is, certainly, supposed to occur in the Roman Forum; the fights in *Romeo and Juliet* happen in a street; Desdemona is murdered in her bedroom. But many scenes are indeterminate. Sometimes the locality appears to shift during a dialogue. Certainly because Othello addresses 'yond marble heaven' in the temptation-scene of *Othello* that is no authority for labelling the whole scene 'The Garden of the Castle'. Hamlet apostrophizes the firmament from what we thought was an interior, and later points out clouds to Polonius from the place where the play has just been performed. It does not follow that the middle action of *Hamlet* takes place mainly out of doors, nor that we have to build or visualize a window. The Elizabethan theatre was, it is true, open to the sky: but let the modern actor point up at any time during the action, and the audience will accept the gesture provided that the set does not present too meticulously realistic and detailed an interior. The scene headings in many modern Shakespearian texts are late additions. It is foolish to list scene localities on the programme: they really mean nothing. The Shakespearian play is a continuous stream of action, thought and emotion, revealing psychic rather than topographical panoramas.

Usually it is best to have a more or less permanent full set interspaced with front-scenes. These latter are not necessarily the less important. Where we have a particularly fine set-speech or any difficult incident or words that we want at all costs driven into our audience's minds, they are best thrown forward. Such are: Ophelia's description of Hamlet's changed appearance, the Queen's account of Ophelia's death, Mercutio's Queen Mab speech which loses much of its power if given from a full setting; Buckingham's farewell in *Henry VIII*, the Welsh Captain's dialogue with Salisbury in *Richard II*, Othello's description of the magical properties of the handkerchief. These are not soliloquies. Soliloquies are often best in a big set where the actor can people the stage with his thoughts and movements. They should not be given direct to the audience; though, when supported by listeners on the stage, a long speech often can and should be so given. Prince Hal's 'I know you all . . .' is clearly best done in the same set as was recently filled by his companions. Hamlet's long soliloquy can effectively use the full stage. But the front-scenes I have indicated fall naturally into such arrangement, and their peculiar quality is enhanced by it: I conclude that they were originally so conceived and planned. Where we have short flashes of opposing armies in turn, as in *Antony and Cleopatra* and the Histories, use of the front-cloth is inevitable and powerful, giving a vivid sense of conflict. Recently I saw such action played from opposite corners of a fairly realistic full setting, and the fault was obvious.

Anything like painted realistic scenery for the full sets is inappropriate. It pretends to be what it is not in a peculiarly annoying and unconvincing way that makes its pretence the more to be deprecated the nearer it approaches success. The first time you see what looked like a solid pillar tremble in the breeze, your faith is ruined; and on the most important point. Your dimensional faith is at stake; and I am arguing that the third space dimension of solidity on the stage corresponds to the extra dimension of psychic reality unveiled, or created, by poetry; so that, if the seemingly solid pillar is suddenly seen to be flat, poetic drama becomes not a revelation but a deception. Today there is a peculiarly annoying trick of using painted curtains for front-scenes, with houses and streets falling in folds. This is not studied symbolism, but slovenly realism. Everything on the stage should seem to be doing well what it tries to do, and such a curtain is doing its job of representing a street horribly badly. A well-graced and richly-robed actor speaking solid and rich blank verse in front of a painted back-drop meagrely representing a house appears, or should appear, devastatingly incongruous. Besides, two utterly different conventions clash. Such attempts pin the action and words to an exactitude and local reference alien to their nature. A street picture, whether full set or curtain, across the stage forcibly relates itself second by second to the words spoken in front of it, which may have nothing whatsoever to do with streets, and probably involve issues far more important. A fairly plain background is important not only in itself, but in that it allows all things said and done and all objects placed in front of it to be in turn exactly and precisely themselves, and not something else:

for everything on the stage is modified by its relations to other visible objects. An action played before a plain curtain, or an object so placed, is seen not in terms of some partial context, but *sub specie aeternitatis*. That is why, to the trained eye, things in front of a plain black, or other reasonably dark, curtain are at once so deeply significant.

A certain dignity and richness of setting is needed for all plays aiming at any kind of intellectual importance or spiritual profundity. Recently I saw Sean O'Casey's *The Plough and the Stars* done with very cheap-looking realistic slum scenes. Walls trembled, colours were non-significant: all cardboard and paper in the worst traditions of the last century. It was utterly wrong. A degree of solidity, formalism, and rich though simple colouring is needed even here: just as, however low the character an actor represents, there are certain ugly because non-significant postures and movements to be avoided. Especially in Shakespeare the spatial element of production has a precise and particular duty: to subserve the rich quality and complex inward significances of Shakespeare's text; to help body forth the concrete nature of poetic, that is of real as opposed to realistic, drama; something more, not less, solid and dimensional than what you find in lesser plays.

Then, you will say, we should arrange some elaborately symbolical modernistic set? But such settings are generally designed by artists not deeply and lovingly versed in Shakespeare's peculiar symbolisms. They are often angular, with cubes and steps and tiers and levels out of all proportion to the action; whereas a Shakespearian play is normally composed rather of rhythm, curvature, and gradation. Indeed, whatever sort of artistic setting we have, there is danger the moment it becomes an art-form in itself. A stage set should not make a pretty picture of its own. The empty stage should look formal and pleasing, but should seem to be waiting for the action to complete it: it should not hold definite significance in itself. If you do work out an elaborated and exactly appropriate set such as that I describe later for *Macbeth*, it should so depend throughout on the action for its meaning that, until you see the play performed, it looks grand, possibly, but certainly incomplete.

There is so much meaning in Shakespeare's text that if you load the eye with a new type of independent visual significance, even though it have a parallel correspondence to the play's quality, the mind cannot take it all in. This is what happens. At first the visual details dominate the attention and you don't get the play, the eye always being a more restful medium than the intelligence; then after a while you take the set for granted, see it no more, and watch the action only. The first part of the performance is ruined, the second not improved. Moreover, it is likely that such an elaborate set will not properly fulfil its function of throwing up the figures and especially the faces of the actors. The designer will have been thinking of other things. The only kind of elaborately planned set that is possible would be one that is all the time reacting closely on the text, one that so interlocks with rather than runs parallel to the action and words that the audience is continually being forced by it, not to neglect them, but to attend with new interest and understanding.

What, then, must we aim at? Something formal, pleasing, dignified. This will be fairly permanent. A plain curtain set disclosing a central platform and steps makes a good start. We can use a sky-sheet very often to good effect. We can break the back curtains with a couple of flats. For a peculiarly spiritual and metaphysical, as opposed to an historical, play, a couple of tall white cubes are sometimes helpful; it is wonderful what you can do by rearranging them and showing different edges. *King Lear* needs a more irregular suggestion; *Twelfth Night* can use a definitely formal garden wall and flowers. The main principle of solidity, some degree of formalism, and permanence, holds good; infinite variations can be invented according to the play and the occasion. For any tragedy, some underlining of centrality is nearly always important: our central steps, for example, and small platform. This helps to universalize the action. But a word of warning is necessary here: I have seen Cleopatra and her girls on a big stage high on a raised level above tiers of steps. This was a permanent set for the early Egyptian scenes. The empty lower level was widely illuminated. She seemed lost in vast spaces. A figure too high up after a while loses dignity and significance, especially if her position is not referred to any persons below. Her chair should, I felt, have been below the steps: visual importance being closely related to weight, or the sense of it.

Because our main plan involves formalism and permanence, we shall often deliberately avoid what seems at first a necessary touch of realism. Juliet's balcony and window will not be too realistically convincing, but rather solidly and plainly formal. As for Desdemona's bed, the more like a bed it is the less suggestion we can get of an altar. Universal as well as particular issues are involved. Permanence is in itself important: if we cut the big scenes too definitely into a street, Juliet's balcony, the Friar's cell, a bedroom, a tomb, we have separate bits of a story in place of a single dramatic statement. Often we find a hopeless succession of unrelated types of setting: plain, symbolical, and realistically painted front curtains; plain formal sets, symbolical-realistic sets; all sorts, in fact, with absolutely no unity of impact. There must be some noble permanence, reflecting the play's quality of wholeness, giving a sense of the end implicit in the start, and helping to build the final stillness of great drama that should crown and surround and interpenetrate the action. Nor will a permanent arch in one convention and a succession of changing realistic pictures in another seen through it be of value, since we end by believing neither in the arch nor in the pictures. Any such elaborate and detailed variations should be seen in front of, not behind and through, the enduring and enclosing whole; and this fortunately tends to preclude picture scenery. The spatial quality of the whole play must dominate in the permanent set, details of the story and changes of properties, which should be varied sufficiently to avoid monotony, significantly taking their place within and before it. The two are not finally distinct and it is because there are usually in Shakespeare certain recurrent, almost static, themes, leading colours of the play's patterned area, that an ideal set might be possible, as I have suggested, where certain symbolic permanences were solidified on a more elaborate scale, to blend variously with and at the same time brood over the action.

4. ON STAGE CONVENTION

The play's time-sequence generates a mental space-area, which in turn enriches the sequence, and so on infinitely. The more you know of the end the more significant the beginning, and *vice versa*. This oscillating reciprocity throws up the space-time quality of the result. The mind is expanded to a rich and complex apprehension; in terms of an art-form simultaneously fluid and solid it somehow focuses the universal in the particular and the infinite in the finite.

This is done, as I have already demonstrated, by use of conventions, especially conventional limits. Now whereas the literary play is limited mainly in time, so that we may not allow reasonings as to what happens before and after the action to disturb our view, the theatre works within a spatial convention as well, whose limits, conventionally accepted, open vistas of universal meaning. All that is necessary is the one acceptance. It is the same with the compressing line units in poetry, and with an actor's speaking: control holds infinite resources. The stage limits are accordingly themselves important. Kill or fog the limits and you tend to blur all grand suggestion in terms of those limits. That is why pools of light and areas of darkness are, normally, bad: we receive no sense of a marked-out area. The audience need not see the whole stage clearly all the time, but they should be visually aware of it. They should feel a significant right or left, up-stage and down, especially a significant centre; and there should be a certain grand permanence limiting the whole. Only so can universal meanings get across. Supposing central steps are made to look too definitely like palace stairs: an actor standing on them no longer commands the universe; he is half-way between his bedroom and the front door. Therefore a too realistic wall or house corner are not good: we feel there are more houses outside the wings, or perhaps a gate farther along the wall. Within our limits we have our world: outside them not houses or gates, but either (i) nothing or (ii) infinity, though under this second heading I should have to include vague suggestion of any particular quality; as when, at a certain point in the action, one side of the stage is impregnated with associations of a particular person and his significance. We must be willing to use the whole stage frankly as a conventionally accepted medium. Often the producer tries to pretend that things are not happening in a theatre, whereas everyone knows that they are, and it is just this that gives him his chance, for this knowledge is to be used and not fought against. Work in full recognition of the convention and you can pack the universe into your theatre.

Conventionally limited, the stage becomes a magic area where every action and position is deeply significant. What is our real reason for producing Shakespeare at all? To hear the words? You could have those by sitting at home and reading. Elaborate visual effects of light and set? I have tried to kill that fallacy. No.

The Theory of Production

Neither the spatial nor the temporal in abstraction reaches the play's essential quality, which exists in mental space-time; and the vitality of any production depends on its power to project this space-time, solid-fluid, quality in terms of *significant action*. This principle, which includes both words and use of properties, involves too continually varied significance in movement and grouping, which in turn depends largely on a properly conventionalized stage area. The result will be a fusing together, a reintegration, of the play's two elements, temporal and spatial, particular and universal, to build a proper re-creation.

All poses and gestures should, in any straight poetic part, be picturesque and dignified.[1] The actor should normally look grand and heroic. Every movement should be significant. A stage fall should be rhythmic, not sudden. Recently I have twice noticed in professional productions a fall done in one sudden, straight, slanting, and signal-like motion, with the body left lying like a log, the feet together and straight. There is no natural gradation in that. A sway and a half-turn is more graceful; and the body should arrange itself in a picturesque position. Nor is it only a question of pleasing appearance: the sudden straight fall is quite negative and you hardly believe in it. A dying man must deliberately act his dying, which involves at least two movements. Similarly, a log-like body does not look so significantly dead as one with limbs more artistically deployed. Gestures also must be melodic, not angular, and normally not too fast or significance is lost. Wide and graceful gestures and picturesque positions generally are demanded not by any considerations of period, as is sometimes supposed, but to establish again the extra dimension of poetic drama (see pp. 236–40, 279–80).

At every moment the producer must have regard to the stage group. He should be continually at work to make grouping significant. I give a few simple instances. Three persons alone on the stage look bad if equidistant. Whether or not they are in a straight line, the equidistance itself leaves them in non-significant relation, whereas one facing two placed together is powerful, since you then get opposition, which implies conflict, and therefore drama.

[1] In my own experience practising before a looking-glass can be very depressing. You cannot see yourself in any particular action, since you see your own eyes, which are necessarily diverted from taking part in that action, and the whole result is at once dislocated. By arranging the glass so that your head is cut out of vision you can, however, get a fairly good idea of your poses, gestures, and turns.

Even though the persons be friendly, this holds; for conversation is itself a sort of conflict. Certainly if you get a quarrel, as with Brutus and Cassius, the opponents must face each other strongly and use the whole stage. Such considerations are important: the formality of grouping at every instant should be significant. In grouping a big informal crowd addressed by a central figure up-stage you must deploy your actors, not in diagonal lines sloping towards the central figure, but rather in small serried ranks parallel to the audience, close against the wing curtains; the ranks getting more central as you work up-stage. Entrances of important people should be given careful ceremonial, the stage filling from both sides to avoid a procession. These are only a few basic ideas: but the grouping should be employed all the time with additional subtlety to express the varying meanings of situation and action.

Each part of the stage has its own significance. Exits should not be chancy matters. Within a scene one side of the stage may quickly get charged with a certain association. You can spoil Mark Antony's entrance after Caesar's murder by making him come in from a conspirator-impregnated side. A conventionally accepted stage is always alive with potential meaning. In watching a student performance of *Berkeley Square* (by John L. Balderstone and J. C. Squire) I was recently struck by the possibilities of stage convention. The lovers part tragically across the centuries, the hero leaving the eighteenth for the twentieth. The girl stood with an Isis-symbol, a cross surmounted by a circle, while her lover, facing her, backed into the curtained wings. The lights were well up. The situation was allowed to play itself and the effect over-powering: the stage wings became vistas of time; time was, for the moment, spatial. By using and welcoming the stage convention we can do things impossible otherwise. How often is the central madness extravaganza of *King Lear* properly done? Only an elaborated use of significant action and grouping can properly join with the words and thunder to build its towering fantasti-cality. The stage limits may create profound significance beyond themselves. See how Shakespeare uses the stage in *Macbeth*; how Macbeth's exit for the murder off takes him from the visible world into infinities of horror. Here we touch the reason why noises off so often hold infinite reverberations.

Suppose the Weird Sisters in the first scene of *Macbeth* are to vanish. A black-out does nothing: but suppose they act the vanishing. Say they speak their words in a still group centre, one standing, another kneeling close, the third kneeling on the other side farther off. They employ appropriately significant, melodic, and clearly visible gestures, such as the hand dropping from the wrist with forefinger pointing down: and how much more effective that is in realizing the supernaturally evil than darkness and green lights. At the close, the group is broken. A twirl and a turn, proper gestures, the words pitched on the note of a whining wind, and the side figures go into different wings, the centre one exits centre. We gain not only the effect of the three parting from each other, but also make a solid group dissolve, melt into air; the action helps to realize the idea of vanishing. It is all done by positive visual suggestion in terms of the convention, with rhythm, gradation and significance. How does this compare with the usual black-out? Or suppose Hamlet is to speak his long soliloquy dramatizing his own inactivity. How is essential inaction to be put across by significant action? I describe my solution later.

Half the errors of modern Shakespearian production are due to misunderstanding of the nature of stage convention. Nowhere is this clearer than with ghosts. Producers are usually weak on *Hamlet*, but are worse with *Macbeth*. Banquo's ghostly entrance at the feast I have seen represented with a magic-lantern projection on to Macbeth's cushion, or as a sliding panel up the back of his throne. I have seen Banquo get unobtrusively in place with his back to the audience and then show himself by turning his blood-bolter'd face, and afterwards scamper out at the wings with his head down, whilst the other actors crowd around holding out their cloaks. Or I have seen the Ghost represented by Macbeth's own shadow cast on the wall, symbolizing the subjectivity of his fear, though I did not get the point at the time. But, after all, what has all this, except perhaps the last, to do with Shakespeare? Or with drama in general?

Behind these tricks is the desire to make the supernatural convincing. The producer completely ignores that willing suspension of disbelief that is his right. In terms of stage convention he has to do certain very difficult things; instead, he wastes his time labouring to replace that convention by something quite superfluous that no one wants. For suppose you did convince the audience that you had a real ghost on the stage, they would only be frightened and leave the theatre. You may call this an absurd objection. Well, say you arrange matters so that the audience knows that the Ghost only seems to appear from nowhere and vanish. Then for the rest of the scene the audience are wondering how it was done and whispering theories to each other, the dramatic tension quite killed. What of a method than which nothing can be more disastrous than perfect success? We should always want our audience to see how effects are accomplished: if this spoils the effect, it is nearly certain to be a bad one. Moreover, the whole point and horror of a ghost in real life is that it looks just like a living person except, I am told, that its movement makes no sound. It does not appear in a green light. Nor does it slide up the back of your chair. As usual, poetic drama turns out to be fundamentally more real than realism: Shakespeare's ghosts come in and go out, like all respectable stage persons, by the stage entrances. If grouping and good acting, by the ghost and still more by those who see it, do not make it convincing, nothing will; and if you want to suggest the infinite, as when a supernatural being vanishes, nothing will do it so well as the skilful use of the wings of a conventionally limited stage; since such a stage suggests the world, and its limits can always be used as frontiers of infinity.

The same principle of conventional acceptance applies to fights. They should be as dramatically powerful as possible, but not just a series of random sword-clinkings and vagabond noise. Often the best effects are attained by suggestion rather than actual blows: a weapon raised and held for a moment above a shrinking opponent in the middle of a mêlée may be extremely effective. Othello has to strike Desdemona: if just before the blow he looks as though he is going to make it and just after both look as though it has been made, the blow will be dramatically convincing. An audience is very kind and sensible where conventional belief is demanded, but utterly heartless the moment you try to deceive them. That, in nine cases out of ten, is why they laugh at the wrong time.

The whole performance should be constricted by a set convention which gives it infinite freedom. The stage becomes a world. For a grand ceremonial it should be filled broadly to the down-stage wings. A small stage thus used with a few actors gives a greater impression of size and numbers than a large stage full of actors less carefully placed, with a yard or so left unfilled at the sides. Opposing armies across a front-scene can give a grand impression if well spaced out, as when Brutus and Cassius confront Octavius and Antony. You do not need a vast army. In a full set four or five well-deployed figures can be arranged to lead the eye towards the wings, widening out and forcing the imagination to construct an infinite proportional expansion beyond the recognized limits; whereas a crowd of thousands in an out-of-doors pageant may well look meagre.

Today we have slight sense of the universal. Our typical plays are pieces of life torn from their context in the whole. But a Shakespearian play is not: it and its stage traffic in universality. Its kings should appear as kings of the whole world; its heroes, as mankind; its happy-ending romance becomes a dream of paradise; its tragedy, solemnizing the principle of sacrifice, touches ritual.

5

Whatever be our views about the theatre, it is clear that Shakespeare cannot be popular on the stage while we clog his plays by unsuitable methods. What is uniquely Shakespeare's own is finally his one hope of popularity on or off the stage. The best sort of performance, and by far the hardest to create, would make the play look as though it had produced itself. With care we must exclude all false short cuts to an outward appearance of elaboration, whilst aiming instead to exploit the inner core and centrality of the drama. But never must the production appear laboured or inhumanly intellectualized. The more graceful effects of poetic gesture should be shot through and varied, like Shakespeare's poetry, by touches of pure naturalism. Sets and properties must be so devised that they lend themselves easily to the action, and blend into the various supposed localities of the performance. There is no point in having Desdemona's bed central and looking like an altar, unless it also is very clearly known to be her bed. Shakespeare touches universality continually, but it is always the intensely human that he universalizes. I hope none of my remarks appear to argue that Shakespeare is a writer of classic formality: I stress most the elements most in danger of neglect. Shakespeare's art shows a unique blend of classic dignity and romantic naturalism. This we forget at our peril. The Court scene in *The*

Merchant of Venice has been played with dummied figures and masked faces sitting in a row: I cannot see Shakespeare's humanism in a masked face. Too often so-called 'symbolic' effects sit on a Shakespearian play like a monkey on a war-horse. Those I emphasize are rather the combing of its mane, the glint of steel on its hoof, the caparison to drape its flank. So we shall lead it out for some great actor, some new Garrick, Kean, Henry Irving or Forbes-Robertson, to bestride as never before was possible. Shakespeare's symbolic effects expand but never oppose nature; his world is no dream world, but a newly-wakened world; his is an inclusive transcendentalism. Therefore all our symbolisms must be warmly human; intensely real, though not realistic; drawn from, not imposed on, the action.

More: if the production is to live, the producer himself must build and create during rehearsal; even sometimes take suggestions from his cast; must use the varied interplay of personality at his disposal to the full. Every true performance, amateur or professional or mixed, is partly a communal creation. The producer must have final control over every detail, but he should use it with reserve. He should not work from an unalterable plan. Who ever painted a picture or wrote a novel in that way? So much depends on the actual personalities of the cast. In my own experience the best points often develop from an accident, some one else's good suggestion, or the necessities of a particular stage. Limitations are usually capable of exploitation. Every true artist knows this. Shakespeare knew it. Art is not a luxuriating of fancy, but a bending of opposition and inertia to the creative will.

CHAPTER III

Some Actual Productions

I

I shall next describe some actual examples. First, I outline the development of Orsino in *Twelfth Night*, a part which I have had the opportunity of playing[1]; next, I refer shortly to my productions of *Romeo and Juliet*, *Henry VIII*, *Othello*, *Hamlet*, and *King Lear*. I use the initials C, R, and L, for 'centre', 'right' and 'left'. Stage right is the audience's left. Up-stage is away from the audience, down-stage towards them.

Hart House Theatre in Toronto has a good fore-stage which suits Shakespeare well and serves to make the change from auditorium to stage gradual and convincing. We ought perhaps before this to have discussed the kind of stage best suited to Shakespeare. However, what we do on our stage is more important than the type of stage we use: often we have no choice. A blend of modernism and fore-stage seems best, such as you have at the Stratford (England) Theatre. I am not myself in favour of an Elizabethan theatre: to incorporate certain Elizabethan principles with our own seems healthier.[2]

[1] On two occasions. One was a production by the late E. A. Dale of Toronto, to whose work for the Shakespeare Society I would here pay tribute; as also to that of Major James Annand, Mr. Raymond Card, and Mr. Leonard Parker. [1963]

[2] I feel, however, that I ought to quote this relevant passage from an article by Mr. T. R. Barnes in *Scrutiny* (IV, iii; December 1935) on the Maddermarket Theatre, Norwich (which I have not yet seen): 'It is very difficult to describe in words the effect of all this in practice; but it is quite unlike the ordinary theatre. The actors do not appear to be in a brilliantly lit box, but seem more three-dimensional and more natural than they do on other stages. The settings form, as it were, a screen in front of which they perform. But in spite of this intimacy and naturalness, the actors (as they should) seem to inhabit a world of their own. The separation between play and audience is created by light, rather than by the structure of the theatre. One can look at the picture without being perpetually reminded of the frame. One gets an

2

Orsino in TWELFTH NIGHT

The current stage misconception that Orsino is a dull part is a symptom of our false valuations concerning dramatic poetry. Difficult it may be, but not dull. It is subtler than the part of Sir Toby. Orsino starts as a romantic lover, with a fiercely passionate nature dominated by Olivia. At his second appearance his words 'Who saw Cesario, ho?' following Valentine's remarks about Viola's advancement, already suggest a new emotional direction. Next, he describes how he has opened his soul to the supposed boy. He talks of his 'passion' when Cesario (i.e. Viola) reminds him of it, only next moment to revert at length to Cesario's suitability as a messenger. This he develops, promising big rewards. Watch how fond he is getting of Cesario. Soon we find them together listening to sentimental music. Orsino is now happier being sentimental over Olivia with the boy beside him than he would be if his suit were accepted. Notice with what new and contrasted cheeriness he enters: 'Good-morrow, friends'. See how he looks forward to a feast of sentiment and song with Cesario. Last night it relieved 'his passion much': we can well believe it. He calls Cesario to his chair, and talks of the day when he too shall love, enjoying the thought. At the words 'the constant image of the creature that is belov'd his eyes can rest on Viola: the action points the quality of the whole scene. Orsino is unconsciously revealing to us a love he has not yet recognized. He asks how Cesario likes the music. 'It gives a very echo to the seat where love is thron'd.' Orsino, delighted, inquires if the boy has himself yet loved, and an exquisite dialogue of cross-purposes ensues: Orsino enjoys associating Cesario with love. The psychology is subtle and delicate. And somehow, listening to Cesario's replies, in a new and finer consciousness, he wistfully speaks the truth of his violent masculine passion for Olivia:

---

impression of height and space which is almost always lacking in the box stage, however painstaking the scenery is; the picture is higher than it is wide—a shape which is more dramatic (if one may speak of a dramatic shape); on stages, for example, like that of the Festival Theatre [i.e. at Cambridge], which is longer than it is wide, you get the effect of a frieze, which is narrative, not dramatic.' [This footnote appeared in the 1936 edition, but was excluded from the 1949 Penguin edition. Compare p. 294 below.)

For, boy, however we do praise ourselves,
Our fancies are more giddy and unfirm,
More longing, wavering, sooner lost and worn
Than women's are.

To which Cesario replies: 'I think it well, my lord.' Watch the contrast in this scene of female sincerity, marked by Viola's short replies, and male flamboyance. Feste arrives. Orsino tells Cesario to mark the song, which he describes. It is 'old and plain', not light and flashy: a significant contrast between the two sorts of love outlined in this scene. So together they listen to Feste, Viola deeply in love with Orsino, Orsino not yet aware that he is already deeply in love with Cesario. He has an arm round the boy, holds his hand, listening to the love-poignancies of Feste's wavering melody, Olivia all but forgotten; for it is a nameless Love only that rules, Cesario by his side. As from a dream, where the touch of Cesario plays a part, Orsino wakes; but I think Feste has to come and stand in front to remind him, coughs perhaps, and receives his payment. We need not fear comedy. Why does Feste get so many tips? Other Shakespearian fools do not. Feste, compact of music and wit, distils the quintessence of the romantic comedies and is the presiding genius of *Twelfth Night*. His habit of getting money out of everyone increases his dramatic dignity: he is *using* them.

So Orsino and Cesario have to be recalled from the paradise wherein the undulations of music still hold their minds. Orsino is irritable. He tells them all to go.

Again he is alone with Cesario. His Olivia-passion, the cheating lure that vulture-like has fixed its beak in his consciousness, has returned. It rises almost as an undesired duty. Lust is a very conscious experience. The mind projects before itself an image not profoundly desired by the unconscious self and therefore finally unsatisfying; and next pursues it almost as a *duty*. A. C. Bradley has noted that Macbeth seems to kill Duncan as a 'duty'; and I have elsewhere noticed the element of lust in the play. Certainly Orsino is tormented by carnal passion. If he in deep thought crosses the stage before 'Once more, Cesario', we can get the change well underlined by action. His love for Olivia, he says, owes nothing to her wealth: it is purely her face and body he desires, or words to that effect. There is no thought of anything deeper. At Cesario's objections to his insistence—how maternal

Viola is compared with Orsino's almost adolescent unreason—
and the apt reference to some woman whose love might with a
like hopelessness be set on him, Orsino scoffs at woman's love,
saying that no woman could sustain so powerful a passion. His
words, in his changed consciousness, contradict the spirit of his
earlier admission of masculine inconstancy. He is irritable, angry,
in that confusion where the baffled mind struggles to unify and
objectify its conflicting levels of consciousness.

Viola helps him. She tells of her supposed sister's love, and for
the first time in this scene lets herself go:

> My father had a daughter lov'd a man . . .

Orsino grows interested. He returns to his chair. She is kneeling
by him. They are again almost in their old positions. Again he
takes her hand. The accents of true love melt the mirage of his
eye-lust for Olivia. 'She never told her love . . .' Orsino is again
rapt in Cesario. But Viola has gone too far, and draws away, tears
welling to her eyes. Turning from him, quickly she speaks: 'Sir,
shall I to this lady?' Orsino is baffled: both at the boy and at himself. Then he remembers his part of dramatic lover, recalls how
he loves Olivia, and speaks perfunctorily:

> Ay, that's the theme.
> To her in haste; give her this jewel. Say
> My love can give no place, bide no denay.

His mind is not in the glib words. Cesario goes out. If during the
action some small object, a rose for example, can be impregnated
with Cesario-associations and left lying about, Orsino can now
stand watching Cesario's exit, then pick it up, look anxious, and,
ending with a gesture of worry, go out deeply thoughtful.

In the last scene, where Orsino is rejected by Olivia, his threat
to slaughter Cesario does not conflict with my reading. His
Olivia-lust is a mad hunger (I. i. 3, 22; II. iv. 102), and, when it
dominates, all-powerful:

> But this, your minion, whom I know you love,
> *And whom, by heaven, I swear I tender dearly,*
> Him will I tear out of that cruel eye
> Where he sits crowned in his master's spite.
> Come, boy, with me; my thoughts are ripe in mischief.
> I'll sacrifice *the lamb that I do love*
> To spite a raven's heart within a dove.

The italicized words should be spoken with an expression of inward conflict. Orsino recognizes the act as one of mad 'mischief': he is spiting himself as well as everyone else. Observe, too, that there may be some jealousy of Olivia's share in Cesario's affections. Anyway he is thwarted on every side and mad with rage. When he knows the truth and Cesario turns out to be a girl, he should look as though scales of blindness have fallen from his eyes.[1] Paradise is found at his elbow and has been there all the time, could he have known it:

> Boy, thou hast said to me a thousand times
> Thou never would'st love woman like to me.

Orsino speaks the final couplet: Viola is to be 'Orsino's mistress and his fancy's queen'. It is a lovely ending. It is not a patched-up conclusion. From the very start this ending is prepared. Orsino, like Benedick, the chief persons in *Measure for Measure*, and Shakespeare's greater tragic figures, is shown on a voyage of self-discovery. He sloughs off the false and is forced by the action to self-recognition. He should not be presented as a sentimental young man, but rather as a barbaric prince, somewhat oriental, of a passionate and violent nature. His name is significant.

3

ROMEO AND JULIET

Hart House Theatre, Toronto; 1932

Our working out of the first fight appeared to me interesting. It is important to get the contrast of the two houses and their retainers branded into the audience's mind, and this cannot be done if the words are lost. The servants start brawling, but as soon as they cross weapons Benvolio enters. They pause at his words; or he beats down their swords. Tybalt's entry draws Benvolio's attention; they speak and start to fight, the servants

[1] Shakespeare's sonnets describe a man's love for a boy, such as Antonio's for Bassanio and the other Antonio's for Sebastian. The Antonio-Sebastian drama is a miniature *Othello*, and most powerful. To what extent may we relate the boys-who-turn-out-to-be-girls in the romantic plays to Sonnet xx? Or other such plots in Elizabethan drama to a general tendency towards such attachments? [Since first composing this note, I have expanded its thought in *Christ and Nietzsche*, *The Mutual Flame*; and elsewhere; 1963.]

supporting them on either side, not actually crossing weapons, but shouting 'Down with the Capulets' or 'Montagues'. Two officers enter, using staves to push back the fighters. Capulet enters from down R. His appearance helps the officers to check the noise and most of the action: his words should get an exact hearing. Then Montague enters down L. They face each other across the fore-stage, each with his lady restraining him. The tableau is important. When they fall on each other there starts a general mêlée. The two officers use action that suggests that they are restraining Capulet and Montague; one between them, one outside Montague, to avoid too stiff an artificiality. There are more shouts, and weapons cross. There is more noise than ever before, thunderous.

For an instant you get a vivid picture: on each side one of the servants sinks to his knee, an arm shielding his turned head from an opponent holding an uplifted weapon. These are up-stage of Capulet and Montague and their wives, and partly obscured. What is wanted is a definitely significant picture to build the effect subconsciously. There is a great noise just before the Prince's entry. Notice how the entrances are built up: servants, gentlemen, lords, and the Prince, in order. He enters on a platform up C and speaks from its steps; the noise dwindles, then rises. The fighting has stopped. He carves a way down centre, the officers pushing people aside. There are still murmurs. He is right down on the words 'Throw your mistemper'd weapons to the ground'. There is complete silence. A pause. Then, 'And hear the sentence of your moved prince'. He turns—the deliberate throwing away of stage presence by a turn up-stage underlines his absolute authority—and walks up C, followed by the officers. Standing on the steps he speaks the rest, officers either side, the whole group, who have had time to get to new positions, listening: many have their backs half-turned to the audience, giving emphasis to the Prince's importance.

Done like this, not a single line need be lost; there has been hardly any actual fighting, but the impression of a fight is strong. We realize the fight by an undulating succession, increasing waves, curving down after the Prince's entrance; the usual Shakespearian movement. Such variation is far more effective than one undifferentiated mass of noise, since without variation there is no significance. Shouts and murmurs in waves are more humanly effective than weapons banging. Usually the words are quite lost; people in odd corners of the stage clink swords in pairs, with no effect of two separate parties, nor any real effect of a fight, which cannot be got by just imitating fighting. The Prince comes on as likely as not from one side instead of appearing high and central. We must use our conventional stage and get significant pictures from our groupings. There is usually no centrality about the set: it is just 'a street in Verona' and looks like one: nothing has been done to spatialize the play's inward centrality, and without such interpretation the production is dead. The various entrances are all important: there is a patterned formality about them which must be not only preserved but emphasized.

Romeo and Juliet presents a love union in contrast to family hostility and civil disorder: the contrast is clearly a variation of the music-tempest opposition throughout Shakespeare. The prologue correctly describes the play. *Romeo and Juliet* is more than a love story, since not only is the lovers' story related to these outward disturbances, but their deaths prove sacrificially creative. The play has an exact and intricate pattern. These wider issues must not be slurred.

In this production we used no sky-sheet, only black drapes with steps and a platform disclosed centre. On the central platform we arranged variously two white blocks, made to appear like solid rectangular cubes, over six feet long with a cross-section about eighteen inches square. For the street scenes one stood perpendicular, the other lay horizontal and diagonally towards the audience, both with corners and edges showing as much as possible. They gave the touch we wanted of rectangular irregularity suggesting city streets and buildings. For the Capulets' dance they became pillars, and were useful for Juliet's tomb. They appeared in all the full-set scenes, giving a helpful impression of permanence. The Friar Laurence incidents and smaller Capulet scenes were done before plain curtains. Juliet's potion speech is most effective with a minimum of furniture: we had one couch in front of a black curtain. Romeo's parting with Juliet we arranged poorly with Romeo going off on one side and a plain back curtain. I have seen it done better by the Ottawa Drama League, Romeo disappearing over a central balcony against a sky background. In most professional performances these inward and emotional scenes are hampered by alien effects. If Romeo ties a rope to Juliet's bed to help him down, and she throws it after him, it is all very convincing but disconcerting. Such action has no depth of inward significance at all, and therefore fights against the words, besides making us too conscious of windows, beds, dressing-tables, hair-brushes, and so on.

In the central fight scene Mercutio and Benvolio must really start in ill-humour with each other. It is a hot day. They are bored and quarrel irritably about each other's aptitude to quarrel. The humour of the situation should be unconscious on their part. They are shown in a mood that makes Mercutio's later actions reasonable. An interesting point arose in Romeo's attack on Tybalt. In contrast to the earlier Mercutio-Tybalt duel, Romeo rushes on Tybalt in a blind frenzy, disarms him with a sword and stabs him with a dagger. At the dress rehearsal I found that I had no time or space to draw the dagger: I just pushed at him with my hand, his body obscuring the action. Though I clearly could not have drawn the dagger, no one observed anything wrong, and we did it that way each night, without losing the effect. In this scene, when the Prince arrives, he is better not speaking from the centre steps. He has done that once. It is better to have him down centre, in the middle of the general distress, as it were; drawn down from his authority by this disastrous civil disorder that has ended in his own kinsman's death. So he stands, surrounded by figures pleading for forgiveness or vengeance, Lady Capulet kneeling over Tybalt. He is a symbol of Verona, torn, distracted by internal conflict.

Romeo grows during the play. First he is a love-sick boy,[1] next an ardent and successful lover; next, a hero suffering for support of his friend. In his 'banishèd' scene with Friar Laurence his emotion is violent, and must be given with *rhetorical* force and abandon. He must on no account sob like a big baby: he so often does. This is the sort of situation that only poetic drama can properly tackle and we must let it do so. At his re-entrance into the action in the Mantua scene he should show a new maturity and manly dignity: the wearing of a cloak and top-boots, a small but effective touch, strikes the right note. His soliloquy recount-

---

[1] His youth should be emphasized by make-up. Picture 1, which was taken during the 1939 production of *Romeo and Juliet* (p. 13 above), shows highlights on the face and a broadened mouth making a 'character' creation quite different from my own appearance.

ing his wondrous dream must be given every chance: this is all clearly to be done on the fore-stage. The dream curiously forecasts *Antony and Cleopatra*, touching a sense of love's victory beyond death. Compare Romeo's '. . . that I reviv'd, and was an emperor' and Cleopatra's 'I dream'd there was an emperor Antony'.

Romeo's hearing of Juliet's death is best taken with a terrible quiet and a mad glint in the eye giving a new depth to contrast with his earlier abandon. His description of the Apothecary is very important, and should be done slowly. New worlds are swimming into his ken. Tragic experience now for the first time opens his eyes to suffering and impoverished humanity: Lear's purgatory is forecast. He recalls having seen the Apothecary; partly because he needs him and partly because his consciousness is tuned in to such things, unnoticed before. Shakespeare uses the Apothecary to strike the required tragic note. Watch how Romeo's values are reversed during his conversation with the man: the world's gold becomes poison, life a sickness. Even so, beyond pleasure himself, he takes a selfless pleasure in the other's advantage: 'Farewell; buy good and get thyself in flesh'. This is the first purely selfless thought he has uttered: Juliet's death has made a Christian of him. All this must be stressed and done simply: we must not spoil it by attempts to photograph Mantua.

When Romeo next enters before the tomb with Balthasar his heavy step and set looks must express his deadly intensity and rigid course. He warns his servant from impeding his almost maniac determination. He gives him gold and says farewell kindly, again kind with an all but inhuman and last-moment charity, like Timon with Flavius. In these latter scenes Romeo should certainly wear a heavy cloak: it gives him the extra power and presence that he needs. We are in the world of *Othello*, *King Lear* and *Timon of Athens*. Alone on the stage he turns and walks *up* towards the tomb, a figure of tragic destiny. It is a tragic *ascent*.

The last scene of *Romeo and Juliet* is nearly always arranged badly. The full set usually shows the interior of the vault. For much of the scene this at first sight appears to have certain advantages; for the end it is weak and for the beginning ruinous. Romeo has to enter far up-stage beyond a grating, he and Balthasar two distant silhouettes. His first speeches are thrown away: instead the picturesque adventure fills the eye with tawdry enjoyment. At the entry of Capulet, Montague, and the Prince it is not very helpful to have the final group within the tomb. The final speeches are better spoken from outside it, from the outside world, overlooking the lovers' tragedy, yet looking up to it nevertheless as to a sacrifice. The Prince's reference to the sun's overclouding comes better this way than if they were already engulfed underground; though this is a minor point.

The tomb should, then, be up-centre and raised. Romeo entered, in our production, down L on the fore-stage: this throws the intensity of his first speeches down close to the audience. As he walks up to Juliet, he is, as it were, climbing, not descending. The mattock-business of the opening of the tomb we did simply by suggestion—though Romeo had an actual mattock—and the drawing of a curtain: a little extra realism could be arranged, if wanted. The middle action is equally good this way, and the final group better. The whole scene acts itself. It might have been written for such an arrangement, and as a matter of fact was. However, we nowadays see it done differently, all to get a pretty effect of gratings and silhouette figures against a night sky and perhaps a twinkling star: disjointing the body of the drama and pushing it out of shape.

The conclusion should be stately and ceremonious, with no hurry, though the Friar's speech will be condensed by cutting. We cut also from Juliet's potion speech to Romeo's Mantua scene. For a production done under un-professional conditions it is safest to cut freely and if possible find a large cut that does not tangle the pattern, generally in the latter half. We had no music, unavoidably; but certain simple sound-effects at act beginnings might have been profitably devised.

4

Henry VIII

Hart House Theatre, Toronto; 1934 (see p. 23)

Henry VIII is a massive play. It is a fitting, one might say the only fitting, culmination of Shakespeare's work. The play was given in three acts. Each movement we preluded with music suggesting, for Act I, tragedy; for Act II, a quality pre-eminently martial and kingly; for Act III, a joyful solemnity. Certain other scenes were given a few bars appropriate to what followed. I tried to play on a recurrent king-theme *motif*. The saturating Christian quality of the play was reflected into anthems and hymns.

As for sets, we used mainly an up-stage central platform and steps between black curtains. On the platform was a table and chair, and behind small red curtains disclosing a stained-glass window. This appeared to blend neatly a permanent and ecclesiastical formalism with historical realism. In front we used thrones, chairs, tables. Once we had the red curtains closed and a heavy lighted candelabra on the platform, for the scene where the King hears of the birth of his child. For the Queen's trial the central platform was filled with standing lords and a bench of bishops below on the steps; the Cardinals' thrones were up L to LC and the King's R. Down L was the Queen's chair. This arrangement distinguished between the King's and Cardinals' authority, and gave the Queen an important cross to a good position between the King and Cardinals for her long speeches. Buckingham's farewell speech was spoken, necessarily I think, on the fore-stage.

Three scenes are worth describing in some detail. The first is that (III. ii) where the King discovers Wolsey's duplicity and leaves him to the merciless baiting of hostile lords. My arrangement illustrates what I mean by 'significant action'.

The set shows a chair and table on the platform in the up-stage central alcove, and another chair and table down R. Throughout the scene we use the platform as peculiarly Wolsey's, its centrality and height relating to the here dominating matter of his high position; the right of the stage belongs to the King. Off-stage L is imagined as Wolsey's world, off-stage R as the King's.

The four lords are discovered discussing their grievances and rumours of Wolsey's impending disgrace. Seeing him coming L they draw down L on the fore-stage. Wolsey crosses R, dismisses Cromwell, who goes out L, and sits at the table down R soliloquizing. Appropriately he sits in the chair later to be used by the King as he plans how to rule the King's affairs. Wolsey next goes up C to the other chair and gets busy with his papers; the movement toning with his unrestful state of mind. The King enters R with an attendant lord, sits by the table down R, and addresses the four lords who have advanced. Two of them go to awake Wolsey's attention to the King's presence, and then go R.

Wolsey comes down C. He faces the seated King and three

standing lords R, who are grouped like a tribunal; the two other lords are L. He is, as it were, surrounded by cold hostility on both sides as he receives the King's anger. All but Wolsey exit R, the two lords L passing behind him up-stage, leaving him high and dry, so to speak, as he comes down looking at the papers that have ruined him, given by the King.

Wolsey, alone, first sits R, sees the whole disastrous situation, and in despair rises and retires up towards the alcove, standing on the steps, back turned. The lords, the Lord Chamberlain, Norfolk, Suffolk and Surrey, re-enter from the King's side R. The Lord Chamberlain and Norfolk get L of Wolsey and demand as from the King his seal of office. Wolsey, who has come down the steps C with great dignity, refuses, then turns to re-ascend. Their words bring him down again. For a while he maintains this central position, the lords taunting and insulting him, two on either side. Surrey, particularly fiery, has moved from R across Suffolk to RC. From there he makes a particularly insulting remark about Wolsey's supposed amours and then turns away up-stage R, the line lending itself to just this movement of disgust. He is joined there by Suffolk, who walks up, R of the table. Wolsey with great dignity crosses down R to the table on the line: 'How much, methinks, I could despise this man. . . .' This movement suggests his yet intact outward confidence, since he goes deliberately to the side—the King's side—from which the insult came; yet suggests subtly his need of chair or table as support. Observe that he has given up his central position. The placing now is: Wolsey standing by the table R, slightly more central than the two lords Surrey and Suffolk behind him up-stage R; and Norfolk and the Lord Chamberlain L. The Lord Chamberlain stands well away, aside from it all, to mark his more sympathetic and kindly nature. Now the other three lords volley a succession of charges at Wolsey. Surrey and Suffolk come down centre from up-stage R, coming from behind Wolsey, each on his first words in a semicircular movement ranging themselves with Norfolk in a diagonal line. The accumulative nature of their accusations is underlined by one following the other; and the coming round from behind gives a touch of meanness to their bullying attack. At one particularly crushing charge Wolsey sinks in the chair. Wolsey's central dignity is gone; he sits crushed on the King's side of the stage where he was recently planning England's future;

and the lords are now one combined force bearing down on him from one side and shutting him off from both the platform and his own world L. One of them might ascend the first step. Finally the lords exit R as before, passing up-stage of Wolsey. Anything slightly undignified in their thus trooping off in single file tones with their bullying behaviour. Surrey makes a final expression of scorn as he passes; the Lord Chamberlain, the last to go, hesitates, looks sorry and baffled, and passes out.

Wolsey is left alone again. His soliloquy is spoken in the chair. Cromwell enters L, and gives his news turned away down L. At 'That's news indeed' Wolsey stands, only to sit again at 'There was the weight that pull'd me down'. At his assertion of loyalty Cromwell falls kneeling by Wolsey's chair. Wolsey speaks sitting, his hand on Cromwell's shoulder, but rises on the line 'Say, Wolsey that once trod the ways of glory', Cromwell still kneeling. At 'Prithee, lead me in' Cromwell rises. They go up C. At the words, 'Farewell the hopes of court' Wolsey turns and looks towards the empty chair R. At 'My hopes in Heaven do dwell' Wolsey and Cromwell are C, backs to the audience, Wolsey looking up toward the stained-glass windows. The scene then closes.

We next notice the scene (IV. ii) where Queen Katharine has a vision of Paradise. This, Shakespeare's last play, shares with the others of his final period a strong religious and mystical quality, here for the first time explicitly Christian.

The sick Queen is discovered in a chair RC with two girls and her gentleman Griffeth. The lights are slightly dimmed, with a predominance of red to create a sunset effect. Griffeth speaks his description of Wolsey's end. The Queen asks for music. Griffeth makes a gesture down L and withdraws there with the two girls, as solemn piano music starts. As soon as the now sleeping Queen is quite alone violins are audible coming over the solemn music which dies down. Faint voices are heard, singing an Easter Alleluia hymn. The voices and violins gather power as three white-robed figures enter from either side. The lights gradually come up. The six, themselves silent, execute a complicated dance, and curtsey to the Queen in pairs. At the climax, when the lights and singing are at their height, they offer her the garland of immortality. The lights are now a white blaze on the snowy figures. The Queen holds out her hands. Then the figures depart, voices and violins growing softer and lights dimming down to their original strength and colour. Finally the solemn bars from the piano come up again and all is as it started. The Queen calls, Griffeth and the girls go to her, having seen and heard nothing.

We amplified Shakespeare's directions to the extent of varying the music, but the effect was essentially true to them. The use of lights was unorthodox: a sleep-vision is nearly always done in queer lights. I chose the opposite, showing off the vision against waking life as daylight against dream. Whether or not we believe in any paradise it is clearly the producer's business to make such scenes convincing; and a paradise of green or blue lights is not attractive (Picture 10).

The whole last movement is optimistic, towering up to the final crest of prophecy. In the earlier parts we had tragedy heavily toned with the religious consolation of Buckingham's and Wolsey's last speeches. Our third act is happier. In Queen Katharine's vision we face the radiance of eternity; in the coronation of Anne Bullen and the christening of Elizabeth we face rather a radiance temporal and earthly. To point a unity here I used the same Easter hymn for Katharine's vision and Elizabeth's christening procession. Easter associations are appropriate to both resurrection and birth. If it were objected that the hymn was a Protestant affair out of period, we could argue that the play significantly contrasts Cranmer and the Cardinals. In this last act Cranmer becomes most important: the three tragic persons were excessively proud and fell; Cranmer is excessively humble and rises. We have three processions in the play: first, Buckingham's execution; second, Anne Bullen's coronation; third, the christening. The first two went across the fore-stage, rather similarly, to help stress their comparison and contrast as noticed by one of the choric gentlemen in the text. Our last procession gained a new dimension of importance by coming up on to the stage through the auditorium.

For our final scene the Lord Chamberlain is addressing the two porters on the fore-stage before a plain curtain. Then from the back of the auditorium the joyful pealing of church bells breaks out, and the procession appears singing the Easter hymn. As it reaches the fore-stage the curtain opens, discovering the full set with a few persons grouped on both sides. The Duchess with the child Elizabeth under a canopy goes up the steps C with Cranmer; the rest of the procession goes mostly L, but some R. This leaves empty spaces R. The Lord Chamberlain speaks his formal salutation down L. Next there are trumpets and the King's guard enters R; and then the King with more lords and preceded by two heralds walks up C to a few bars of the king *motif*. Notice that the empty spaces are now being filled. The deliberate and *gradual* filling of such spaces in a scene of pageantry is effective. We gain a sense of mass by watching the building piece by piece, and one of plan and purpose that lends the whole significance. In this instance we have seen the Alleluia procession arrive, leaving Cranmer and the child in the centre; and, as the waiting gaps in stage grouping, which give us a sense of something lacking, are filled at the King's entry, we watch royalism complement religion. The interplay of Church and State is vital in *Henry VIII*. So now the King ascends the steps, stands opposite Cranmer, and kisses the child; and then starts to descend, taking Cranmer's hand. But Cranmer holds back after coming down one step and asks leave to speak. This gets the King a step lower than Cranmer, who remains high and central for his prophecy, the culmination of the whole play and, indeed, Shakespeare's last word to the world.

Additional Note, 1963

Buckingham's farewell on the way to execution in *Henry VIII* (ii. i) is among Shakespeare's most remarkable long speeches. It is patterned on the deposition scene in *Richard II* (p. 32); both show humility giving way to anger. This is my reading:

A great and loved nobleman, Buckingham is attended by a crowd of sympathizers. He forgives his enemies and accusers, imitating Christ, and means to maintain this high state. Lovell's interruption should be regarded as a painful, because *specific*, test, but after a pause Buckingham recovers himself and assumes a yet more spectacular, though now slightly artificial, pose of universal forgiveness.

When Vaux refers to his lordly status there follows a yet more severe test, touching Buckingham's pride. He is projected into the *Timon* world of bitterness at betrayal and ingratitude, and the stifled passions within him are released, as he denounces his enemies. Fingering by chance a cross that he is wearing he realizes how far he has fallen from the Christ-like state he had aimed at.

He is silent. Then, struck with remorse, he asks for his followers' prayers.

In this speech of Shakespeare's last play the long line of his tragic heroes is brought to the bar of Christianity, and found wanting. If the overtones and variations here indicated are preserved, the scene is among the most dramatically moving in Shakespeare. A more detailed examination of it is given in *The Crown of Life*, 274–8.

5

OTHELLO

Hart House Theatre, Toronto; 1934

We divided the play into three movements; one leading up to Cassio's dismissal; the second composed only of the big temptation scene; the third, the rest of the play. That is, the hatching of Iago's plot; the success of it; the result of it.

The early scenes were done simply, but a difficulty arose at the change from the Duke's council-chamber to Cyprus. There was furniture to be moved. The gap was filled by an interesting expedient. We want something here to indicate and help realize the change in locality; and the tempestuous voyage of Othello and the rest is of great importance and needs underlining. Its symbolic force is this: Othello and Desdemona conquer adversity. They arrive safe over hostile and tempestuous seas. The Turks are drowned and Othello when rejoining Desdemona is shown victorious in both war and love. All this contrasts with the more fatal spiritual tempest to be raised later in Othello's mind by Iago. So we arranged a miniature orchestra of sounds, using a wind-machine, a surf-machine, a thunder-sheet, a big drum, and a bugle. All lights are down. Waves of elemental conflict crash in the darkness, and through them comes a faint strangled bugle; again, waves of sound booming and thundering, dying and rising, a crescendo of fury; but next the bugle comes strong and clear over the tempestuous waves, suggesting the victory of man over hostile nature. These sounds last quite a while and are very loud. Meanwhile the curtains have been drawn, and the lights go up on Cyprus.

On the central platform there is a plain balcony against a darkened sky-sheet, where men are watching the waves. Montano

strides about anxiously below. The lights are still a little dimmed.
News arrives by hurrying messengers. All is warlike preparation
and bustle. Intermittent wind and surf still sound. A messenger
tells of the Turkish disaster and of the arrival of Cassio's ship. It
is growing lighter. Cassio enters L, thronged by citizens. He wears
armour and a helmet. Cries of 'A sail, a sail!' are heard. Soon—
not directly—after, guns thunder a salute. Cassio's arrival was not
so heralded beforehand. A messenger goes off to inquire of this
new arrival, while Cassio tells of Othello's marriage, emphasizing
Desdemona's excellence. The messenger returns, saying that it is
she who has arrived. Cassio in figurative language imagines her
divine prerogative of safety against tempests. He prays for
Othello, speaking of him as of a god coming to breathe life-fire
into the Cypriots. The glamorous situation is being built, heaped
up, one entry on another. The lights are well raised. Desdemona,
Emilia, and Iago enter from the centre platform, and descend the
steps, holding their raised position for a second or two while the
crowded stage kneels at Cassio's command and Cassio speaks his
welcome. Watch Desdemona descend, immortal beauty un-
touched by storm. The lights are bright on her. No more wind
and surf is audible: the tempest is being crushed by human excellence. Now again, in quick succession, cries of 'A sail, a sail!'
and guns. Cassio was unannounced by such effects; for Desdemona they were separated by a few lines; now they come both at
once. While they go for the news, Desdemona talks playfully to
Iago: an exquisite contrast and delicate irony. She is gay and
colloquial. A divine domesticity breathes from her. A trumpet
sounds: our third entry has this additional ceremony, by contrast
rising over the others. 'The Moor—I know his trumpet!' Cheers
sound off. Desdemona runs to the steps. Attended by soldiers
Othello appears up-centre on the platform, with steel breastplate
and tall Viking helmet, and stands amid a din of welcome from
the now packed stage, an arm raised both in recognition and to
command silence. There is next utter quiet. He starts to come
down, and holds out his arms as Desdemona steps up to his
embrace. Notice that she, no 'moth of peace', goes *up* to meet
him, up to his glamorous world, he does not descend all the way.
'O my fair warrior!' The light falls brilliant on them, central.

The scene progresses in waves, like the first scene in *Romeo and
Juliet*, each entry more striking than the last. Consider the skilful

technique by which normal time is telescoped to make such a swift-gathering crescendo of dramatic effect, depending as it does on the arrival of several ships, possible. My arrangement brings out only what is already in Shakespeare. The poetry here is highly decorative and richly inflated with universal significance. As Othello and Desdemona kiss, Iago, down L, mutters: 'O you are well tun'd now . . .' It is a great scene: but its grand artistry can be slaughtered by inconsiderate production.

After Othello's exit we had Bianca give an inviting eye to Cassio, who reciprocates her interest; and shortly after introduced a dance for her and two others. My reasons were: (i) the part of Bianca needs building up, and it is as well to let the audience know who and what she is or her later entry loses force; (ii) in this way we help to illuminate the part of Cassio, his attractiveness and moral laxity; and (iii) it all serves to create a sensuous suggestion, in tone with the change in locality, that helps the later action.

The Herald announces the general holiday on the fore-stage. Then the curtain discovers our recent full set, now with a table and benches L. Montano, Iago, and others are lounging about. The dance starts, given by Bianca and two girls. It is a southern riotous affair with tambourines. Bianca follows with a solo turn, very colourful and sensuous. All this lends point to Othello's warning to Cassio—they enter down R after the dance is over—about over-stepping the limits of merry-making. Cassio's drunkenness follows more easily. When Othello enters after the fight we can get a good effect by letting him stalk about in dead silence. Seeing Bianca solicitous for Cassio, holding on to him perhaps, he gives her a stony and puritanical stare, as though his high morality is doubly shocked by scenting sexual in addition to imbibitory vice. These are the kind of additions I defend: unless they seem to be doing quite a lot of useful things at the same time, they are probably unsafe.

We come now to the important middle act, where we find some interesting examples of significant action. The set shows the steps and central platform between dark curtains. Over the balcony is thrown a rich purple cloth. The sky is bright behind. On the main stage we have two light-grey seats by a table with a golden tasselled cloth R, a little up-stage, and a colourous divan L. On the table are papers, ink, and pens. Up to now Othello has

1, 2. *Romeo and Juliet*, Toronto 1939 (p. 13); Romeo (pp. 86 note, 216); Juliet, Grace Irwin

3, 4, 5, 6. *Hamlet*, Toronto 1933 (p. 23; for the variations, pp. 44, 105–21)

7. *Antony and Cleopatra*, Toronto 1937 (pp., 13, 164 note). The death of Antony: Antony, Edward Roberts; Cleopatra, Betty Markham; Charmian, Patricia Murphy; Iras, Valentine Barrow; Dercetas, William Shelden; Eros, Robert Anderson

8. *Antony and Cleopatra*, Toronto 1937 (pp. 13, 164 note). The death of Cleopatra: Cleopatra, Betty Markham; Dolabella, Norman Maclean; Octavius Caesar, Fred Mann

Henry VIII, Toronto 1934
(pp. 23, 164 note)

9. The Duke of Buckingham

10. Queen Katharine's vision
of Paradise (pp. 91–2): Queen
Katharine, Frances Rostance

11. (*above*) *Macbeth*, Brownlow Card's production, Toronto 1938 (pp. 134, 173; notes), showing the incident described on p. 134 note: Banquo, Armand Gardner; Fleance, Nancy Ann Fetherstone. Macbeth watching

12. (*left*) *Macbeth*, Toronto 1938 (p. 134, 283, notes)

13. (*right*) *The Tempest*, Toronto 1938 (pp. 13, 274): Ariel, Josephine Koenig.

dressed in European style; from now onwards he wears an oriental costume; a purple gown with, in this scene, a loose gold and red robe over it.

Desdemona, Emilia and Cassio are discovered talking. Just before Cassio's exit R Othello and Iago enter on the fore-stage down L. This entry with Iago tends to impregnate stage-left with suggestion of Iago and render it slightly hostile to Desdemona, who will throughout exit and re-enter R. Othello hears Desdemona's solicitations, sits at the table R on the inside, more central, chair, and there succumbs to her caresses and gives in. The ladies exit R. Iago crosses up R above Othello, gazing after them. He is now beyond the table, R. Othello is signing papers. The action of this long scene will show us Iago driving Othello from up-stage R to down L. The table suggests the civilized Europeanized Othello; the divan L something of oriental passion. Iago will exit and re-enter L.

At Iago's first words Othello continues with his papers. Afterwards he puts them down. Iago sits R on the outside chair far R at 'My lord, you know I love you'. Othello stands at 'By heaven, I'll know thy thoughts'; Iago stands and draws back. Othello's 'Ha!' is uttered as he strides suddenly C; a significant move according to my plan. Iago follows close up with 'Beware, my lord, of jealousy'. Othello is C or RC at 'O misery'; then, recovering, turns to Iago, and speaks his reassurance; lays his hand on his shoulder, crosses below the table to the *far* seat R, sits down, and restarts on his papers. This long walk indicates a strong recovery; yet the fact that he has gone too far and finds that he now has to regather his papers for his new position at the wrong chair reflects the excess and uncertainty of his assurance. Iago now comes up close, kneeling on the other more central chair—the one Othello first occupied—and continues, Othello glancing sideways nervously as though afraid of having his confidence blasted by an awkward truth. Quickly he is standing again, Iago also, solicitous. Othello, now very perturbed, asks to be left alone. Iago goes out L. Othello with steady deliberation crosses to the divan and stands by it as he considers his wife's possible unfaithfulness. Up to now Othello has been comparatively subdued in word and action compared with what is to follow. Notice the acute psychology by which terrible news is shown as not having its full effect at the start: it has to work in the constitution. Iago's

lines on 'dangerous conceits' suggest as much. Othello's soliloquy is meditative. His mind is numbed, the full pain not yet felt.

Desdemona re-enters on the platform up RC with Emilia; there is the short conversation and the dropping of the handkerchief. Othello and Desdemona go out up RC. Othello can stop, study Desdemona's face, and then go out alone, she wondering at it. Emilia, left alone, picks up the handkerchief. Iago returns and gets it from her. Dismissing her, he goes down L for his soliloquy about dangerous conceits. He watches Othello stride back across the platform C, and speaks his 'mandragora' lines, standing in the position, down L, where he is finally to drive Othello. He waits, his back half-turned to the audience, mesmerizing, drawing Othello, who now re-enters C descending the steps. 'Ha! ha! False to me?' Iago gets up-stage, L of Othello, on 'How now, General, no more of that'. Othello should already show a great increase in passion: a few minutes off the stage can often be allowed to correspond to hours.

Othello speaks his first words 'Avaunt, begone . . .' from the steps, with great, though controlled, intensity; then crosses Iago to LC on the words 'What sense had I . . .' He has come a little down-stage, and maintains the position for 'O now forever . . .' facing diagonally L away from Iago. During his next violent speeches he turns on Iago C, his wrath rising, and attacks him, throwing him to the ground close to the table; then walks back L and paces down-stage, then up, distractedly, on 'I think my wife be honest and think she is not'. He is violently agitated. This section of the scene is using mainly the left of the stage as the first part of it used the right. Iago is driving Othello down-stage, and to the left. At 'Death and damnation!' Othello sinks on the couch: the first time he has actually touched it. Iago draws close, telling him of Cassio's supposed dream. Othello is projected by this down C. The movements are getting more violent and rapid in succession. Iago quickly follows up on his L and drives in the final nail with his words about the handkerchief. This finishes Othello. He crosses to the down L corner. 'Now do I see 'tis true . . .' He blows his love to the winds and invokes hell-vengeance.

The scene was rounded off by Othello striding back to the steps RC on 'Blood, blood, blood!' Iago follows to LC. Both pray to the marbled heaven of the sky-sheet. Othello crosses Iago

L as he asks him to go with him 'aside' and find 'swift means of death' for Desdemona; then stops; turns; and puts his hand on Iago's shoulder: 'Now art *thou* my lieutenant.' Iago kneels as the curtains close. Othello's cross shows that they are to exit L; that is, away from Desdemona to the Iago-world. Iago's kneeling gives a useful touch of Mephistophelean servitude.

For this crucial scene we have used the whole stage, squeezing out every drop of its potential significance as a conventional area: for the first half, the right; for the second, the left; and for Othello's middle exit and entrance, the centre. Iago's positions are often up-stage of Othello, but he keeps drawing level. Othello does most of the moving, impelled by the words of an outwardly passive Iago. I considered the possibility of keeping Othello central and Iago weaving spiders' webs round him; which would mean Othello moving at first violently and far, then less and less. It has points, and justification in the play's imagery, but it would be less effective. Othello would have to become more still as his language became more violent and this is illogical, or at the least extremely difficult. Also it might seem too definitely part of a studied scheme. Iago is on the whole a calm force behind a violent and active Othello: and that is what my arrangement reflected. We have the change in Othello spatially embodied: up R to down L. Movements should never appear artificial, but should grow naturally from the producer's spontaneous visualization and during rehearsal. There are none here that are not dramatically of a very obvious sort, but they are used significantly. Such a blend is exactly what we want. The audience need not be aware conceptually of the intellectual plan, which should work rather as an unnoticed auxiliary.

The handkerchief is Iago's conclusive point, its importance being underlined by our central down-stage position and Othello's vivid cross to the down L corner. Our third act starts with the scene where Othello demands the handkerchief from Desdemona. Its peculiar quality and importance necessitate a plain fore-stage arrangement. Every word must be driven in and the attention concentrated.

In poetic drama the action often crystallizes into some thing or person suggesting the universal or supernatural. Such are, in Shakespeare, the Ghost in *Hamlet*, the Weird Sisters and their Apparitions in *Macbeth*, the vigorous and elemental tempest in

King Lear, the squadrons of blood-drizzling soldiers above Rome in *Julius Caesar*, the mysterious music in *Antony and Cleopatra*. These are powers which bind the action, about which the action clusters; or which at an especially poignant moment help to crystallize and universalize it. It may be a nature-force, or a god-force, or a magical force. Or it may dominate and all but fill the whole action, like the spirit of war in *Journey's End*, or the orchard of Chekhov's *The Cherry Orchard*.

What is Shakespeare to do in *Othello*? We have seen (p. 54) that thunder and tempest is not a suitable accompaniment for domestic tragedy, and Shakespeare consequently here edges his tempest in differently, making it for once contrast with rather than accompany the later conflict by means of the stormy voyage to Cyprus. That however is over now. What can take over as a universalizing symbol? Shakespeare chooses an eminently *domestic* article and saturates it in a supernatural significance, so that it becomes a symbol of domestic sanctity. It serves to bind and focus the action: Othello, Desdemona, Emilia, Iago, Cassio, and Bianca all possess it in turn.[1]

The lines are spoken with frightening yet controlled intensity. Othello's mind is *above* his passion. He enters with feline grace and slippered softness. From now on he wears his long, straight, purple gown, the coloured robe discarded. He holds Desdemona's hand, finding it moist. At ' 'Tis a good hand' he studies it, like a palmist: the action prepares for what follows. Desdemona cannot produce the handkerchief. Othello describes how it was given to his mother by an Egyptian charmer who 'could almost read the thoughts of people', as a security against losing her husband's love. Desdemona is frightened. Othello's words gather intensity:

> 'Tis true: there's magic in the web of it:
> A sibyl that had number'd in the world
> The sun to course two hundred compasses,
> In her prophetic fury sew'd the work.
> The worms were hallow'd that did breed the silk;
> And it was dyed in mummy which the skilful
> Conserv'd of maidens' hearts.

Such speeches are lost on a modern audience in a furniture-

[1] Byron observed the ethnological exactitude of Shakespeare's symbol, noting that 'the handkerchief is the strongest proof of love, not only among the Moors, but all Eastern nations' (Thomas Medwin, *Conversations of Lord Byron*; 1824).

cluttered stage. Throughout until his exit Othello should neither rage, nor appear pathetic: his words are the channel of a terrible and irrevocable fate, and stern control and reserve in their utterance, like a channel's limits, gives them force and direction. Othello becomes here a terrific force. The powers of the handkerchief are being in the same speech described and proved. So Desdemona, staggered, murmurs: 'Sure, there's some wonder in this handkerchief.' She has already seen its powers in operation.[1] After Othello's exit, Emilia uses his behaviour to justify her cynical remarks spoken just before his entrance: Shakespeare does his best to forestall criticism as to her later silence. From now on the handkerchief dominates the action. It is not too much to say that Othello kills Desdemona not for an act of physical unfaithfulness, but for parting with the handkerchief.[2] For that is an act suggesting the desecration of a universal sanctity.

We grouped the next few scenes together against a green curtain half-pulled to reveal a black curtain background C, with a single chair in the opening. The chair proved very useful. Othello is discovered beside and slightly in front of it facing down-stage, Iago one knee on the chair towards him, instilling verbal poison. The tableau compresses a miniature of the play's meaning. You see Othello's mind thinking away on its own, Iago preying on it. Othello's words should be wanderingly half-delirious, not passionate and violent: the usual view of Othello as, to borrow Bottom's phrase (*A Misdummer Night's Dream*, I. ii. 32), 'a part to tear a cat in' is off the point. His expression here should be one of extreme *intellectual* agony. His mind is shown in pieces. See how Iago keeps bringing back his attention to the handkerchief and the reiterated part it plays in his delirium just before he falls. It is Iago's main instrument of torture.

The chair was useful for Othello to sink in after witnessing Cassio's meeting with Bianca and the handkerchief business between them; and later for Desdemona, and Roderigo. But first we get Lodovico's entry. We had a tall actor in the part: at this point, where he strikes Desdemona, it is helpful for Othello to lose some of his former dignity. Lodovico comes in as a challenge to his high position, informing him of his recall and Cassio's

---

[1] I owe this vital reading of Desdemona's remark to an article by J. Middleton Murry incorporated into his *Shakespeare*, 1936 (XIV; 'Desdemona's Handkerchief').
[2] Pope had the point. See *The Rape of the Lock*, V, 105–6.

advancement. Fate is assisting Iago[1] to torment Othello, whose words to Lodovico 'Cassio shall have my place' and 'You are welcome, Sir, to Cyprus' hold a bitterly ironic note. This last speech to Lodovico is on the border of insanity, and the final 'Goats and monkeys!' not shouted, but laughed, with a demonic, dry laugh. We cut Othello's next interview with Desdemona, arranging for her to re-enter with Emilia. She sits on the chair and later kneels to Iago. She does not touch him, nor he her. The effect on Iago is left by Shakespeare unregistered. To follow Shakespeare, let Iago turn up-stage after Desdemona's exit and stand with his back to the audience. Iago must not be shown as positively callous of her pathetic position, nor as deeply moved by it. He speaks courteously enough to her. It is just outside his inhuman attention. I do not think that the producer should commit himself: hence my arrangement.

Roderigo next sits in the chair, ludicrously dignified, at 'What I protest intendment of doing'. Seeing this new self-assertion, Iago plays on his pride and suggests 'removing' Cassio. Roderigo rises and advances nervously towards Iago at 'How do you mean, removing of him?' Next he retreats behind and up-stage of the chair, sliding his hand tremblingly along its back, as though to put it between himself and Iago, on 'And that you would have me do?' The use of this single chair for occasions of such varying quality since Othello and Iago were first discovered there helped to bind and knit the play at a point where its action is, comparatively, limp. There is intentionally less grandeur of action here: we just watch Othello slipping. His dignity is temporarily gone.

It returns, however, in the last scene. No protagonist of Shakespearian tragedy attains a richer dignity at his end: it is almost formalistic, statuesque. This quality must be preserved. We had Desdemona's bed central between dark curtains, above the steps. We were offered a real old-style bed, but it looked uncomfortable and self-conscious up there, and we did better with a built-up arrangement of simple blocks, laying a rich purple covering over the sheets. The results held suggestion of both bed and altar. We want some such formality. The candle tones with it, while the

---

[1] This is usual in Shakespeare. Events are as important as psychology. Shakespeare's heroes do not altogether carve out their own course. Fateful circumstance does half the work, pressing them to evil in *Macbeth* or to nobility in *Antony and Cleopatra*. Here fate is ironical.

more universal moon and star references contrast and blend with the candle. Throughout the scene those gems of poetry referring to stars, the moon, the world 'of one entire and perfect chrysolite' should be given with measured and underlined emphasis. Othello can catch the same beam from the wings for the stars and moon: though this is not really necessary. Observe the reiterated references to the handkerchief, both before and after Desdemona's death. Just as the handkerchief caused the final overthrow of Othello's love, so not until Cassio's explanation does Othello recognize the depth of his folly. The explanation is withheld till the last possible moment; then it is decisive. Thought of the handkerchief dominates the situation.

An interesting point arose at Othello's attack on Iago. If that synchronizes with Montano's trying to stop Othello, and Iago's stabbing of Emilia, while Gratiano is drawing near ready to hold her afterwards, you get the whole stage scrambling round Emilia like a football scrum. So we had Emilia down LC, Iago down L, and Gratiano close by. Othello is up-stage on the steps at their right end. He stands there, towering, for 'Are there no stones . . .'; and at 'Precious villain!' charges directly down-stage so that he faces Iago across the stage with his weapon drawn, Montano outside him, R, catching his uplifted arm. Coming directly down-stage often gives a more powerful effect of approaching a person on the other side than going diagonally towards him. Besides, the instant's tableau across the stage was effective. Notice, by the way, Shakespeare's usual trick of showing his people greater than you or they had guessed in his use here of Emilia.

When playing Othello I felt convinced that there is nothing in him particularly primitive or of negroid savagery. He is not to be confused with O'Neill's magnificent study in *The Emperor Jones*. Othello's pain is largely an intellectual pain at the ruin of a romantic faith. There are certainly moments of barbaric fury, others of neurotic disgust, and some of delirium; but nothing of a sub-human and jungle violence. At the last he attains a serenity, killing Desdemona as a sacred duty. The Renaissance poet idealizes human love in the Provençal romantic tradition of modern literature: Othello, Desdemona, and Iago are Man, the Divine, and the Devil. That a Moor should be the protagonist in a play of this type is not strange. I have read that the romance-cult came to the Provençal troubadours and thence to Petrarch and Dante through the Moorish civilization in Spain. Shakespeare has a habit of getting significant colourings right, as when Richard III continually swears by St. Paul, who according to one tradition was deformed. Iago is in the poetry explicitly associated with the Devil, but only in somewhat the same sense that Bosola is implicitly a sort of devil; in a typically Renaissance and humanist play, where the divine is approached through the human, the Devil logically must be human too. This may help to explain the almost absurdly villainous persons in Elizabethan drama, the universal essences of the Mystery plays recurring in human form. *Macbeth* provides an interesting contrast.

The producer must have some sense of these more universal suggestions. The symbolic effects I have emphasized in my arrangement are all in the poetry: Iago knows that he is in league with hell-forces and often says so, while Desdemona is equated imagistically with divinity. But the moment such thoughts are allowed to interfere with the expressly domestic and human qualities of the drama, there is disaster. We neglect either aspect at our peril: we must realize both. There can be alternations in emphasis, but no mutual exclusion, for in our feeling for the whole there should be no distinction.

Additional Note, 1963

A difficulty arises regarding Othello's appearance. Is he to be negroid or semitic? I have always, with regard to the high degree of civilization reached by the Moors at a time when the southern Africans were less advanced, tended to see Othello as semitic; and this is the usual way he is represented. He has, however, had a notable representative in Paul Robeson; we have the Shakespearian phrase 'thick-lips' (i. i. 66) as evidence; and in *Poetry and the Physical Voice* (157) Mr. Francis Berry has convincingly related the peculiar quality of Othello's poetry to the orotundity of African speech.

Whatever we decide, we must respond to both his nobility and his sensitivity. A good Shakespearian pointer is the sketch of Morocco in *The Merchant of Venice*; though Mr. Berry rightly observes that the first orotundity of his speaking is not maintained. Two noble Moors in our dramatic tradition may also be adduced: Zanga in Edward Young's *The Revenge* and the superlatively noble hero of Browning's *Luria*, whose respect to European civilization and will to its service matches Othello's final speech.

Othello invades his tidy world as an unknown quality. He is unpredictable. It is not simply a matter of the soldier up against domesticity. In *Essays in Criticism* (IX, 4; Oct. 1959; 358) Mr. Laurence Lerner groups Brabantio's charge that Othello has been using black magic with Othello's own statement on the handkerchief to suggest a derogatory reading of Othello's primitive nature. Instead, I should suggest that Brabantio's accusation helps to build in our minds a sense of Othello's mystery; he, as a *person*, houses in this domestic play categories of the supernatural elsewhere carried by symbolism or persons of more than human powers.

Once we accept this mysterious quality as a key, much of the play's difficulty disappears. If he be an African negro, then all the wizardry of black Africa is in his blood, collaborating, through the handkerchief, with Egyptian arts. He exists at the point where *others* accuse him of satanic practices, but *we* respond to the 'prophetic fury' of the 'sibyl' (III. iv. 71–3) who wove the handkerchief. He is imaginatively a composite of the Moorish, the negroid and—by association—the Egyptian, as baffling to commentators as he is disturbing to Venice.

Othello subscribes to Christianity, but after a fall to ugliness and dementia he presses on and through to a poetic sublimity entirely his own, with its own lonely valuations in terms of which he is for a while justified. His final admission of Christian and Venetian values does not detract from it. His speech on his service to Venice may be read rather as a Shakespearian conclusion in anti-climax following the climax of 'It is the cause' and his other marvellous words.

Othello has a mysterious stature beyond anyone or anything in his context.

HAMLET

Rudolf Steiner Hall, London; 1935[1]

Production here should stress (i) the death atmosphere of the play; (ii) the balanced opposition of the King and Hamlet, not shirking the good or evil in either; (iii) Hamlet's change of

[1] I had previously done *Hamlet* in Toronto in 1933.

appearance; and (iv) sound-effects. Much of the play is indecisive and enigmatic: this quality must be preserved. We find death-forces paradoxically allied with moral good, and life-forces with evil. The dominant sound-effects touch neither music nor tempest, but are set between: there is a particular sequence peculiar to this play of drums, trumpets, and cannon. It is as though Shakespeare's own axes of reference in the imaginative world are here themselves suspect. The Ghost, the sound-effects, the King, Hamlet himself, the final duel, indeed the whole play, are strangely both clear and precise in one sense but extremely baffling in another.

We used curtains with no sky-sheet but a repeated set of dais, thrones, chair, inset central platform, and steps. Often we had a semi-front scene made by drawing a curtain half-way on one side, yet spacing the action up to a curtain behind on the other: which both enabled us to keep the throne-dais on the stage throughout and also suggested the play's see-saw enigmatic quality, close-twined more than once with 'policy' and deceit, clarity and uncertainty mixed.

ACT I

We start with the traditional twelve beats, lights down. The curtain is half drawn, and we discover Francisco on guard in the deep half of the stage R. There is a sound of whining wind not too loud, repeated during the early part of the scene at appropriate intervals.[1] There is a bench L. The lights are a little dimmed, toning to a suggestion of blues and greens on the deep area R where the Ghost will appear. Marcellus, Horatio, and Bernardo, who have all entered L (no one but the Ghost enters or exits R), are L, Bernardo sitting on the bench. At 'Peace, break thee off...' the Ghost enters C from behind the curtain: the entering from the same side of the stage, only farther up, as persons already on it, is often effective when one party is to be for a second or so

[1] Wind is a natural ghost-effect. Compare the wind-ghost association in Claudio's death-speech; in Tennyson's lines on Gawain in *The Passing of Arthur*; and at the end of *Hassan*. Compare the impression of 'cold' in *Hassan* with reference to ghosts and Hamlet's remark: 'The air bites shrewdly: it is very cold'. There is a certain communal store of imaginative impressions possessing a logic of their own throughout literature that has not yet been studied.

[Since composing this note I have learned that there is a spiritualist basis for these associations; 1963.]

unaware of the other. The Ghost comes down R, facing across at the others. Horatio, between Marcellus and Bernardo, addresses it without moving, to contrast with his action at its next entrance: the contrast suits his words and is important. The Ghost goes out down R. On its re-entrance down R, Horatio, now bolder, crosses C past Marcellus and addresses it. As it turns up-stage, Horatio crosses it R, swinging round with his back to the audience and calling to Marcellus to stop it. Marcellus attacks it, moving diagonally up-stage across the curtain edge C, while the Ghost goes off LC behind the curtain. Their words ' 'Tis here', ' 'Tis here', ' 'Tis gone', are variously spoken about the stage, helping to disembody the Ghost. The Ghost should give no appearance of hurry: a deliberate and dignified turn and pause before finally disappearing helps the impression of its invulnerability. You should see Marcellus miss it; and also clearly see it go off. The rest of this scene is easy. The dawn lines are spoken down L. Horatio and Marcellus go out L, leaving Bernardo on guard.

Curtains are drawn and the seat removed while an elaborate flourish sounds, and immediately afterwards the full Court set is disclosed: carpeted steps and platform C; two thrones on a dais L; Hamlet's chair R. The King and Queen are C descending the steps, everyone, including Hamlet, who stands by his chair, bowing. Hamlet wears a rich dress of black and white. In this production the King spoke his lines about drinking and cannons down C, and went off with most of the others L: but perhaps they should have been spoken up-stage on the steps with a corresponding exit. The lines are so very important. At the general exit Hamlet bows again: it is essential throughout the play to show that the King is King. If he is taller than Hamlet[1] and generally made to seem more dominating in appearance, the play is assisted. Every Shakespearian king has to be understood on two levels: (i) as a man and (ii) as a king. Generally the interweaving and contrasted implications of these two views are vital to the plot.

Hamlet helps to impregnate the thrones by indicating them during his soliloquy at appropriate phrases, visualizing the King and Queen. On their entry he draws Horatio and the two officers down-stage, while the curtain is pulled behind them. His hearing of their news is best concentrated as a front-scene. Observe Horatio's delicate aspersions on the courage of the other two:

[1] The King was played by Mr. Clement McCallin; Ophelia by Miss Ida Gilbert.

here and both before and after this occasion, in the first and second Ghost scene, there is a running series of more or less good-natured hostility, sarcasm and contradiction between the scholar and soldiers. The soldiers have had to call in a scholar to deal with a supernatural fear. We tried to give a touch of this hostility, but I doubt if it registered; it was too difficult to stress heavily. After Hamlet's exit the action continues with Laertes and Ophelia. In this scene Ophelia can show a sense of humour with Laertes and a note of sullenness at 'I shall obey' to Polonius: we don't want her too much of a weakling.

We return to our half-curtain set. Lights change for the Ghost scene; this time without the bench L. The wind is heard again. The flourish and cannon off are done as from a distance blending into mystery. Hamlet, Horatio, and Marcellus all show a momentary start, their nerves on edge: 'What does this mean, my lord?' Hamlet laughs bitterly and explains. This flourish and cannon come shortly before the Ghost's entrance, which follows the sooner through our cutting Hamlet's long speech and also throws forward to similar effects in the last scene. Its peculiar significance is enhanced by delicately relating it to the Ghost from the start (and see p. 118 below). Like the whining wind, the bugle and cannon strike a balance between music and tempest suiting the enigmatic nature of the Ghost.

The Ghost enters this time down R. Hamlet crosses C, leaving Horatio and Marcellus L, and addresses it. His speech is subtly varied. We start with awe, amaze, love (in the word 'father'): then a pause, awaiting an answer. 'O answer me!' Now agony, pathos ('quietly inurned'), and another pause after 'cerements'. Now almost hysteria, a mind distraught, violent. The Ghost beckons. Hamlet half turns back, indecisive, at 'It will not speak: *then will I follow it*'; is more determined at 'It waves me forth again; *I'll follow it*'; and is violently so at 'It waves me still. Go on, *I'll follow thee*'. He breaks from Horatio and Marcellus at 'Unhand me, gentlemen', throwing them back far L and springing R himself, drawing his sword: 'By heaven, I'll make a ghost of him that lets [i.e. hinders] me!' The Ghost has been moving up while making his successive gestures, and is now RC, Hamlet down R. Hamlet has broken from the world of his companions to join that of the Ghost: his struggle with Horatio and Marcellus is important and must be clearly seen, and his breaking from them R must make a new picture. Hamlet now goes up R far into the up-stage Ghost area, and says, 'Go on, I'll follow *thee*', the new emphasis on 'thee' marking Hamlet's sense of allegiance to the Ghost. Both exit L behind the half-drawn curtain.

The drawing of the half-curtain reveals the throne dais as a plain platform *without the throne* against the curtains L. There is wind again, or surf, louder than before. The lights show a pre-dominance of blue, but the whole stage is clearly visible. The Ghost LC near or on the dais, perhaps resting one foot on it, addresses Hamlet C. Hamlet sinks with a moan as his mother's sin is described. Saying farewell, the Ghost comes down holding out his arms, and Hamlet totters towards the embrace of death. The Ghost ascends the platform and disappears through the curtains, leaving Hamlet with his head clasped in his hands. Left alone Hamlet addresses the stars, earth, and hell. He reiterates the command to 'remember', looking L and building the platform into a Ghost symbol. Whilst declaring his renunciation of past trivialities he tears off his rich cloak and leaves it, almost as an offering, on the platform: if it has metal or glass sequins it should glisten there tellingly. 'So, Uncle, there *you* are' is spoken care-lessly with an emphatic 'you'; but, 'Now to my word—it is adieu, adieu, remember me' is done solemnly, looking L. The contrast is significant. Horatio and Marcellus enter R. Hamlet twice on appropriate words wards them off from the dais platform as they eagerly question him, thus further impregnating it with Ghost significance. At the first subterranean 'Swear' he takes them from RC down C; and at the second and third towards the dais platform. The Ghost is breaking down Hamlet's reluctance to initiate them. I have no clearer idea in mind, but this is the only arrangement so far as I know that has ever given any point to these strange, enigmatic, but important movements. Hamlet stands with one foot on the Ghost platform, high priest of the occasion, while the others kneel before it and swear on his sword hilt. He looks L at 'Rest, rest, perturbed spirit'. The rest is easy: they go out R, Hamlet breaking away on his 'The time is out of joint', and falling back weakly into their arms just before the exit.

In this scene I would point to the use made of the throneless platform and the cloak: objects thus loaded with meaning can be most powerful. The cloak is left there to the end, the wind rises over an otherwise empty stage, and the curtain closes. A roll of drums concludes Act I.

Act II

The act starts with a roll of drums. Polonius is discovered L in front of a plain curtain, Ophelia entering through it C, looking over her shoulder and showing fear. Her description of Hamlet's terrifying experience must be given intense narrative concentration. She is to act her words, as the text implies.

The Court set is disclosed with a table by Hamlet's chair R. The King and Queen speak with Rosencrantz and Guildenstern, and after with Polonius. Polonius is then alone. Hamlet enters L and walks slowly across to his area R and sits in his chair.

His dress is now a plain black tunic—earlier he wore black and white—unlaced; the traditional open white shirt; disarranged hair; a soiled white rag tied in his belt, hanging limply; and his right arm through a black torn and tattered cloak not fixed to the other shoulder so that it drags on the ground behind. In preparing my earlier (1933) Toronto production I had found no disorder of a normal costume of any use: it either looked neat from the front or as though I had dressed carelessly. It must be done, like everything else that is important, by some positive and significant addition. That is how I came to use the white rag and tattered cloak. Hamlet can pick up the loose train and throw it over his left arm to look tidy; curled round his feet it makes him a king of grief; holding his arms out, tatters falling, he looks fantastic; alone, he can sometimes remove it altogether. His appearance now must contrast strongly with that in Act I: he must seem disintegrated, gone-to-pieces, the glamour and light of life have left him.

He talks to Polonius sarcastically from his corner R and then greets Rosencrantz and Guildenstern happily, walking C, and perhaps arranging his cloak sanely, throwing the loose end over his arm. They say that 'the world's grown honest'. He laughs merrily for his 'then is doomsday near'; then reality weighs back on him suddenly: 'But your news is not true' is spoken bitterly. Thereafter he is suspicious and bitter, his cloak trails, he moves about near his chair. We find a similar rhythm in his first meeting with Horatio: first, spontaneous pleasure, then—'I pray thee, do not mock me . . .' Everything is sooner or later related to his own obsession. It happens again with the Players; and with Ophelia. At the Players' entry he is happy and thoroughly excited at the prospect of a 'passionate speech'. But the words 'moblèd queen' he repeats, referring them to his mother, and again the light is extinguished. The Players go; he gets rid of Rosencrantz and Guildenstern. 'Ay so, God be wi' ye' is spoken with irritation. He puts the manuscript of the play on the table and throws off his cloak. 'Now I am alone . . .' This soliloquy demands close attention.

Hamlet's chair is R, and from that corner his more bitter speeches have been delivered. The two thrones are L: they suggest the world ranged against him. His more subjective fears come from his own side, R. He starts the soliloquy standing near his chair. At 'What's Hecuba to him . . .' his irritation is marked by a determined advance down C. Soon this fails in disgust, and he retreats R, falling hopelessly in his chair at 'Yet I, a dull and muddy-mettled rascal . . .' At 'Who calls me villain?' still sitting, he looks R as at an unseen enemy of his own imagination. Then he rises with new virulence and marches LC facing the thrones for 'this slave's offal'. Next a left turn up-stage to the steps C marks a failure, which is followed immediately with a recovery, another left turn, so that he speaks the words 'bloody, bawdy villain' over his left shoulder, again looking at the thrones: this gives an impression of scorn that can be helped by not greatly stressing the words. Careless disgust is wanted: Hamlet's failure is not cowardice so much as mental inability to find a working basis for even a hostile relation to his surroundings. His speech gathers power at 'Remorseless, treacherous, lecherous, kindless villain'. The rhyme can be given a touch of mad humour. He sways, drawing a dagger, then leaps down-stage at 'Vengeance', attacking the King's throne, the up-stage one of the two. His attack is cut short, dagger in mid-air, by his critical judgement that now throws him into more disgust, as he sinks on the dais beneath the throne, defeated again by circumstance. The dagger held in mid-air seems a more controlled and precise effect than a series of hysterical stabs at the throne. He rises at 'About, my brain', goes to the table R, picks up the manuscript, throws his cloak over his shoulder and walks down L while the curtain is half-drawn behind his new position, leaving the chair and table R still visible. This pulling of the curtain whilst Hamlet walks round it gives an impression of stealthy movement from one room to another, along corridors, which suits his plotting lines.

If you trace out these movements on a diagram you will see how they aim to express futility and inaction in terms of stage action, zigzags being the obvious solution. The half-drawing of the curtain suggests a new line of action, but an indirect one, away from the thrones: which is apt. It also leaves our set ready for the 'nunnery' scene.

Ophelia is left sitting in the chair R with the spies behind the half-drawn curtain. The lights are dimmed a little for this scene of mental twilight. Hamlet enters L. It is a mistake to let Ophelia go off during the 'To be or not to be' soliloquy. She, a creature of beauty and young life, is in Hamlet's mind to be contrasted with his own death-obsession. You therefore want them both as a visible contrast during the lines. There might even be more light on her than on him. When Hamlet advances, he can first kneel, but rise and retreat at 'I never gave you aught'. He speaks these early speeches gently, with an occasional touch of bitterness and perhaps of fun, too; as he catalogues his faults he could be almost playful, and she might smile, and we feel that he may succumb after all to her old appeal. A touch of flirtation helps. He dallies with her hand or hair. Eventually he turns at 'Go thy ways to a nunnery', spoken lovingly. Now there is just a faint sound of the Ghost-wind. It raises in Hamlet the demon of mistrust. You see it in his eyes. 'Where's your father?' She shows guilt, and lies. He steps back in horror against the curtain and registers that he has felt the presence of spies. His final speeches are done on the borderland of insanity, but not with shouting. 'It hath made me mad' should come in a tense, agonized whisper. Controlled insanity is the line to take, and a very difficult one.

The full set is used for the Play scene. Hamlet and Horatio are discovered on the steps C, and then come down. At the King's entry, done formally from C and down the steps to elaborate flourishes, Hamlet gets in front of the thrones, blocking his way. The King pauses. Hamlet laughs devilishly. 'How fares our cousin Hamlet?' Hamlet's answer is as fantastically and luridly given as possible. This picture captures and compresses the essence of our middle action: we don't get enough of such significant tableaux in the average production. The tall and thriving King at the head of his train in full ceremony finds himself faced by the less imposing figure of Hamlet that mocks his painted glory. Contrasted with Hamlet's forced humility when they last met in Act I, it shows how the pretence, or partial truth, of madness gives Hamlet a freedom impossible before.

During the play, done up C on the platform, Hamlet sits on the ground by Ophelia R watching the King, who steadies himself with a drink. 'Have you heard the argument? Is there no offence in't?' is best spoken to Polonius, L. Hamlet immediately rises, and goes C, telling the King 'they do but jest, poison in jest—no *offence* i' the world', with ironical reference to the King's easy conscience. Hamlet goes up-stage, one foot on the steps RC indicating Lucianus, and drawing his sword at 'The croaking raven doth bellow for revenge'. This can be ranted. On the decisive words 'He poisons him i' the garden . . .' he walks diagonally down L to the King, speaking not too loud and carelessly fingering his sword with both hands. I sometimes held the point poised towards the King: I do not know how it looked from the front. When the King rises the words of Ophelia, Hamlet and Polonius must all be heard, while the King holds for a second his rigid position, standing. This is a powerful and precise effect, better than a general hurly-burly. The King dashes out. Hamlet, alone with Horatio, is triumphant. His calling for music reflects a psychological release and a new sense of freedom in action. He is king of the situation. His words to Rosencrantz and Guildenstern are done sharply, they come like the crack of a whip, especially the 'recorder' pieces. Horatio is the last to leave Hamlet; he goes up to him as though realizing the crucial nature of this moment in his story; Hamlet clasps his hand and puts him aside. What follows he must do alone. Soliloquizing, his thoughts are first violent with revenge-images of blood; then, his eye catching the thrones, he recalls his coming interview with his mother; the two thoughts coalesce and he prays that he may not confuse the issue and use 'daggers' on her. During this speech the lights, which have been varied appropriately before, during, and after the play, are toned with red.

The King's prayer follows in a front-scene. The King should really enlist the audience's sympathy here. Hamlet enters C, speaks his lines without any white-washing of their horror, and then recalls his mother: she seems more important to him than the King. All this must be going very quickly.

Now to the Queen's closet. The mid-stage curtain is drawn across the stage and obscures throne and steps. There is a chair and table L and a couch R. Polonius hides up C. The Queen arranges herself with dignity in the chair L and Hamlet enters R. Their first words go swift. The Queen rises. Hamlet draws his sword. She cries for help, thinking that he means to murder her. Hamlet kills Polonius. The Queen screams and crosses far down R. Hamlet draws the curtain and the body falls: it should be visible during the scene. Hamlet, L, lays his cloak, which was thrown over his shoulder, on the table, and his sword beside it. Pointing to the couch R he tells the Queen to sit down. She approaches from her far position, mesmerized by his determination. At the word-picture of his father he comes close, sitting or kneeling on the couch: both pictures are, I think, best regarded as mental. As the speech grows in violence Hamlet draws away C. At 'O shame, where is thy blush?' he turns down L, speaking rhetorically. What started as a righteous lecture has become introverted rhetoric. It grows worse. 'Nay, but to live . . .' is spoken right away from the Queen: Hamlet is overcome by his own nausea. He grows pathological. He is close to the table L fingering the sword. Nausea turns to insane hysterics. 'A murderer and a villain . . .' It comes in spasms, jerks. The King stole the crown from a shelf and 'put it in his pocket'. Maniac laughter. He now has the sword. At 'a king of shreds and patches' he charges across the stage R at the Queen, whose head in her hands sobbing is turned from him. In mid-volley, about to stab, he stops; drops the sword; slowly turns left facing the audience and with utterly changed voice says the words: 'Save me and hover o'er me with your wings . . .' He turns farther, is being drawn left by the Ghost, who has entered behind him, L. Notice that Hamlet is aware of the Ghost before seeing him physically; and how his prayer is used to refer partly at least to his attack on his mother. This is a good example of a way by which supernature can, without any play on lights, be presented in direct and positive dramatic action. Polonius's body should be up-stage LC. Then the Ghost's entrance L can be related to it: the first shedding of blood since the Ghost's command brings the death-figure again on the stage. Having turned completely to the Ghost, Hamlet with bended head addresses him again. The Queen comes up to him, and both face L.

At the Ghost's exit L and Hamlet's words, 'My father in his habit as he liv'd!' the Queen shows anger and sits in the chair L, remarking on Hamlet's madness. Her defence is roused; she is a woman who hides unpleasant things from herself and is angry if forced to face them; and Hamlet's reference to his father troubles her. This chair L, which she used at the start, is her position of self-assertion; the couch, of humility. Hamlet tells her to confess herself to Heaven and leads her R as though to go off. Passing the couch, however, she sinks suddenly on it, sobbing. Hamlet stands C, baffled and distressed, and asks that his virtue be forgiven. Repeated 'good-nights' reflect his indecision. Turning to Polonius he expresses repentance. The weeping Queen is on one side, Polonius dead on the other: he looks at them in turn. He sinks by the Queen, his head on her knees: 'I must be cruel only to be kind.' Next, fearful of this weakness, he draws back from her and utters voluble sarcasm. His phrase 'mad in craft' should be so spoken that you doubt it. The strain is telling on him. As he refers to his going to England, and talks of outwitting his enemies, his eye glints with insane cunning: it is best done close up to the Queen. Hamlet's expression suddenly changes for 'This man shall set me packing'. Solemnly he regards Polonius and comments on the body. He kneels by it, says 'good-night' for the last time, and the curtains close.

There follows a short front-scene. The King sends for Hamlet, who is brought in between Rosencrantz and Guildenstern as a prisoner. At this moment we should certainly feel that the King is a force of order,[1] Hamlet a danger. Continually we need to get some such contrast: the King is a finely material, Hamlet a darkly spiritual, force. So the fine-robed King now faces Hamlet, who with a hideous and unabashed assurance reminds him how a painted outside can veil an inward corruption, and all kings are merely meat fatted for death-worms. Hamlet's words are spoken with a Feste's jest-accent, to deepen their horror. Arrested, guards either side, guilty of murder, Hamlet bears a charmed life; he knows it; so does the King. All now hinges on England. 'For England!' Hamlet speaks the words with a devilish smile. The significance of this voyage is enigmatic; Hamlet's expression must help make it so.

[1] See III. iii. 7–23. I might well have quoted this passage to support my view of the King in former essays.

The act ends with the King's speech, 'Do it, England', and a roll of drums.

Act III

We preluded the third movement with a few muted trumpet notes to tone with Ophelia's mad scene. The Hamlet-Fortinbras incident had to go. For the mad scene looped curtains would do well, but we had no time to arrange this and used a plain background. I have in *The Imperial Theme* shown how, after Hamlet has been revealed as a dangerous force, opposing values of life-excellence are sublimated: we are made aware of Fortinbras' soldiership, Ophelia's pathetic madness caused by Hamlet's act, the King's admirable courage and regal dignity, and Laertes' manly determination. To dress Ophelia in black seems to me therefore wrong: hers is a pretty, flowery and colourful insanity. The King's remarks during Ophelia's madness should appear sympathetic, springing from a kind heart. The Laertes riot should be big waves of shouting. Finally the King leads Laertes off and reappears with him immediately for a front-scene. The plot should show the King in a new light. Hitherto only the very subtlest suggestions of an essentially villainous nature, if that, should have been apparent: a spectator viewing the play for the first time should never be quite sure, in spite of the Play scene and the King's two soliloquies, whether Hamlet's view has full justification. But now the plot thickens. The Queen's description of Ophelia's death is best done before a plain curtain, but a gentlewoman, perhaps two, should enter with her. To bring in Ophelia's body on a bier borne by four hooded figures appears to me gratuitously weak. Attempts at enriching Shakespeare by additional action are often ill-chosen.

For various reasons we cut the Second Gravedigger. This is an unusual but satisfactory cut. The scene opens with our half-drawn curtain, the Gravedigger singing in the grave up R, Hamlet and Horatio entering down L. The lights are suggestive of evening, with sunset red. Hamlet is more assured, dignified, and controlled. His journey to England may be taken to mark a spiritual or psychological advance.[1] He voyages through to a new serenity. The change was suggested by his wearing new and colourful clothes, reddish-purple tunic, and a cloak of the same colour; a

---

[1] Compare Stavrogin's voyage into the far north in Dostoevsky's *The Possessed* as interpreted by J. Middleton Murry (*Fyodor Dostoevsky*, 1923 edn.; 160).

colour suggesting dignity and spiritual authority, and also toning with the Graveyard scene. He also has a small greyish beard and white streaks line his hair, marking an increase of age that assists the suggestion of spiritual advance and also has some justification in the text; compare the sense we receive of Romeo's advance to manhood and Macbeth's to old age. 'How long hast thou been a *grave*-maker' should be curiously spoken with a dwelling emphasis on 'grave': Hamlet is so interested in graves, skulls, death, and all that concerns them. For the speech on Yorick's skull he is L of the grave, but R of Horatio, the centre of a small group. At Toronto we had a platform leading up to the grave. First Hamlet addressed the Gravedigger with one foot on this level, but later advanced to take Yorick's skull, high and central, Horatio moving to Hamlet's first position to make a formal group for what is an apex of imaginative intensity. The Yorick lines should be taken slow; the whole scene up to this should go smoothly, and its emotional quality be allowed to luxuriate at leisure. The stillness of eternity should brood over it.

This stillness is next violently disturbed. The funeral procession enters to a tolling bell. After the struggle with Laertes Hamlet is between Laertes C and the grave R. The King LC restrains Laertes. Hamlet's ranting speech is spoken in controlled fury and cynical abandon, a bitter self-critical rhetoric. 'I'll rant as well as thou' means to suggest that Hamlet's strangeness derives from his possession of more, not less, feeling than others. Laertes is by comparison a child in emotional experience. Hamlet's love was 'forty thousand' times his. We might have Laertes in mourning here, getting a happy contrast to Hamlet's brighter clothes; as though Laertes has crossed the threshold into the state Hamlet has come through. Hamlet is a giant in spiritual stature:

> Let Hercules himself do what he may,
> The cat will mew, and dog will have his day.

'Cat' is spoken to Laertes, his grief a mewing only; 'dog' as Hamlet passes opposite and pauses in front of the King. This reference is not usually brought out in production. The King's phrase 'living monument' refers to Hamlet's projected death, and must be spoken with meaning.

Hamlet and Horatio re-enter for a front-scene. Hamlet's 'Providence' speech ending with 'the readiness is all' witnesses his new acceptance and serenity. After Osric's exit the King enters L with Laertes. Hamlet, now polite, bows to the King, takes Laertes' hand, speaks courteously. The play is highly formal and ceremonial, both here and during the fight. Hamlet calls for the foils. The curtains are pulled revealing the Court set, without Hamlet's chair.

The King and Queen take their places. The King describes the drums, flourish, and cannon that shall sound when he drinks to celebrate Hamlet's success.[1] This speech throws back to his similar speech in Act I where these sounds were to accompany the King's celebration of Hamlet's willingness to stay in Denmark (I. ii. 121– 128). Hamlet is involved in both. In both instances the sounds serve as a warning to Hamlet: first, in the way I have already described, making Hamlet and Horatio start nervously on the platform before the Ghost's entry; and now in a way I shall indicate. Hamlet and Laertes salute the King, the salute marking Hamlet's new and formal respect. The courtiers, all but Osric, are grouped up R. Laertes and Osric are L, Hamlet and Horatio down R; the King and Queen on the thrones and one Gentleman, looking after the cups, up L. At Hamlet's first hit the King drinks and sends an attendant across to Hamlet with the cup. Meanwhile the drums, followed by the trumpet, are sounding. Just as Hamlet is about to take the cup, the cannon go off ominously. His mind changes: 'I'll play this bout first; set it by awhile'. This is the warning referred to just now. I have no explicit interpretation, but this is the sort of enigmatic but precise effect that characterizes *Hamlet* throughout, and it comes straight from the text: I was not aware of it till it happened in performance. Hamlet scores another hit. The Queen comes across to him with her napkin and then takes the cup from the attendant, who has stood RC since Hamlet told him to 'set it by'. This gets the Queen well away from the King, who can be talking to Laertes, when she starts to drink. Notice Hamlet's polite 'good madam': his behaviour suits his new clothes. The King, too late to prevent the Queen drinking, goes up C in great anxiety. Hamlet, hurt, registers to Horatio; then gets Laertes' weapon, drives him down L, and wounds him. The Queen falls.

[1] The last big production I saw let the cannon off during this speech, as well as later. Great care had been taken over many inessentials of sets and lights; but the things that matter are so often slurred or muddled.

The duel is very important, and should be as striking and powerful as possible. It holds the see-saw indecisive *Hamlet*-quality, enigmatic yet precise. It balances the whole play: a hair's weight will turn the scales. Laertes is poised against Hamlet, healthy normality against neurotic genius. It must be breathlessly exciting, assisted by attentive watchers. Hamlet once attacks Laertes and runs past him, so that they have changed positions; then he works back. The more variety the better, using the whole stage. The fight condenses the drama. As Hamlet becomes almost evil, is anyway a channel for evil so that the King's crime may be rammed back on him, his 'poison'd chalice' *actually* commended to his own lips (*Macbeth*, I. vii. 11–12; *Hamlet*, v. ii. 340), so Hamlet, wounded by Laertes' treachery, gets the poisoned rapier to return the blow. Whatever the opposing forces do to Hamlet comes back on them. On the voyage to England he changes the commands and hoists his adversaries with their own petard. The King sends him away, but the seas cast him back. It is a curiously reiterated rhythm; the fight sums it up in sharp, significant action.

The King in terror has gone up C on to the steps. Hamlet gets RC ordering the doors, imagined up L, to be locked. The crowd R prevents the King escaping there. He is hemmed in. As Hamlet rushes to kill him he descends, bravely meeting his end, perhaps trying the king-divinity assurance again. Horatio comes between the crowd and the steps, holding up one hand as though warding them off from what is a necessary act. The gesture may sound weak, but is nevertheless dramatically powerful and significant. It provides a reason for the crowd's failure to stop Hamlet; it is in tune with the part played by Horatio; and together with the altar-like platform and steps it lends the deed an almost ritualistic suggestion which tones with the formality of the last scene and Shakespearian tragedy in general. The position need not be held long. Osric moves C, then R. Laertes lies dying down L, the Queen lies at the foot of her throne against the dais L. The King totters down the steps as Hamlet puts the cup to his mouth, again almost a ritualistic and ceremonious touch, and then falls, lying against the steps. Hamlet and Horatio struggle for the cup C; then Hamlet, supported by Horatio, ascends the throne. All the dead or dying are now grouped in a diagonal line from C to down L, variation being preserved by their positions: Laertes flat, the Queen against the low dais, the King against the central steps, Hamlet sitting on the throne. Hamlet has three times walked down from up C to the King's throne: once when attacking it during his soliloquy; once while terrorizing the King during the play; and now. Here we may see the advantage of a permanent set for recurring big scenes: we can play on cross-sections of meaning which have a valuable, if only subconscious, effect.

Horatio kneels by Hamlet LC. Distant drums beat a steady march. Hamlet inquires their meaning, and hears that it is Fortinbras come victorious from Poland. In prophesying and blessing Fortinbras' accession Hamlet sits up, his eye alight with fervour. All his dying speeches are taken happily, on the brink of 'felicity'. He falls back dead. Horatio speaks. The march comes up again, this time near, rapidly nearing; very close, insistent, victorious. 'Why does the drum come hither?' The addition of some noises off, the grounding of arms and military commands ('Stand!'— 'Pass the word along!'—'Stand!') helps to project Fortinbras like a winged arrow on to the stage.[1] He should be young, fair, and have a rich voice, wearing a Viking helmet, Mercurially winged, and fine armour. He enters R, the crowd makes way for him, and he stands in front of them facing the line of dead.

The group here is important. It is often complained that the end of Hamlet is absurd, the stage so cluttered with dead. But death is throughout our dominant theme. Hear Fortinbras' words:

> O proud death,
> What feast is toward in thine eternal cell,
> That thou so many princes at a shot
> So bloodily hast struck?

The dead are in a single group L. We must, as so often in Shakespeare, make a special point of the very thing we feared. There is another advantage. Where should Hamlet die? Is not the throne, giving him a formalized and victorious dignity his rather indecisive course has scarcely warranted, inappropriate? But if he lies on the ground Fortinbras' final honouring of him to the exclusion of the King is visually and dramatically absurd. Our group solves all difficulties. Hamlet is now King; but king only among the dead. He rises over the group of corpses. The place next in

[1] William Poel's arrangement of off-stage sounds for Fortinbras' entry was similar, and mine may indirectly derive from him (see Robert Speaight, *William Poel and the Elizabethan Revival*, 1954; 52).

honour is held by the King himself, central, on the steps. This position preserves a correct balance, and prevents Hamlet's new ascendancy being too dominant: to the last we must preserve our see-saw indecisiveness. Fortinbras does not however *face* the King, and Horatio's central position tends to lead the eye to Hamlet.

Horatio has risen to meet Fortinbras, in his own person linking the two worlds, of death and life: we may remember how he, the scholar, was called in by soldiers to deal with the Ghost at the start. Horatio on the steps offers a general explanation, and then returns among the dead, kneeling by Hamlet's chair, praying. Fortinbras speaks his final speech. At 'Go, bid the soldiers shoot' he draws his sword and holds it steadily at the salute. Horatio is still kneeling. The drums start, a long roll; the trumpets swell out in an elaborate call, a sort of last post, sinking and rising, trumpet and rolling drums together, a vast roll of sound, waves rolling on and up. Then one cannon; a pause, in silence; then a second. The curtain is drawn, the group still, Fortinbras at the salute, sharing with Hamlet and the King the honours of the stage; Fortinbras, strong-armed, with the material strength of Claudius and the spiritual strength of Hamlet, a white light on him, the new hope for Denmark.[1]

There is no need to carry the bodies off. My arrangement preserves the spirit of Shakespeare's conclusion. The two final cannon sum up the dualistic nature of the play, and together with the other similar effect in this scene throw back to the flourish and cannon before the Ghost's first entry to Hamlet, thus giving an inevitability and implied necessity to the conclusion, a kind of 'consummatum est', helped also by our use of a permanent set.

7

KING LEAR

Hart House Theatre, Toronto; 1935

I describe shortly my arrangement of the middle action. After their repeated unkindness Lear confronts his daughters as a pathetic figure. He seems to be breaking under their flint-hearted behaviour. Here realistic touches are called for in the acting of

---

[1] My comment may be attributing to Fortinbras a spiritual status for which the text gives us no evidence. The producer will nevertheless do well to believe it. [1963]

Lear, in voice and gesture. The play is throughout unique in its blend of homely realism and cosmic grandeur. He is an old man in distress. He prays that the heavens may save him from the shame of tears, asking for 'noble anger'. The prayer is answered. He will not 'weep'. He grows swiftly in stature. This is the turning-point in his story. Ascending the central steps his poise and gestures assume a grand manner he has not touched before as he flings defiance at his daughters. 'O fool—I shall go mad'. He preserves his manhood, but at a terrific cost. Low thunder—there is authority of stage-direction for it—accompanies this, the end of our first long movement. We are prepared for our middle action.

In our first act-division we used against our black curtains two white blocks a little over a man's height. In the first scene they were together, central, suggesting order and government. We used them for the stocks scene as pillars on either side to suggest, vaguely, a courtyard. For our middle action something more is needed. The scene is, superficially, a wild heath; and, psychologically, a sort of eruption. The poetry shows subterranean forces in volcanic burst and leaping flickers of lunacy devil-dancing about titanic and heroic passion. Something of vast and awful psychic significance is upthrust. The inward world is now our stage and we are to explore fantastic territories. I have a book which warns the actor that *King Lear* shows the breaking of a strong man and leaves it at that. But he is only broken, as a man, as an eggshell breaks to disclose new action, new strength of grander, beyond human, stature. Something about our stage is needed (i) to break the monotony of plain curtains, (ii) to suggest rugged country, and (iii) to solidify the spiritual content of our middle action. So we had constructed two other white elements, larger than our rectangular blocks, well above a man's life-size in height and breadth, showing irregular edges and slants whichever way they were placed. These were put vertically, and our former blocks laid flat, diagonally, down-stage on either side: the old tidy world fallen and shattered, and central the grand ruggedness upward towering. The use, for the first time, of four symbolic elements on the stage together provided the sense of a new richness in imaginative content that was needed. Such elements should be understood not as directly representing spatial facts but as a kind of visual grammar referring to deeper significances, though they are at the same time not altogether independent of the supposed scene, here one of rugged country. Of course, had the two 'icebergs' been too much like real blocks in shape and colour, their psychological meanings would have been lost and their relation to the other blocks destroyed. The use of a *ramp* in place of central steps leading to a platform C and the tone of the sky-sheet disclosed C between curtains helped to give a sense of desolation in wide open spaces. The draping of the curtain at one side of this central opening in a curved downward sweep *inwards* helped to build an impression of harmonious irregularity.

The four elements and the ramp we used variously for our main scenes during the rest of the play, without too great a positional stress on the rugged pair after the middle action. But not until the last scene of the play are the two rectangular blocks found together and upright, as at the play's beginning, only now placed at one side and sharing honour of position with the others.

Our thunder was alternated carefully with the words. Such sounds must come in at the right time, and only then, the cues properly prepared. Sounds must not form a vague running accompaniment to words: we must aim at rhythmic alternation. This is why some people thought our thunder more effective than is usual in the theatre, where rival noises are too often left to fight things out as best they may. After hesitation I succumbed to a reserved use of lightning: what there is should always be held for a fraction of a second, too sudden a flash being mechanical and artistically non-significant. Our lights were kept fairly strong always, precluding certain tableau-effects but preserving other more important effects of acting.

I offer an example of interpretative action. The Fool counters Lear's breaking mind with witticisms, trying to resolve by humour the tugging dualism that otherwise wrenches open the abysms of insanity. This is why his wit concentrates on the subject of Lear's pain, and not away from it. In their first tempest scene Lear goes out hand-in-hand with the Fool, who is singing his 'wind and rain' song as they exit. In the next, Lear meets mad Tom, and *leaves the fool for the madman*. Both were played, with variation in the position of the elements, around the centre ramp. Tom is mainly central, but moves freely right and left during his big speeches, returning to the ramp in the centre. Action must underline an opposition between the Fool and Tom. We must see the

Fool's repeated fear whenever Tom comes near him, and also his painful loneliness at Lear's desertion. Lear's interest in Tom is necessarily crucial. When they go out Lear and Tom are together, Tom muttering his 'child Rowland' verse, this exit making a close replica of the former, only on the other side of the stage. The Fool follows, a pathetic lonely figure. The similar yet contrasted conclusions to these two scenes underline the relation of Tom to the Fool with reference to Lear.

On the strength of reports from people who saw the play I believe that such a presentation of the middle action proves the conventional attitude to the acting of *King Lear* unsound. If Lear's apostrophe to the elements is acted in dim lights, or in front of a picture of the English countryside, and interrupted all along by thunder, even the greatest actor is helpless; done after the fashion I have suggested the problems are at most not much harder than those in *Othello*. It must be remembered however that the technique of grouping, gesture and voice should harmonize with the setting. Before the middle action Lear is an old man; during it, though with recurrent reminders of age and pathos, almost a cosmic force. Here you can employ a more extravagant use of gesture and need worry less about age in the voice. Such contrasts in the patterning and development of the poet's plan should be reflected, as far as possible, in the technique of presentation.

The ramp lent itself to a slow winding purgatorial climbing effect when Edgar leads Gloucester off, and to the Lear and Cordelia conclusion. Compare my arrangement of the last scene in *Romeo and Juliet* and contrast my *Macbeth* arrangement, described later, with its suggestions of descent, especially on the two occasions when Macbeth meets the Weird Sisters.

Additional Note, 1963

When we were doing *King Lear* at Leeds in 1951 Dr. Louie Eickhoff, who was playing Cordelia, objected to my making the mad king begin to recognize Gloucester as though after an effort ('I know thee well enough . . .' IV. vi. 182). Instead, he should first fail to recognize him, but, when the time comes for it, with the discontinuity of madness, recognize him quite easily and obviously.

CHAPTER IV

The Ideal Production

I hold up none of my examples for other producers necessarily
to copy. We could have Hamlet perfectly well leaning against
the King's throne for his long soliloquy: it would look quite
effective. That, too, would be significant: whatever we do on a
formally devised set must be significant; just as, whatever we do
on an unduly realistic set, is non-significant. The play's central
wholeness is implicit all along its circumference, and the stage-
centre, and other permanent centres of interest elsewhere, should
be used to spatialize that ideological centrality and core of wholeness discussed in our first chapter and lend point and balance to
conflicting persons facing each other across the stage. Therefore
for any one producer at any one time certain movements will
usually be far better than others; some will be excellent, some
disastrous.

Such productions as I advocate, you may say, would never be
popular. I am not so sure. I suggest no return to an archaic
Elizabethanism, robbing the theatre of its usual appeals and
putting nothing in their place. I urge something positive which
if well done should be exciting. I admit that my own productions
have erred in the direction of plainness. That has been inevitable.
But, supposing the chance offered, could an elaborate and colourful presentation be devised, one with sense-appeal, general richness and grandeur, not conflicting with my arguments? I think so.
A Shakespearian play is a rich creation and we need not deny it a
rich setting.

For *Romeo and Juliet* we could arrange some permanent blazon
consisting of the coats-of-arms of the two houses surmounted by

the Prince's coronet. For *The Tempest* we might for once play on darkness for the first scene. *The Tempest* holds within its patterned profundity suggestion of a spiritual parable. The loss of the ship in tempest reflects the tempests of mortal error and must be contrasted with the miraculous survivals on the island of music. The contrast could be pointed by acting the first scene in semi-darkness with confused cries and mazed circlings, as of lost souls; and we could have Ariel disclosed as a creature of angelic lightning, poised flaming on the mast-head, as he describes himself to Prospero afterwards. It could be done, and would assist the play's meaning more than the elaboration of realistic seas.

For any extrinsic aids and decorations we invent, there is one essential condition: they must point and be pointed by the significant action of the drama itself and must lend themselves to human and naturalistic touches in the acting. The setting must be *interwoven* with the performance: it is not enough, as I have argued earlier, to devise an elaborate artistic background, however suitable, running all the time a parallel and rival appeal to the eye. All additions must interlock with both the poetry and the action. I now outline some rough suggestions for the ideal production of (i) *The Merchant of Venice* and (ii) *Macbeth*.

2

The meaning of *The Merchant of Venice* is never sufficiently brought out. We must take the play seriously. Its deeper significances do not correspond at every point with a surface realism as they do in *Macbeth*, but for this very reason we must take care to bring the inherent meaning out as harmoniously and as naturally, yet powerfully, as we can.

The play, as I have shown in *The Shakespearian Tempest*, presents two contrasted worlds: Venice and Belmont. The one is a world of business competition, usury, melancholy, and tragic sea-disaster; the other, a spelled land of riches, music and romance. Many of our Venetian scenes are comparatively jovial; but Gratiano is scarcely a pleasant man. Venice has romantic associations, but here they are darkly toned. The supposedly pleasant people are not all that they might be. Antonio is cruel to Shylock, Bassanio a spendthrift, Gratiano vulgar, and honesty certainly not the strongest point of Lorenzo and Jessica. Shylock towers over the rest, grand but scarcely amiable. The tragedy depends on sea-wreck, tempests, and such like, Shakespeare's usual tragedy associations. At Belmont all is changed. The people become noble as soon as they arrive there: Bassanio is the loyal friend, Lorenzo the perfect lover, Gratiano comparatively subdued. The name 'Belmont' suggests a height overlooking the water-logged world of Venetian rivalry and pettiness. At Belmont we have music: at Venice, none. The projected Masque does not, so far as our persons are concerned, come off after all (II. vi. 64), but it serves for Shylock's line about the 'vile squealing of the wry-neck'd fife' (II. v. 30), which might be compared with his even less pretty 'bagpipe' reference later. Certainly, Venice is not here a place of romantic music. Belmont is. The Belmont world is dominated by Portia, expressly Christian as against Shylock, her only rival in dramatic importance, and of infinite wealth as against the penurious Bassiano and thieving Lorenzo. Everyone in Venice is in money difficulties of some sort, even the rich ones. Antonio's fortune is all at sea. Shylock has to borrow from Tubal, loses a great part of his wealth with his daughter, and bemoans his lost ducats in the street. But Portia is infinitely rich. Her riches hold dramatically a spiritual quality.

Our permanent set must help to mark out these contrasted worlds. I suggest dividing the stage into two levels, the rise making a straight diagonal from up L to down R. The higher level is thus mainly on stage right. Half-way along this diagonal steps can be used to lead from one level to the other. Venetian scenes will concentrate on the lower, Belmont on the higher, level. I do not mean that no Venetian in Venice should ascend the higher: merely that the Venetian action should focus on the lower with a force proportional to the particular significance. Certainly in the Belmont scenes the lower space must never be quite empty, which would tend to rob the figures above of any dignity their raised position gives them. We can arrange a background that gives a wide and variable range of tones according to the lights. For the casket scenes the suitors enter down R or down L and ascend the steps ceremoniously. Nothing must seem too rigid. Portia, standing aside during Bassanio's meditations, would probably come down L on the lower level and afterwards meet him as he descends the steps, an action that suits the submissive femininity of her speech and his victorious choice.

The three caskets will be large and solid-looking, and must be
allowed to dominate. They are symbolically central. At the heart
of this play is the idea of riches, of false and true wealth. Jesus'
parables are suggested. Venice is lost in the varied complexities
of the false; Portia possesses the true. Love and beauty are regularly in Shakespeare compared to riches; Portia is vitally associated
with Christianity; and she is an heiress with an infinite bank-
balance. In this play of greed her serene disregard of exact sums is
supernal:

> PORTIA: What sum owes he the Jew?
> BASSANIO: For me, three thousand ducats.
> PORTIA: What, no more?
> Pay him six thousand, and deface the bond;
> Double six thousand, and then treble that . . .

He shall have gold 'to pay the petty debt twenty times over'.

Portia's office in the play is to demonstrate the futility of
business and legal exactitudes. The action drives home the truth
that money is only an aspect of life, and that life itself must come
before money and the laws of money.[1] The contrast is pointed by
a man giving a pound of flesh as security. Everyone wants to save
his life, but there seems no loophole. His life is now subject to
laws made only for money. Observe how Portia deals with the
absurd situation. She dispels the clouding precisions and intellec-
tualities of the law court by a serene common-sense, not unlike
the common-sense of Jesus. Her 'mercy' speech exactly reflects His
teaching. The white beam of her intuition shows, as genius has a
way of showing, as Jesus' teaching so often shows, that the
academic intelligence is vulnerable to its own weapons. Shylock's
worst danger is to be allowed the rights he fights for:

> The words expressly are 'a pound of flesh':
> Then take thy bond; take thou thy pound of flesh;
> But, in the cutting it, if thou dost shed
> One drop of Christian blood . . .

This is what comes of not distinguishing between the counters of
finance and the bread and wine, the silver flesh and golden blood,
of life itself. The serene wisdom of life works by refusing validity

---

[1] I acknowledge a debt in my thinking around this point to Mr. Max Plowman's
illuminating note, 'Money and the Merchant', *The Adelphi*, New Series, II, vi;
Sept. 1931.

to false abstractions. We may cut money into bits, but not life; there any piece involves the whole. Such are the lines of Portia's poetic and holistic reasoning. As soon as we begin to think in such poetic and holistic terms there are certain supposed exactitudes that lose all meaning: so next Portia supports her first argument by insisting that Shylock shall take exactly a pound of flesh, neither less nor more. His whole position crumbles.

At Belmont Portia's caskets of gold, silver and lead, containing respectively death, folly, and infinite love and wealth, must be solid and dominating.

Venice and Belmont alternate. The play works up to the climax of the Trial scene, where the protagonists of the two worlds, Portia and Shylock, meet for the first time. Portia descends from Belmont almost as a divine being: her office is that of a *dea ex machina*. Morocco has compared her to a 'shrine' and called her a 'mortal-breathing saint' (II. vii. 40), and her wooers will have faced her as she stands above them on the steps, as pilgrims before a sanctuary. For the Trial I would have the court sitting on the high level R, some using the level itself for a seat. The Duke's chair will be half-way along. Bassanio and Antonio are down R; Shylock moves between up L, L, and C. Some spectators can edge in down L and Gratiano stand L between them and Shylock, coming forward for his big speeches.

Portia enters down R, circles up-stage to the steps, and ascends the higher level, standing beside the Duke. Her doctor's gown is better neither black nor red. Her doctorate is one of Christian wisdom and feminine intuition. Let her therefore wear a correctly cut doctor-of-laws gown of spotless white, making a blend of realism and symbolic meaning suiting the nature of Shakespearian drama. She stands high and central dominating the whole court. The light should be intensified on her gown and golden hair just showing under her cap as she speaks her Mercy speech. As the situation ripens, she descends, the movement using our levels to capture the essence of her arrival in Venice to render assistance, her *descent* from the happier world of her home. She comes nearly, but not quite, down at: 'I pray you, let me look upon the bond'. Shylock gives it her. She warns him: 'Shylock, there's thrice thy money offer'd thee'. She is kind, is meeting these people on their own terms, descending to their level. But Shylock will have none of it. She tries again. He returns to his corner, talking to Tubal, adamant. Portia, on the steps, begins to prepare judgement. She asks for balances and a surgeon, and addresses Antonio. Antonio says his farewell. Now, swaying slightly, she pronounces judgement, the speed gathers as the whirl of her repetition gains force, the whirl of a lasso:

> The court awards it and the law doth give it,

and

> The law allows it and the court awards it.

Shylock in ecstasy of hatred cries 'A sentence! Come, prepare!' Unleashed, he springs down-stage. Bassanio shields Antonio. The Duke stands. The crowds murmur. But at this instant Portia takes the last step down to the lower level and cuts off Shylock's attack with a raised hand. 'Tarry a little.' There is silence. In a quiet voice she continues:

> . . . there is something else.
> This bond doth give thee here no jot of blood . . .

The terrifying judgement of a fathomless simplicity and a divine common-sense.

It is an amazing scene, its impact deriving from the clash of the two dominating forces in the play, Shylock and Portia, and all that they stand for. Our set of two levels and Portia's descent will assist; so will her white gown and her barring of Shylock's attack at the crucial moment, which must be given expressive action. We must work from the profound issues implicit in the dramatic thrill if it is to have full power. Portia's standing on the same steps where previously we have seen her meet her suitors, with the caskets behind, priestess of the knowledge of true and false wealth, helps this scene. We are aware of her bringing her own world and all that it symbolizes into the new context.

For the rest of the scene we need not be afraid of an anticlimax. Portia must be firm and not too pitiful. Shylock's exit, C to down L through the crowd, can be as pathetic as you will, but not too long delayed. The play shows a Christian, romantic and expressly feminine Portia against a down-trodden, vengeful, racially grand, usurious Jew. I do not claim that all the difficulties inherent in this opposition are finally settled, but I would claim that this dramatic opposition is a profound one. We must not suppose that since Portia has all our sympathy Shylock can have none: poetic drama can be paradoxical. Portia stands serene in white purity, symbol of Christian romance. Shylock, saying he is ill, picks up his cloak and goes out robed in purple: the purple of tragedy. Two vast imaginative issues conflict: the romantic dream and tragic realism. Later on Shakespeare is to reconcile them. Here the opposition must be stark: neither must be watered down.

The last scene at Belmont acts itself easily, but I object to so unfortunate a back-cloth as one with *waves* painted on it. Our set here might for the first time dispose of the change in level. The action's dualism may not have been perfectly unified, but we are not supposed now to be worrying about it. Or again, we might keep it, and get significant comedy out of the lovers chasing each other, as they usually do, from one level to the other. On second thoughts, I think this best. It would have meaning. Lorenzo and Jessica would be comfortably placed on the steps at the beginning.

3

We have referred continually in this book to *Macbeth*. Here is an outline of my ideal production. The general purpose will be: (i) to use a more or less permanent set; (ii) to arrange a rich production to bring out and solidify *with the help of the action* layers in the play's imagery and symbolism which it usually takes years of sensitive appreciation to remark and hold in the mind; and (iii) to give at last the element of supernature an adequate projection. I shall not attempt to describe sound-effects: I have already indicated my principles in this matter. My arrangement exploits dramatically the more philosophical ideas of my essay on *Macbeth* in *The Imperial Theme*.

The stage will be mostly draped in black. There will be a semi-circular background with a ledge half-way up, and two or more high entrances there. There are entrances below variously as may be convenient. A flight of steps leads down from the ledge C, or possibly a little L of C, so that it points inward at a slight angle. There is a big dais R supporting a heavy and elaborate golden throne. Opposite the throne there is, L, a niche containing a raised Madonna-figure and Child and an altar-like level, having a step in front, but none of it too definitely ecclesiastical. Possibly the black drapes all round are streaked with gold zig-zags here and there. Two of the entrances to the ledge show red curtains, but

The Ideal Production

these and other gaps can also disclose sky for out-door effects. The stairway is carpeted first in green, later in crimson, and finally again in green. The lighting will be subtly used throughout: especially important will be its varied play on the Madonna and the throne. These will, however, nearly always remain visible. There will be no obvious stress on coloured lights.

ACT I

The first scene is given on the fore-stage: I assume that we should have a good one. Next Duncan stands before the throne, the bloody Sergeant entering down L. The Madonna is well lit and wide patches of sky show above the ledge.

The lights would then change for Macbeth's meeting with the Weird Sisters, dimming on the Madonna. Through the openings over the ledge irregular patches of sky-sheet could show to suggest a mountainous and craggy gorge. Our set lends itself to effects of descent which can be used to suggest a Dantesque circle of Hell. Having a very definite permanent set we need be less afraid of dimming corners, since the audience are conscious of what is there and have a feeling for the proper limits. The throne and Madonna are dim. The Weird Sisters meet and circle C. Macbeth and Banquo enter on one of the ledge openings, silhouetted for a second against sky, and walk round and descend the steps. They are coming over mountain crags. The Weird Sisters prophesy grouped in front of the throne, and facing Macbeth and Banquo, who have walked down L. Macbeth advances: they melt away, and he finds himself confronted significantly by the throne, on which the lights have slightly risen. Macbeth gazes on it, as he says 'Your children shall be kings'; then starts at Banquo's '*You* shall be king', and turns away from it as though uninterested: 'And Thane of Cawdor, too . . .' During his soliloquy he stands near, and on appropriate lines regarding, the throne. Banquo and the lords group down L. Macbeth comes down to meet them, while the curtain closes behind. They go off together.

The curtain is drawn and Duncan is discovered on the throne, his sons on either side. No sky is visible: it is an interior. The Madonna and Child are bright. Macbeth and Banquo enter down L—not down the steps—and approach the dais. The King's

132

proclamation of Malcolm's accession must be done ceremoniously, Macbeth and the others kneeling before the throne-group; this will be effective, and brings out the meaning of the situation, besides throwing forward to a later group.

The lights change and direct the eye to Lady Macbeth appearing through one of the ledge-entrances. Morning sky might show, as through windows. She is on the steps, reading the letter. At 'Glamis thou art . . .' she swiftly descends, facing the throne from the bottom step at '. . . shalt be what thou art promis'd'. The servant tells of the messenger. 'He brings great news' takes Lady Macbeth up-stage. She refers to her 'battlements', arms raised to the sky openings, back to the audience; then swings round to face the Madonna and Child. She deliberately challenges the figure for a second, then scornfully turns and invokes the spirits of evil against her sex and motherhood; or she might speak boldly facing the image. Macbeth enters down R crossing the throne, and does not look on it until his wife urges him. They go out.

Duncan and his following enter down L, and look up to the ledge, as to a battlemented castle. After Duncan's 'martlet' speech, Lady Macbeth descends the green stairway to meet him. He confronts her standing with his sons and lords grouped before the throne.

The curtains are drawn and the feast procession passes to music across the fore-stage.

Next the full set is discovered with now a *red* carpet on the stairs. Macbeth is standing on the lower steps of the stairway for his soliloquy. His references to Duncan are made looking at the throne. As his speech grows impassioned he rises, walks downstage, and faces the Madonna for his lines on 'pity like a naked new-born babe' and 'heaven's cherubin'. Finally he falls on his knees on the steps before the Madonna, looking back at the throne for the words 'vaulting ambition'; then prays. At Lady Macbeth's entry he rises. She draws him down L, away. Laughter is heard from the feast, from time to time, during their dialogue. Then we have a ceremonious procession. Duncan and the rest enter R. There is business of some sort between the King and his hosts. He, with his sons, ascends the red stairs and, half-way, turns and holds his arms in blessing over the crowded stage. The grouping tends to mask the throne. Then all go out, some up the stairs and at different openings on the ledge, others at up-stage ground entrances, others at the wings. You should see the red-curtained door of Duncan's exit on the ledge.

The lights change. Night sky is seen at openings over the ledge. Banquo enters below with Fleance[1]; then Macbeth and a servant. During this subtle dialogue the throne, close to Macbeth, can catch Banquo's eye on the words 'To you they have show'd some truth'. Macbeth stands with his back to it, for 'I think not of them'. The Madonna is dim. Macbeth is left alone. The air-drawn dagger points up the red stairs. He follows it a step or two. Then he banishes it, turning, and facing the darkly glowing throne with lustful eye. He now succumbs utterly to evil and speaks the Tarquin lines. He regards the throne again at 'Whiles I threat, he lives'. The bell sounds. He crouches up the stairs and along the ledge to Duncan's room.

Lady Macbeth enters up R, lower level. Macbeth's reappearance is easy. You watch his zig-zag course, along and down. For his agonized 'sleep no more' speeches he sinks on the dais step, a puny, miserable figure under the vast throne. You see how it offers him no pleasure; indeed, is clearly not his at all. Lady Macbeth ascends the stairs and returns. The knocking is ominous. They go out and the Porter enters, and then Macduff and Lennox. Macduff is all efficiency, sharp with the Porter, afraid of being late, precise and military. He and Macbeth confront each other before the Madonna and throne respectively. Macbeth offers to take Macduff up, but his nerve fails, and he points: 'This is the door'.

At the general discovery of the murder people crowd in from all the entrances. Banquo and Macduff are respectively in front of the throne and Madonna, Malcolm and Donalbain down R. The King's people are massed down R and L. Macbeth stands at the foot of the red stairs, his retainers slanting off on either side and above, the apex of a wedge spined with crimson. A kind of arrow-head. Macduff L speaks his 'Wherefore did you so?' with a challenging ring; Banquo his lines

---

[1] Suppose that during their short dialogue Fleance sits, and that the first article handed him by his father is held like a sceptre, and that Banquo next gives him his own head-piece, looking like a crown. Notice how the incident and dialogue proceed to flower. This suggestion I owe to a production by Mr. Brownlow Card in 1938 (revived 1940), in which I was privileged to play Macbeth to the Lady Macbeth of Patricia Card. See pictures 11 and 12.

In the great hand of God I stand, and thence
Against the undivulg'd pretence I fight
Of treasonous malice

with one foot on the throne steps. After the rest go, Malcolm and Donalbain can show a definite suspicion of Macbeth.

The choric commentary of Ross and the Old Man is to be done as a front-scene. Macduff, entering later, must appear meditative, unwilling to express his full suspicions, but darkly meaningful and thoughtful. This ends Act I.

ACT II

Banquo enters in the full set and uses reference to the throne freely to point his words, standing C. Then Macbeth and Lady Macbeth enter from above with a couple of attendants, and come down the crimson-carpeted stairs. Banquo draws R to the throne-step. The stage fills from lower entrances LC and down L. Macbeth is again the apex of a crowd, as he comes down C. The repetition is significant. Banquo, with Fleance, is R, and seems for a second to be barring Macbeth's approach to the throne. Then he bows and the incident melts, as he steps aside and Macbeth and Lady Macbeth cross. This is the second of a series of incidents where Banquo is related to the throne. Now we have a small wooden throne for Lady Macbeth down-stage of the gold one, beside it: which points the proper quality of Lady Macbeth's position, subsidiary to Macbeth's kingship. Her unselfishness is a platitude of commentary. Macbeth in his throne looks lost. It is so big. An all but ludicrous effect is wanted; for which there is authority in the text:

> Now does he feel his title
> Hang loose about him, like a giant's robe
> Upon a dwarfish thief. (v. ii. 20)

After Banquo's exit, the others go and leave Macbeth alone. He rises quickly from the throne as if with relief. 'To be thus is nothing . . .' Referring to Banquo's royal descendants he looks on it, bringing to our minds the two incidents when Banquo has, as it were by chance, seemed positionally to possess it. Macbeth asserts himself as he defies fate. He can, as it were, attack the image of Banquo, sweeping it from the throne, banishing it like the air-drawn dagger: then swiftly turns, nervous, at 'Who's there?' He stands on the throne steps as he addresses the murderers; then goes out. Lady Macbeth returns. The Servant goes out down-stage. Lady Macbeth sees her husband re-enter and stand gazing at the Madonna. She quickly draws him away, telling him to banish 'sorriest fancies' and all thoughts that should die with the dead. She leads him to his throne, would put him there, and try to love seeing him there, as a mother puts her baby to rest. He sits in it for 'We have scotch'd the snake, not killed it . . .' She kneels, and caresses him. 'Gentle my lord, sleek o'er your rugged looks . . .' Macbeth breaks from her, but still sitting, and hints aside of some 'deed of dreadful note'. She, anxious, rises and importunately draws to him, holds his arm. 'What's to be done?' Now he breaks from her altogether, rises, and from the throne steps invokes night and evil. She is fearful, bereft of speech.

The murder of Banquo is done as a front-scene.

For the feast we have our full set. There is one big table running diagonally down L at whatever exact angle may be most convenient. Macbeth and Lady Macbeth are in their thrones. Guests are at the table. Macbeth's other chair is at the table's upstage end, which is near the base of the stairs. Macbeth talks to the murderer on the stairs where the Ghost is to come from. Then he comes down R. On his lines referring to Banquo the Ghost walks slowly and deliberately down the red stairs and sits in Macbeth's table-chair, which is slightly raised, giving the Ghost a dominant position. Lady Macbeth comes down R and talks to Macbeth aside. The Ghost exits into the shadows up R behind the throne. On its next entrance it appears down R, stalks to the dais and *sits in the throne*. Macbeth on his second reference to Banquo has taken possession of the table-chair as if to make sure of no more accidents, but only finds that he has driven the Ghost to a still more terrible position: the very one he most hates to associate with Banquo. Macbeth finally advances to the throne steps and violently banishes it, repeating the movement I introduced earlier. Note Macbeth's *courage in face of the supernatural*.[1] Every time he shakes portentous nightmares from him. It was the same with the dagger; and he curses the Weird Sisters later. He treats them like dirt. His humanity never bends under these sub-human horrors. He never abrogates his human status. This is important

---

[1] Before the Ghost's second entry Macbeth's deliberate use of Banquo's name and the words 'would he were here' are, as it were, *daring* the ghost to reappear. [1963]

and forms, or should, a large part of our admiration. His bark is thus 'tempest-toss'd' but 'cannot be lost'. The Ghost's exit is a simple turn left and round along the dais into shadows, quickly obscured behind the tall throne. The guests go out L and up R. Alone together Macbeth and Lady Macbeth stay by the thrones; Macbeth is sunk on the dais, his wife kneels, ministering to him. At 'Come, we'll to sleep' they cross and start to ascend the stairs, slowly, like Adam and Eve, hand-in-hand. Half-way up, Macbeth stops and speaks his last couple of lines, looking on the disordered remains of the banquet: 'My strange and self-abuse . . .' Again they move up, slowly, laboriously.

The Hecate scene is done on the fore-stage. Then we go back to the feast scene. All is just as we left it, overturned chairs and all. But the lights have changed. The Madonna-figure is picked out brilliantly. Lennox and a Lord enter looking surreptitious and stealthy, up-stage. Their dialogue is done more or less C. They speak softly. At Lennox' lines 'Some holy angel . . .' they come down, perhaps kneel, to the Madonna. The advantages of doing this dialogue from our full set are obvious. The Lord can point to the disarranged remnants, tumbled cups, and so on for his words:

> We may again
> Give to our tables meat, sleep to our nights,
> Free from our feasts and banquets bloody knives . . .

The words point the moral of the Banquet scene; let the action do so, too.

We cannot run on at once to the Cauldron scene, as the table has to be moved. I suggest that we draw the curtain, and all lights are down. In the darkness we hear the thunder and the Weird Sisters' first speeches; this can go on as long as may be necessary. Then the lights come up on our full set showing the cauldron C and the three figures at their work around it. The sky shows in craggy strips above. We are in one of the lowest circles of Hell, the 'pit of Acheron' (III. v. 15). The Madonna figure is dim for this Black Mass: if we use Hecate's entrance, she will appropriately obscure it, down L. The Weird Sisters between their chants can variously twirl away a little up the stairs or on to the dais. Macbeth appears above and speaks from half-way down the steps: 'What is't you do?' The throne is not clearly visible. Macbeth stands before it. The Sisters are now down-stage of the cauldron and when the Apparitions are to appear group themselves diagonally LC facing up-stage, close to the cauldron. The Apparitions come from the cauldron C, very solid and distinct. They could be dummy figures and their words spoken in turn by each of the Sisters: this may be the original intention. The thunder is very loud. Macbeth cowers instinctively before the Crowned Child: though part of the little conflict-drama[1] it is itself a powerful life-symbol. The words, however, reassure him. Macbeth demands to know more. The Weird Sisters get C above the cauldron. Macbeth, back to the audience, fiercely advances, and the cauldron sinks, obeying the text. It almost seems as if Macbeth has stamped it out of existence. The Sisters and Hecate draw back, moving backwards, up the stairs as though fearful, as they should be, of what follows.

Macbeth, C, sees the throne loom out, the lights coming up on it and the Madonna. Music sounds. The kings enter up R and down R variously, each pausing before Macbeth, and in turn grouping themselves round the throne, like a photograph group. Pauses are no difficulty: let it be all done with deliberation and ceremony. Balls and sceptres and the glass should be visibly solid. Last the Ghost of Banquo enters and takes his place in the throne itself. Banquo's continual possession of the throne during the middle action is most significant. His royalty is spiritual, creative, and real; Macbeth's selfish, lustful, and unreal. This is why Banquo worries Macbeth so much. Now the whole group is complete. Macbeth stands C between it and the bright Madonna. The effect is splendid and solid. The kings as they enter must give Macbeth a good look: usually they just peep at him through gauze. The group then melts away, ceremoniously, moving with dignity, the lights on them dimming. Lights could for once go down all round the stage leaving Macbeth alone illuminated C, a pin-point of burning consciousness in Hell.

There is thunder and the galloping of horses. Later we have a realistic explanation, but meanwhile they can be associated with the Weird Sisters' departure, riding through midnight storm-wrack. In Shakespeare a realistic structure may provide a sound of more general import, as in the music preluding the middle action of *Othello*, and the sound-effects in *Hamlet*.

---

[1] See either *The Shakespearian Tempest*, pp. 192–3, or *The Christian Renaissance*, 1933, 63–4; 1962, 45–6. See also p. 166 below, note.

Now all the lights go up, the sky-strips are again red-curtained doors, the wild nightmare crags are the corridors of his own palace. He stands dazed, in sudden daylight. He stares at the throne and dais recently occupied by Banquo and his descendants; and the stairs, where the Weird Sisters were hunched up. He covers his eyes in agony. Lennox enters.

Consider our use of the throne in relation to Banquo during the middle action. Just before the murder, Macbeth, himself in front of it, confronts Banquo's innuendo speech. After the murder, Banquo stands on its steps for 'In the great hand of God I stand'. Banquo, in the soliloquy that starts our second act, will have gazed on it at the start, 'Thou hast it now . . .', and also as he remembers the prophecy concerning his own sons. Macbeth next finds him significantly in front of it, but sits in it himself whilst questioning Banquo about his journey. Now follow three incidents of rising intensity. First, Macbeth images Banquo in the throne during his own soliloquy; next, Banquo's ghost sits there at the banquet; and, third, Banquo and all his line possess it in the Cauldron scene. We may remember the early group of Duncan and his sons. Our production must reflect the poet's skill in keeping before our eyes Banquo's 'royalty of nature' and all that it stands for of creative kingship. Thoughts of Banquo dominate the middle action.

ACT III

The murder of Lady Macduff can be best done before simple curtains. Generally it gets laughter. It is, however, not meant to hold any grandeur of action. Macbeth's exploits get less and less dignified and more mad. They are meant to. Duncan's murder was tragically grand; Banquo's melodramatic; and this is almost ludicrous. The producer must bring out its quality of ghoulish horror fearlessly and no one will laugh. He must avoid a lot of screams at the end.

The English scene is done also before a plain curtain: a green background would do well.

We return to our main set for the sleep-walking. Lady Macbeth comes down the red stairs and later reascends them. Her candle will be put on the throne dais, or the stairs. She fingers the throne with the action of blindness. At one point she comes near the

Madonna, perhaps touches the altar-level in front, and shrinks away whimpering. She moves about the stage, living its significances. The Doctor's 'God, God, forgive us all!' can be spoken with some reference to the Madonna, which should be palely lit.

From now the action speeds up. A short military front-scene, accompanied by martial drums, shows troops gathering to meet Malcolm. Then we have our full set: the sky-sheet shows in places above to give some effect of battlements, but lights are gloomy and autumnal for Macbeth's passage of tragic loneliness and the Doctor's lines on Lady Macbeth. The stairway is now green again. Now follows a second short scene, martial music getting louder and nearer for Malcolm's and Macduff's approach. The play is growing brighter. We want our lights to grow sensibly brighter during this last movement, but this does not mean that all the middle action must be done in half darkness. All that is necessary is for this movement to start dark; quickly get bright enough for clear expression but with a certain toning of atmospheric and autumnal suggestion; and gradually increase to a brilliant conclusion. Notice the repeated direction 'drum and *colours*' for Malcolm and his supporters; also for Macbeth; and Macbeth's 'Hang out our banners on the outward walls'. Both sides share in the awakening. Macbeth is reckless and flings himself in the throne. He is almost happy. There is action, colour and sane purpose at last, replacing nightmare and actions that beat only the dark and torment the doer. Macbeth no longer fears a nightshriek; he has all but won through. Hearing of his wife's death he first moves towards the Madonna, as if to pray, but turns away:

> She should have died hereafter;
> There would have been a time for such a word . . .

The messenger announcing the movement of Birnam Wood comes from above. Martial music sounds louder and very close for another front-scene: 'Now near enough: your leavy screens throw down . . .' I think these are best suggested off-stage. Then our full set, for the last time. The sky-sheet shows more than ever before. The stage is bright. Macbeth fights Young Siward, and goes off. Macduff enters. During his short speech—'My wife and children's ghosts will haunt me still'—he might get some business with the Madonna-altar, dedicating his sword to her and praying. He goes off up the stairs. Malcolm and Siward enter from down L and cross, going out down R. Macbeth re-enters, and is by his throne as Macduff confronts him coming down the stairs. He is killed finally below the Madonna and Child. The body lies on the steps before it, sacrificed. We remember Macduff's slaughtered wife and children, and Lady Macbeth's speech invoking the desecration of motherhood.

The rest is easy. At the conclusion Malcolm ascends the throne, or at the least stands on its step. Macduff remains close to the Madonna for the final group. Malcolm might in some way use the Madonna for his phrase 'the grace of Grace'; as might Old Siward earlier. The lights are bright, the sky above as brilliant as possible, for the first time exposed all the way round the curving ledge, crowning the stage with a wide circle of light.

I have hurried these last descriptions, not because the last scenes are weak or unimportant, but because they depend more on a quick time sequence and martial sounds than on spatial significances.

Such is my outline. I have used a permanent set for all big scenes and have preserved an impression of weight and solidity. The main impressions used are:

(i) *The throne*, which covers the various royalty-symbolism of our play, gold crowns and sceptres, etc.; and the whole matter of kingship, rightful for Duncan and Malcolm, wrongful for Macbeth, spiritual and prophetic for Banquo.

(ii) *The red stairway*, mainly suggesting blood, which is a powerful impression throughout. My arrangement of the carpets will be best understood by considering that the play moves from social and natural order through nightmare and blood to daylight sanity and a new harmony.

(iii) *The green stairway* at the beginning and end, suggesting nature and social harmony generally, an integral conception to be contrasted with the unnatural and nightmarish evil and related to the child-with-a-tree, the martlet's nest, the wren passage, the Birnam Wood incidents, and numerous other nature references; and also thoughts of honour and integrity generally.

(iv) *The Madonna and Child*, relating to the frequent Christian imagery of purity, angels and divine grace, closely associated with child-thoughts, Lady Macbeth's invocation of evil to dry up in her breasts the milk of human and feminine tenderness, her 'I have given suck . . .', the 'naked new-born babe', the two child apparitions, Macduff's family. The symbolism blends with the creative royalty of Banquo and his descendants.

I have not attempted to discuss sounds.[1] They must be given exact attention: music for Duncan's feast and the show of Banquo's kings and, if we use it, the Weird Sisters' dance with Hecate; thunder continually, especially for the Weird Sisters and the three Apparitions; continually nearing martial sounds for Malcolm's army; and the strange effect of horses galloping, twice at least, which relates to the nightmarish atmosphere very aptly. By working this—as, indeed, on occasion other sounds—with growing volume from behind the audience, you can temporarily enclose the whole theatre in the play's action. The ideal performance would also embody many strands and trains of imagery and thought too subtle or intangible for static visual projection. The questions, the mazed bafflement, the essential darkness of the play, might be reflected into appropriate turns and gestures.[2]

If my description here appears to lay too much emphasis on universal meanings, and seems rather like an X-ray of the play, exposing its skeleton, that is because I have concentrated only on certain moments. These should not appear obtrusive when embedded in the whole.

I claim that some such production is called for. I have not explained all the significances, but if studied these arrangements will be found to vitalize the play. The objects used are drawn from and react on the story and the poetry of its expression. We must aim to reveal the profound issues implicit in particular events; to bring into prominence the things which make *Macbeth* great dramatic literature rather than rhetorical melodrama. The average production rarely gets beyond good melodrama, and sometimes fails to reach that. Sometimes, of course, effects are imaginatively right and powerful by subconscious understanding, but there is little conscious and systematic exploitation of the author's pattern. There is little beyond a direct realistic abstraction from the concrete significances of Shakespeare's poetry; or, if there is anything

[1] The flourishes, sennets etc. in *Macbeth* are well handled by Mr. Roy Walker in *The Time is Free*, 1949.
[2] Compare E. Gordon Craig's demand for such actions in order to prepare for the supernatural effects. See pp. 220-1 below.

'symbolic', the symbols come, not from the play itself, but out of the producer's mind.

Additional Note, 1949

I reprint this essay with certain reservations:

(i) It should be read as an extreme and purely suggestive development of certain sound principles. What is important is not the details but the *direction* of my attempt. No such intellectual plan is likely to stand in practice without modification. Possibly the solids suggested might be of more use in rehearsal, to focalize action and grouping, than in actual performance; or even held merely as images in the producer's mind.

(ii) The Madonna-figure, in spite of my 'not too ecclesiastical', points rather dangerously to a rigid orthodoxy. It may be safer to feel the play's Christian tonings, which are richer than is normally supposed,[1] as part only of a wild naturalism of birth and creation, while limiting the specifically Christian to the English court. There appears to be too much domesticity in the carpet, though there again the textual authority is strong. The throne may be allowed.

(iii) If used, the objects might be slabbed out in rough modernistic fashion from a setting of not dissimilar substance, being themselves denied a too assertive particularity; so that the throne and Madonna could be taken, under certain lights, for rocks. Under such a treatment many difficulties might dissolve.

Additional Note, 1963

The compromising 'reservations' of my 1949 note under heading (i) above seem to me too pusillanimous. My scheme has already to some extent proved itself in production (pp. 17, 260). The coloured carpets are however wrong: many of the audience would not see them, and lighting might play havoc with the colours. Perhaps I was thinking of the *Agamemnon*. If a change in colours is wanted, it would have to be done by careful lighting on banners or other drapes set high.

When I produced *Macbeth* at Stowe in 1942 the three Apparitions were done as follows: from a temporarily darkened stage the Armed Head was picked out by a green spot; for the second and

---

[1] See F. C. Kolbe's *Shakespeare's Way* (1930); my own *The Wheel of Fire* (1930; enlarged 1949); and Mr. Roy Walker's *The Time is Free* (1949).

third apparitions, figures bare from the waist up were picked out
by red and white lights respectively, the third with his crown and
tree making a brilliant unit. It is an exceptionally difficult scene
and our resources were limited; but, given the situation, such was
our expedient, and it succeeded.

Two last thoughts: (i) Those who find my general scheme
distracting should turn to the—perhaps deceptively—simpler
instructions of John Masefield's *A Macbeth Production* (1945).
(ii) My symbolic solids might radiate strong and needed thematic
powers (e.g., the Throne up-stage and the Madonna down-stage,
facing up) on one of our new 'open' stages (see pp. 288–9, 294):
perhaps that is where they belong.

4 [1963]. THE WINTER'S TALE

I add a few notes to develop further what could be no more than
an attempt in my production of *The Winter's Tale* at Toronto in
1936.

The story, though superficially loose, is bound together by
Apollo and his oracle. We tried to suggest a statue, but our
resources were inadequate. Some such figure might nevertheless
be an effective symbol.

Probably it should be high, embossed and bronze or gilded
against an iron-dark, metallic, wall, and beneath it an altar-shelf
and braziers. It could be the centre of a silent ritual before the
play opens.

If however we use a statue it should at first be vaguely lit and
seem no more than a palatial decoration; or a silhouette holding,
in so far as it is noticed, a slightly ominous suggestion. It would
be partly draped: Apollo here is not quite the Apollo of our
expectance, seeming often as near Jehovah as Apollo; and the
folds will be needed to vary its appearance under illumination.

The figure's full significance is first revealed by Leontes' gesture
at:

> I have dispatch'd in post
> To sacred Delphos, to Apollo's temple,
> Cleomenes and Dion, whom you know
> Of stuff'd sufficiency. Now from the oracle
> They will bring all . . .   (II. i. 181)

If a statue, lights will here for the first time show its lines of

The Ideal Production

majesty. When Cleomenes and Dion enter to describe their awe-inspiring experience in Apollo's temple some ritualistic observance would be in order.

At the trial (III. ii) it will dominate. Hermione cries

> I do refer me to the oracle:
> Apollo be my judge!

The Officer stands below it as he reads the oracular pronouncement. At 'Now blessed be the great Apollo' some of the company kneel. Leontes' blasphemous 'There is no truth at all i' the oracle' is rendered the more terrible by the deity's visible presence, and we respond with greater awe to his

> Apollo's angry; and the heavens themselves
> Do strike at my injustice.

At

> Apollo pardon
> My great profaneness 'gainst thine oracle!

Leontes falls, grovelling, and remains there, below the figure, by the steps, while above Paulina, from nearer it, speaks her denunciation.

When Antigonus enters on the Bohemian coast, panels might be removed to disclose sky on either side of the embossed figure, and rocks in silhouette; or the statue could be so lit that it seems a rock-pinnacle; some supporting objects might help. It may seem a pity to destroy our iron permanency by removing these panels, but we must make of it a special effect, letting them slide apart to thunder as though some cosmic disturbance were opening new vistas. The stage will be dark and the sky stormy, but Apollo meanwhile well-lit and dominating so that he, and not the producer, *appears to be doing it*. We not only solve our problem; in the process we make our Apollo an obvious *agent*, just what he should be. As the scene develops the sky-openings become lighter. For the country scenes that follow they will be bright.

Antigonus' reference to the oracle keeps Apollo in our minds, and as he lays the child at the figure's base we should become delicately aware that the child is safe.

During the sheep-shearing festival, sky will show and colour be bright with Maypole-like streamers and garishly be-ribboned

145 K

dresses. The Apollo will be a centre of country ritual, floral decoration, and harvest offerings. Apollo is remembered and given precedence over other gods:

> The gods themselves,
> Humbling their deities to love, have taken
> The shapes of beasts upon them: Jupiter
> Became a bull, and bellow'd; the green Neptune
> A ram, and bleated; and the fire-rob'd god,
> Golden Apollo, a poor humble swain,
> As I seem now.

The others are nature deities, Apollo human. 'Fire-rob'd' gives the electrician his chance. Perdita and others will honour Apollo with flowers.

When we return to Sicilia Paulina's position in relation to the figure is the same as when she denounced Leontes after his blasphemy. The curse is not yet removed; Sicilia has been static for sixteen years. 'The divine Apollo' is still remembered (v. 1. 37).

For the final revelation we are in a 'chapel' and incense should be freely used and sensed by the audience.

If we have our statue, two statues are awkward, and it might be possible to let Apollo turn out here to be Hermione, theology and resurrection becoming identical. This smacks rather of trickery, though it would not be untrue to the play. The humanistic Apollo is our deity, and the final revelation deliberately referred to 'that rare Italian master Julio Romano' (v. ii. 108), signifying the Italian renaissance. Also Hermione is regarded, in the manner of these last plays, as herself all but a divinity; words of royal and pietistic reverence applied to humanity sprinkle the text; there is a numinous halo over our people, especially towards the end. Our scheme has a general justification in that Apollo, our presiding deity, is pre-eminently, according to Nietzsche's *The Birth of Tragedy*, the god of sculpture, while the statue of Hermione makes our climax. There is a unity here.

The statue would certainly make heavy demands on lighting if it is to assume so many different forms while remaining itself. But, considering the amazing skills which are so often put to the service of irrelevant distractions, it is not too much to ask that such skills should be used in a better cause. Another thought: if a real stroke of creative interpretation is involved, many of our objections regarding spectacle and lighting become foolish, if not meaningless. The 'if' is important: as Touchstone reminds us, there is 'much virtue in if'.

I suspect nevertheless that the metaphysics of our statue conclusion are dramatically unsound since they set the audience thinking when they should be experiencing. Our gilded embossment against dark iron is probably more satisfactory, because more truly a setting, whereas a statue is throughout in visual rivalry with the stage persons. Apollo should exist in a different, here a flat, dimension. The altar-shelf, votive offerings and incense come off best this way; and it should not be hard to suggest open-air for Bohemia. For an ordinary stage I prefer the embossed figure: it would look grand. On an open or arena stage the statue might be excellent.

Audiences normally receive no consistent impression of Appolo's importance here as sun-god. Our projection enforces their response.

CHAPTER V

Shakespeare and Ritual

G reat drama is more than entertainment. Rather I would call it a ceremony in which actors and audience share in the formal unfurling of some deeply significant pattern. The better you know a great play, the richer your gain: there should be little element of excitement as to what shall happen. Or rather your knowledge of the future disclosure actually increases your delight in its awaited surprise. Remember Bottom's remark—'You shall see, it will fall pat as I told you: yonder she comes'. That goes deep into the nature of dramatic art. Greek and Elizabethan dramatists alike were fond of well-known tales. For, by knowing the future and overlooking the whole, whether we be actor or audience, we become fully conscious of life's patterned progress, for a while entering a state unattained in actual affairs except at rare moments. We rise above the story's purely sequential nature. People often ask whether an actor should feel and live his part or rather work from a cold and impersonal intellectual height; but the question is futile, since he must do both. He must be lost in his part while rising above it. He must live it intensely, but with the intensity of art. An actor's efforts must always be given with a certain conscious precision, often signalling to the audience the kind of reaction desired. An audience will often laugh at or take seriously a certain effect according to what they think is expected of them. This is a psychological fact, apart from theory, that must not be forgotten. There must be, therefore, a blend of conscious artistry and spontaneous feeling. This very blend is the supreme necessity. As in a dance you may lose your self-consciousness to realize it differently in terms of acquired technique and orchestral rhythm, so audience and actors lose themselves for a purpose, and, living in that purpose, attain an awareness wherein the temporal succession becomes the edge of some more solid and rounded dimension. There is a still wider analogy: that of the saint whose consciousness enjoys perfect freedom in subjection, wherein the antinomy of free-will and predestination is resolved.

A famous painter used to advise beginners to make their work 'look as though it were painted', and not to attempt to 'deceive the eye'. But how often do we find 'naturalness' the only criterion of popular and even enlightened dramatic appreciation? It is all wrong; or, at least, some of it is. A production should look like a production, and look as though it knows it; an actor should even look as though he were acting, since if he did not we should all accuse him with one voice of incompetence. I ask only that we acknowledge what we already know, and consciously accept the conventions on which drama rests and of which Shakespeare makes superb use. This is the way to a convincing and honest sincerity and the only medium of a richly human appeal. I would blaze a trail to no esoteric and stiff intellectualism, but to a proper projection of Shakespeare's synthesis of flexible detail and permanent architectonic, of varied human insight and universal meaning. I approve a permanent and solid-looking set whose clear definitions and constraining limits give point and power to the human action enclosed. Without a consciously artistic compression in set, general arrangement, and acting technique we rob the play's explosive force of its right detonation and lingering reverberations.

Shakespeare demands in places an almost ritualistic performance. There is explicit suggestion of this even in the romantic comedies. We have the formal song conclusions to *Love's Labour's Lost* and *Twelfth Night*. *A Midsummer Night's Dream* ends with ceremonious dance and formal procession. *Much Ado about Nothing* has a dance. Hymen's entry towards the close of *As You Like It* is important, and our critical reception, or rejection, of it a characteristic symptom. *The Taming of the Shrew* ends with a feast. These romances exploit and expand the dream-desires of a romantic aspiration. They are variously toned with transcendental suggestion. Each dreams a world of melody where mistakes are rectified, desires fulfilled, and all live happy ever after. Shakespeare exploits to the full the deep content of the happy-ending romance, perhaps the world's most universal art-form. We must not let twentieth-century cynicism have its way with such creations: they existed long before our time and will exist after. Our failure to recognize profundities here is our, not their, limitation. Each such romance is a day-dream, if you will, but one that outlines Paradise, and as such must be read and performed.

The early Romances explore paradises of personal desire: they are visions of harmony, of union. But the Histories pursue a sterner task, developing the antagonisms of England's story in terms of military ardour, honour and the ideal of kingship. A Shakespearian play, aiming at the universal through the personal, finds the king, in whom these two categories blend, a pregnant centre. The problems of England converge mercilessly on Shakespeare's kings. The succession is epic, almost biblical, the swing and ceremony of England's story. Remember the divinity of Richard II, and how the curse of his deposition and death is not lifted until Henry's noble prayer before Agincourt. To all these kingly plays we must bring a sense of the sacramental. They challenge our modern understanding on a vital issue. Kingship is closely related to the essence of poetic drama, which seems never properly to have recovered from the execution of Charles I. Today the problem, to the would-be dramatic artist, is baffling. How many plays of Shakespeare are without their king or duke? Even the fairies are a royalistic community. Kingship is central to Shakespeare's life-pattern and whatever our political philosophy we must receive such significances correctly and unfold them on the stage with due ceremonial and a willing suspension of disrespect. They are grand plays. In them surges the tumultuous energy of the soul of a nation; they are rich in the pride, pomp and circumstance of earthly power. Here is Henry V meditating on kingly 'ceremony':

> No, thou proud dream
> That play'st so subtly with a king's repose;
> I am a king that find thee, and I know
> 'Tis not the balm, the sceptre, and the ball,
> The sword, the mace, the crown imperial,
> The intertissued robe of gold and pearl,
> The farced title running 'fore the king,
> The throne he sits on, nor the tide of pomp
> That beats upon the high shore of this world,

> No, not all these, thrice gorgeous ceremony,
> Not all these, laid in bed majestical,
> Can sleep so soundly as the wretched slave . . .
>
> (*Henry V*, IV. i. 277)

This intuition of kingly grandeur is vastly different from Marlowe's: Shakespeare would never allow the indignities suffered by Edward II. Shakespeare's kingly sequence celebrates the unfurling of a nation's history towards the destiny outlined in Cranmer's prophecy in *Henry VIII*.

There are kings of material and kings of spiritual authority; and I often think the noble sleep-speeches of Shakespeare's three royally-burdened Henrys reflect his own, spiritual, royalty and its pain. Often in the Histories there is sharp interplay and psychic inward drama between these conflicting authorities: in Richard II, in all the Henrys. The saintly Henry VI outlines the contrast:

> My crown is in my heart, not on my head;
> Not deck'd with diamonds and Indian stones,
> Nor to be seen. My crown is called content;
> A crown it is that seldom kings enjoy.
>
> (*3 Henry VI*, III. i. 62)

On the spiritual kingship in the heart of man turn the great tragedies. In them also worldly power twines with hierarchies of spiritual initiation. The tragic hero is usually a king, or at least a great soldier. In *Hamlet*, in *Othello*, in *Timon of Athens*, in *King Lear*, in *Antony and Cleopatra*, an overmastering spiritual force batters at, interlocks with, overthrows the more material ceremony with its own, ritualistic and mystic, rite. Earthly power is seen as incomplete and, its royalty renounced, forced into the dwarfing context of the infinite and the eternal.

What is then this mystery dwarfing life's positives with a seeming negation? It is close-entwined with the ritualistic concept of *sacrifice*. We have authority in Shakespeare's own words. His mind thinks variously in such terms. Here is a pagan and militaristic expression:

> Let them come;
> They come like sacrifices in their trim,
> And to the fire-ey'd maid of smoky war
> All hot and bleeding will we offer them:
> The mailed Mars shall on his altar sit
> Up to the ears in blood.
>
> (*1 Henry IV*, IV. i. 112)

So Hotspur. Orsino is similarly pagan:

> I'll sacrifice the lamb that I do love
> To spite a raven's heart within a dove . . .
> (Twelfth Night, v. i. 134)

But the pagan intuition can accompany a more strictly ethical fervour. To Brutus the assassination of Caesar is a spiritual and ritualistic act:

> Let us be sacrificers, but not butchers, Caius.
> We all stand up against the spirit of Caesar;
> And in the spirit of men there is no blood.
> (Julius Caesar, ii. i. 166)

For Caesar's death is demanded not by man's envy and greed, but by a divine necessity:

> Let's carve him as a dish fit for the gods,
> Not hew him as a carcass fit for hounds.
> (Julius Caesar, ii. i. 173)

This recalls a similar phrase from *Antony and Cleopatra*. Just before Cleopatra's death, the peasant, during a dialogue pregnant of suggestion deeply concerned with the nature of her end, sees that end as a sacrifice:

> . . . I know that a woman is a dish for the gods, if the
> devil dress her not. But truly these same whoreson devils
> do the gods great harm in their women; for in every ten
> that they make, the devils mar five.
> (Antony and Cleopatra, v. ii. 274)

The protagonist's tragedy is itself a divinely ordained sacrifice: we are close to a more Christian concept.

The end of *Othello* is sublimely formal; the bed an altar, with wedding sheets; the candle beside it, as an altar-flame; and the chaste stars and virgin moon without. The word 'sacrifice' occurs:

> O perjur'd woman! Thou dost stone my heart,
> And mak'st me call what I intend to do
> A murder, which I thought a sacrifice.
> (Othello, v. ii. 63)

Othello's words and acts in this scene have a religious and ritualistic colouring. In *King Lear*, Lear and Cordelia reunite in a temporary paradise where the mind is waked from distraught

agony to music. She is 'a soul in bliss', but he still bound on
'a wheel of fire' (*King Lear*, IV. vii. 46–7); like Desdemona meeting
Othello 'at compt' and hurling his soul from Heaven (*Othello*,
v. ii. 272–3). They are later to be 'God's spies', living only for
simple love, and seeing therefore the 'mystery of things':

> Upon such sacrifices, my Cordelia,
> The gods themselves throw incense.
>
> (*King Lear*, v. iii. 20)

For this is the renunciation of all pride of mind, 'all passion spent':
but spent, as a temporal price, for an eternally enduring wisdom.
Sacrifice is a recurrent conception. We find the word as early as
Romeo and Juliet. Looking on the dead lovers, who die that Verona
may learn to live in peace, Capulet knows they are 'poor sacrifices
to our enmity' (v. iii. 304); and in what is, perhaps, the finest
tragic passage in Shakespeare, Buckingham would have the
citizens

> Make of your prayers one sweet sacrifice
> And lift my soul to Heaven.
>
> (*Henry VIII*, II. i. 77)

Shakespeare sees human tragedy as essentially a sacrifice. A writer
of very similar cast of intuition, Hardy, in his greatest book,
follows the thought in the noble passage where Angel Clare tells
Tess that she lies on an ancient ruined altar to the sun, at Stone-
henge.

Here we draw close to one aspect of the tragic mystery: its
relation to morality. Is Hardy fundamentally an unchristian writer;
or *King Lear* a dangerously pagan play? Wherein lies the morality
of tragedy? Life flows and ebbs in rhythms. There are necessary
rhythms of creation and destruction throughout animal life and
natural evolution. Within man's personal existence these take
on the shapes of (i) self-assertion and (ii) self-sacrifice. The universe is patterned on such rhythmic alternations, and in the tragic
sacrifice we watch objectified the essential grandeur and positive
thrust of the sacrificial act. Quite apart from the morality of the
hero—or the justice of his end—this general principle claims our
assent. We are held by a metaphysical rather than a moral recognition. We share its direction; but the direction becomes next
inevitably conscious and moral; we begin to know sacrifice as a
positive rhythm, twin to creation. This positive quality is finely

pointed in the prologue and action of *Romeo and Juliet*. The lovers themselves do not act with specific moral intention, but we watch their love-sacrifice prove creative. The result in us is to induce an understanding and a temporary living of the sacrificial thrust. In all high tragedy we are initiated into one vast and difficult swing of the piston-pulse of the universal law conditioning and enclosing all existence. Morality is the living consciously the difficult principles implicit in the unconscious processes of nature: it interprets into self-conscious action the existent laws of the universe.

Marlowe's heroes die unromantically: Tamburlaine from a sudden disease, Faustus in terror, the Jew in his own booby-trap, Edward in a dungeon of filth. But Shakespeare's are best dying upstage, usually, though not in *Macbeth* for obvious reasons, central; raised as on an altar. Shakespeare suggests a ritualistic close continually: the four captains carrying off Hamlet, Bolingbroke following Richard's 'untimely bier', Brutus lying in state in Octavius's tent; the 'tragic loading' of the tomb in *Romeo and Juliet* and the bed in *Othello*; the stark picture of Cordelia in Lear's arms; Cleopatra in state, her girls dying before and after. There is a pictorial and positive quality about these which we do not find so consistently exploited in other tragic artists. Notice the formality, the noble reserve, of the final speeches; or the final sounds, as in *Hamlet*, *Timon of Athens*, and *Coriolanus*. We may even find a suggestion of height, raising the dignity of the tragic act:

> Come, Dolabella, see
> *High* order in this great solemnity.
> (*Antony and Cleopatra*, v. ii. 366)

Or, with more exact relevance to my argument:

> Give order that these bodies
> *High* on a stage be placed to the view . . .
> (*Hamlet*, v. ii. 391)

I recall another and greater tragedy: 'I, if I be lifted up, will draw all men unto Me'. Shakespeare's heroes are raised in turn as sacrificial offerings: they go robed and garlanded to their end. I am thinking of Cassius' wreath, Ophelia's garland of flowers, Lear's crown of 'idle weeds' (*King Lear*, iv. iv. 5), Desdemona's bridal sheets; above all, of Cleopatra robed and imperially diademed for a new Cydnus and the spousal ceremony of death: 'Husband, I come' (v. ii. 289).

In *Antony and Cleopatra* the tragic sacrifice becomes a pure positive, an adventure and an expansion. The great tragedies break the shell of the poet's tragic intuition, and henceforth a new and miraculous life-intuition takes our stage. The result is not unlike the romance dreams of *As You Like It* and *Twelfth Night*, which were, in their own kind, serious plays enough. And yet Shakespeare never subjected his mind wholly to romance; always parallel was the history succession, presenting burdened kings and martial conflict in place of dreams. The Tragedies blend the more personal and spiritual essence of the comic Romances with the communal and realistic essence of the Histories. Next, the broken shell and new-winged intuition of the Final Plays show youthful dreams mystically reopening beyond the sacrificial agony. These plays demand an understanding that recalls parallels in ancient myth of death and rebirth.[1]

We need not emphasize that sensitive and significant planning in production are here more than ever necessary. Here for the first time Shakespeare has left elaborate and careful directions for ceremonial. But we have no easy task. In *Pericles* think of Cerimon the recluse raising Thaisa from the dead in a scene insistently recalling the raising of Lazarus; of Pericles and Marina at Mitylene reunited after the night of fasting sorrow, to the onrush of a spheral music; of the vision of Diana that follows; of the descent of the priestess Thaisa from Diana's temple, meeting her lost lord, as the dead unite beyond the grave:

> No more, you gods! Your present kindness
> Makes my past miseries sport.
>
> (v. iii. 40)

In *The Winter's Tale* there is the oracle of Apollo and its decisive message; there is the contrast of wintry passion and tragedy with the rebirth of the year and summer-time festival; and the young Perdita, a seed sown in winter, but blossoming in spring. Is it chance that Perdita talks of Dis and Proserpina? Is there not a clear relation between this play and season myths of antiquity; and between those and our own concepts of death and resurrection? And here Hermione descends to the repentant and suffering Leontes, as Thaisa to Pericles, a marbled and memorial statue new-waked in the 'chapel' by Paulina's music. Temples, chapels,

[1] To these last plays I have now given a detailed study in *The Crown of Life*.

oracles, resurrections, and the rhythmic swing of seasons, of death
and rebirth: plays rich with mythical symbols and religious
formalism. In *Cymbeline* there is more. Here we have a close-
enwoven pattern and similar reunion themes. We have the pagan
glory of the sun-worship of the royal boys Guiderius and Arvira-
gus; the apocalyptic Vision of Jupiter with full and expanded
direction for ceremonial; the prophetic tablet, the Soothsayer and
his dream of 'Jove's bird' (IV. ii. 348); and the formal and ceremonious conclusion. The others were kingly plays: here the King,
as king, is still more important. The union of the realms of Britain
and Rome is deeply significant, and the new peace is ratified by
sacrifice:

> Laud we the gods;
> And let our crooked smokes climb to their nostrils
> From our bless'd altars.

> (v. v. 477)

There is more, very much more, in *Cymbeline*, than has as yet been
realized.

What of *The Tempest*? It is too packed with relevant material
to be considered now. Let me point instead to Mr. Colin Still's
book, *Shakespeare's Mystery Play*[1] and to my own analysis. It sums
and completes the more spiritual progress of Shakespeare's genius,
compacting dominant past symbols and expanding a highly condensed pattern of universal suggestion closely related to ideas
embedded in the myths, ritual and poetry of all ages. Here, too, we
have a sovereign figure, and temporal and spiritual lordship are
contrasted. As for *Henry VIII*, we have already referred to its importance: its tragic mysticism, its vision of Paradise, its sense of
a sacramental kingship in Henry himself, and, in Cranmer's
prophecy, of England's almost Messianic destiny. Here Shakespeare blends all his worlds; of tragedy; of romance, in Henry's
marriage with Anne Bullen, to which we are forced by the text to
give a purely romantic assent; of paradisal vision; and of England,
her king, her imperial future. The whole is impregnated heavily
with a ceremonial and ritualistic grandeur and a stately, orthodox,
Christianity.

That is not strange. Christianity has all the time been implicit
in Shakespeare's work and the two today form a necessary and

---

[1] Published in 1921; revised and reissued as *The Timeless Theme*, 1936.

most fertile commentary on each other. Each of Shakespeare's tragic heroes is a miniature Christ. That is why I have urged the importance of Romeo's tragic ascent, his little Calvary. Richard II makes the comparison, and the analogy is pointed twice in *Timon of Athens*. Commentators from time to time make such a cross-reference in discussing *King Lear*, suggested partly perhaps by his crown of country weeds. The New Testament is a tragic art-form of unique force and unique reality. And if its 'My God, my God, why hast thou forsaken me?' is spoken from the *King Lear* or Hardy sense of bleak cosmic desolation, the sublime τετέλεσται nevertheless circumferences the whole nature of the tragic sacrifice: the consummation, the positive thrust, the creativeness. Yet also the references to Paradise from the Cross and the last 'Into thy hands . . .', and especially the resurrection, all these correspond to the resurrections and reunions of the Final Plays. Shakespeare was influenced by Christianity, no doubt. Who in the modern world was not? But primarily I stress, whatever our private views on the New Testament or Shakespeare, that both are recording the same facts, whatever the nature of those facts and however strange and indecipherable they appear to a less sensitive generation.

Today orthodox Christianity and Shakespeare confront each other with a contrast and similarity that challenge our attention. What is the relation of the Shakespearian play to the Christian Mass? The Mass or Communion Service is at once a consummation and a transcending of pagan ritual. The organic growth was continuous. Paganism knew sacrifice to be essentially a creative and life-giving force; hence their various ceremonies, sometimes cruel and sadistic; often superstitious, bearing an unprofitable and usually dangerous relation to actual affairs; sometimes closely approaching Christianity.

The king was important in pagan ritual; his life, the life of the community; his death, their death; his renewal, their redemption and resurrection. In paganism too we have the dying and resurrected god. In Christianity we find these themes blended, with a king not of temporal but of spiritual power and authority and one whose sacrifice is a consciously willed act wherein ritual and ethic become one. In the New Testament the Christ's kingship is contrasted with temporal royalty, with Herod and Caesar; and yet again is itself given the tragic insignia of purple, the proclamation written over the cross and the crown of thorns. These are the two kingships whose interpenetration recurs continually in Shakespeare. In the Christian Mass we act over again Christ's sacrifice, remembering it as a willed and purposeful self-surrender to destruction and recognizing the creative power of such surrender. We are to feed on the bread and wine of that once-given sacrificial act; and afterwards, the praise, the opening hope, the remembered resurrection of the Christ and renewal of ourselves. In the world of Shakespearian tragedy this unique act of the Christ sacrifice can, if we like, be felt as central. Shakespeare gives us a human and infinitely varying interpretation of the sacrificial ceremony, but the relation is important. Moreover, Shakespeare's final plays celebrate the victory and the glory, the resurrection and the renewal, that in the Christian story and in its reflection in Christian ritual succeed the sacrifice.[1]

The meaning of these last plays is not properly recognized as yet. While we stumble on the threshold of Shakespearian tragedy we can scarcely approach those inner shrines; and until we do, we shall not further see the significance of *Henry VIII* for England today. Indeed, how can we? we who find Shakespeare's kings a stumbling-block and the other spiritual kingship of the Christ an enigmatic dream, and are therefore unable to follow the significance of their union.

But we must never, in emphasizing Shakespeare's more universal significances, forget the intense and subtle human psychology and sympathy on which their value depends. The two co-exist in a dynamic and vital reciprocity. Conventional acceptance and recognition of the purposeful and ritualistic quality of art opens the universal; but not necessarily by denying the particular. Only in so far as we accept the necessary dramatic compression and telescoping of incident and psychology of the Shakespearian art-form can we focus the infinite minutiae of human sympathy, such as we have in this book explored in the person of Orsino, the essentially poetic psychology, that functions within and in terms of the dramatic art-form itself. The Shakespearian convention blends and balances the personal and the universal, and this balance is closely related to his use of kings.

[1] This paragraph appears to risk overstatement unless balanced by the remembrance that Shakespeare has as much in common with Aeschylus and Sophocles as he has with Dante. [1949]

A worldly king is expressly this: the communal brought to a focal point in the personal, the state known as personality. The other king, the spiritual king, presents in his person not the communal only, but the universal: hence, the Christ. The theological problem of the two natures, divine and earthly, each equally inhering to the full in the Christ reflects the nature of the balance, the organic cohesion, of the two qualities, the highly universal and symbolic and the realistically human, of the Shakespearian play. Through acceptance of the convention the apparent antinomy is resolved: more, its resolution is known to be the inmost purpose of the drama. In other words, the drama exists to demonstrate the necessity of its own convention, which is its ritualistic nature; for ritual and artistic convention are one, or almost one. Ritual is a deliberately willed acceptance in terms of which the barriers between the universal and the personal, God and man, are broken. In a Shakespearian production the conscious element of artistry must be apparent; we must know the play as a play and make a willed act of conventional acceptance, without which deliberate and consciously desired submission we cannot richly receive it. If conventional acceptances were not demanded by the play itself, we should have to invent others: they are the entrances to initiation. A certain active and partaking generosity is necessary in order to receive generously and the production must force its audience to share, consciously and willingly, in its own artistic creation. Our performances of Shakespeare will never be truly powerful till they are also consciously and sympathetically artistic; till they are given with reverence and dignity; with understanding and intellectual humility.

If this were accomplished Shakespeare's work might do many strange things for us. It might awake in us an understanding of great art at once communal and intelligent; might help to harmonize groups of our people of various classes and casts of mind in one common fusion of spiritual understanding, which means an understanding of the fundamental laws of life; be a bridge between the various complications of human existence and the central truths of Christianity; give us again, as a nation, a sense of national and Christian purpose—I am thinking especially of *Henry VIII*—revitalizing in us that which is behind Shakespeare's sublimation of kingship and faith in warrior-virtue, and helping us therefore either to cut out what new expressions may be necessary for the positive powers in man, or refurbish the old; and, finally, make possible a new contemporary drama of similar quality to Shakespeare's, which cannot exist till we understand and know how to use that which we already possess.

I plead for a sensitive production of Shakespeare; a performance as deeply understanding as that which we would give to an oratorio of Bach; a production at times matching the reserve and dignity of military ceremonial. I have stressed particularly the ritualistic element in Shakespeare's conclusions; but this final objectivity crowns the tumultuous subjective violence thrown up by the middle action, whose tempests and alarums should be as a crucible of sound to weld stage and auditorium in one living architecture. Then shall we listen afresh to the blood-pulse of human existence and its laws. And, as when we listen with a stethoscope we are appalled by the Atlantic rushing and seething and thundering in a human body, so Shakespeare awakes us not to realism, but to reality; not to the face and limbs and sculptured body only, but to the greater solidity, the rhythmic breathings of the spirit, the thunderous music, the domed and quivering palace.

PART II

[1949 and 1963]

CHAPTER VI

The Body Histrionic [1949]¹

An introduction to the staging of *Timon of Athens*

The production of Shakespearian plays eventually raises the important problem: what precisely is, or should be, the proper place and use of the unclothed body in serious dramatic performances? Certain recent liftings of communal taboo necessarily react on stage practice. Tight clothes were recently used, and sometimes are still, to imitate nakedness; and though one meets instances of a bolder technique, these are usually far from satisfying. Here the ballet is in advance of the drama, while the films have probably done better than either; but the somewhat unnaturally stylized idiom of the ballet lends itself more easily to exotic costume design than to any profoundly significant use of physical detail, while examples in film production have normally been limited by triviality of theme. Neither art has, it would seem, understood and developed the finer potential significances, as have, for example, the arts of sculpture and photography. I here offer tentative suggestions from a new angle. My remarks are limited to consideration of the male form, since the female enjoys a fairly generally accepted definition in both moral reserve and exploitation of significant appeal, while its more directly sexual significances are, in our present era, clearly different in direction from those which we are to analyse.

But stage technique remains indecisive and rudimentary. It is not enough for Edgar in *King Lear* to appear with only a waist-cloth and a level make-up: the peculiar part he plays will need a

<hr>

¹ Composed in 1940 and published in the 1949 Penguin edition of *Principles of Shakespearian Production*. I have omitted some passages.

careful body-design and the waist-cloth must be significantly arranged. Nor can Ariel rely on a figure, however beautiful, with some characterizing accoutrements for waist, shoulders, and head, and nothing more but a straight application of body-wash or powder. Colours should be thought out and applied, using a delicate modulation suiting physical contours, to realize the Ariel quality on and through the actor's body itself. We should not be aware of the actor as undressed; that is, of a negation, and one which plunges us away from art into the wrong kind of reality. The first necessity is a careful make-up. To what extent the body should be shaded, moulded and accentuated must be left to individual experiment according to the conditions obtaining; the shading is easily overdone. For a performance of Caliban I have myself used an arrangement of heavy grey furs for waist, shoulders and back arranged over a complete covering of green grease-paint and purple variations, which in its blend of the slimy-reptilian and the savagely human is surely an improvement on the traditional tights, hump and imitation skin, while aiming at an elemental dignity and rendering possible a significant body-action for which the usual costuming leaves no scope. Nakedness alone, however skilfully coloured, may not suit a conception that seems at first to demand it and I doubt if Caliban would be properly characterized without some heavy addition for the shoulders (Picture 15). When playing the Messenger in *Antony and Cleopatra* I have found arm-bands, Egyptian collar and head-dress help to supplement a loin-cloth and sash in building a stage personality (Picture 16).[1] Whatever the amount worn, the effect must have conviction: tights can never give this, missing the sheen of life. Nor will a body-wash that does not react to lighting prove adequate. Grease-paint, or some similar and more tractable preparation, will be necessary. We must through make-up as well as clothes and minor accoutrements give the impression rather of something carefully created than of something removed. The body should not merely be exposed; it must be used.

The words and thoughts of my present analysis probably appear more bold than would the corresponding creations on the

[1] The photograph was taken at some try-out scenes a few months before our 1937 *Antony and Cleopatra* (p. 13). This and *Henry VIII* (p. 23) were probably my most finished Toronto productions, since my own acting parts were brief. Antony was played by Edward Roberts, and in *Henry VIII* the King by E. A. Dale and Wolsey by A. J. Rostance.

stage where one should not be directly aware of nakedness in isolation owing to make-up, setting, lighting and action. Any such figure must be felt to grow out of his setting. The normal need for atmospheric unity is here even more urgent. The middle scenes in *King Lear* must provide a wind-swept support to Edgar's uncouth yet vivid appearance. If Prospero's cell is designed with any sort of civilized, even though rustic, artistry, a naked Ariel will appear at once slightly indecent and too compellingly human for so elemental a conception as he represents. The impact of *Antony and Cleopatra* will depend throughout on atmospheric unity. Moreover, any striking bodily appearance, even of necessarily statuesque figures such as Nubian slaves, must be carried off by very assured acting. An amateurish indecision will be far more noticeable than in costume and risk an annihilating judgement; so will any too purely 'naturalistic' a manner, any failure to use the limbs boldly with precision and effect; for naturalism, when at grips with nature itself, will paradoxically be found unnatural. The intellectual content of the performance must keep continually ahead, as it were, of the sensuous impact, and to do this the actor must sink his consciousness properly within his body, act through it, and transmit a sense of artistic poise and vitality. This lifts the audience's mind to the creative dimension, and it is probably because ballet is always on the move that undress has been there more freely developed. In acting, where repose is continually also necessary, nothing but a sincere creative consciousness radiating through the total physique will enable every held gesture and posture to be, as they must be, vitally significant. The physical must be continually shot through with spiritual meaning, as well with Caliban as with Timon and Edgar. Finally, lighting may be allowed to contribute more striking effects, akin to those used in modern photography, than is normally proper, according to my own principles, in Shakespearian production. Since the specifically human is visually broader there is the less fear of its dissolution under the electrician's art. Such lighting effects must however be carefully watched lest they blur rather than assist the specifically physical creation.

All this might seem of secondary importance. But, as I have already (p. 60) written:

The visual and spatial effects of production should primarily subserve the play's emotional quality and poetic colour. They will solidify the spiritual, make real that dimension of profound and solid significance that great poetry possesses. Thus the visual side of production will be concerned with the play's more significant, universal, and poetic qualities.

Our main spatial and visual effect must always remain the actor himself, and where figures of elemental and universal meaning are to be portrayed a direct use of his body exploits the farthest visual resources of the actor's art. *Timon of Athens*, in this as in other ways, is found to express the central essence of tragic drama.[1]

I have often discussed the peculiar symbolic exposures of Shakespeare's greater plays. *Hamlet* shows, as it were, a stripping away of accepted values, the hero's very nerves laid bare before the nakedly spectral appearance of his father's spirit and the tearing down of all deceptive covering from society around. In *Julius Caesar* and *Macbeth* exposure is rather metaphysical than psychological. In the one state-order is rudely shattered to disclose the blood and fire of its own pulsing heart as ghostly strife burns and battles above Rome; in the other, the inward mechanisms of time and history are nakedly bared in the compressed and vitally significant drama of the three Apparitions[2] and the procession of future kings. In *King Lear* there is a revelation through madness and a break from conventional appearance into universal and elemental, what Nietzsche called Dionysian, significance, with a return through nature and wild sources of energy to fantastic exhibition of subterranean forces in the dialogue-extravaganza of Lear, the Fool and Tom. All these visions concern some sudden stripping away of surface deceptions, leading eventually to expression through physical nakedness, both in Lear's attempt to tear off his clothes and in the dramatic conception of Edgar as 'poor Tom', whose 'presented nakedness' (II. iii. 11), like his elaborated madness, far outreaches in formal suggestion the plot-logic that is its superficial motivation.

Next, this whole sequence curving up to *King Lear* is given an intensely human consummation and condensation in *Timon of Athens*. The play is itself a bare, almost indecently direct, statement of the experience present behind the more realistically

---

[1] *Timon of Athens* has been the most influential of all Shakespeare's plays in our dramatic tradition. See my article '*Timon of Athens* and its Dramatic Descendants', *A Review of English Literature*, II. 4; Oct., 1961.

[2] They symbolize (i) iron destruction; (ii) life born out of conflict and (iii) creation victorious. See my note on p. 138.

motivated and subtly modulated surfaces of earlier works. Their essence is presented in naked simplicity. Moreover, at a moment of terrific dramatic pressure the swift reverse movement of the titanic action, concerned as in former tragedies with a shattering of conventional appearance, pivots on Timon's suddenly throwing from him the trappings of civilization. The act should come as a sudden stab, an electrifying shock. Those visionary disclosures that have hitherto appeared as a complex interaction of many persons with heightening of attendant symbolism, all swirling round and through the tragic hero but not directly housed in him as a person, become now incarnate in the protagonist. In this sense, as in others, Timon is expressive of pure 'personality', including all those overtones of the infinite that the term suggests, as distinct from the earlier 'persons', more than one of whom in complex dance, together with heavy symbolic machinery, were needed to generate a super-personal presence. Timon himself is now just such a 'presence' and his play accordingly dispenses with auxiliary symbolisms, no thunder or tempest of the usual Shakespearian sort accompanying the tragic redirection. He is himself utterly symbolic; in him the Apollonian and Dionysian principles coincide. He is at once single, whole and universal, and his appearance during the later scenes, themselves set by the seashore, blends naturally into the many poetic impressions of the elemental, the cosmic, and the eternal. The artistic kinship of physical nakedness to spiritual profundity will always be close. Nor must we be deceived by Shakespeare's complete lack of Marlovian fascination—as in *Hero and Leander* and *Edward II*— with his theme. He rather uses it, and stands alone among the world's dramatists in his peculiarly striking, profound and even metaphysical, impregnation. Moreover, he deliberately counters the visual attraction in both *King Lear* and *Timon of Athens* by associations of suffering and degradation. There is no verbal sensuous delight whatsoever: but there should be a most impressive stage impact. We here face merely one very important aspect of the usual process whereby in tragedy material disaster is countered by an inward and spiritual royalty. Connotations both bestial and prophetic are in the two-way significances: Caliban himself should have aesthetic dignity. In *King Lear* a new rush of imaginative power takes the stage after the preliminary indecisions, and in *Timon of Athens* a new and striking direction is outlined by the protagonist's solitary, at once human and in-human, grandeur during the final acts.

Stage representation must be both strong and subtle. The central act of Timon's disrobing can easily be rendered nugatory. I have seen Timon, recently in rich robes, enter suddenly on a fore-stage under full lights with a single rough cloak, and throw it violently from him, to reveal a rough loin-cloth. The action was crude, non-significant and unconvincing. How did he come to be wearing that rough loin-cloth? No. Let him be wearing under a loose cloak a rich kilt in similar style; and let him appear for this difficult action up-stage central, lit from one side, unwrapping and throwing his cloak from him with pictorial movements. The action is held for a moment in mid-flight, a cameo.[1] Then let him appear later in the rough loin-cloth of his prophetic savagery. It is, you see, an important, semi-ritualistic, act, an unveiling of the universal; yet one to be carefully realized in terms of possible behaviour and set within a graduated sequence. During the later action we must have a setting of wild and rugged power, Timon being first revealed as a statuesque silhouette among gaunt rocks and the dawn gradually gilding, throwing up, creating, his body, preparatory to his first address to the sun. Thereafter various strong lighting and shadow effects can be used, both on his body and on the rocks. Meanwhile the intermittent sound of surf will hint that ocean of being towards which the action moves.

Though in Shakespeare actual examples of such elemental figures, while more frequent than in other great dramatists, are strictly limited—we might add Oberon, and possibly Puck, to our list—they nevertheless present a challenge to our stage conventions. We are still far from the necessary understanding. Our freedom today from so-called Victorian taboos is perhaps not wholly a cause for satisfaction, since it may derive not so much from insight as from a dangerous insensibility where a deep concern would be more creditable. Blake, Nietzsche, Whitman, and Lawrence all attacked our want of a significant body-conscious-ness, and we need not search far for examples of body-desecration. Surely few people sensitive to the human form can sit through some of our recent cinematograph cartoons with open eyes; those, I mean, where limbs are transposed or blasphemously pulled into absurd and nauseating proportions. A similar indict-

[1] The action is more fully described below, pp. 177–8; and see Picture 19.

ment can, and indeed must, be levelled against much that gains respect among the more esoteric advances in modern painting and sculpture, where artistic strength may yet be a reflection of a disease in the community. Such things offend against the closely-related natural and spiritual dignities of man. But all this we accept; and in contradistinction we are seriously ignorant where the more profound values are in question.

Dress is symptomatic of the communal consciousness, and the limitation of human appearance to heads emerging from clothes reflects the excessively mentalized concentration of our era. The head expresses human 'character' in the objective and individualizing sense. The body beneath is less individualized and may suggest equally the sub-mental and the super-mental states, while also emphasizing their close interdependence and continuity. As Nicolas Berdyaev in *Solitude and Society* (London 1938; v. i. 169) observes, the truly Christian culture will be centred rather in the heart than in the head. We are pointed to categories more universal, less characterizing, less egocentric and egoconscious; to the greater potential self as phrased by both Christ and St. Paul in strong physical terms. The Crucifixion image offers an extreme example of this process, showing the human form on the edge, as it were, of some further, indefinable universalization. In doctrine and symbolism alike Christianity is over and over again felt to be the religion *par excellence* of the body: and so, with the greater boldness and precision, of the spirit too. In Christianity the body is an almost mystical entity, the 'temple', as St. Paul calls it, of the spirit. The title of my chapter was suggested by that of Mr. Frederick Carter's monograph *D. H. Lawrence and The Body Mystical* (1932). The finest art may often derive from a recognition of physical significance and, in the heart-area of the male form especially, of spiritual strength. I am urging something new; something that has never hitherto been attempted. But there is no clear reason why the theatre should henceforth lag behind the sister arts of sculpture (of the traditional, Greek, kind, obeying the laws of nature), and photography. In it bodily appearance and action can compass a whole gamut of new meanings from the savagery of Caliban and O'Neill's hero in *The Emperor Jones* to Ariel and Shelley's Prometheus; while Timon includes them all.

Such suggestions hint at what may prove a task of primary importance in the future history of the drama, and one which may well react sharply on dramatic composition; though not to be lightly undertaken, to be carefully watched and given closest technical attention. Yet, again, any instinctive diffidence must also be closely examined. The average summer beach today dispels suspicion of fundamental aesthetic disapproval or moral hostility. Nor does the active movement of limbs or muscles on the stage itself constitute an added objection, since in swimming, boxing, and wrestling this is evident enough. Wherein, then, lies the difference? Precisely in what I have called 'significance'; and, moreover, significance of a peculiarly subtle and powerful kind, beyond any such simple beauty of athletic energy as that of a diver's flight or a boxer's poise. Our reserve may therefore be not quite what we think it. Where undress is required a stage costume draped diagonally over one side of the body on occasions where such is not strictly appropriate, since on the stage a very little will suffice to kill the body line and give a fully dressed impression, may often appear to be intended, most illogically, to help render the other half respectable; with a consequent and I think semi-purposeful destruction of the finer significance. For, if any diffidence concerned primarily with the stage and the additional effectiveness of artificial lighting exists, as in my experience it does, that diffidence will be found to derive less from any moral or aesthetic scruple than from a semi-conscious fear of what might prove a source of electrifying dramatic power, exerting less a sensual attraction than a spiritual domination. We are in danger of deploring the impotence of poetic, that is of spiritual, drama while fearing one medium through which the poetic essence might powerfully revitalize our stage. The visible breathing of a human body alone, closely entwined as it is with both the mystery and the mastery of poetic speech and the rhythmic essences of life itself, might in certain dramatic contexts hold compelling force.

The possibility of giving adequate stage representation to Aeschylus' or Shelley's *Prometheus*, Milton's *Samson Agonistes*, the early books of *Paradise Lost*, or Byron's *Cain*, depends on such recognitions. Our neglect of *Timon of Athens* is symptomatic. It is normally either not produced or so costumed as to constrict its power.[1] Wherever human drama touches the vast and elemental

---

[1] I should however record that in Mr. Bridges Adams' Stratford production some years ago, with Mr. Wilfrid Walter as Timon, the costuming had the boldness, though scarcely the deeper significances, demanded.

it will tend towards some such projection as you have in *Timon*. We might remember the vivid image of Laon's naked mountain exposure in brazen bonds against the burning sun in Shelley's poetic narrative *Laon and Cythna* (or *The Revolt of Islam*). Such dynamic impressions pierce through the physical to the spiritual that is nevertheless indissolubly one with it, dramatizing through visible yet picturesque agony and destruction the living mystery of this interdependence. We have tragedy concentrated as light through a lens to the fiery centres of physical consciousness. Flecker's *Hassan* is powerfully constructed to drive home a similar statement through actual stage performance. The latter scenes of *Timon of Athens* aim to dramatize a slow, spiritual, crucifixion, the technique resembling the skilful use of a physical to express a psychological disclosure in O'Neill's *Emperor Jones*; and, more distantly, the central incident of Masefield's *Everlasting Mercy*. By such works as *Timon of Athens*, *Prometheus Unbound*, *Laon and Cythna*, *Hassan*, *The Emperor Jones*, we are pointed to that archetypal imagination, at once act and image, which rises over them as an Everest above foothills: the Crucifixion of the Christ. This, the central drama of our Western culture, may be felt as the fountain-source of all tragic art and creative action in the Christian era. It dramatizes the final interpenetration of the human form by Significance; shows that Body 'given' for mankind in utter subjugation to an ultimate, if indefinable, purpose; and has therefore a faint reflection in even the humblest examples of the actor's art.

CHAPTER VII

Timon of Athens and Shylock

───────────────────────────

I

TIMON OF ATHENS

Leeds University Union Theatre Group, December 1948; repeated for the National Union of Students Arts Festival at Leeds, January 1949 and for the British Drama League, The Royal Hall, Harrogate, June 1949. My first production was given in Toronto, February and March 1940. Excerpts from the later scenes were presented in *This Sceptred Isle* at the Westminster Theatre, London, July 1941 (p. 14). Press notices and other particulars are included in my 'Dramatic Papers' (p. 14 above). My account here follows the Leeds presentation, in which I would record the help given me by Mr. Peter Tillott and Mr Trevor Lennam as production assistants.[1]

Problems are raised by *Timon of Athens* unlike those to be faced in any other Shakespearian tragedy. Its effects are studied and planned, and its structure is in simple blocks: it is, within Shakespeare's scale of values, a kind of morality play. Its later scenes forecast the Romantic period. It has generally been supposed that the play as we have it is an uncompleted or unrevised version. Perhaps it is. It seems that Shakespeare was pushing beyond his own time, interpreting his tragic vision as the Romantics were to interpret theirs, and he may have found the experiment disquieting. *Timon of Athens* is a peculiarly self-conscious work.

---

[1] Accounts of my various *Timon* presentations and their reception are given below, Appendix C.

Timon of Athens *and Shylock*

Our setting and costuming were vaguely those of ancient Greece. We had two intervals. For our first two acts we used front-scenes before a down-stage curtain; a full-stage area backed by two strong, white, pillars decorated at the tops, between which steps rose C to a platform, forming an inset alcove, with a balcony, a rich cloth sometimes thrown over it, against the cyclorama; and sometimes a medium-stage area backed by an up-stage curtain which when drawn obscured the pillars and steps. At Toronto the costumes were Byzantine, the pillars richly coloured, and a dome visible against the cyclorama.[1]

ACT I

We open with a front-scene. The Painter L is holding a picture; the Poet crosses to him and they talk; grandees enter and go out C between the curtains, drawn aside for them by servants. The Merchant and Jeweller are now talking R. More grandees, senators, enter and go out as before. The Poet's long speech on Fortune, which serves as a prologue, gains from being spoken in a front-scene.

Trumpets sound and the curtains disclose a glittering assembly. Timon enters on the platform up C, coming from L, and begins to descend the steps, his descent interrupted as he greets suitors on either side. Coming down, he moves about the stage, greeting his friends and looking at the picture. At Apemantus' entry down R people are grouped behind Timon who becomes the apex of a wedge looking down R as he addresses Apemantus whose words are greeted by the rest with amusement, scorn or anger. Afterwards Timon meets Alcibiades and takes him up the steps C and then off up L. The crowd dissolves and Apemantus comes downstage so that the lower curtain can close behind him for a front-scene.

For the following brief conversation we replaced the 'lords' of the text by the two ladies to appear later as Phrynia and Timandra. The building up of the two female parts has obvious advantages.

The curtains draw to disclose the Banquet. The pillars are wreathed with leaves. One long table,[2] its cloth elaborately

[1] The costumes were made by Patricia Card Costumes and the pillars, which had been used for his *Macbeth* the previous week (p. 134, note), were generously loaned and painted by Mr. Brownlow Card. See Pictures 11, 17, 18.
[2] As our picture shows, at Toronto we used small tables.

festooned, crosses the stage, and there is a small one down R for Apemantus. Timon will sit C, Alcibiades at the table's end and Flavius dominates with a staff of office on the steps behind. Timon rises for his speech. Before and during this speech the guests must express amusement, approval and sentimentality in ways appropriate to a dinner speech. Soft approving murmurs can be richly effective. The lords should show no obvious flattery; to perform them so is as foolish as to make Cressida an obvious minx in the early part of *Troilus and Cressida*. Timon's friends are not to be regarded as flatterers; rather we watch a friendly meeting of fine people in mutual trust. They drink freely.

For the Masque we used a dance done by girls with tambourines, working up excitement, the guests grouped around the table, some high on the platform and steps, and some down-stage at the sides, the whole company a glittering spectacle as the Bacchanalian music and dance work to a crescendo. This dance, excellently arranged for us by Mrs. Olive Hewetson to music from Moszkowski's 'Spanish Dance', gave lift and impetus to the occasion. People are near intoxication from wine, music and mutual affection. They touch each other freely. Cheeks are flushed and eyes sparkle. From such a soil Timon's exaggerated presentations flower naturally. Even so, the guests receive their gifts with an honourable diffidence. The darker notes sounded by Flavius' aside can be punctuated by laughter from a group talking to Timon who are unaware of his words. Timon's brief dialogue with Apemantus makes an ominous conclusion.

Act II

The Senator's interview with Caphis is done as a front-scene, and we next turn to Timon's hall, the table removed and a chair down R. Flavius enters and after him retainers with demands for money. Timon enters C on the platform from R with Alcibiades and is confronted by the demands. He comes down. We cut the dialogue with the Fool and went straight on to Timon's interview with Flavius, the others temporarily dismissed.

Timon has the full stage for his anxious movements; he strides up, stands silent, back to audience, and turns again; being gradually made to realize the truth. He decides to send out requests for assistance and moves down-stage with Flavius, the curtains closing behind. In the front-scene he hears of the Senators' refusal; servants are dispatched to his friends.

We now disclose a medium-stage scene for the interview with Lucullus, a curtain obscuring the steps and pillars. We return to a front-scene for Lucius and the Strangers; then back to medium-stage for Sempronius. Acting details for these Jonsonian miniatures need not delay us, their satirical nature being of a kind likely today to be readily projected. The responses of the three friends must be as admirably differentiated in performance as they are in the text. The effect needed is the disclosure of a natural, if ugly, selfishness from within the externals of conviviality and affection previously shown. We should recognize a dramatic compression of what would probably be our own change of attitude if we heard that one of our friends or a distant relative had suddenly fallen from affluence to penury; or it might be a question of wanting help in the literary world. Our refusals might be more gradual and camouflaged, but a suppliant is always on a lower plane; the old easy contact would be gone; and few of us would go out of our way to restore it. In these scenes the choric commentary of the Strangers and Timon's servants must be underlined as pointers enforcing our sympathy for Timon. Everything possible is done to direct our response.

We return to our full stage, lights darkened. Servants cluster with their masters' bills. Flaminius enters, they push to him like a pack of hounds, he eludes them. Next comes Flavius 'in a cloak, muffled'; they corner him; he replies, and tries to get away; some of them cut off his escape; he half fights his way out. The creditor-servants' movements should be crisp, official, jerky, having an almost military, team-like, or pack-like, precision.

Timon enters C on the platform from up L and comes down the steps, not as at first attending to suitors, nor as afterwards brushing interruption away, but being attacked and hampered; impeded as before, but very differently. Such cross-references made of similarity in position and difference of action are often helpful. The shouts of the servants, crying their amounts, rise to a crescendo. Their insistence draws, pulls, Timon down among them, to their level; he is tall and splendid, they are bent round him like yapping curs. Timon's 'tear me' suggests a great stag or bull, baited by hounds. He breaks from them and goes off L. Immediately the front curtain draws and he enters L, breathless,

for a brief front-scene, Flavius following. His broken phrases
—'I'll have it so'—suggest something terrible to follow. At his
concluding rhymed couplet

> I charge thee, invite them all; let in the tide
> Of knaves once more—my cook and I'll provide

he strides swiftly off, crossing the proscenium from L to R. This
move had a precise effect. Timon has hitherto always entered
from the platform up C, coming in, except after his hunting with
Alcibiades, from the left. This vivid down-stage move from L to
R indicates his entry into a new world, leaving his ivory-castle
consciousness for recognition of the world of human viciousness;
it cuts across the stage like an attack.

The Senate scene that follows is on medium-stage, curtains
obscuring the steps. Our second Banquet scene is set like the
first, but without Apemantus' chair and table. The nature of
Timon's speech is only gradually revealed. The guests expect
conviviality; at 'lest your deities be despised' one or two attempt
a laugh, thinking a joke may be intended, and break off, nervously; comedy is in place. They grow embarrassed: 'What does
his lordship mean?' Timon's purpose is at last revealed. The
speech gathers to its crest. The splashing of water is not enough.
Timon hurls a heavy dish-cover, and another. There is a general
tumult, the guests rise; the table tilts and Timon deliberately
hurls it over, the whole long table, plate and crockery crashing. In
real life the breaking of crockery always arouses a peculiar shock,
depending in part on the reversal of so fundamental a life-joy as
food and its careful preparations, so that we experience a poignant
pathos; even tears may be awakened. In our play this normal
experience is raised to a fearful power as the long table, like a
breaking wave, crashes over. The effect is more nerve-racking
than thunder or an explosion.

This is the kind of climax that must at all costs not be under-
played. The professional theatre here will use all its dangerous
resources to get through the awkward moment smoothly with
the minimum amount of trouble, making an easy transition of
what should be a cataclysmic terror. That, to transpose Hamlet's
phrase, is 'villainous'.

The table overturned, Timon leaps on to the steps, seizes
Flavius' staff, and raising it appears for an instant a gigantic,

14. *King Lear*, Toronto 1935 (p. 23): Kent, Lyndon Smith; Edgar (pp. 46, 163–6), Robin Godfrey

15. *The Tempest*, Toronto 1938 (pp. 13, 274): Caliban (for the colouring, p. 164)

16. *Antony and Cleopatra*, experimental scenes preliminary to the production, Toronto 1937 (p. 13): the Messenger (p. 164 and note)

17. *Timon of Athens*, Toronto 1940 (pp. 13, 172–3; 173 notes). Timon and his guests in the first Feast scene

18. *Timon of Athens*, Toronto 1940: Creditor's servants, led by Caphis, attacking Timon: Caphis, John Hayes

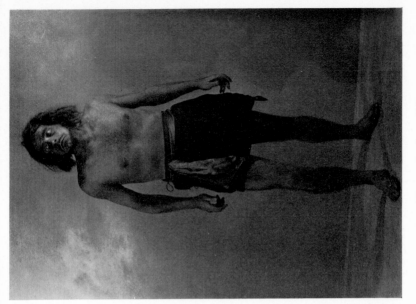

20. Timon in the wilds
(for the artistic effect, p. 164–8)

19. *Timon of Athens*, Toronto 1940. Timon
disrobing (for the action, pp. 168, 177–8)

21. *Timon of Athens*, Leeds 1948 (pp. 15, 172-4). The first Feast scene: Apemantus, Michael Bampton; Flavius, Richard Gendall; Alcibiades (without a beard), end of table, Trevor Lennam

22. *Timon of Athens*, Leeds 1948: Timon and the Bandits, 'The Moon's an arrant thief' (p. 183): Bandits, Stuart Shaw and John Fricker

towering, figure of judgement well lit, though lights elsewhere have lowered; then he descends, moving about the darkened stage as he speaks the lines

> Live loath'd and long,
> Most smiling, smooth, detested parasites . . .

and closing at 'a welcome guest'; we reserve the final couplet for a later use. As he speaks Timon wields the staff, making as though to beat his victims, driving them off down-stage this side and that, sweeping round in a curve, the tall staff causing him to loom darkly gigantic, while the guests cower, some on hands and knees, ludicrous, hiding behind objects. The effect should resemble that we imagine of Christ when He belabours the temple money-changers.

Timon goes out L, and the guests have a few brief speeches. Timon returns from up L, up-stage C on the platform, the lights picking him out, to speak the lines 'Let me look back upon thee . . .' He is visually alone, a cameo, the rest of the stage quite dark. The strain on the actor of Timon from these violent actions and thundering speeches has been severe, and lines must be cut. We cut from 'matrons . . . parents' eyes', 'Maid . . . brains', 'Instruction . . . laws', 'Thou cold . . . merely poison', and instead of the concluding 'Amen' used the couplet (III. VI. 115) omitted earlier:

> Burn, house! Sink, Athens! Henceforth hated be
> Of Timon, man and all humanity!

Timon goes out on the platform R. He has broken with Athens.

Timon's embracing of 'nakedness' (IV. I. 33) during this speech is important, but his clothes are not such as can be effectively unwound before the audience. After belabouring the guests, he has only a few moments off-stage: in those his upper robe is removed and his long under-dress lifted over his head. He wears underneath a kilt *of similar rich style* and now wraps his main robe loosely round him. When he returns on the platform he can un-robe easily; but the action is to be done with deliberation and artistry. Timon is facing L, catching a vivid light from L. He is clasping the robe round him with both hands in front. He un-wraps the robe with his left hand holding its corner out, and letting his right unwind it behind him, so that his body from the waist is shown *against* the robe, stretched between the two hands across his back. Then, with a sweeping movement, he hurls it away in front of him L with his *right* hand, after having loosened the grip with his left, so that it curls round him as it falls away. For 'take thou that too' he throws a chaplet worn on his head (at Toronto it was a metal circlet), with both hands. The sudden appearance of the naked body, picked out by the wing-light, makes a vivid cameo.

From Timon's address to the guests till this last exit the strain in speech and physical action, including the swift costume-change, has been unrelieved. The cutting of his long speech is technically forced; and anyway, spoken as it is in the up-stage inset, it is better abbreviated.

We go straight on to the parting of Timon's servants, using the full stage, among the debris. To conclude our second main movement at a climax would be un-Shakespearian and this scene makes the correct end. It should be spoken with a measured, elegiac, solemnity. During this scene Timon's discarded robe will be visually vociferous.

Act III

Our third movement must be preluded by music of appropriate elemental force, and demands a strong setting. Shakespeare's 'Timon will to the woods' must be amplified by recognition of his subsequent references to the sea. The conception is from now on Promethean and romantic, and the obvious choice will be a background of rocks, making a rhythmic line rising from R towards C, broken low at C, and rising highest at L, the sea imagined behind. L will still be Timon's area, R for other persons. Our blocks at Leeds (Picture 22) scarcely got the line needed; at Toronto we used a simple ground-roll. Perhaps more successful was the painted setting for these scenes in *This Sceptred Isle* at the Westminster Theatre. At Toronto foliage was, if I remember correctly, roughly suggested above and at the sides. The lighting must be so arranged that the cyclorama does not tire the eye. Sea-surf sounds intermittently from now on.

We are to watch a succession of visits to Timon, and we arranged them in this order: (i) Alcibiades and his army; (ii) Apemantus; (iii) Poet and Painter; (iv) Flavius; (v) the Bandits; (vi) the Senators. These were given lighting as follows: (i) morning; (ii) and (iii) day; (iv) sunset; (v) moonlight; (vi) starlight. Our

Suggested setting for the second half of Timon of Athens
(*drawing by Michael Wright*)

order is not quite that of the text but there is some authority for a change, since Apemantus' 'Yonder comes a poet and a painter' (IV. iii. 358) is not followed by their entrance, though it is dramatically pointless if they are not to come next, for such remarks are made to stimulate immediate expectance; and once we start transposing, the advantages of having the Bandits by moonlight are sufficient to justify our placing. The text of *Timon of Athens* may not be reliable.

Timon's curses need cutting. They are unlike Shakespeare's long speeches elsewhere in that they do not gather and accumulate; his curses are *lists* of items, ungraduated additions, not organic growths. For this there is a reason. *Timon of Athens* appears to have been written as from the sophisticated consciousness of a later period, intellectually patterned and purposeful; the poet knows what he means his spokesman to say instead of giving him the chance to work it out for himself; conscious manipulation replaces natural flowering. In this respect *Timon of Athens* resembles the dramas of the romantic period—Professor Allardyce Nicoll aptly calls it 'Byronic' (*Shakespeare*, 1952; 61)—and speaking is the more difficult: the actor has to make his own structure from speeches that lack rhetorical organization. Much of the difficulty may be remedied by cuts. The problem only applies to some of the longer speeches as units; the shorter ones and the scenes as scenes work up to their climaxes well, and have all the organic flowering we expect. So does the whole later movement.

Our coast scenes open to show Timon up R among the rocks, darkly silhouetted against the cyclorama. Surf sounds. He wears a loose, leather loin-cloth, devised with falling folds, longer one side than the other; his hair is long and beard wild. It is dawn. Timon's silhouetted body is gradually gilded by light from the wings R as he lifts his arms to the dawn: 'O blessed breeding sun . . .' During the speech Timon comes C, speaks a while from there, and ends up digging for roots down L, which is to be his own natural area from now on. We imagine a cave off-stage L. He finds gold.

This gold is to take on symbolic properties and must look worthy of them. Historically Timon is said to have found 'treasure', but whatever the original meaning our text is concerned with gold, as gold, and solid blocks are needed, heavy nuggets. One of these Timon raises, and addresses.

Alcibiades enters R between Phrynia and Timandra, with his soldiers. The dialogue needs no commentary except to say that at the lines

> Put armour on thine ears, and on thine eyes,
> Whose proof nor yells of mothers, maids, nor babes,
> Nor sight of priests in holy vestments bleeding,
> Shall pierce a jot

Timon's speaking should give full value to the pathos and sanctity which is being repudiated. He is moving beyond these softer values; but they still exist in him and their existence must be pointed. Alcibiades and his company leave R.

Then follows Timon's soliloquy to the earth, to be given from where he digs down L in a measured utterance against a monotone of surf, his calmness when alone contrasting with his anger

when interrupted. Apemantus enters R. The following dialogue can be made to act better than it reads. During his long
verse speech Timon rests on his spade. He stands strongly, one
leg advanced and the spade planted vertical, not too near him,
almost as a third leg. Strong, elemental positions with firm limbs
and torso must be preserved, or Timon's nakedness lacks stage
power; certain positions, natural and good in costume, will look
weak.

The effect of Timon's dialogue with Apemantus should weigh
the balance strongly in Timon's favour. Some of his reasoning,
based on the aristocratic values, may not appear to us valid, but
all we need to understand is that Timon's hatred is being shown
as motivated and noble whereas Apemantus' is ingrained and
ignoble. Timon's is an agony to him, Apemantus' an enjoyment.
Some of the interchanges are subtle. Timon at one point dismisses
Apemantus with 'Get thee gone', but then shows him his gold
with a touch of pride, as though assuring Apemantus that his
own spiritual worth has been maintained: the stage gold visually
helps to build and therefore symbolizes his new, semi-prophetic,
status. Apemantus, rationalistically impervious to imaginative or
spiritual radiations, observes that there is here 'no use for gold',
and offers Timon instead a medlar, or apple: food is all he, as a
materialist philosopher, can understand. He is *tempting* Timon
to come down to his own level. We are reminded of the temptation of Christ in the wilderness. Timon is going to accept it, then
refuses: 'On what I hate I feed not'. He proceeds, with a pun, to
associate the 'medlar' with Apemantus himself. He turns away.
Apemantus pursues him, following up with a more subtle temptation as he invites Timon to discuss his wrongs, and here Timon
meets him for a while on equal, philosophic, terms, only to
recover himself, recognizing that Apemantus' philosophy is
bestial and Apemantus an 'ass'. His escape infuriates Apemantus.
Timon's wrath rises. They part.

Timon stands C, alone. We postpone his lines on the sea and
go straight on to his address to the gold: 'O thou sweet king-
killer'. He speaks to it as to a living person. The gold essence,
which is close to his own essential nobility, must be good; and
yet it leads in practice to evil. Its significances are accordingly
ambivalent; it is a great and living power, a 'visible god', a
ruler of human 'hearts'. That Timon still possesses gold has a

significance, which means nothing to Apemantus, that must be vividly put across.

The Poet and Painter, to whom Apemantus has recently referred, enter R; Timon is down L, eating. The satire against these two is here strong, and the actors should burlesque their parts slightly in contrast to their earlier courtly behaviour. They are now *obvious* flatterers. The full stage is used for Timon's play with them, leaving him C after beating them off with his spade, so that he can go up C to the gap between the rocks for 'I am sick of this false world' and his lines on his death:

> Lie where the light foam of the sea may beat
> Thy grave-stone daily.

These are the lines split off and postponed from the earlier speech, the advantage being that in this way we maintain another strong soliloquy between visits from the outer world. Timon speaks them looking sideways out to sea, the surf sounding, this position up C being Timon's position of ultimate authority, where he communes with the eternal.

The lines set the note for Flavius' entrance. Lighting on the cyclorama L suggests sunset. After his first distrust Timon softens: 'I do proclaim one honest man'. His following 'no more, I pray' indicates a certain weakness, a desire that his all but universal condemnation be proved right. He kneels down, picks up some gold, and offers it, still kneeling, to Flavius, the position indicating his temporary loss of dramatic status: Flavius is momentarily his superior. The words 'the gods out of my misery have sent thee treasure' hold a suggestion well beyond the obvious meaning: we may call the gold 'tragic' gold, the wealth of a great soul's suffering, mysteriously beneficent.[1]

Timon quickly returns to his uncompromising hatred, but even his most terrible lines, his

> Hate all, curse all, show charity to none,
> But let the famish'd flesh slide from the bone
> Ere thou relieve the beggar

somehow *stimulate their opposite*. One is the more, not less,

---

[1] The spiritual significances of gold and other rich metals I have discussed in the 1962 reprint of *The Christian Renaissance*, Epilogue, 288–92; *Christ and Nietzsche*, 156–7 and 193–4; *The Golden Labyrinth*, 249–50; and in '*Timon of Athens* and its Dramatic Descendants' in *A Review of English Literature*, II, 4; Oct. 1961.

Christian for having heard them. The lines serve to throw into relief a goodness which we all recognize but *have no right to* while our falsities, the falsities which the play has been defining, persist.

Timon has been dramatically reduced, almost deflated, since Flavius has shown his philosophy to be relative and not absolute. He goes up C, back to the audience, meditating. The lights change, darkening, and a spot from above C begins to suggest moonlight. The Bandits enter R and move about, crossing to Timon's area L as they search for the gold. Suddenly they see him silhouetted up C. They are down L of him as he approaches them C, where he speaks to them, rocks behind and moonlight faintly picking him out from above: 'Behold the earth hath roots . . .' The lines are spoken wearily. He comes down, and breaks through them L while they, fearful, step aside out of his way. Timon picks up some gold and offers it. Things are coming rather too easily for safety, and the Bandits back away, afraid of Timon's power. They are now variously down-stage or R, Timon a little up L. He is still speaking dully, ironically. But suddenly he moves to his position up C and turns, so that he is again moonlit, the light stronger, the Bandits now down-stage of him on either side. This is his position for the following elemental lines, which must be given with a sudden access of force and fling, the fantasy built up, stressed eerily by what he calls the moonlight's 'pale fire' on Timon's body. From 'I'll example you with thievery' onwards his gestures are fantastic, conjuring up the great cosmos, sun, moon, sea and earth:

> The sun's a thief, and with his great attraction
> Robs the vast sea. The moon's an arrant thief,
> And her pale fire she snatches from the sun.
> The sea's a thief, whose liquid surge resolves
> The moon into salt tears. The earth's a thief,
> That feeds and breeds by a composture stol'n
> From general excrement: each thing's a thief . . .

He points to moon, sea, and earth in turn; surf sounds strong before 'The sea's a thief'. The sun itself cannot be indicated, unless a gesture L can be made to suggest its earlier setting, as though it had escaped, like a thief. During Timon's lines the Bandits, now thoroughly uneasy, look across at each other, or follow Timon's gestures and indications, as though fearful of magic. They *are* being magically attacked, by poetry and all its cosmic contacts and extensions, far beyond their ken: the effect on them can be comic.

After 'each thing's a thief' Timon, still violent, comes down, breaks through, and gathers more gold, urging the Bandits to engage in riot and murder. And now we find clear evidence for what we have already hinted, that Timon's anarchic poetry contains in itself, as Apemantus' dour philosophizing does not, a saving grace that acts on others not for their harm but for their good. Of this good the new-found gold may itself be regarded as the symbol: it, together with Timon's poetry—they are aspects of the same thing—makes Timon still a princely figure, a mine of bounty, an outradiating power more strong in his new life-way than in his earlier ease. The Bandits have been offered gold. One of them remarks: 'He has almost charmed me from my profession by persuading me to it'; another will 'give over' his 'trade'. As to whether the Bandits actually take the gold, we have a choice: we could show them as afraid to touch it, feeling unworthy.

The stage darkens. Timon has gone up C, and is now a dark silhouette only. It is starlight. Flavius and the Senators enter. Despite our night setting, Timon's 'Thou sun, that comfort'st, burn' can be allowed, if spoken in an off-hand manner, though we shall find a difficulty a little later. The visit of the Senators, coming to implore Timon's aid to save the city from Alcibiades, is our climax. What has happened is this: Timon has been recognized by the community that had rejected him as a magical power, like Sophocles' Oedipus in the *Oedipus Coloneus*. The plot of neither play may seem, to our minds, adequate to the impact expected. We cannot feel all the significances which Oedipus' story held for ancient Athens, and the lustre held by the aristocracy of Shakespeare's time is to us alien. These themes were however no more than a rough basis for Sophocles and Shakespeare to develop far beyond their first content. On the stage all we need is a production which follows what is demanded, and the audience will respond. In any age personal greatness, or genius, is likely enough to find itself at first rejected and subsequently wooed as a saving power. This is all that we need to recognize.

Timon, lit by a steel or blue-steel light, remains unforgiving: his stand is firm, and must not be softened, except that the lines

Timon of Athens *and Shylock*

> But if he sack fair Athens,
> And take our goodly aged men by the beards,
> Giving our holy virgins to the stain
> Of contumelious, beastly, mad-brain'd war . . .

must be spoken with full regard to the excellences which the viciousness of man has given over to desecration. Timon has moreover—his speech to the Bandits recognizing relativity as implanted in the universal scheme suggested as much—passed beyond particularities, beyond ethic and satire. Life is now a 'sickness' and death's 'nothing' brings him 'all things'. So he, who had first aimed at love's perfection, can now see only one wholly satisfying solution to the human enigma: death. If the Athenians really wish to avoid the agonies of mortal existence, they can always commit suicide. Timon's thinking has gone beyond mortality; the words are spoken from his position up C, touched by gleams of starlight, the surf as a low thunder. For his last lines he moves to a position *higher* than ever before, as though on the edge of a precipice falling to the sea. Then he turns to face us:

> Come not to me again: but say to Athens
> Timon hath made his everlasting mansion
> Upon the beachèd verge of the salt flood;
> Who once a day with his embossèd froth
> The turbulent surge shall cover: thither come,
> And let my grave-stone be your oracle.
> Lips, let sour words go by and language end:
> What is amiss, plague and infection mend!
> Graves only be men's works, and death their gain!
> Stars, hide your beams! Timon hath done his reign[1].

Again, death is Timon's panacea: he is already there, or nearly there, within a sort of Nirvana the presence of which is realized by the *sound* of the surf and the suggestion that has run through all these last scenes of a vast ocean of mysterious being beyond the line of rocks. The others go. Left alone, Timon's gaunt figure stands majestic, silhouetted against a purple cyclorama, the surf his only music. The curtains close.

It will be observed that we have changed Shakespeare's 'Sun,

---

[1] As on pp. 52 and 279 I put accents on the syllables '-ed' to assure a correct pronunciation. Elsewhere in this book I follow the Folio by assuming pronunciation except when the 'e' is omitted. In this matter I fear that some of my books have been misleadingly inconsistent.

hide thy beams' to 'Stars, hide your beams'. If the words are spoken at all, our lighting precludes a second use of 'sun', and to speak the text in a setting which contradicts it is an example of the type of mis-placed idolatry of which modern producers are too often guilty. If the addition of words seems sacrilegious, the couplet must be cut; but that leaves a poor ending. Besides, this adjustment is less important than our use of rocks and surf, for neither of which have we any explicit directions. We must oppose objections which hamper an honest deviation. Provided that the producer has first penetrated inward into the deepest spiritual mechanics of such a work as *Timon*, which as we have it looks like an uncompleted, at the least an unpolished, work, we may allow him a certain liberty of adjustment.

The two following brief scenes are better cut: the first merely reports what we already know, and the second, by bringing Timon's grave too near to us, arouses awkward questions as to how he buried himself instead of letting us bring to his death the kind of acceptance which we bring to that of Sophocles' Oedipus. So we pass on directly to Alcibiades' entry before the walls of Athens, set effectively as a front-scene. This is the finest ritual conclusion in Shakespearian tragedy, and should be done with full civic and military conviction.

Produced according to the directions we have been outlining, the greatness of *Timon of Athens* as a stage-piece becomes apparent. The masterly structure of the Athenian action in all its simplicity and strength needs no advertisement and raises no unusual problems. Afterwards more spiritual and philosophic categories are involved, and they, as the romantic dramatists found, are less easy to put across. These difficulties we have countered by a free exploitation of hints already in Shakespeare's poetry: by a bold use of Timon's nakedness, usually shirked, driving home under a free play of varied lighting—for the elemental significances of an unclothed body demand such effects (see p. 165 above)—the Promethean and cosmic part assumed by the protagonist; and also by the recurring sound of surf, which is best made by tilting a trough filled with lead shot. In addition, we must throughout the play preserve a sense of certain stage areas as possessing this or that significance. Stage left is Timon's side, stage right is for the rest of humanity. In the later scenes we have three main areas: L for Timon's cave entrance, and his digging; R for the entry of visitors; and up C, at the break in the rocks, for Timon's communing with the sea-as-Nirvana. Respect to these areas should never result in moves or groupings that do not seem realistically natural; all should go smoothly and inevitably and the audience should not necessarily be aware of any particular significances being driven in by them, though it will do no harm if they are. The effect of such a production on a reasonably intelligent audience will be strong.

A caution may be expressed. Should any producer wish to follow the plan we have been describing, much will depend on close attention to details. The avoidance, through anxiety to save labour, of the crashing table, will affect all the subsequent scenes; the shock is essential. Again, if we give Timon tinkling little coins for his new-found treasure instead of weighty ingots—as was done in a recent Old Vic production—his address to it

> Think thy slave man rebels; and by thy virtue
> Set them into confounding odds that beasts
> May have the world in empire

falls limp. If Timon, fearing the impact of a naked torso, wears a drape that covers one shoulder, the elemental challenge is gone. Success in Shakespearian production will only mature from an honest piling up of various effects in exact attunement to the drama's inner meanings.

2

SHYLOCK

The Leeds University Union Theatre Group; February 1960

There is perhaps no other of Shakespeare's heavier parts so rewarding to the actor as Shylock. The great tragic roles are conceived as a series of poetic adventures which only Shakespeare's skill prevents from being too refined for stage production. So many problems are raised. Othello is a superb enigma, and the readily appreciated Iago only makes the actor's problem worse, like Mercutio beside Romeo; Macbeth, even when he is supposed to be talking to another, is generally soliloquizing; Lear as a tyrannic old man is easy to characterize, but elaborate resources are needed to make the last two-thirds of the play grip; and Timon will, if care be not taken, only too easily look less superman than fool. In all these both producer and actor have to *lift* the audience; sometimes, it seems, *drag* them. The response has to be won. Hamlet certainly is easier, because of the variety and because we have enough prose in the main part to re-engage contact when it might be lost.

Behind these great personal conceptions lie two precursors: Falstaff and Shylock. In them the greater powers are felt bursting the bounds of an otherwise normal drama. I wish here to record some experiences in the acting of Shylock.

The actor can rely on a number of assumptions: the audience all know, roughly, what kind of a man Shylock is, and what is his relation to a Christian society. This made Shakespeare's task easier, and the actor has today an even greater advantage than the actor of Shakespeare's time in that the racial problems are the more vividly present to us. Shylock is from the start a recognizable and convincing figure. He does not need to be built up for us gradually; he is already there, and the dramatist and actor can get down to the important matters without diffusion of their poetic or histrionic energies. This is why it is possible for so comparatively short a role, and one scarcely holding 'protagonist' stature—and in a 'comedy' too—to assume so great a tragic power. There is a compacted force in Shylock made from the fusion of local realism with spiritual pointing that is like nothing else in Shakespeare.

I did not play the part until 1960 when I was invited to do so by the Leeds University Union Theatre Group in a production by Mr. Frederick May. I record my gratitude to both. Portia was Miss Susan Lee. The experience convinced me that Shylock's dramatic status should be rated even higher than it normally is.

Though a compact study, Shylock develops; his every entry marks a step in his progress in a manner which Shakespeare was to repeat with the very similarly compacted Caliban in *The Tempest*—the details I have analysed in *The Crown of Life*—who resembles Shylock in that he holds protagonist quality without protagonist status. At Shylock's first entrance we are introduced to all those facets of his personality which are to be our subsequent concerns. He wears a Jewish cap, an underdress bound by a coloured sash and a rich gown or 'gaberdine' above. He carries a stick. As the scene unfurls, we become aware of his slightly off-centre, Jewish idiom; his Jewish faith and customs and the

Timon of Athens *and Shylock*

Biblical background to his thought; his ugly hatred of Antonio and expectance of revenge countered by evidence of the wrongs and insults that he has endured. Shylock has a Hebraic dignity alternating with moments of obsequious respect ingrained from centuries of oppression. A difficulty occurs in his proposal of the bond. Somehow it must be made to look like a 'merry sport'. The lines starting 'If you repay me not on such a day . . .' may be spoken quickly, half-carelessly; there is a pause before 'an equal pound', which comes with a shrug and a gesture, as though it were the first thought to occur; and the conclusion is almost thrown away, off-handedly.

Shylock's stick is slightly above walking-stick length, yet not a staff, so that it rests on the ground with the hand holding it reasonably high. During his description of Jacob's tricking of Laban he can use it to illustrate the peeling of the 'wands'. Shylock's gestures suggest his nation. Normally a Shakespearian actor has to use expansive gestures unhabitual to modern behaviour; Shylock's are a natural element in a 'character' study. The basis of them will be made by turning the hands in, palms up; for normal 'poetic' parts, Othello or Macbeth, the basic position will be palms down, as when one points at something. Shylock will, of course, on occasion break free from character gestures into the wider range of poetic acting.

On his second entrance the note to be struck is racial dignity. He may be a hard master to Launcelot Gobbo, but he is not conscious of it and genuinely sees himself as a kind one. As he talks to Jessica his 'I am not bid for love' has pathos and his sense of foreboding has tragic radiations. Depth is conveyed by his dislike of popular music and the 'shallow foppery' of masques in comparison with his own 'sober house'. The grand phrase 'by Jacob's staff' sums up these weighty impressions. Shylock still has his stick. The scene is short but pregnant.

We do not meet Shylock again until after his daughter has absconded and he has been robbed of his wealth by her and Lorenzo. His entry is, however, prepared by Salanio's earlier account of his passionate misery and the mockery being made of it by others. This account serves a dual purpose: if the audience is going to find Shylock's passion amusing they have been given authority for it, but authority of so dubious a kind that it is more likely to work the other way. On Shylock's entry Salarino and

Salanio maintain the mockery until Shylock's power bears them down.

Shylock has shed his main over-robe and wears his simple underdress and the coloured sash. His Jewish cap has gone and his hair is wild. He does not have his stick, for gestures must be free. The passion is such that he must move about freely, going up-stage, turning round, and coming down, the movements underlining his thwarted anger, like a torrent searching for a channel.

The famous 'Hath not a Jew eyes' was spoken less for power than for pathos, avoiding too strong a climax at the end: 'and it shall go hard but I will better the instruction'. We want to save our climax for later, and Shylock has not as yet found his way: he is blindly threatening, and the threats come almost through tears, certainly a catch in the voice. The note is pathos; but, the conception following the inevitable rise of a Shakespearian hero, we shall not stop there. Shylock is to tower beyond all claims to pity.

The dialogue with Tubal is the hardest part to perform. It has the intensity of Hamlet's 'nunnery' scene with Ophelia: in both, prose is used to forbid, as it were, the flow and freedom of Shakespearian verse. Passion is thwarted, half-choked. We are up against real life, whereas poetry is an interpretation of life, a conventional medium for a fluent expression of what would in actuality be a series of half-smothered, volcanic, eruptions. That is what we find here; the changes will be sudden, though—and this is where the acting becomes difficult—the poise and grace of the actor's technique must be preserved.

Shylock has met Tubal up-stage R. He hears that his daughter has not been found:

> Why, there, there, there! a diamond gone, cost me two
> thousand ducats in Frankfort! The curse never fell upon
> our nation till now: I never felt it till now: two thousand
> ducats in that, and other precious, precious jewels.

Shylock's grief for his wealth, which is for him his soul's symbol, as Timon's new-found gold is his, his integrity and power against an alien community, becomes one with his nation's tragedy throughout the ages. The word 'nation' elevates the speech. The words are deep and quiet, holding the sob of a race's agony. Then there is a pause. Shylock is quivering, the bow is strung, and now, in sudden abandon, turning away from Tubal a step down-stage, and speaking frontally:

> I would my daughter were dead at my foot and the jewels in her ear! would she was hearsed at my foot, and the ducats in her coffin!

At 'my daughter' one hand is raised, as though proclaiming an invocation, a reversed blessing; then, like a hawk's plunge, it comes down, pointing almost vertically to the ground. Shylock is acting a solitary drama, Tubal forgotten. The anathema is the more terrible for the family love and loyalty ingrained in Shylock's nature. The use of 'ear' marks an absurdity like some of Othello's prose agonies; the meaninglessness is wanted. The awkward repetition of 'foot' is of similar type. The lines are dramatically overpowering, and the more frightening for being on a realistic rather than a poetic level.

After this fearful outbreak Shylock is exhausted. He turns L, makes a weak circling movement, back to the audience, and comes completely round to face Tubal again, and with a changed, tremulous voice and a pitifully weak, Jewish, gesture asks plaintively:

> No news of them?

Tubal is silent, or shakes his head. Shylock turns away, and now, all loose in his abandon, arms falling limp and body swaying, makes a long circular move across from up R to up L, down L, and across to down R while he speaks the despairing lines:

> Why, so: and I know not what's spent in the search: why, thou loss upon loss! the thief gone with so much, and so much to find the thief; and no satisfaction, no revenge; nor no ill luck stirring but what lights on my shoulders; no sighs but of my breathing; no tears but of my shedding.

Again, he is a figure of pathos. But at Tubal's hint of Antonio's 'ill luck', his eye and voice quicken:

> What, what, what? ill luck, ill luck?

Hearing of Antonio's lost argosy, he answers:

> I thank God, I thank God!

Timon of Athens *and* Shylock

A dark paradox lies in his finding of God's grace in another's misfortune; the thought descends from the Old Testament, from the Psalms, seeing in God the protector of a single race.

From now on the dialogue see-saws from the height of 'good news, good news' down to 'thou stick'st a dagger in me'; and again from 'I am very glad of it: I'll plague him; I'll torture him . . .' to 'I would not have given it for a wilderness of monkeys'. Tubal acts as tempter; Shylock is being goaded into the position he is shortly to take up, and maintain. The scene towers up to culminate in his request for an officer and 'I will have the heart of him, if he forfeit'. It is typical of Shakespeare that our nobler sympathies are immediately countered by 'for, were he out of Venice, I can make what merchandise I will'. The stage brilliance of the exit lines 'Go, good Tubal; at our synagogue, Tubal' needs no underlining, except perhaps to observe that the conclusion on 'synagogue' drives home the thought that for Shylock his intended course has religious sanction.

For the short scene where Shylock confronts Antonio and the gaoler Shylock has again his full gaberdine, Jewish cap and stick; he has a new kind of authority; he is feared. As for the underlying emotions, we note that his words are not those of one to whom implacability comes easily. He repeats himself, is afraid of listening to pleas, reasons in self-justification:

> Thou call'dst me dog before thou had'st a cause;
> But since I am a dog, beware my fangs.

His repeated 'I'll have my bond' marks a fall not only to a too absolute trust in a *thing*, the bond, apart from all human considerations, but also, in its *repetition*, to a kind of subhuman level, like that of Aeschylus' Erinyes, who are impervious to argument and similarly repeat themselves. His statement that he has sworn an oath that he will have his bond marks the will to bind himself for fear of his kindlier tendencies. Shylock is, not without an effort, giving himself over to a demonic power. We watch him doing it:

> I'll not be made a soft and dull-eyed fool,
> To shake the head, relent, and sigh, and yield
> To Christian intercessors.

Clearly, as we found in Timon's curses, the rejected tendencies are still present. Shylock is *trying* to say, like Milton's Satan, 'evil be

192

thou my good'. True, he cannot, and that is part of his problem, see what he is doing as evil, but his nature does not find cruelty easy. All this the actor can convey if he feels it. At 'therefore speak no more' he can turn from Antonio and speak the lines 'I'll not be made . . .' almost as an aside, self-troubled, turning back for 'Follow not . . .' He is *afraid* of Antonio's pleading.

In the Trial scene Shylock has surpassed his uncertainties and become a wholly dedicated and unitary force. There is now no pathos, nor any temptation to weakness: he has given himself over to the demoniac course, and the audience, knowing the situation, should be dramatically impressed.

He now accordingly speaks fluent poetry, and in Shakespeare such poetry, if closely inspected, may often reveal self-diagnosing contrapuntal subtleties of considerable importance. These represent the elements that have been incorporated into the one flow. In his opening speech Shylock first reminds himself and those present of his oath, but does not say a word of his wrongs and makes no mention of Lorenzo's theft of his daughter and his jewels. Instead he speaks directly from the demoniac consciousness to which he has given himself up, confessing that his actions spring from an antipathy that does not lend itself to rational definition; from, that is, what we might call some 'complex' in the 'unconscious mind'. We can, if we like, trace the 'complex' to centuries of oppression, but Shylock himself does not; and there may be some yet deeper, racial, antagonism at work antedating, and perhaps itself originally causing, or helping to cause, that oppression. That Shylock finds this dark force repellent even while he identifies himself with it is witnessed by his use, which must be spoken with a full sense of disgust at its *sickening* quality, of repellent imagery: 'carrion-flesh,' 'rat', 'gaping pig', the 'bagpipe' singing 'i' the nose', 'urine'. For such antipathies as his there is 'no firm reason to be render'd'; the cat some people loathe is really 'harmless' and 'necessary'; and the sufferer is forced on, he freely admits, to

> yield to such inevitable shame
> As to offend, himself being offended.

Shylock has with full consciousness given himself up to a course of action which he himself recognizes, not as evil, but as ugly.

The speech is beautifully composed, the impressionistic argument unfurling and rising. Shylock's vocal expression and Jewish, explanatory, gestures and shrugs, witness his struggle to express a difficult thought as well as his dislike and disgust at the whole situation in which he has become protagonist. But from these anxieties his final certainty breaks free. At 'So can I give no reason' his hand is raised, well before the reason for its raising, and gradually and remorselessly falls to level finally at Antonio, as his name is uttered. The words 'a losing suit' mark Shylock's recognition that it is, in the deepest sense, a 'losing' suit. The speech is a notable example of that gathering and rising power which Shakespeare's longer speeches regularly show.

His brief stychomythic interchange with Bassanio must be given with venom: 'serpent' and 'sting' carry on the earlier vein of repellent imagery. For Shylock's

> If every ducat in six thousand ducats
> Were in six parts and every part a ducat
> I would not draw them; I would have my bond

a peculiarly pleasing effect can be gained by speaking the first line explanatorily and the next line and a half unemotionally and quickly, the speed from the opening at first gradually and then swiftly increasing till there is no pause whatever at the end of the second line, all sense of metre and even syntax *deliberately* broken by the run-on. The movement is halted after 'draw them', and 'I would have my bond' spoken slowly and with weight.

Shylock's second long expository speech 'What judgement shall I dread, doing no wrong?' is more rational than the first. He is growing impatient and wants to clarify the issue. Rationally, he is, from his view, 'doing no wrong' and is consequently in no fear of 'judgement'. It is a simple matter of law and possession, and no one but he need concern himself with those darker issues of unmotivated loathing which he has already handled. The imagery is still denigratory: asses, dogs, mules. The reference to slavery serves to assert that all society is built on suffering, and that absolute standards cannot be adduced by his opponents without self-condemnation. The lines are spoken with expostulatory gestures, and shrugs. This speech of thwarted impatience ends on a strong climax: 'I stand for judgement: answer: shall I have it?'

Timon of Athens *and Shylock*

Shylock's interchanges with Portia need no comment: the obvious reading and relevant actions come easily. After the reversal, Shylock registers his reaction in face and eyes. This is not easy but to have him turned up-stage is a weak expedient. There is however a limit to what can be done, and during Portia's long speech 'Tarry, Jew . . .' and its staggering content Shylock can, at an appropriate moment, cover his eyes with his hands, his head well up, not lowered. At 'Down, therefore, and beg mercy of the Duke' Shylock, half-driven by the crowd, kneels. As he hears the Duke's sentence of confiscation, he slumps lower, lying on the ground. For his following lines, he lifts himself a little, palms on the ground, still half lying but his head and shoulders raised;

> Nay, take my life and all; pardon not that:
> You take my house when you do take the prop
> That doth sustain my house; you take my life
> When you do take the means whereby I live.

It is not easy to account for the extraordinary stage power of these lines.

They were spoken in a long, slow, wail with the vocal contrasts simple and strongly modulated; up on 'all', and changing to a deep note on 'pardon'; a measured utterance for the next line and a half; a rising wail on 'life', sinking again, like a corpse into the earth, at 'whereby I live'. The modulation fixed, the actor's main business here is to make every syllable exaggeratedly clear, if only because, being on the ground, his figure and even face may not be clearly visible to everyone. This is what he should be thinking about himself, while the audience is being emotionally transfixed. The thoughts and rhythms are simple, and may be called either universal or platitudinous, according to taste; but their impact is terrific. We can say that they drive home the nature of Shylock's central life-way wherein his wealth is all but his soul; but we knew all that before. What really happens is this. The situation is before us; we already feel with Shylock to the limit, and need no new thoughts. At this point intellectual concentration would blur the feeling, and that is precisely why they must be spoken so clearly; not that the thoughts are in themselves important, but that the audience should expend no jot of psychic power in listening, inquiring or thinking; they must simply be allowed to *feel*, and these four lines exist mainly to fill out space for their feeling, without raising irrelevant issues. This is masterly stage-composition.[1]

Shylock rises, pauses, and says 'I am content', hesitating after 'am'. Before 'I am not well' he almost falls, no one coming to his aid. 'Send the deed after me and I will sign it' is spoken weakly before the attorney's desk, a pathetically weak, Jewish gesture of both hands made towards the desk while his face and voice register a horror away from it. At the last of our ten performances I found myself emphasizing the horror by actually withdrawing a step while the hands were out, using an even more strongly contradictory action than before; but since this seemed to me very effective while it was being done, I suspect that it was overdone. Shylock's exit is made cowering, followed by jeers. He is back where he started, or lower; his bearing has the repellent humility of a pariah.

What we find here is a maximum of external humiliation supervening on our sympathy and our clear sense of a richness in Shylock's personality beyond anything apparent in his dramatic associates. The darker elements have not been diluted by the author and must not be diluted by the actor; but if played as we have described, the effect is, in its own way, deeply tragic. Such disasters in real life will often enough be accompanied by condemnation and humiliation, but we should seldom allow ourselves to feel that such an outcome covers the human problem. After Shylock Shakespeare develops a series of tragedies wherein the inward soul-worth of Shylock, even his soul-worth-while submitting to the demoniac powers, is given a more poetically explicit formulation in heroes whose possession by such powers is an accepted element in a purposive scheme, and who are accordingly *not humiliated*. In them the Dionysian principle takes over, at least for a while, and has its fling; we are subtly made to accept its provisional authority, as an inalienable part of the universal structure; and condemnation becomes irrelevant. The great tragedies are metaphysical explorations of that which lies behind, or within, the human enigma; Shylock is a study drawn more directly from that enigma, from life itself, as we know it. Neither is more 'true' than the other, but having regard to the high degree of tragic

---

[1] My thoughts on these lines which in performance I found so strangely interesting have been both stimulated and clarified by a subsequent conversation with Mr. John Boorman.

sympathy aroused by Shylock we can perhaps suggest that in him Shakespeare has left us, brief though the treatment be, a more convincing and perhaps even a more comprehensive reading of man than in the more famous works. Ethic and society have more rights, and it is just because these rights so violently and even crudely assert themselves against our tragic sympathies that the end of the Trial scene appears so deeply shocking. The shock, made of the crushing together of two seemingly incompatible and yet unavoidable truths, should leave the audience disturbed.

3

The problems posed by Falstaff and Shylock forced Shakespeare on to his more metaphysically patterned dramas; he had, as it were, to attempt deliberate interpretations of the mystery, to render the sympathy which we accord Shylock more central. In Shylock many elements intrinsic to these later dramas are contained, swirling like electrons in an atom. Shylock has atomic quality, compact yet explosive.

His motives, like those of the tragic heroes, are complex. He himself asserts at his first entry that he hates Antonio not only because he is a Christian

> But more for that in low simplicity
> He lends out money gratis, and brings down
> The rate of usance here with us in Venice.

Later, as we have seen, he repeats, at a climax, this same ugly thought. At Belmont Jessica tells the company that Shylock has often ruminated on the thought of gaining his pound of flesh. On the other side, we must realize that his wealth is his only safeguard against social enmity, and remember the persecution he has endured, the shameless robbery of his house, and the whole tenor of the action forcing a revenge which his own religious beliefs, as expressed in the Trial scene, underwrite:

> An oath, an oath, I have an oath in Heaven!
> Shall I lay perjury upon my soul?
> No, not for Venice.

We have seen moreover that he does not find actual revenge as easy or palatable as in fantasy he had expected, and our final definition of his motivation is given in terms of an uncontrollable, and to that extent in itself forgivable, antipathy. We find compactly presented just such a vagueness of motivation as we are to find in Hamlet ('I do not know why yet I live to say "This thing's to do"'; *Hamlet*, IV. iv. 43); in Iago's various explanations and self-diagnoses, so like Shylock's, his 'I hate the Moor' (*Othello*, I. iii. 373) corresponding to Shylock's admission of a central loathing; Macbeth's willing submission to powers he repudiates; and Lear's volcanic irrationality.

Timon's actions, which exist on yet another level of dramatic composition, have a greater rationality. He sees the truth of the human heart and his course is fixed. But here again, Shylock is a precursor. *The Merchant of Venice* and *Timon of Athens* are Shakespeare's two dramas on gold, playing very similarly on its ambivalence as both money and soul-symbol. Now in the later scenes of *Timon of Athens*, Timon as denunciatory prophet might well be called 'Hebraic'; he is also, like Shylock, an outcast; and yet both are finally sued to in vain for favour, as was Sophocles' Oedipus, by the community that had scorned them. It would be to lay too limited an emphasis on the fictional surfaces to fail to see in these dramas signs of poetic genius taking a mighty pleasure in putting the community in its place. Despite obvious differences, Timon and Shylock show a common emphasis which persists across the centuries, and it is no chance that Byron, in a Timon mood, should in a letter to John Murray on 6 April 1819 address the British public with an adaptation of Shylock's

> I will buy with you, sell with you, talk with you, walk with you, and so following: but I will not eat with you, drink with you, nor pray with you.

This letter I have discussed in my lecture 'Byron's Dramatic Prose' (Byron Foundation Lecture, 1954; to be reprinted in my study *Byron and Shakespeare*). For both Shylock and Timon riches —I refer especially to Timon's new-found gold—are important symbols. Timon's becomes a symbol of his soul-worth and Shylock's may be called at the least a symbol of his own personal integrity, his safety and power as a personal unit in a hostile world. The nature of such symbolisms I have often discussed (see my note on p. 182 above).

It is accordingly hard not to see in Shylock the essential elements of subsequent heroes compactly defined and balanced neatly against social necessity; and in that he is more closely localized and defined as a recognizable person and part of a dramatic pattern that not only envisages the inevitable revenge of society but even envisages that revenge as *humiliating* the hero —though there is no degradation such as we find in Marlowe— he is more, in the obvious sense of the word, 'realistic'. Were Shakespeare's genius not such that critical rulings are left at a loss, it would be, from a strictly 'critical' standpoint, a tenable judgement were we to conclude that in the general handling of the two parts of *Henry IV* and in the semi-tragic conception of Shylock Shakespeare had his masterpieces. Fortunately, our concern is not here with literary, or any other, criticism, but with acting. The actor should love his part and the producer his play, and should make the best of them, slurring or hiding any technical slips and bringing to fruition the strength; and so I suspect that it may be the actor in myself who is letting his interest in his most recent dramatic adventure tempt him to an honourable extravagance.

CHAPTER VIII

Tree and Craig; Poel and Barker

I draw on the authorities here listed. Reference designations, where used, are shown in brackets.

Herbert Beerbohm Tree, *Thoughts and After-Thoughts*, 1913 (*T and A*); *Nothing Matters*, with other stories, 1917 (*N M*). Mrs. George Cran, *Herbert Beerbohm Tree*, 1907 (Cran); Max Beerbohm as editor, *Herbert Beerbohm Tree*, essays by various hands, undated (Beerbohm); Hesketh Pearson, *Beerbohm Tree*, 1956 (Pearson); A. E. Wilson, *Edwardian Theatre*, 1951 (Wilson); *Oscar Asche; his life*, 'by Himself'; contains valuable passages on Tree; undated (Asche); Joseph Harker, *Studio and Stage*, 1924 (Harker); W. Macqueen-Pope, *Carriages at Eleven*, on the Edwardian theatre, 1947; for Tree, 31–44; and *The Curtain Rises*, 1961, 290–4. Material is held by Mr. A. J. Nathan (p. 18).

Edward Gordon Craig, *On the Art of the Theatre*, 1957, first published 1911 (*A of T*); *Towards a New Theatre* (mainly designs), 1913 (*T N T*); *The Theatre Advancing*, 1921 (*T A*); *Scene*, with a foreword and poem by John Masefield, 1923 (*Scene*); *Henry Irving*, 1930. Enid Rose, *Gordon Craig and the Theatre*, undated (Rose); Janet Leeper, *Edward Gordon Craig, Designs for the Theatre*, King Penguin, 1948 (Leeper); Denis Bablet, *Edward Gordon Craig*, L'Arche, Paris 1962 (Bablet).

William Poel, *Monthly Letters*, 1929; Robert Speaight, *William Poel and the Elizabethan Revival*, 1954 (Speaight); Harley Granville Barker, *The Exemplary Theatre*, 1922 (Barker); C. B. Purdom, *Harley Granville Barker*, 1955 (Purdom); W. Bridges Adams, *The Lost Leader*, 1954.

Maurice Willson Disher, *The Last Romantic*, on Sir John Martin Harvey, undated; Bertram Joseph, *The Tragic Actor*, 1959

(Joseph); Norman Marshall, *The Producer and the Play*, 1962 edn. (Marshall); W. Moelwyn Merchant, *Shakespeare and the Artist*, 1959 (Merchant).

1. TREE

My staging of the final scenes of *Timon of Athens* suggests certain extensions of some of my earlier views on scenery and lighting. In this connexion we may profitably think back to the productions of Herbert Beerbohm Tree (1853–1917) before the First World War.

Our stage history includes no personality more expansively important than Tree's. During the early years of this century, in the great period of actor-managers of which Henry Irving had set the style, Tree stood pre-eminent. A man of wide literary, political and social interests, he was more than an actor-manager; he was a great public figure, patron as well as artist, active in a number of good causes. He founded the Royal Academy of Dramatic Art.

After a distinguished management of the Haymarket he built Her Majesty's, opened in 1897; and it stands today as a record of his quality. Under him it was almost as much temple as theatre, as though entertainment had become one with religion. Its liveried attendants, its presentation souvenirs, its spacious programmes with strong lettering printed black and red on buff paper; the courtesy extended towards every part of the house; in all this Tree was host as well as artist and high-priest to his community. In terms of the commercial theatre and a living society, he created a royal foretaste of that for which civilization strives. His own social sympathies were advanced, tending to what might be called a 'socialistic royalism'.[1] He named his theatre 'Her Majesty's'; and since it was a living symbol, the name changed to 'His Majesty's' on the accession of Edward VII.[2]

As an actor-manager he avoided some at least of the attendant dangers. He surrounded himself with eminent performers, aiming

---

[1] He once designated himself an 'anti-Gladstonian socialist' (*T and A*, 165). A fervent anti-militarist, he looked to the 'workers of all nations' and the women to prevent future wars by 'a holy strike' (*N M*, 248–50; and see 143–4). He was peculiarly fond of Falstaff's 'honour' speech and played the Tolstoyan Frithiof in Israel Zangwill's *The War God* in 1911.

[2] The atmosphere of His Majesty's under Tree is well described by W. Macqueen-Pope in *Carriages at Eleven*, 35–6. A comprehensive set of Tree's programmes is held in the Enthoven Theatre Collection of the Victoria and Albert Museum.

at a star cast, often to his personal disadvantage. His expansive genius assisted methods not his own. Companies contributing to his annual Shakespeare festivals included those not only of H. B. Irving, Lewis Waller, F. R. Benson, Arthur Bourchier and Herbert Trench, but also of William Poel; and Granville Barker was, in 1911, invited to produce for him on a gala occasion (Pearson, 209). His Majesty's, with its Shakespeare festivals, varied revivals and guest-producers, has been called 'the greatest repertory theatre the world has seen' (Macqueen-Pope, *The Curtain Rises*, 292).

The actor-managers of Tree's day used their personalities to lift mediocre plays of potential strength to the plane of dramatic artistry, so blending greatness with appeal. Irving in *The Bells*, Forbes-Robertson in *The Passing of the Third Floor Back*, Martin Harvey in *The Only Way*, Fred Terry in *The Scarlet Pimpernel*, Lewis Waller in *Monsieur Beaucaire*, Oscar Asche in *Kismet*, all attained successes impossible for Shakespeare. Such successes sometimes paved the way for Shakespearian productions; but often they themselves, through the living performance and the power of the central actor, became dramas of weight.

Tree had a number of such successes, perhaps the most notable being an adaptation of George du Maurier's *Trilby*, on the proceeds of which he built Her Majesty's. The plays favoured by the actor-managers may generally be distinguished from melodrama by their central emphasis on some powerful dramatic figure, like Svengali in *Trilby*, expanding the imagination in the tradition of great drama. Tree was not however content with such successes alone; he had an eye for work of higher quality. He instituted matinée performances to bring out important plays of limited appeal. He was our first to popularize Ibsen, in *An Enemy of the People*. His major productions included dramatizations of Tolstoy, Dumas, Dickens, and Thackeray; and he once planned a Dostoevsky. He was himself a writer of quality in essays, fiction and dramatic adaptation. Shaw wrote that he had 'a very marked literary talent' showing 'finish of style and sureness of execution' (Shaw; Beerbohm, 245–6).[1]

Opposition was frequent (Cran; 11, 95) and Tree's eminence was not at any time easy. His position was less assured than it

[1] The short stories in *Nothing Matters* (1917) show qualities of suspense, humour, irony, invention and fantasy that would lend themselves admirably to broadcasting.

seemed, since he spent freely, refusing the financial advantages of long runs while he strove for great things in a great way.

His personality was a field for the play of opposites. A social figure-head, he yet revelled, according to W. L. Courtney, in all that was 'unconventional' (Courtney; Beerbohm, 256). Though the leader of his profession, his attitude to it was notoriously unprofessional. Chaotic rehearsals led to results of finish and precision; reverence for his art was interrupted by practical jokes during performance; disregard of finance made money. Unconscious of time, he was never for any important appointment late; with little apparent reading, he had extensive literary knowledge and resource. It was as though he were drawing on 'some kind of queer instinct' unknown to science (Max Beerbohm; Beerbohm, 194-5); without learning he '*knew* things' like 'an inspired water-finder' (Lady Tree; Beerbohm, 164). Louis N. Parker, after travelling with him to Egypt for archaeological detail and being worried by his unconcern, found that he had seen and remembered more than the scholar (Parker; Beerbohm, 211-2).

His most strenuous activities were suffused with humour; in this, as in much else, he was Byronic. His wit had brilliance, though his neglect of the business in hand while pursuing his peculiar vein of paradox must often have been trying. According to Gordon Craig, Oscar Wilde and Beerbohm Tree were 'two men of genius and wit' in whom the fun had sometimes to be forgiven for the genius (E. Gordon Craig, *Henry Irving*, 95-6). Bernard Shaw, after recounting his experiences with Tree during the rehearsals of *Pygmalion*, said that he should and could have written his own plays:

And it would have given him what he was always craving from authors, and in the nature of the case could never get from them: a perfect projection of the great Tree personality. What did he care for Higgins or Hamlet? His real objective was his amazing self.

(Shaw; Beerbohm, 251)

Tree pleased Shaw best when he broke through his stage disguises:

They were his robes of state; and he was never happier than when he stepped in front of the curtain and spoke in his own immensity to the audience, if not as deep calling unto deep (for the audience could not play up to him as splendidly as that), at least as a monarch to his courtiers. (Shaw; Beerbohm, 252)

Tree and Craig; Poel and Barker

A man who was recognized by both Craig and Shaw as a genius demands something more than respect. In studying Tree and his methods we are up against a mystery.

My present purpose is to lay an especial emphasis on his qualities of vision. Among his contemporaries he was regarded as a 'dreamer' and 'mystic' (Cran, 4). His daughter Iris wrote of him:

It was to London that he belonged, or rather his brain and body belonged to London, though in his spirit I think he belonged to no land; he seemed like an exile from some country whose name he had forgotten, but whose beauty came back to him and left his eyes bewildered at gazing upon things to which he had no kin. Most men bear traces of their environment, are typical of some place or age or coterie, but he seemed always the singular being, a wanderer from far roads whose dust had not dimmed his face, a seeker for some star whose rays had dazzled his eyes.

(Iris Tree; Beerbohm, 182)

Without recognition of this mystical centre, so delicately conveyed in Iris Tree's sonnets on her father (Beerbohm, xi; 267), we shall not appreciate Tree's accomplishment. He was labouring to realize a vision.

As an actor, Tree had a wide range. Shaw preferred him in a straight part; most contemporaries rated highest his more fantastic rôles such as Svengali in *Trilby*, Fagin in *Oliver Twist*, Macari in *Called Back*; or, in a different vein, Colonel Newcome from Thackeray; or, with a striking and even *technical* realization of musical genius, Beethoven in *Beethoven* (Parker; Beerbohm, 209–11). His expertise in make-up was phenomenal. More, he could appear to change his build, the 'inner man' according to his own account, somehow convincing the audience of fatness or height or kingliness (*T and A*, 112). As both Colonel Newcome and Beethoven he changed his bearing and stature miraculously (Pearson, 196–7). When acting he could smoke cigars which would have normally made him ill (Courtney; Beerbohm, 257). According to Joseph Harker he could change not only his appearance but his whole character by 'a few deft touches of greasepaint', applied with lightning speed; he normally allowed himself ten minutes for make-up and five for dressing (Harker, 146). Many photographs bear witness to his brilliant visual impersonations.

His speaking was unusual. Some critics note a slight accent attributed to his Dutch paternal descent; there are criticisms of a lisp; the term 'guttural' is sometimes used. In conversation it could however be 'soft' and 'purring' (Pearson, 206). It was a light voice. The late Leslie Harris, formerly of his company, told me that he worked hard to lower its register; he seems to have lowered it for Cardinal Wolsey in 1910 (Pearson, 169). Shaw said that his elocution showed no sense of traditional skills, as did Forbes-Robertson's, or of blank verse (Shaw; Beerbohm, 247-8); but Asquith in a memorial speech tells us that he added to his natural endowments 'all the resources of elocution and make-up' (Asquith; Beerbohm, 275). He seems to have given much thought and labour to his Shakespearian speaking. He had to build on what Shaw, noting his foreign voice, calls a verbal 'music of his own' (Shaw; Beerbohm, 248). The remark rings true: I myself recall from his *Othello* in 1912 his 'Have you prayed tonight, Desdemona?', the words soft and slow and the 'o' of 'Desdemona' thinned and drawn out, on a spiritual, wraithly, note; and I was deeply impressed in the next year by his inspired chant as the patriarchal Jacob of Louis N. Parker's *Joseph and His Brethren*. Mrs. Cran refers to the effectiveness in *Richard II* of 'his cob-webby voice with its haunting tones of grey'; for Falstaff however, he laboured 'with infinite patience' to gain the 'fruity', 'bibulous' voice recorded on the gramophone (Cran; 63, 21).

The British Institute of Recorded Sound holds records of Tree's speaking of this Falstaff speech; of Richard II's survey of tragic kingship; of Hamlet's 'To be or not to be'; and of Antony's 'O pardon me thou bleeding piece of earth' in *Julius Caesar*. Despite Shaw's aspersions on Tree's inability to 'build up vocal climaxes with his voice through a long crescendo of rhetoric' (Beerbohm, 247-8),[1] this 'build up' is precisely what the recorded speech, as though of set purpose, exemplifies. This Antony record I possess. It was given to me in 1949 by Mr. Robert A. Morton after seeing my acting of Timon, and it at once suggested to me that my own sense of the gathering power of Shakespeare's longer speeches must have been trained by hearing Tree in my youth. *Julius Caesar* in his 1911 Shakespeare Festival was my first experi-ence of professional Shakespearian production, but my recollec-tion of the speaking is dimmed. Mr. Pearson's statement that 'the rhetoric' of Mark Antony was beyond Tree's 'declamatory powers'

[1] There is a record of Shaw's own speaking of Shakespearian verse at the Institute which does little to establish his authority.

(Pearson, 119) may conceivably have been true of the actual stage performance. What he could do on a record he might of course be unable to accomplish in a large theatre, though according to his wife his acting in the scene of Caesar's murder was most impressive (Lady Tree; Beerbohm, 108). The record remains as evidence of a rare vocal understanding and poetic sensitivity. The speaking is slow and deliberate, but it gradually accelerates; the blank-verse units are—countering Shaw's other aspersion—given almost too great a respect; but the long, suspended, yet inevitable up-building reaching its climax on 'dogs of war' is a remarkable feat of sustained and exactly articulated declamation. The artistry is a spiritualized artistry. The architectonics of such a speech demand a sense of it as a whole; the whole is to be felt throughout each detail; and this can only come through intuition of a soul-centre, for 'soul' and 'wholeness' are interdependent categories. What I am most aware of in this record is the spiritualized, yet strongly sensuous, quality of Tree's speaking.

His Hamlet and Richard II records have superb intonations of a haunting, ethereal richness, almost more a poet's than an actor's. He was by nature drawn to impersonations of artist-types, (Joseph, 384–5) such as Hamlet, Richard II—among his greatest successes—and Beethoven; and his love of *fantastic* 'character' rôles was an extension of the same instinct. Joseph Harker recounts how rapidly he transformed, as with the artistry of a portrait painter, his 'pale, ascetic face' into whatever guise he desired (Harker, 146).

Mrs. Cran's phrase on Tree's 'haunting tones' bears out my own youthful memories and present conclusion regarding the spiritualized quality of his work. So does his daughter Iris Tree, who writes of

his voice, which had that far, clear quality of voices on summer waters, his laughing eyes under brows that frowned from the habit of thought, and his hands that were more expressive than his words, and seemed as though they would draw on the air the thoughts that flashed upon his mind . . . (Iris Tree; Beerbohm, 183)

His acting was of similar tone:

It was in those parts of sinister fancy, of whimsical humour, of nightmare and dream, that he let his spirit loose, leaving the audience haunted and bewitched. (Iris Tree; Beerbohm, 185)

According to Desmond MacCarthy his acting was more inspirational than technical (MacCarthy; Beerbohm, 225); it varied from night to night, sometimes just a walking through (Viola Tree; Beerbohm, 178). He was often uncertain of his words. He had the virtues and also the failings of an amateur. To put it higher, we could call him a 'mystical' actor; and mysticism is always unpredictable.

His abundant imagination could lead to excess: his Malvolio seems—I did not see it—to have been a *tour-de-force* of burlesque that stepped out of Shakespeare's frame into a life of its own; and it was neatly countered by Granville Barker's directing of Henry Ainley in the part as a dry puritan in his 1912 production of *Twelfth Night*. Tree's Malvolio was however no distortion of Shakespeare, but rather an expansion, following the instinct of stage improvisation which Gordon Craig regarded as a main constituent in the original creation of all Shakespearian comedy (*T A*, 'Shakespeare's Collaborators', 131–42). It was an extremely subtle burlesque. Despite the extravagance and despite his apparent independence of any formal technique, Tree's characterizing quality as an actor was 'delicacy' (Cran, 39–40; Max Beerbohm and MacCarthy; Beerbohm, 201, 226). His hands were sensitive agents. His use of facial expression, and in particular of his eyes, was remarkable; of it we have evidence in the many photographs, and in the pictures of him by Charles A. Buchel, the best known being the King John in Her Majesty's Theatre. We reproduce Buchel's portraits of Tree's Malvolio and Othello (Pictures 24, 25).

Tree is famed for his elaborate productions. In these the tradition of historical spectacle given impetus by Charles Kean and developed by Irving attained its climax. Though his rehearsals were chaotic (Shaw and Parker; Beerbohm, 244–5, 211–2; Pearson, 178, 197) it seems possible that Tree's apparent unconcern may have been in part deliberate. Louis N. Parker records that he worked himself and others day and night for *Henry VIII*, leaving Parker exhausted but himself fresh for performance (Parker; Beerbohm, 211–2). He seems to have liked postponing the real work until late at night (Asche, 98). He had 'an infinite capacity for making other people take pains' (Pearson, 119) and let results mature from multiple suggestion and divergent authorities, the process being not so much dominated as permeated by his own personality. In place of discipline there was an anxious and devoted community willing success. Shaw, writing of the rehearsals of his own *Pygmalion*, regarded Tree's entourage as 'courtiers' (Shaw; Beerbohm, 244); and the implied royalty was a spiritual power. Tree was less the dictator than the soul of what was going on. Meanwhile there seemed to be no respect to authority. 'It was amiable and modest in him', wrote Shaw, 'not to know his own place, since it was the highest in the theatre; but it was exasperating in him not to know any one else's' (Shaw; Beerbohm, 245). Mr. Pearson writes:

> Out of chaos Tree created cosmos; out of vagueness came clarity; from conditions that reminded many people of a more than usually riotous playground, there emerged a production of admirable smoothness, carefully considered detail, and unrivalled magnificence. It seemed, and was, a miracle.
>
> (Pearson, 200)

Such was the process behind Tree's, as I have elsewhere called it, 'spiritualized showmanship'.

Showmanship it was, and when applied to Shakespeare it held grave dangers. The delays caused by excessive, if admirable, pageantry; the waits between scene-settings or textual rearrangements to avoid them[1]; the distracting detail; the deflating of imaginative belief by the momentary quiver of a painted castle; the ever-present possibility of some justified realism in a part countering the imaginative atmosphere needed for the whole—on these we need not expend labour. The issues are known, and have, if only provisionally, been settled.

By pushing spectacle and historical exactitude to new extremes, Tree was a pioneer and an adventurer. His methods were continually attacked. The school of plain-style Shakespearian production, of which William Poel was the leader, was already vocal. Tree's defences, set out in his *Thoughts and After-thoughts*, are deeply considered and in parts convincing. He is willing to agree 'that the modern move towards greater simplicity' is right for highly imaginative works, suggestion being often stronger than actuality; he records that his own *Hamlet* had always been played before simple tapestries and claims that his 1911 *Macbeth* was characterized by 'simple grandeur'; and he expresses admiration

---

[1] Modern techniques in mobile and revolving sets such as those used recently in the musicals *Oliver* and *My Fair Lady* would, had they been available, have gone far to solve the problem.

23, 24. Beerbohm Tree as Malvolio and as Othello (pp. 207, 21). Reproduced from coloured portraitures by Charles A. Buchel (Malvolio, from a souvenir booklet; Othello, originally designed for a poster); (see pp. 17–18).

25. Beerbohm Tree's production of *Julius Caesar*: the Forum scene (pp. 209, 229, 232). Tree as Mark Antony

for the 'rugged simplicity' of a recent *King Lear*. But he denies that the historical plays can be adequately represented without a high degree of realism (*T and A*, 223–4; and see p. 232 below).

We need not make any too final a distinction between historical and other productions. There was no ultimate difference in the experiences of colour and delight transmitted by the Roman Forum or Cleopatra's palace and his famous wood and garden settings for *A Midsummer Night's Dream* and *Twelfth Night*. A. E. Wilson writes:

His artistic mind revelled in the opportunity to heap upon the stage rich and glittering fabrics and to load it with every detail of luxury and extravagance. The ample proportions of his theatre enabled him to give full play to such Byzantine splendours and elaborate effects, done on a scale in which expense seemed to have been disregarded.

(Wilson, 76)

Tree was exploiting to the full what Aldous Huxley in *Heaven and Hell* (p. 287, note, below) shows to be the spiritual powers implicit in such theatric brilliances. His wife, Lady Tree, observed his delight in bringing woods, streams, skies and mountains onto the stage, and also 'pillared palaces and long-drawn aisles', castles, battlements, forests and 'fields jewelled with daisies, and yellow sands' (Lady Tree; Beerbohm, 124). For his nature-settings W. L. Courtney regarded him as a 'magician' (Courtney; Beerbohm, 260–1). Tree's 'realism' existed as a basis for manifold excitements. Realism is often thought of, as Gordon Craig thought of it, as a constricting and imprisoning force, impeding vision and draining art of colour. Tree's was the very reverse of that; anything 'drab' he loathed, loving light and colour (Lady Tree; Beerbohm, 163); his was a sensuous and a liberating realism, opening splendours. His dislike of modernistic symbolisms (as at *T and A*, 290–5; Viola Tree; Beerbohm, 176) was the dislike of a man for whom realism and mysticism were potentially identical.

Though he was himself a man of the town, he loved to bring nature into his theatre. Behind this love lay a long tradition of nineteenth-century melodrama and pantomime. Nature artificially lit in an enclosed theatre may radiate a magic that only the born nature-mystic, a Wordsworth or a Powys, can receive directly. Once when, after complaining at a rehearsal of the inadequacy of some thunder, Tree was told that it was real thunder, 'Ah,' he said, 'that may satisfy the people outside, but we must do better at

Her Majesty's' (W. Macqueen-Pope, *The Curtain Rises*, 292). All theatre-nature is magical. The result is achieved in part by lighting and in part through our sight of some natural effect isolated, seen *sub specie aeternitatis* and without hampering associations. And yet without human reference such visual delights become soon cheapened, facile and irresponsible; the marvels of pantomime and revue are quickly forgotten; what we want is theatre-magic related to human drama. This is what Tree gave us. For an example of it we might point to picture 23, of Tree's *Macbeth*, in Norman Marshall's *The Producer and the Play*.

Since my own Shakespearian commentary has been so largely given to exposing, by a mental spatializing or staging, Shakespeare's more elemental, colourful and spiritual properties, its relation to Tree's productions may be assumed. His Weird Sisters floating among smoky clouds at the opening of *Macbeth*, together with the wailing pitch of their voices, were for me seminal. His Brocken scene in Stephen Phillips's adaptation of *Faust* was famous (Wilson, 72). Apart from the numinous, some of Tree's nature-effects held a precise poetic validity. The use of rabbits in *A Midsummer Night's Dream* may be criticized, but when we hear of a garden interlude composed entirely of bird-song being introduced into *Much Ado about Nothing* (Wilson, 77), our first temptation to smile should be countered by the consideration that, as I myself, following Caroline Spurgeon, have pointed out (*The Shakespearian Tempest*, 87–90), bird-imagery is here a characterizing element. In this instance Tree's methods are found revealing a vein of Shakespearian ore only subsequently handled by scholars. Despite their unquestioned achievements neither William Poel nor Granville Barker had either the equipment or the desire to make their productions in this visual sense interpretative; they were content to let imagery remain locked in poetry. Rightly or wrongly, Tree's methods took a different course.

He naturally found *The Tempest* a congenial field. I have in my possession a copy of his acting text made on the occasion of the play's fiftieth performance on 27 October 1904. It has a preface on his methods of production, the text as spoken, and elaborated directions in red type; and thirteen coloured pictures by Charles A. Buchel. In his preface (reprinted except for one passage in *Thoughts and After-Thoughts*), he defends his methods as true to Shakespeare's directions while maintaining that whatever in his production was not actually contained in the 'letter' of Shakespeare's text sprang 'from the spirit which animated it' (*T and A*, 221-2).

His arrangement of the masque of Reapers and Nymphs is, with its close resemblance to the Masques of Shakespeare's day, to which he refers in his defence, and also in its truth to the sexology of *The Tempest*, amply justified. Here is another direction:

They all creep stealthily to the entrance of Prospero's cell. Enter Ariel. Darkness and thunder. Shakespeare's stage directions are as follows:— 'Enter divers spirits in shapes of dogs and hounds, hunting them about'. Prospero's magic wand is once more at work. To Caliban, Stephano and Trinculo is now revealed a monstrous cave. At first there is an uncanny silence. The three are paralyzed with fear. They attempt to creep off, but are met at every turn by strange shapes which, appearing from behind the rocks, bow to the drunkards with a mocking and haunting politeness. The three men rush up the steps, but are again met by divers spirits with terrible and unearthly shapes. They are hunted about and tortured as Shakespeare directs. Once more they seek to rush from their tormentors, but the air itself is now inhabited by the denizens of night-mares which afflict conscience-stricken men. The shapes laugh a hollow laugh. The punishment of the drunkards is now complete—the comic Inferno dissolves and we are once more in Prospero's cave.

This description, with the accompanying illustration of serpentine and dinosaurian 'shapes', is truly frightening; and it is exactly true to the spirit of Shakespeare's play, though belonging more nearly to our own recognition descending from Colin Still, who may well have been influenced by Tree's production, of 'ponderous and substantial' meanings within *The Tempest* than to the academic commentaries of the Edwardian period.

That Tree should have taken care to build up the part of Caliban is not strange. Not only is it the obvious star-part lending itself admirably to his genius for make-up and bizarre characterization, but there is a more condensed dramatic poetry in Caliban than elsewhere; just as there is a deeper drama in Shylock and Falstaff than elsewhere in *their* plays. Such works are to this extent artistically imperfect, as is *Paradise Lost*, since each contains a cancerous growth which we are tempted to regard, and may even be right to regard, as more valuable than the body it threatens. The producer has a legitimate choice as to how he will place his emphases; and though we shall probably say that he must strike a balance, few of us will object if on occasion an actor-producer concentrates on one of these wonderful stage-parts.

Here is Tree's Caliban, summoned by Prospero:

He strikes the rock with his magic wand; the rock opens, disclosing Caliban, 'a savage and deformed slave', who crawls out with a fish in his mouth. His dress consists of fur and seaweed, and round his neck he wears a necklace of shells and pearls, amber and coral, and other precious jewels of the sea.

The description is illustrated by a picture: the stage creation blending earth and sea is in tune with Shakespeare's conception. When Caliban hears Ariel's music he 'becomes transformed and is moved to dance, making inarticulate sounds as if attempting to sing'. Tree concluded the drama's text with 'Ye elves of hills, brooks, standing lakes, and groves', transposed, with an apology, to replace Prospero's epilogue. But the play did not end there: Caliban had, if not the last word, at least the last gesture. There is a 'final tableau' as follows:

Prospero breaks his staff, at which there is lightning and thunder, followed by darkness. Through the darkness we gradually see once more a picture of the Yellow Sands enveloped in a purple haze. The Nymphs are again singing 'Come unto these yellow sands'. But their music is broken by the homing-song of the sailors, and we see the ship sailing away, carrying Prospero and the lovers, and all their train. Caliban creeps from his cave, and watches the departing ship bearing away the freight of humanity which for a brief spell has gladdened and saddened his island home, and taught him to 'seek for grace'. For the last time Ariel appears, singing the song of the bee. Taking flight at the words 'Merrily, merrily shall I live now', the voice of the sprite rises higher and higher until it is merged into the note of the lark—Ariel is now free as a bird. Caliban listens for the last time to the sweet air, then turns sadly in the direction of the parting ship. The play is ended. As the curtain rises again, the ship is seen on the horizon, Caliban stretching out his arms towards it in mute despair. The night falls, and Caliban is left on the lonely rock. He is a King once more.[1]

'King' is exactly Shakespearian, since Shakespeare regularly, as I have elsewhere insisted ('The Shakespearian Integrity', *The*

[1] This ending, presumably Tree's invention, appears to have become traditional on the Continent. See the conclusion to the review of Jan Kott's *Shakespeare notre Contemporain*, *T.L.S.*, 27 Sept. 1963; 744.

Sovereign Flower, 224), establishes the soul-worth, which is the royalty, of his every person: and among such achievements Caliban is perhaps of all his most impressive.

There is a picture showing the rocks and sand, the distant ship, and Caliban, a little drama of poignant appeal; and the reader may receive some faint impression of what was actually experienced at His Majesty's in 1904.

Drawing by Michael Wright after the painting by Charles A. Buchel

We can disagree, naturally. One of Tree's directions approaches a sentimentalizing of Caliban. But how often does one of our modern producers show such loving care, not so much of Shakespeare's text as of what he regards as the spirit within that text? How often do our modern adaptations show just this kind of integrity? Do their deliberate falsifications of the Shakespearian soul-centre not sometimes constitute a vandalism of which Tree could never have been accused? What producer today handles the more numinous and magical elements in Shakespeare *as though he believes in them*? When Tree offended, it was through his own creative exuberance; he offended as an artist; and as a deeply Shakespearian artist.

Despite his reputation for spectacular realism, Tree's greatest contribution appears to me to have been this: a realization of the spiritual, almost one might call it the 'eerie', in terms not only of sepulchral or demonic horrors or macabre characterizations but of colour and grandeur too. He devoted the same care to spiritual categories as he did to archaeological exactitudes, and was at pains to make them, too, realistic: or rather real, because if they exist they should be at their best no less colourful, indeed more, than normal existence. A typical achievement was his way of synchronizing plaintive, wraithly, speech with spectacle: I heard reports from the late Leslie Harris of the wraithly effect of the faintly drawn-out cry 'U-lys-sees' in his production of Stephen Phillips' *Ulysses*. More directly relevant here, and this I experienced myself, was the conclusion to a revival of *The Darling of the Gods*, a spectacular heroic drama of Japan by David Belasco and John Luther Long described by Mrs. Cran as 'a tale of honour, of love that betrays for the sake of love, of love that expiates for a thousand years in hell the sin against honour, and that meets finally, after the passage of the river of souls, in the first celestial heaven' (Cran, 64). The text is slight; the production was impressive. At the conclusion the heroine Yo-San was shown in vast sky floating up to meet her lover Kara while crying in a voice of spirit-timbre, 'Ka—ra, Ka—ra'. Today spectacle, colour and the sensuous are the preserves of trivial pieces. Tree aligned them with spiritual power.[1]

I do not hold up this particular scene as on the Shakespearian wave-length. I do nevertheless hold it up as an example of high theatric art of a nature which the future will perhaps understand better than we can today.

2. FORBES-ROBERTSON AND POEL

A contrast might be drawn between Tree and Sir Johnston Forbes-Robertson (1853–1937), whose elocutionary powers have been admirably discussed by Mr. Bertram Joseph (Joseph, 389–94). His vocal range was such that he could infuse the depth and colour of Shakespearian speech into an utterance that seemed perfectly natural. Nevertheless, I suggest that even so fine a technique may not, for all occasions, suffice. In the nineties he was regarded as

---

[1] A reviewer of Mr. Hugh Hunt's *The Live Theatre* in *The Times Literary Supplement* of 28 September 1962, in complaining of an illustration exemplifying 'the Actor-Manager's Theatre', writes: 'He would have done better to find an illustration of Tree's production of *The Darling of the Gods*, for its visual impact involved one young play-goer so deeply that it is still vivid in his recollection of its lyrical and terrible fascination.' Souvenir pictures are in the British Museum.

the exponent of a newly unostentatious style, called by the *Athenaeum* 'limpid' and 'quasi-realistic' but lacking in 'electricity' (Joseph, 386). Records of his speaking, done admittedly in old age, are held at the British Institute of Recorded Sound. The great voice we recognize, and the noble modulations, but the speeches do not, like Tree's, take wing.

I have discussed the architectural quality in Tree's record of Antony's speech. His range was limited, and his voice light; but something was re-created beyond any simple phrase by phrase repetition, however good. Forbes-Robertson's accents as the Stranger in *The Passing of the Third Floor Back* are among my most treasured stage memories; but for Shakespeare, we might argue that our results should flower less from the text than from the text's hinterland, or basis. Put otherwise, Shakespeare must be acted from within and not merely spoken, however perfectly.

Maurice Willson Disher in his study of Sir John Martin Harvey *The Last Romantic* observes in Forbes-Robertson a lack of facial vitality and regards his Hamlet as memorable not for what we 'saw' but for its speaking. He recounts his extraordinary ability in old age to perform a part movingly, seated and without facial expression. 'How much', he asks, 'of his spell as an actor had been created by his voice alone?' (Disher, 227). Whereas photographs of Tree in his parts almost leap from the page in animated variety, those I have seen of Forbes-Robertson's—except perhaps for one of Othello—show comparatively little change; there is the one grave demeanour. Nor does the whole figure appear to be acting, nor always organic to the various costumes. My suggestions may seem to be countered by Forbes-Robertson's 1913 *Hamlet* film, which I was privileged to witness this (1963) summer (see p. 18). A notice of it which appeared in *The Times* of 25 April 1960 referred, among passages of strong commendation, to 'the macabre expressions of a gaunt face with high cheek-bones, wide eye-sockets and a wide inflexible mouth'. The 'craggy face', though 'lacking in subtle expression', was called 'harshly virile'. I agree. For me, the performance was almost *too dynamic*. Gesture was restless, the torso's proper repose broken, and the whites of the eyes violent. Age was—as I found it at Drury Lane in the same year—a grave impediment, and a silent film, perhaps over-rapid, no fair test of acting developed for the stage. With these reservations, I suggest that the performance appeared, except for some superb moments of tragic terror, slightly off-centre and inorganic, as though Jerome K. Jerome's Stranger were being forced into galvanic actions unnatural and unworthy. It seems that Forbes-Robertson was, visually at least, most 'inside' his parts when varied acting was less important than vocal modulation and classic poise. At his 1913 farewell season at Drury Lane I recall being dissatisfied by the grey hair and heavily lined face of his Hamlet, which, despite his being a painter of distinction, were surely symptoms of a disregard to the stage importance of visual appeal. Youth may be more difficult than age to convey by make-up, but much can be done, as in the use of high-lights in my Romeo (Picture 1). Tree could make his face bulge for Falstaff without reliance on any devices beyond the artistry of grease-paint (Harker, 147). Was Forbes-Robertson's heart not wholly in his work? He himself writes, at the conclusion to his auto-biography: 'Never at any time have I gone on the stage without longing for the moment when the curtain would come down on the last act. Rarely, very rarely have I enjoyed myself in acting. This cannot be the proper mental attitude for an actor, and I am persuaded, as I look back upon my career, that I was not tempera-mentally suited to my calling' (*A Player Under Three Reigns*, 1925; 288).

In Shakespeare a total mental and physical re-creation is, both in acting and in production, always hazardous; it may lead to disaster; it may also be the one way to a result of genius; but genius is rare, and we are treading dangerous ground.

Forbes-Robertson had been trained by Samuel Phelps, whose unostentatious staging and emphasis on correct speaking may be aligned with the long campaign of William Poel (1852–1934) for new methods in Shakespearian production. Poel's life-work has been described by Mr. Robert Speaight in *William Poel and the Elizabethan Revival*. He demanded respect for the text, good speaking, continuity of action, and a stage approximating to Shake-speare's. Elizabethan staging, he maintained, was stately and not, as sometimes supposed, drab. Shakespeare's dramas were made of action and movement; these should be contained within a worthy architecture; but pictorial scenery he rejected. A Shakespearian play was largely a thing heard, and extraneous appeals to the eye dangerous. Poel was a master of stage grouping, and in terms of actor and architecture gained effects of dignity and strength.

Atmospheric lighting was allowed. His tenets are neatly summed by Mr. Speaight:

On the picture stage, the eye demands a picture. Poel himself would have been the first to admit this. The only point of constructing a frame is that you put a picture inside it. Poel admired the rich pictorial effects achieved by Irving at the Lyceum and by Tree at His Majesty's. All he maintained was that they were irrelevant to the imagery of Shakespeare's plays and destructive of their rhythm.

(Speaight, 80)

Whether all 'pictorial' effects are necessarily irrelevant to the imagery may be arguable, but the main contention that the picture-stage seen through a proscenium arch does not easily fit a play made for Shakespeare's Globe is valid.

Among Poel's most valuable contributions was his emphasis on fluent verse speaking dependent on a close regard to the natural emphases of rational speech and the avoidance of irrelevant and laboured stresses elsewhere. The right words were to be selected for emphasis and a pounding on others avoided. This is admirable advice; metric and stage-instinct may tempt us to irrational resonances and luscious vowellings out-of-tune with meaning; and these may have to be countered. Nevertheless, metric and stage instinct have their rights and a balance must be struck. Poel's principles go far to cover the problem provided that we have the vocal resources of a Forbes-Robertson to put them into practice. Sir Lewis Casson in a fine appreciation reported in *The Amateur Stage* of April 1963 tells us that Poel laid great stress on his text's 'tune', worked out for it a 'score', and cast his actors by their voices. Certainly rationality alone, without vocal colour—we are forced into a spatial metaphor—will not suffice; and Poel was as interested in verbal music as in verbal reason. The overtones of poetic speech are admirably discussed in Francis Berry's *Poetry and the Physical Voice* (1962).

Mr. Speaight tells us that despite his tenets Poel was on occasion too free in the cutting of his Shakespearian texts (Speaight, 104, 151, 173, 197–8, 258–63); whereas we find Shaw praising Tree for his truth to Shakespeare in *Henry IV*, and we are told that he always kept as close to his texts as exigencies allowed (Pearson, 92, 117–8). Our investigation bristles with paradoxes. Tree invited Poel to do a production at His Majesty's, for which he arranged front lighting and an 'apron' stage, or fore-stage, both of which were used subsequently by Tree for *Henry VIII* (Speaight, 121). Poel, on his side, not only admired Irving's and Tree's scenic effects but took a keen delight in W. Bridges Adams' 'stage pictures' at Stratford (Speaight, 235).

My only experience of Poel's work was a production of *The Taming of the Shrew* presented by John Martin Harvey at the Prince of Wales's Theatre in 1913, which I recall as either directed by Poel or at least done in accordance with his principles, with which Martin Harvey was in sympathy. Our general debt to Poel is inestimable. Much of what he fought for we today take for granted, and his achievement is the less definable for its success.

3. Craig

The four pillars of dramatic wisdom whom we are discussing show a divergence regarding the respective rights of (i) the sound and sense of spoken poetry and (ii) visual effects. In contrast to Poel and, as we shall see, Barker, both Tree and Gordon Craig (1872—) lay a heavy stress on the visual; it is not to be merely adequate, or formally pleasing; it is to be an interpretative element.

In *The Exemplary Theatre* Granville Barker regarded Edward Gordon Craig as a genius 'retired to' an 'absolute supremacy in a theatre of the clouds' (Barker, 209), cut off from the practical theatre by his uncompromising tenets. In discussing Craig's theories I shall rely mainly on the 1957 edition of *On the Art of the Theatre*.

After acting under Irving Craig became a producer, rejecting realism for more imaginative styles of simplicity and power. He quickly became renowned as an artist of atmospheric designs, especially in Europe, and has been vastly influential. He believed in colour and motion, and in 'significant actions' (*A of T*, 36); but, though he did a number of chosen productions, he tends to regard the body of fallen mankind as so intransigent to the mental will that true acting remains impossible, and what the producer, envisaged as an artistic despot, needs is accordingly some kind of perfected marionette (*A of T*, 54–94). He experimented with models and claimed to have devised a method by which the shifting planes of mobile screens under a variegated and colourous lighting could create a kaleidoscopic theatre (*Scene*, 19–27; Leeper, 19–20; Bablet, 185–6). He stated that Shakespeare, if performed at all rather than simply read, demands a scene, and a scene of a special, 'mobile' nature (*Scene*, 19–20, note), together with acting of heroic proportions sufficient to match the overpoweringly tall blocks of his own designs (pp. 224, 229 below).

Craig was not embarrassed by great dramatic texts; he looks deeper, behind all texts, to the essence. For the 'written play' (*A of T*, 53) he has slight respect, since the theatre—as indeed the name implies—is for seeing and not for listening or thinking; in the Barker-Vedrenne management of the Court Theatre he considered that authors dominated too strongly (*A of T*, 110). Shakespeare's fecund imagistic artistry, superb for reading, should not be confused by mixing it with appeals to other senses, and the plays should be only seldom performed. What Shakespeare says in poetry can be stated by other means. Painter and musician are, as such, dismissed; let all these keep to their own preserves (*A of T*, 118–23). Music itself is merely a derivative of 'the supreme force—movement', which the theatre serves (*A of T*, 47). It—though not scene-painting—may nevertheless be valuable as a constituent. Craig's early London productions (1900–1903), which included Purcell's *Dido and Aeneas*, admirably described by Denis Bablet, blended music, motion and soft-coloured lights (Leeper, 7–8; Bablet, 52–61). But silence may, it seems, be still better. A new art is announced within which a religion will be contained:

That religion will preach no more, but it will reveal. It will not show us the definite images which the sculptor and the painter show. It will unveil thought to our eyes, silently—by movements—in visions.

(*A of T*, 123)

Craig would appear to be envisaging some higher plane of existence, the realization of which is to be drama's final end and aim. Drama is to advance 'beyond reality' (*T A*, 120). His ranging imagination surveyed all manner of productions, closed or open to the air. At one point he describes an ideal theatre composed of costly metals worthy of the New Jerusalem (*T A*, 15).

'A new form of acting' is demanded based on 'symbolical gesture' (*A of T*, 61; compare pp. 224, 287, 299 below). Action is emphasized, the dance being regarded as the dramatic origin, and though words, colour and rhythm may be used, the action seen, and not anything heard, is his key. Man's 'keenest sense' is his eye and audiences are right when they flock to see, not hear, plays; he regards *Hamlet* as better read, whereas a truly theatric art should be incomplete without performance (*A of T*, 141–3). Craig nevertheless knew what was needed for a literary drama, stating that, given a text, a director will first feel its colour, tone and rhythm, and work from these (*A of T*, 149, 155–8). This *is* how a director should start. What may seem his excessive concentration on the dramatic essence enables him, when he does descend to earth, to get his priorities right. His Shakespearian practice must be judged by his Moscow *Hamlet*, done for mobile screens and lighting with Stanislavsky in 1912, to which Denis Bablet devotes a fascinating chapter. *The Times* accorded it high praise, but Craig was not satisfied, finding the combination of Shakespearian abundance and the inadequacies of contemporary stage-craft unassimilable to his cherished schemes. He today prefers to recall his earlier adventures in spectacle (Bablet, 194).

His main complaint regarding contemporary Shakespearian productions was levelled against their inadequate projection of the more supernatural elements. In 'On the Ghosts in the Tragedies of Shakespeare' he stresses the centrality of ghosts and spirits in Shakespeare's dramatic world:

These spirits set the key to which, as in music, every note of the composition must be harmonized; they are integral, not extraneous parts of the drama; they are the visualised symbols of the supernatural world which enfolds the natural . . .

(*A of T*, 264)

The producer of *Richard III*, *Hamlet*, *Macbeth*, *Julius Caesar*, *Antony and Cleopatra*, *A Midsummer Night's Dream*, or *The Tempest* must first 'woo the spirits in those plays'; only by becoming one with them will he become a 'master' of Shakespearian production (*A of T*, 266–7). They should not come as interruptions but should appear to grow from an atmosphere of 'unseen forces', whose 'presence' must be felt throughout (*A of T*, 270–1). When of *Macbeth* he wrote that 'we must open this play high up in an atmosphere loftier than that in which we generally grope' (*A of T*, 276) we may remember Tree's Valkyrie figures. Craig's essay is dated 1910, the year before Tree's production; there may have been an influence, one way or the other, perhaps in correspondence. The performance of *Macbeth* should be saturated in supernatural feeling:

And on the faces of the actors, on their costumes, and on the scene, by the light, by line, by colour, by movement, voice and every means at our disposal, I would repeatedly and repeatedly bring upon the stage some reminder of the presence of these spirits . . .

(*A of T*, 279)

We should be *expecting* the ghost of Banquo, feeling it before it appears. Here we have a master-mind at work. Craig writes as one to whom 'spirits' are a 'reality', and for whom Shakespearian production should be a means to a 'revelation of the unseen' (*A of T*, 278, 280).

For Craig the human drama is not only shadowed but itself interpenetrated by spirit-powers. That is why his actors must be able to perform in exact physical obedience to, or unison with, the over-ruling design (*A of T*, 165–72); acting is an art which demands a perfect fusion of spirit and body; and it is because, in his fallen state, man has lost this unity that Craig, at the limit, demands the 'über-marionette', which is his symbol of perfection.

He nevertheless recognized that a great actor can sometimes touch what he demands, and herein lies the importance of his study *Henry Irving* (1930). Irving's genius is usually described in terms of magnetism, or even mesmerism;[1] Craig, at home with the imponderables, can view it as technique. In answer to complaints regarding Irving's idiosyncratic speech and mannered walk he argues that his strange pronunciation restored to our language vowel-sounds once its own but since weakened; that his interrelation of words and actions was exactly devised; and that his walk was a kind of dance. More; that the total rhythm created from words and action was a Shakespearian rhythm. Irving created dances in exact attunement to Shakespeare's words and brought similar rhythms to the improvement of weaker plays (*Henry Irving*, 76–8). Since he 'was an actor and not the playwriter's puppet', a poor text could often draw out what was greatest in his art (Craig's *Irving*, 202–3). For his Moscow *Hamlet* —with no Irving—Craig counselled a minimum of movement, because so much was covered by the words (Bablet, 183).

Craig's study of Irving's genius is in direct line with his other, more uncompromising, manifestos; for in Irving he found, and

[1] Of his own dramatic lecturing, John Cowper Powys is reported to have said that 'it was from Irving that I learnt how to be a vampire, how to suck the blood from your audience while you yourself remain unexhausted' (Evelyn Hardy in *The Aylesford Review*, V, 1; Winter, 1962–1963).

for a while served, an actor in whom physique was malleable to mind. Craig claimed to see spirits and to have conversed with Irving after writing the book (*Henry Irving*, 241–7).

To return to *On the Art of the Theatre*. Irving's powers were a sign, a hint, of that yet greater art for which Craig is fighting. The theatre, he says, must develop its own creative, rather than interpretative, art, with no 'play' in our sense but a rich deployment of action, scene, gesture, colour and lights in significant dance-drama, any words used whether spoken or sung being such as are not devised for *reading* (*A of T*, 176–81). He would rediscover the lost art of the theatre as it once existed; the result will be the highest instruction through revelation (*A of T*, 236, 247–52); it will be an experience not of thought but of 'enchantment'. Of it he admits that he may know little, but this is the right 'direction' (*A of T*, 261).

He writes as from experience of some higher dimension beyond mortal existence:

This flesh-and-blood life, lovely as it is to us all, is for me not a thing made to search into, or to give out again to the world, even conventionalized. I think that my aim shall rather be to catch some far-off glimpse of that spirit which we call Death—to recall beautiful things from the imaginary world; they say they are cold, these dead things, I do not know—they often seem warmer and more living than that which parades as life. Shades—spirits seem to me to be more beautiful, and filled with more vitality than men and women; cities of men and women packed with pettiness, creatures inhuman, secret, coldest cold, hardest humanity. For, looking too long upon life, may one not find all this to be not the beautiful, nor the mysterious, nor the tragic, but the dull, the melodramatic, and the silly: the conspiracy against vitality—against both red heat and white heat? And from such things which lack the sun of life it is not possible to draw inspiration. But from that mysterious, joyous, and superbly complete life which is called Death—that life of shadow and of unknown shapes, where all cannot be blackness and fog as is supposed, but vivid colour, vivid light, sharp-cut form; and which one finds peopled with strange, fierce and solemn figures, pretty figures and calm figures, and those figures impelled to some wondrous harmony of movement—all this is something more than a mere matter of fact. From this idea of death, which seems a kind of spring, a blossoming—from this land and from this idea can come so vast an inspiration, that with unhesitating exultation I leap forward to it; and behold, in an instant, I find my arms full of flowers. I advance but a pace

or two and again plenty is around me. I pass at ease on a sea of beauty,
I sail whither the winds take me—*there*, there is no danger.

(*A of T*, 74-5)

Craig's 'über-marionette' will not 'compete with life' but rather surpass it:

Its ideal will not be the flesh and blood but rather the body in trance—it will aim to clothe itself with a death-like beauty while exhaling a living spirit . . .   (*A of T*, 84)

Art's life reflects 'the likeness of the spirit':

And in that picture, if the form be that of the living, on account of its beauty and tenderness, the colour for it must be sought from that unknown land of the imagination, and what is that but the land where dwells that which we call Death? So it is not lightly and flippantly that I speak of puppets and their power to retain the beautiful and remote expressions in form and face . . .

(*A of T*, 89-90)

In ancient times the divine was symbolized in puppet form; the symbol heralded 'the existence to come, which is veiled by the word Death' (*A of T*, 91-2). People copied it, and human performance arose; but the copy was a parody. We need, as fallen creatures, to re-engage that primal vision, retrace our steps through 'the return of the image', the 'über-marionette', to the theatre, until we learn again to honour creation and make 'intercession' with Death (*A of T*, 94).

What does it all mean? This: that Craig has his eye not on drama alone but on *that for which it exists*. Drama is to honour creation and make friends with death; put otherwise, it is to use earthly experiences and spectacles with spiritualized pointing, simultaneously ratifying 'life' and raising it to the higher power known as 'death'. Though he can write of marionettes and masks with enthusiasm, he can also tell us that his 'über-marionette' is a semi-divine 'symbol of man' that has nothing to do with metals and threads (*T A*, 111), and in his 1924 preface to *On the Art of the Theatre* he writes:

The über-marionette is the actor plus fire, minus egoism: the fire of the gods and demons, without the smoke and steam of mortality.

(*A of T*, ix)

That, crisply, sums the actor of genius. Much of it he found in Irving.

When he descends to human and Shakespearian terms, Craig's insights are keen: he knows where we go wrong, as when in 1921 he complained that Shakespeare's 'grand Ghosts', 'Autocratic kings' and 'splendid Aristocrats' were apparently in our century 'considered a bore' (*T A*, xxxi). He demanded actors who could cope with 'the heroic size' of Shakespeare's 'thought' and 'the stupendous force of his passion' (*T A*, xlvi). The lifting masses of his many vertical designs were impelled by an instinct for greatness, and to that extent were calculated to force the actor *up* to a commensurate stature (*T N T*, 33): if these masses appear excessive, the excess is the measure of a salutary discontent. Group these statements with his call for a new art of symbolical—which does not mean *unnatural*—gesture (p. 219 above; pp. 229, 287–8, 299 below), and we have Craig's most valuable contribution to Shakespearian production.

4. BARKER

Harley Granville Barker's Savoy productions of *The Winter's Tale* and *Twelfth Night* in 1912 and *A Midsummer Night's Dream* in 1914 remain for me, as I have earlier (pp. 21–2) recorded, vivid memories.

Barker (1877–1946) was a disciple of Poel. Both strove for fluency of speech and continuity of action; both eschewed picture scenery and aimed at breaking down the proscenium barrier. But there were differences. Poel's tendency was towards a kind of old-world, semi-Elizabethan, stateliness; Barker's productions, influenced perhaps by Gordon Craig,[1] were impressionistic. The result was quite new. The dominating impression, as I recall it, was one of whiteness, in stage, fore-stage, scene and pilasters; lighting from the front was white; and within flowered, as though by nature, formalised objects of various tone, and drop-curtains and costumes of exotic colour and bizarre design.[2] Though the productions were modern in conception, Cecil Sharp's Elizabethan airs infused them with an Elizabethan spirit. The result was *simultaneously solid and buoyant*. Formality might seem unimaginative; there was little thought behind the Noah's Ark garden trees for

---

[1] The relation of the two men is discussed by C. B. Purdom (Purdom, 162–3).

[2] Albert Rutherston (Rothenstein) designed the costumes for *The Winter's Tale*, Norman Wilkinson its settings and both costumes and settings for the other two plays. Coloured lights and green curtains were used in the third production.

Twelfth Night; I recall only one stroke of visual *interpretation*, in the gilded *asiatic* fairies of *A Midsummer Night's Dream*. But an intangible quality, a fragrance, an atmosphere, was created that was the more amazing for the restriction to solid objects and the refusal of atmospheric lighting and scenic vista. Various arts were fused to create, though in terms rather of fancy than of deep imagination (p. 290 below), a marvel.

The promise of these three productions was never subsequently fulfilled. Their note was pastoral and Barker seems not to have had the psychological equipment for the great tragedies; though the early scenes of *The Winter's Tale* were fierce. There is some truth in Mr. Bridges Adams' comment:

... I am glad the Barker of the Savoy didn't try his hand at *Everyman* or *Faustus*. Both Irving and Poel delighted, in their different ways, in stage-magic, whether in the form of a Witches' Sabbath or of a bloody Duncan[1] coming up with a bump through the supper-table. Barker, I believe, had some brilliantly thought-out Witches at the blue-print stage when the war cut him short—but they might have proved to be the Witches of a man who didn't hold with Witches.

(Letter to Robert Speaight; Speaight, 201)[2]

Barker was ready to accept the dubious scholarship of the time (see, for example, the introduction to the old Arden edition) in finding the Witch scenes in *Macbeth*, which aroused Tree to his Wagnerian best, as in part sorry 'stuff' to be dismissed as spurious (Purdom, 267). Barker's Shakespearian prefaces, despite their merits, lack the glamour, the tang and smell as it were, perhaps one might even say the vulgarity, of theatric art; despite their stage references, they are products of the academic rather than the histrionic intelligence. We may question whether his instincts would ever have been adequate to such typical Shakespearian powers as the Ghost in *Hamlet*; the Apparitions of *Macbeth*; the elemental grandeurs of *King Lear* and *Timon of Athens*; the sensuous and physical appeal of *Antony and Cleopatra*, which Tree developed to the full; or the vision of Jupiter in *Cymbeline*; though to the resurrection of Hermione in *The Winter's Tale* he brought an exact insight (see Marshall, 153–4).

[1] Poel followed Charles Knight in relating the Ghost's second appearance in the Banquet scene of *Macbeth* to Duncan (Speaight, 188–9).
[2] Mr. Bridges Adams' extended views on Granville Barker are set out in the booklet *The Lost Leader*, 1954.

My impression is borne out by some remarks of Bernard Shaw in *Drama* (New Series, 3; Winter, 1946):

Barker's productions of his own plays and Galsworthy's were ex-quisite: their styles were perfectly sympathetic, whereas his style and taste were as different from mine as Debussy's from Verdi's. With Shakespeare and with me he was not always at his happiest and best; but he was absolutely faithful to the play and would not cut a line to please himself; and the plays pulled him through with the bits that suited him enchanting and the scenery and dressing perfect . . . His only other fault was to suppress his actors when they pulled out all their stops and declaimed as Shakespeare should be declaimed. They either underacted, or were afraid to act at all lest they should be accused of ranting or being 'hams'.

To this Barker has his defence. In *The Exemplary Theatre* (1922) he states that while opposing old fashions he stands for a new 'virtuosity' in performance, though he leaves this 'virtuosity' undefined.

Theoretically *The Exemplary Theatre* often, perhaps again influ-enced by Craig, goes deep. Here Barker cannot be accused of a too academic reliance on texts:

Before ever the literary man and his manuscript appeared acting was there, and it remains the foundation of the whole affair.

(Barker, 89)

Though he is often thinking of modern plays like his own, his contentions cover all drama:

The better the play, the more full of matter, or the more brilliantly effervescent in style, the less excuse has its performance for being dull. But the more does it need acting; not only a fuller understanding, but a greater virtuosity of interpretation.

(Barker, 90)

That is precisely my own contention; but when Shakespeare is touched on *The Exemplary Theatre* gives no help as to what exactly will constitute this 'virtuosity of interpretation'. In his well known study of *King Lear* Barker tells us that the storm is to be acted with a more-than-realistic technique; but he explains no farther.[1]

[1] Contrast my own more explicit formulations on pp. 279–80 below. I did not see the 1940 *King Lear* at the Old Vic, in which Barker was joint producer with Lewis Casson. Barker's letters to Gielgud at the time contain some suggestions for perfor-mance. A fine direction comparing Mad Tom and the Ghost in *Hamlet* might seem

It seems that where the more numinous effects were in question, Barker knew in general and theoretical terms what was needed, but sheered off in practice. *The Exemplary Theatre* contains many exciting thoughts which bear various resemblances to Craig's doctrine and Tree's methods. Barker's theatre as a 'church of art' (Barker, 34) corresponds to the hieratic atmosphere of His Majesty's. His insistence that not the literary text as itself but rather its hinterland of suggestion should be our basis allows a freedom one might not have expected from him, but to be expected from Tree and Craig. The text, he says, is not to be learned first and then rehearsed; all is to grow organically; improvisations have their value, gestures and actions should not be dictated; performances may vary from occasion to occasion. Instead of a fixed plan and dominating producer (Barker, 209) the company is to be a democratic society working in selfless yet instinctive co-operation in service to the whole. Much, though it differs sharply from Craig's autocratic principles, has direct analogies to Tree's unorthodox and inspiratory methods in both performance and production. There is, however, one great difference: all depended on Tree's personality as a royal essence, or soul, permeating and inspiring the endeavour; and he engaged casts including star-performers. Barker's theories are sound, given one condition: a company of actors such as those Craig wanted, with genius but without egotism.

The most interesting concrete suggestions in *The Exemplary Theatre*, are, as one might have expected, the emphases on formal design and good craftsmanship for all stage objects and on the avoidance of any blurring by soft lights. Barker is an Apollonian artist; he likes what is sharp and clear, avoiding the Dionysian. We may complain that this will not cover all of Shakespeare, or Aeschylus. Barker's rationalistic limitations, as a man, are diagnosed by Mr. C. B. Purdom in his admirable study (Purdom, 280–3). As a producer however Barker has a great defence: 'Only the craftsman can make simplicity fine' (Barker, 211). And the Savoy productions had in them more than craftsmanship.

---

to counter my doubts regarding his sensitivity to the supernatural. See also the tribute and quotations included in Sir John Gielgud's recent *Stage Directions*. According to C. B. Purdom the production had 'little of the real Barker quality'. See Purdom, 261–3.

5. TREE AND CRAIG

It might be argued that much of what was best in the contributions of Poel and Barker has been assimilated but that the
challenges of Tree and Craig still face us.

It may seem strange to align Tree, our supreme example of
actor-manager and realistic showmanship, with their great
denouncer who in his dissatisfaction with actors made a plea for
the 'über-marionette' to take their place and for whom realism
was anathema. But Craig was himself a good actor, he respected
the great personalities of the stage, and his *Henry Irving* is the finest
study of an actor's genius in our language. As for 'showmanship'
we find Tree and Craig at one in the emphasis placed by both on
the visual. The labours of both grow from a natural soil. In his
Thoughts and After-Thoughts Tree regards Wagner, that great
pioneer of an inclusive theatre, as an exemplar; and in one of his
fictional dialogues Craig specifically asserts the greatness of Bay-
reuth, of the Lyceum and of His Majesty's in order to deflate the
over-confident superiority of a would-be disciple:

> You say you want to come to my school.
> I tell you you had better keep away unless you realize that you have
> firstly *no right* to despise the old stage, and secondly *no chance* of practis-
> ing the new Art until you have paid the very humblest tribute to the
> old institution, by studying all those things which at present you dare
> to despise. (*T A*, 234)

That is a characteristic and considered statement.

It was a period of dramatic vision, and it is not strange that
Tree's maturity should have synchronized with Craig's early manifestos. The dual challenge of both may be measured by the
opposition they have aroused. Craig's has been a life-long battling
and the yet-living challenge of Tree is witnessed by the denigratory falsehoods rising to gratuitous insult that still spatter, on
occasion, his name. Opposition is, as Tree knew, and once said,
a sign of impact. He forgave it in as attractive a dedication as our
literature affords, in *Thoughts and After-Thoughts*:

> To Mine Enemy I dedicate the faults of this book: to My Friend I
> dedicate what virtue it may have: hoping thus to give pleasure to both.

Both Tree and Craig had their limitations. Tree's we have
admitted; Craig incurs the criticism of letting his own artistry run

wild, too often, as T. S. Eliot has suggested (in *Drama*, New Series 36; Spring 1955), making designs that dwarf the actor with a visual assertiveness as dangerous as the conventions he was opposing. Craig on his part insisted that his designs were merely analogies in a flat medium to what he would realize very differently on the stage (*T A*, 93). He denied that he put a first emphasis on the scenic, claiming that he was primarily an actor (*T A*, xxxvi; *Scene* 13–14). His vertical set-designs were challenges to make the actor act greatly (*T N T*, 33); and he records that Salvini regarded them as a *liberating* medium (*T A*, 246–7).[1]

In contrast to Barker's more democratic tendencies Tree and Craig had what may be called 'royal' intuitions. Royalty exists at the meeting-point of earthly and beyond-earthly concerns; it signifies a spiritualizing of society. Craig writes:

I use the word 'Kingdom' instinctively in speaking of the land of the Theatre. It explains best what I mean. Maybe in the next three or four thousand years the word Kingdom will have disappeared—Kingdom, Kingship, King—but I doubt it; and if it does go something else equally fine will take its place. It will be the same thing in a different dress. You can't invent anything finer than Kingship, the idea of the King.   (*A of T*, 45)

Shaw found royalistic phrases necessary to define the enigmatic personality of Tree (pp. 203, 208 above), whose theatre was well named. The concept of royalty sinks deep into dramatic tradition and dramatic practice.

Tree and Craig, in different ways, laboured to make staging expand earthly perceptions. Tree, like Craig, laid a strong emphasis on the importance of ghosts and visions in Shakespeare (*T and A*, 305). Both believed in the necessity of a great style on every level for Shakespearian performance. Tree loved gesture, grandeur and crowds, for the manipulation of which he was renowned (Marshall, 143–4); of Antony's oration he wrote, 'The breath of the surging multitude is necessary to fill out the sails of his splendid rhetoric' (*T and A*, 306). Tree's skill in artist-types such as Richard II, his brilliance in fantastic characterizations and love of human pageantry and spectacle were all imaginative approaches from mankind as we know it towards Craig's human-

---

[1] For a criticism of Craig's claims see Norman Marshall, 35–41. Mr. Marshall, of course, admits his great value as an influence.

divine image glowing with 'earthly splendour' and yet 'unearthly simplicity' (*A of T*, 93). Tree worked from an *inclusive* and therefore complicated use of human and natural manifestations. He enlisted every possible sense-appeal, including music from his fine orchestra, physical sensuousness (as in his *Antony and Cleopatra*), and even incense (p. 21 above). Craig's interest in music falls below his delight in colour; he is mainly visual, striking directly for that spiritual essence towards which human creation drives, by-passing the complications. Tree too had his simplicity, though perhaps it needed the genius of Shaw to see it, recognizing a personality (p. 203 above) outspacing literature and even drama, rather as Craig saw Irving's genius as its own, non-literary, sovereign.

Whatever we think of Tree's silent Caliban on his island rocks watching the distant ship depart while Ariel sings, until all is silence speaking to the eye alone, the miniature drama is exactly what Craig would, or should, have liked, since he rates highest the drama of silence (*T A*, 13).[1] Of Irving he wrote:

Sometimes a whole scene was merely a succession of things done—acting, with the poor words used as props which hold up plants. Then it was we all drew up to attention; then we were moved; then we understood what it was to be an actor.

(*Henry Irving*, 202)

This comment serves to characterize Craig's approach. Beside it we may place Shaw's description of Tree's scene in *Richard II* showing Bolingbroke and the deposed Richard riding through London:

Shakespeare makes the Duke of York describe it. Nothing could be easier, with a well-trained actor at hand. And nothing could be more difficult and inconvenient than to bring horses on the stage and represent it in action. But this is just what Tree did. One still remembers that great white horse, and the look of hunted terror with which Richard turned his head as the crowd hooted at him. It passed in a moment; and it flatly contradicted Shakespeare's description of the

---

[1] For silence as ultimate reality compare Julian's trance-experience in Ibsen's *Emperor and Galilean*, 'There invisibility clothed itself in form and silence became sound' (*Caesar's Apostasy*, III); also 'the great silence' of the conclusion to *Little Eyolf* (see my study, *Ibsen*, 1962). In his *Four Quartets* Mr. T. S. Eliot writes of words reaching 'into the silence' (*Burnt Norton*, V) and 'music heard so deeply that it is not heard at all' (*The Dry Salvages*, V). This is the plane to which Craig's theories belong.

saint-like patience of Richard; but the effect was intense: no one but Chaliapine has since done so much by a single look and an appearance for an instant on horseback.

(Shaw; Beerbohm, 249)

The 'contradiction' is perhaps over-emphasized. Shakespeare's speech (V, ii, 23–40) describes a hostile mob, and Richard's 'tears' and 'smiles'. A moment of 'hunted terror' does not necessarily contradict Shakespeare. The look probably came without fore-thought, from living the occasion.

Tree's danger was his devotion to archaeological and other details; Craig's, the temptation to shirk the means in asserting the end, for it is the fate of fallen humanity to lift its weight, to transfuse materiality, unravel complications, to give impetus to inertia.

Craig, like Shaw, recognized Tree's genius (p. 203 above); and Barker praised the 'public spirit' with which he founded the Royal Academy of Dramatic Art (Barker, 39). Once when thinking of possible patrons for a proposed college of 'sound, light and motion' Craig writes:

That Sir Herbert Beerbohm Tree's name will be found in such company is far more likely than that he should join issue with those weary gentlemen whose love of adventure has left them.

(*A of T*, 240, 244)

For, as he knew, Tree was nothing if not adventurous, maintaining throughout his life a youthful expectance and a delight in new things.

Tree, on his side, invited Craig to offer designs for *Macbeth* and was 'delighted' with them (Pearson, 215). But something went wrong, he is said to have been persuaded by the scenic artist Joseph Harker not to use them (Leeper, 23), and the collaboration did not materialize. According to Harker's account, which does not mention Craig by name (Harker, 175–6), Tree did not like them. The main trouble appears to have been their height. The incident is discussed by Norman Marshall (Marshall, 39). Tree and Craig nearly came together again for a production of Gilbert Murray's translation of *The Bacchae* (Speaight, 172).

Tree could certainly be critical of the new styles, a letter to his daughter Viola of 4 October 1912 referring to Barker as 'preten-tious' and Craig as 'really not much better', though his talk was 'wonderful'; he claimed that his own *Hamlet* and *Macbeth* were simpler than such advanced productions, and that most of Shakespeare's plays, *Julius Caesar* especially, 'are entirely unsuited to the impressionistic treatment'; the forum is the forum 'just as Caesar is Caesar, a man'. The last point is well made: it is just because drama uses human forms that it cannot engage too far in the modernistic distortions that characterize the other arts; it *must*, to this extent, be realistic; and it was, in part, because he was up against this difficulty that Craig had to invent his 'über-marionette'. Tree accused the modernists of lack of reverence to Shakespeare; 'Craig *says* Craig is the most important thing' (Pearson, 160–1).

Nevertheless, this letter must not be supposed to cover Tree's views. The very next year he took his stage-manager to see Craig's *Hamlet* at the Moscow Art Theatre. Iris Tree records that though her father was often baffled by the extremities of modernism, he was deeply impressed by Craig's result:

However, some of the really great modern things, notably Gordon Craig's *Hamlet*, which he saw in Moscow, he admired infinitely. He described this as a wonder of gold kings and courtiers from which background the tiny black figure of Hamlet detached itself—described it as he alone could, very slowly, sometimes using gestures to fill the gap of words, which made us hold our breath for fear of losing the sense.

(Viola Tree; Beerbohm, 176; and see *T and A*, 155)[1]

Her comment runs:

Two parallel lines, they say, never meet, and it seems cruel that these two great figures, Craig and himself, born to work together, should have been parted by a sea of misunderstandings, though they occasionally tried to throw rocket signals to each other across the void. Together they would have been gigantic.

(Viola Tree; Beerbohm, 176)

[1] In *Towards a New Theatre* Craig includes a sketch of the scene, writing (81): 'This is the Second Scene, First Act of *Hamlet*, as it was produced by me, with Mr. Stanislawsky's assistance, in the winter of 1911 at the Moscow Art Theatre. You see the stage divided by a barrier. On the one side sits Hamlet, fallen, as it were, into a dream, on the other side you see his dream. You see it, as it were, through the mind's eye of Hamlet. That which is behind him is like molten gold. It is the Court of the King and Queen of Denmark. It is the grotesque caricature of a vile kind of royalty.' By 'one side' Craig means 'the down-stage part' since the stage is divided across. Craig would have the King speak his long speech as a kind of 'automaton'. The particular reading appears rash, but the design has interest as an example of Craig's Shakespearian practice. The production opened on 8 January 1912 (Rose, 100).

We have understood neither until we understand this to be an inevitable comment. Tree and Craig in their own fashions upheld the more spiritualized and cosmic traditions of dramatic art. Both Tree in his histrionic transformations and Craig in his scenic inventions might be called men of 'kaleidoscopic' genius. More generally both are chameleon-like; when you think you have crushed either with criticism, he turns into something else. They and Irving might be called the three men of compelling genius in our stage history of the last hundred years.

6. Some Conclusions

A distinction may be drawn between what is desirable for the future of dramatic art and what is best for Shakespeare. For us, as Craig, who makes this distinction, realizes, Shakespeare is the right start (Craig, *T A*, li–lii); but even so the instinct for visual artistry must not be ignored. For theatric art widely considered futurity is likely to justify it: the cinema has already to some extent done so and for drama itself there are fields awaiting exploration. Of this general movement Shakespearian production cannot remain wholly independent.

To my mind, the best contributions of Poel and Barker to Shakespearian production were themselves visual in that, while rejecting the flatly pictorial, they threw a newly rounded emphasis on architecture, formal design, solid objects, and human figures. They did little in visual design as a means to interpretation: that was left mainly to the acting and the speaking, and many will regard this as right. But a difficulty arises.

In poetry both sound and sight play their parts, the sound being actual, the sight mental (p. 60 above). We, living in a peculiarly visual age, have been able, for the first time, to unlock the visual powers in Shakespeare, to see more precisely his colourings in image and symbol, and detect their hidden meanings. My own work has been analogous to the splitting of the atom; it has *let the pictures out*, and they can never again be rehoused as formerly. A modern audience, anyway, needs more interpretation of the spoken poetry than did Shakespeare's. Both Tree and Craig were up-to-date; they realized the needed direction for their century. So did the poet-dramatist, John Davidson when, in the Prologue to *Scaramouch in Naxos* (1888), he wrote:

Which of the various dramatic forms of the time may one conceive as likeliest to shoot up in the fabulous manner of the beanstalk, bearing on its branches things of earth and heaven undreamt of in philosophy? The sensational dramas? Perhaps from them some new development of tragic art; but Pantomime seems to be of best hope. It contains in crude forms, humour, poetry, and romance. It is the childhood of a new poetical comedy.

'Undreamt of in philosophy': Hamlet's words were quoted by Craig too to support his cosmic dramaturgy (*A of T*, 280). Davidson was thinking presumably of fairyland effects such as those in Planché's extravaganzas.[1]

Professor Merchant has recently complained of the 'puritanism' by which 'sight' is today regarded as of lower dramatic status than 'word and character' (Merchant, 235). Disrespect to the visual rights of drama leads to confused and untidy settings, or settings which contribute, which indeed are, nothing. And yet they can never quite be that; if they are not pleasing, they will be displeasing. Poel's Elizabethan architecture, Barker's formality, Tree's splendours, Craig's atmospherics, all alike witnessed a respect for setting. Simplicity may be meaningful but untidiness, drabness, emptiness, *the will to visual nothingness for its own sake*, these are fatal. The action becomes rootless and the actors weak. The only way to dispense with setting is, as Tree observed (*T and A*, 59), to dress your actors in ordinary clothes, and refuse further pretence. Craig once said much the same, demanding either everything real or everything conventionalized (*T A*, 204–7; and see pp. 218–9 above). It is true that a rehearsal may often achieve an intensity rare in performance (e.g., Speaight, 79–80); and somewhere near this field we shall find the open stage (pp. 284–300 below) asserting its claims.

All our authorities would agree that the *human figure in action* is our base. It must not be crushed by scene or dissolved by lighting; and as for words, words themselves are a variety of action. We have accordingly, for Shakespeare three choices: (i) to speak the unrealistic poetry in a fairly plain set while acting more or less realistically, like normal men; (ii) to act normally, but support the poetry by scene and illumination; and (iii) *to act the poetry itself*, on every level of performer and production. The first concen-

[1] An account of Planché's extravaganzas is given in my study of British Drama, *The Golden Labyrinth*, 1962.

trates on temporal flow; the second on spatial sight; and the third may be related to 'space-time'. There is a necessary interplay between (i) and (ii), which in any case correspond to the constituents of all drama discussed above (pp. 35–41). But, where acting is concerned, our third choice has never been properly developed, though Craig and Barker talked of it in general terms. Of our four pillars, as I have called them, of dramatic wisdom, Tree alone came near it. Some suggestions of my own are given below (pp. 279–80). I claim that my own stage work, with all its blunders, has made the needed advance.

We must start from a firm recognition that poetic acting is not simply a matter of speaking well. Of Irving, Craig, in a passage of the utmost importance for every actor, wrote:

> Irving was essentially an actor, not an orator. While every sentence of a role was to him of the utmost importance, he was ever mindful to act before he spoke, and then to follow up the words by acting again.
>
> Before a phrase or a word Irving would always do something, so that the spectator should never be in doubt as to what the phrase or word was intended to mean; and he gave words special meanings. He was an actor, and not the playwriter's puppet.

(*Henry Irving*, 202)

If such a technique is right for ordinary acting, it is still more necessary where the deeper content of poetry is our concern. Shakespeare's *poetic* meanings are likely to be far from clear to the audience. Physical expression can do much to make them clear (pp. 279–80 below).

Tree's liking of fantastic parts that lent themselves to a visible projection corresponded to his love as a producer of spatial excitements and extravagances. In the many pictures of his characterizations every detail of physical posture, expression and costume expresses the conception. Above all, note his eyes. The actor's eye should be no passive reflector merely, but an *agent*. To account scientifically for its power, we should have to fall back on the physics of an earlier period. Irving too was a master of facial expression (Joseph, quoting Clement Scott, 374). Craig, in theory at least, preferred finely executed masks (*T A*, 113–27).

An extraordinary example of Tree's artistry occurred during his *Othello* in 1912. Mr. Hesketh Pearson, who was a member of his company, writes to me:

Once, in the first week, he walked about nervously beneath the stage muttering 'This is a dreadful part, a terrible part—my voice won't stand it—it's going already'. It went all right, and for the last weeks of the run he acted in a whisper, which however was more audible than the average actor's full-lunged voice.

I myself attended before that happened, but could wish that I had experienced so extraordinary a *tour-de-force* of visual acting.

No clear line demarks the acting of 'character' creations from those sublime and poetic; both equally depend on a permeation of the physical organism by the soul. Pictures of Tree in Stephen Phillips' *Nero* (Cran, facing p. 94) and *Richard II* (Pearson, facing p. 130) show that he had as an actor the requisite poise and grandeur and the will to their use, corresponding to Craig's demand for a great style in Shakespearian acting and expectance of new techniques based on symbolic gesture (pp. 219–24 above).

Nothing *less* than an acting equipment such as Irving's or Tree's will be needed for the fully *embodied* acting which we aim at of Shakespearian poetry; or rather for the acting from within of that which is within the poetry, so that face and gesture momentarily live (see pp. 49–50, 279–80) the phantasmagoria which it contains. Shakespeare's Richard explains the process:

> Say that again.
> 'The shadow of my sorrow.' Ha! let's see.
> 'Tis very true, my grief lies all within;
> And these external manners of laments
> Are merely shadows to the unseen grief
> That swells with anguish in the tortur'd soul.
>
> (*Richard II*, IV. i. 293)

The 'external manners' are both words and actions. The actor must aim *deliberately* at the actions, since paradoxically an attempt at physical expression will often force him within the otherness, putting him, as we say, 'inside his part', whereas immediate concentration on the words, which will nevertheless have given him his general direction, may not in fact do this. By concentrating on the physical, which is the spatial, we touch the soul-centre; by thinking mainly of the words in temporal sequence we remain within the prison of the abstracting intellect. As so often materiality and spirit are found on the one side, intellect on the other.[1]

---

[1] For the acting of poetic meanings I am a little uncertain whether the old rule of action preceding speech holds good *at the moment of performance*. Probably it does, the eye at least registering an infinitesimal moment before the phrase.

Tree and Craig; Poel and Barker

What then of the speaking? Tree was at pains to dissociate himself from any too great a reliance on eye and scene (*T and A*, 47, 57–8); his instincts were Wagnerian and inclusive, as when in *Antony and Cleopatra* he used 'voluptuous music' for Cleopatra countered by 'sterner notes' for Rome (Pearson, 133); with some justice he claimed to be serving Shakespeare in letter and spirit with every means at his disposal. But more is needed than the rational pointing on which Poel rightly insisted or the rapid flow which Barker, in reaction against a heavy tradition, was in danger of over-emphasizing.[1] Some of the further necessities are discussed below (pp. 275–84); a sense of verse-architecture is needed, of the formal, and so spatial, nature of any one long Shakespearian speech, or movement of speeches. Beyond that, the voice's actual timbre should transmit overtones which cannot be easily defined. George Henry Lewes writes: 'The tones which stir us need not be musical, need not be pleasant even, but they must have a penetrating, vibrating quality' (*On Actors and the Art of Acting*, 1875; 'Shakespeare as Actor and Critic'; 91). Such a voice Tree pre-eminently had. In 1949[2] I wrote:

Our age is one of poor dramatic understanding, but great dramatic interest. We feel that the theatre has something for us, but we fear this very 'something'; we love drama, but remain in terror of the dramatic. It is a pity; for the noblest dramatic art must always be steadied on a firm basis of over-statement, over-emphasis and exaggerated action; only so can one equip oneself for the greater roles and free one's powers for rhetoric and subtlety alike.

'Over-acting' is a dangerous misnomer. There is good acting and there is bad acting. Bad acting, if at all powerful, will be found to be putting the emphasis at the wrong place, finding a climax where no climax exists, like the over-swinging of a golf tyro violently sweeping the air and merely tapping the ball. Good acting hits the ball much harder—but it is the ball that it hits.

And yet the actor does not express an ordinary emotion. He expresses an artistic, a stage, emotion. One often finds to-day a fear of

[1] I saw the Savoy *Winter's Tale* on its second night. Henry Ainley's speaking seemed to me—admittedly I had been used to His Majesty's where the words were very exactly articulated—far *too* rapid. It may have been slowed down subsequently. Both Mr. Bridges Adams in *The Lost Leader* and Mr. W. A. Darlington in *Six Thousand and One Nights* have paid memorial honour to the power of Ainley's Leontes.

[2] This and my subsequent passage are taken from my essay 'Drama and the University' which was printed as an appendix to the 1949 Penguin edition of *Principles of Shakespearian Production*.

'over-acting' together with a faulty exhibition of raw, personal feeling. For stage-work a stage speaking must be developed; almost you might say a certain vocal convention mastered, within which a whole gamut of emotional and intellectual themes can be rendered without strain. It is not merely noise and ranting that we distrust: these can be left to the tender mercies of any audience. The danger is more subtle: we fear stage speaking itself, with all its varied artistry of pause and climax, its calculated emotional effects, its colour and resonance. We are morbidly afraid of anything 'old style' in voice or gesture; all grandeur is taboo. We are far too contented with our own impoverished period, and the result in reading or performance remains—what it is.

The actor does not merely imitate; he recreates, from the depths within, a new and strangely variable personality. He is not just disguising his ordinary self; he is always making, or discovering, a new self. He is continually, in religious phraseology, being 'born again'.

An actor's stage speaking may well show a tonal difference from his normal speech, as though mined from some deeper level within the personality, whose rough but glittering quartz waits to be wrought into vocal, or other, artistry. Some people are born with a 'golden voice'; others by labour develop what is given them. Too good a natural voice may certainly prove dangerous; while to take conscious pleasure in one's own speaking is always fatal. Many a professional Shakespearian actor remains content with the voice and a few stock variations, without attuning it to every shade of the required emotion and splitting it into the variegated tints of meaning. The golden voice has then become an overdose of treacle. Such an actor is at the best always painting the same picture. But for most amateurs, and many modern professionals, the danger is the reverse. The film technique of muttered asides has vitiated our judgements.

My definitions are vague: for a more closely reasoned study of the sound-values in spoken poetry I would point again to Francis Berry's *Poetry and the Physical Voice* (1962); and for a more esoteric account, to the theories of Rudolf Steiner.

The rival rights of sound and sight in poetry cannot be easily distinguished; for the *reading* of poetry sound may come first; for the *staging* of poetry, sight has equal, or greater, rights. My own literary labours have been largely concerned with what might be called the visual staging of poetry, its symbols, images and colours, within the mind's theatre; they are basically *theatrical*. In the theatre the visual is not only a way of transmitting intellectual meanings; it has also its own peculiar importance. The eye is the source equally of lusts and visions: 'vision', 'seer', 'imagination', 'intuition', 'theatre'—all connote some kind of *seeing*. The eye is potentially the 'most pure spirit of sense' (*Troilus and Cressida*, III. iii. 106) and we go to the theatre for its purification. There, as Craig tells us, the 'divine power of Movement' is to reveal the 'invisible' things seen 'through the eye and not with the eye' (*A of T*, 46). Stage action prompts speech; but speech, and especially poetic speech, is to be crowned by action. T. S. Eliot once wrote that words in Shakespeare are merely 'shorthand' for the 'acted' play, the beautiful phrase standing 'for a greater beauty still' ('Seneca in Elizabethan Translation', I). The greatest Aeschylean or Shakespearian poetry, itself first prompted by *realistic* events and actions, may be next regarded as subsidiary to the creation of *poetic* actions, poses and groupings. Irving's instinct for actions before and after speech (p. 235) may suggest as a typical unit for poetic drama (i) some realistic event and action; (ii) colloquial blending into poetic speech; (iii) poetic acting. Such sequences, small or large, will be always being repeated, and the final poetic poses, after having been rendered substantial by the poetry, will exist in their own right as the poetry's consummation, awaking the consciousness. Human advance depends on the imagination; on *seeing* what we next attempt to *think*; only so can man surpass himself; and the greatest dramas are agents in this process. Their business is not to make us feel at home, but rather to awake the imagination and expand the consciousness through experiences both prompted and ratified by visible grandeurs.

All converges on the actor. I quote again from my 1949 essay:

There are two main deficiencies in our twentieth-century acting. One is the inability, or lack of desire, to use the full spectroscope of the voice, confining its tones to a monotonous grey, and missing therefore not only the rhetoric and emotional song of great drama, but, since all depends on relation and contrast, the real grip of the colloquial too.

The other limitation is the confining of acting to heads and hands. True acting must search for expression throughout the body; and here the *Comédie Française*, to judge from their performance of *Phèdre* in London in 1945, have developed a technique in advance of our own performers. This is why Timon is so interesting a part and why his play has been, on the whole, so strangely ignored. The last acts demand body-acting. A true understanding of *Timon of Athens* might point the path to a new extension in dramatic art, using the body more freely and thereby the more able to sound depths of universal and poetic meaning.

That last statement points ahead to investigations that go beyond my present study.[1]

Nietzsche saw the origins of drama in music, Craig in the dance. Already in Shakespeare's day Ben Jonson is found complaining of the way spectacle in the Masques detracted from his poetry; and the appeal of opera has often enough been attacked. It would however be waste of time to argue at any length on the respective metaphysical rights of sound and sight, for the simple reason that drama aspires to the higher plane envisioned by Craig in his more extreme statements; there we may suppose the separate sense-inlets to be so transcended that reality is not by them any longer constricted; and in this state, which will be the state beyond death on the 'astral' or 'etheric' plane, spirit-communicators assert that sound *is* sight and music colour. Craig with his visual insistencies does not quite say this but it is precisely what he achieved in his early productions (Bablet, 55-6, 244); and he later planned a production in the round to accompany Bach's *St. Matthew Passion* with symbolic action (Ifan Kyrle Fletcher; *The Amateur Stage*; April 1963). Here we are at the philosophical heart of the dramatic enigma. Of our four pillars only Tree, whose life was so largely devoted to the harmonization of sensory experiences, appears to have left us an explicit comment. At one point in his story *Nothing Matters* there is a sudden merging of 'abstract and concrete'; and 'in such moments', we are told, 'sight, sound and thought are of one substance' (*N M*, 17; and see 50, 191). In the essay appended as 'Epilogue' to his drama *The Triumph of Mammon* (*The Golden Labyrinth*, 312-6) John Davidson wrote:

Once as I walked in Westminster a sunbeam touched the knell of noon with amber light. Touched it? No; the deep-throated vibrant noise, a rich integration of many sounds, mingled with the dazzling sunlight, a rich integration of many a rainbow; and the twain became one flesh; the sound the soul of light, and the light the soul of the sound. When the ultimate analysis is made, it will be found, I believe, that light and sound are identical . . .   (156)

Such was Davidson's intuition of 'light and colour, sound and music, the ethereal warp and woof of the matter of which we ourselves are woven' (162).

[1] Some years ago I composed an elaborated and illustrated exposition analysing the significances of the human form in various postures according to the system of François Delsarte. It is however a study which appears to be too far in advance of our time for immediate publication. Craig refers slightingly to Delsarte (*T A*, 82).

'We ourselves'; once again, however far our flight and deep our metaphysic, we return to the human form; to the actor himself.

In poetry sound and sight are one; the poetic image, itself single, is made from both; and stage art exists to *expand poetry* into a more than intellectual experience. It is an error to suppose that anyone of literary intelligence listening to perfect speaking in a plain setting will experience *all* that is contained in the Shakespearian poetry: he will merely remain as he was, in his intellectual prison. Seeing, as the saying goes, is believing; and the imagination of man is the mechanism by which he surpasses himself through the adjustment of thought to vision. Music, colour, action, words: that is our sequence. This is why in our traditional theatres we have first music, to attune us to Dionysian acceptance; then, the curtain draws, revealing our set in Apollonian design; and so, the eye filled by this and next by figures in action, we not only hear but live the spoken poetry as it flowers naturally from the total drama and becomes embodied before our eyes in human form.

CHAPTER IX

Contemporary Presentations

───────

1 [1949][1]

That my views on Shakespearian production are in our society heterodox, I well recognize; but it seems best to state, unequivocally, that my objection to much that passes current remains deep-rooted. There is room for divergences of opinion on detail, but to certain basic Shakespearian realities our contemporary stage is, as I see it, blind. It is not that the workmanship is bad; on the contrary, one cannot but feel respect for the efficiency shown. But something, some soul-essence, some metaphysical centrality, some heart to the organism, is missing. Too often the production is all surface, all body, all pieces, like the animal in *Julius Caesar* in which they 'could not find a heart within the beast'. Sometimes a very little would be needed to turn a third-rate into a first-rate effect: let that actor hold his fine position a second longer; remove that one unfortunate setting; let that particular sound-effect be correctly timed and then allowed to reverberate as it should instead of being done perfunctorily; why then, an improvement would be registered out of all proportion to the labour engaged. Our technical skill lacks guidance.

The implications go deep. For what is it that is being suggested? The very thing against which the current artistic intelligence is set with consistent hostility. I am urging the build-up of the great, the grand in manner, the elemental, the universal; in short, and to avoid all misunderstanding, the romantic. We live in an un-

───────

[1] This section is composed of selections, adjusted with a few link-phrases for my present purpose, from my chapter 'The Professional Stage' in the 1949 Penguin edition of *Principles of Shakespearian Production*. In reprinting my paragraphs on Sir Donald Wolfit I use the title with which he was subsequently honoured.

romantic age, and it may be argued that it is necessary to produce and act Shakespeare unromantically. This however one must say: we are not performing Shakespeare: we are acting only so much as a modern audience can without trouble assimilate. Shakespeare accordingly entertains, up to a point; he is not allowed to dominate.

I offer first a review of the 1946 Old Vic *King Lear* at the New Theatre in which Sir Laurence Olivier was both producer and protagonist.

The conception of King Lear's first scene was original. One is brought up to expect, and usually one gets, a fierce, intolerant old man striding to his central position and casting a fiery eye on his subject family and lords. Here we had a very different conception. The throne was up-stage, centre. The stage centre itself was occupied by some six attendants bowing first right at Goneril's, then left at Regan's, entry. The main persons were grouped at the sides. Lear entered from one side, quite informally, and threaded his way among the attendants. Arrived at his throne, he was partly masked, his stage centrality and dignity discounted. He struck one from the start as a slightly fussy, almost roguish and very lovable, if at times irritating, old man. He whispered to Cordelia on his way as though enjoying a private joke with her. This reading was maintained. The renunciation of his love for Cordelia was light in carriage; his 'on thy allegiance' to Kent lacked ferocity and finality. Lear was shown as a wilful, almost naughty, old man, but not, even momentarily, as sinning. All was done with a delicacy of touch that was, after its fashion, satisfying. But only with reservations.

For is this a possible reading? Does it follow the curves of the dramatic rhythm? More: does it grow organically from the play's heart? If Lear and Cordelia enjoy a private whisper here, surely that implies a mutual understanding and confidence that makes her later repudiation peculiarly cruel, whereas if one regards her as having been kept at a distance by a dominating and rather tyrannic, though greedily loving, father, then her sulkiness falls into place. Moreover, can we possibly associate with this reading such lines as these:

> For, by the sacred radiance of the sun,
> The mysteries of Hecate and the night,
> By all the operation of the orbs
> From whom we do exist and cease to be,

> Here I disclaim all my paternal care,
> Propinquity and property of blood,
> And as a stranger to my heart and me
> Hold thee from this for ever! The barbarous Scythian
> Or he that makes his generation messes
> To gorge his appetite, shall to my bosom
> Be as well neighbour'd, pitied and reliev'd
> As thou, my sometime daughter.

and

> Peace, Kent!
> Come not between the dragon and his wrath!

The lines demand to be mouthed. Their ferocity is of a recognizable Shakespearian type. Tyrannic fathers are usual in Shakespeare and when thwarted imprecate hideous doom on their children: it happens with Capulet, Egeus, York in *Richard II*. Their unnecessarily harsh and bombastic manner recalls the outburst of Isabella against Claudio. At such moments we are aware of some repressed unease stung to sudden fury, as when Leontes is confronted by Paulina holding his child. Lear's early passages are barbed by this irrational fury. They witness psychic energies not properly geared to his conscious mind. They *are* indeed precisely the substance of his later madness, and a whimsical Lear cannot grow into the Lear of the Storm scenes; the stuff is not there. I conclude that the traditional reading is correct and necessary; that certain qualities of the stagey old actor—why does every age talk of that undying type: is it possible that we merely mean the experienced actor?—is required to make sense of this stormy opening.

The later action suffered in consequence. Had the opening been given with more gravity and fury, then the central performance would have been, in the main, admirable. But it could not properly register after this questionable start. It was as a pillar with no foundation.

So much necessarily depends on the gradual reduction of Lear's false dignity and the final enthroning, by the way of madness and humility, of a more spiritualized royalty. The shock and pathos of his gradual breaking lose greatly if he is not first shown as an almost repellent tyrant. Certainly he must have some obvious dignity to be broken. If he is too lovable at the start, he ceases to be tragic later, not just because the correction of a fault is at stake, but because tragedy depends on depth, or weight. The light, humorous reading was dangerous on yet another count. Lear is essentially humourless. It is because the Fool dimly realizes that if Lear could be brought to laugh at himself his sanity might be preserved that he so remorselessly concentrates his own witticisms on the crucial issue. Twice Lear becomes, unknowingly, comic: when he caps his own violences with 'But I'll not chide thee' and 'No, I will be the pattern of all patience; I will say nothing'. These were given boldly, if subtly, as comedy, raising once a legitimate laugh. But Lear is comic only because he has no humour in him where his own behaviour is concerned. He can scarcely therefore be a whimsical type. This dangerous reading caused one of Lear's neatest later scenes to suffer: I mean his entry in full madness decorated with flowers. This can be done—normally I should say it should be done—as a scene of greatness in pathetic ruin. Here it was taken as essentially lyrical, pretty, lovably so, not unlike Ophelia's madness:

> Thought and affliction, passion, hell itself,
> She turns to favour and to prettiness.
>
> *(Hamlet*, IV. vii. 187)

The reading is risky, but consistent with the text, and one which renders the risks Shakespeare has forced the less dangerous; for here the 'mouse' and 'toasted cheese' passage and the cruelly difficult running exit grew naturally from the conception. Lear was a child again. Had this been grafted on to, or rather flowered from, a performance starting with suggestions of a despotic grandeur, it would have been of an extreme, if delicate, poignancy, darting light into the gloomiest caverns of mental agony. As it was—one must return to the complaint, if only because certain tiny tricks of expression kept reminding one that this was the same whimsical figure of the opening—Lear had already shown a Puckish humour; he had from the opening been a lovable, child-like figure. The contrast, and Shakespeare works continually by such contrasts, was gone.

The play's heart is the Storm scene, or scenes. These provide a complex of fascinating problems and the New Theatre production raised them in a peculiarly interesting fashion. Here, if anywhere, the critic of romantic and metaphysical leanings is likely to have reason for attack; here, if anywhere, I found myself all but whole-hearted in admiration.

Normally such imaginative set-pieces as Lear's two opening declamations demand some static formality, imprinting, if only for a moment or two, the temporal with eternal status. Here the first words were spoken in complete darkness; then the lights came up sufficiently to show Lear and his two[1] companions separated, or at least separating, Lear walking apart, alone, across, and down. The heath was suggested by a ground-roll upstage and lightning intermittently thrown on the cyclorama in fiery zigzags. The main lighting was used intermittently, the stage being dark and illuminated by turns; words were spoken under both conditions. The general result was not chaotic. By careful orchestration, Lear's walk took him down-stage to catch a sudden beam for an important piece of declamation; then he was moving again, in darkness. Sometimes all three figures were close together under a level lighting. There were accordingly at least four sorts of light-effect: (i) complete darkness, (ii) zigzags, (iii) Lear picked out alone, (iv) reasonably full lighting showing all three actors. These effects—there may have been others, such as silhouettes against a half-lit cyclorama—were interwoven with continual movement. The persons were felt as coming together and parting; they were, very clearly, wandering about a tempest-riven heath. Sound-effects were adequate and not allowed to smother the words. This is purely a matter of timing and to talk of an actor as 'dominating' the thunder is therefore meaningless. No actor has ever existed whose voice could register through a really effective thunder-clap. Though Granville Barker in his essay on *King Lear* was right in wanting the actors to act the tempest themselves, he was wrong in simultaneously discounting—as he did, it seems, intend—the dramatic power of sounds. No—let the two effects of voice and thunder intershade. In this the opening of the Olivier tempest-scene succeeded. The orchestration of voice, sounds, lights and stage movement was efficient.

The method was risky. It was fundamentally realistic rather than symbolic, except in so far as an artistic realism in such a scene inevitably becomes symbolic. One was less aware of man elevated to an elemental challenge than of distraught wanderers having poetry drawn out of them by fits and starts. The play on darkness, the picking out of separate figures, the sharp intermittency in place of gradation—all are, normally, dangerous in

[1] Kent presumably was the second, probably at a distance. [1963]

Shakespeare. Yet here, at this moment—for we are still considering Lear's first two speeches—of this drama, and with this actor,
they succeeded.

I say 'with this actor' for an especial reason. I have seen Olivier
in a number of films: his Heathcliff especially appealed to me. In
Shakespeare, I have seen only his Coriolanus, Justice Shallow,
and his film of *Henry V*. Of his film work, both as actor and as
director, no one will do anything but speak in the highest terms.
Of his verse-speaking there is a possible criticism. I observe a
tendency to rely on sudden changes of voice; to speak some lines
quietly, colloquially, and then, without warning, two, three, or
four—not many as a rule—with full rhetorical force. The result
is a shout, since without gradation relevance and significance are
lost. The two terms of the Shakespearian poetry, the realistic and
the rhetorical, are present; what is strange is their discontinuous,
ungraded, intermittency. This characteristic, which appears to be
a deliberately considered technique, was less noticeable in *King
Lear*, but it was not absent. The part, however, lends itself to this
technique, jerking from colloquial triviality to poetic grandeur,
or *vice versa*. Lear talks quietly to Regan, attempting gentleness,
and then breaks out 'Who put my man i' the stocks?' These inter-
mittences throughout Lear's long preliminary torment are vital
and the treatment was correspondingly successful. In the Storm
scene the sharp alternations of light synchronized with chosen
positions exactly lent themselves to Olivier's technique. A few
muttered words in darkness; a sudden beam catching Lear in a
new position, his hand lifted and a line or two of declamation to
the heavens; then moving to a huddled group and colloquial
speech—it was a remarkable piece of co-ordination.

The effect of dim, greyish, wind-swept heath, the low roll of
ground, the silver of Lear's beard and hair, the blue and white
of his robes, the cyclorama studded by shots of golden lightning,
all made a memorable picture. The result was, perhaps, rather
pleasing than awe-inspiring, lyric rather than tragic. Often one
longed for a position to be held, in order to allow its beauty to
impress itself, to take form in a dimension of symbolism never
entered. But the pleasure—for it was pleasure—was so keen that
complaints are pointless: a moving study in which the senses were
momentarily integrated in a super-sensuous whole.

One cannot expect more than a few moments of such success,

and should be grateful for any, especially at such a central moment in great drama as this. The tension—but that is too strong a word —the harmony was not maintained after the arrival of mad Tom, and this from no fault of Tom's. The production was at fault.

The part played by Edgar in the tempest is central. His appearance has been elaborately described; he has long fantastic speeches. All this should be given a bold presentment. Here we were confronted by a healthy, robust figure with various rags draped about him, shoulders and all. This gets no effect of 'presented nakedness' (II. iii. 11) and does little to realize the 'forked' animal Lear talks of. Quite a little on the stage suffices to render a person fully dressed; it is a matter of line; a few rags in the wrong place kill the body-line and the effect has gone. Edgar should wear as little as possible, but that little carefully draped and the body made up with care. The actor should be cast for these central scenes. He should be of ballet build, agile and lithe, able to act with all his limbs as he pounces after his imaginary devils. With his arms up-flung in fantastic gesture he is a veritable Flibbertigibbet, a dancing light, a demon, the genius of the storm-riven heath; a forecast of Ariel as described by himself who 'flam'd amazement' (*The Tempest*, I. ii. 198) above the tempest-racked ship. This is the true Edgar. He, like Ariel, is poetry incarnate, a poetic and dramatic force, fulfilling throughout as madman, choric commentator and agent of judgement a peculiarly poetic role. Instead we had merely a robust young actor, sitting still, stolid, in his heavy rags, mumbling gibberish muffled by thunder which no one listened to. His speeches were given as speeches no one *need* listen to; there was no attempt to act them. Necessarily, the subtlety by which Lear is gradually attracted to this demon of madness whom he calls 'my philosopher' away from the Fool did not well appear, though the Fool certainly had a lonely exit that helped. The farmhouse was poorly devised: a troublesome hut demanding a belief unlike anything else in the production and failing to support the fantasia for which it was the setting.

The play opened in an interior shading off, above an arch, to a view of many old-style houses, courtyards, turrets, seen semi-bird's-eye fashion. The scenery, though not unpleasing, did nothing to support the poet's or the actor's art. For the rest of the middle action, except for the open heath scene, a house-side was used at alternate wings for Albany's and Gloucester's households. For the conclusion we returned to the first setting, or one very similar. There was an effect of (i) an interior, and (ii) a light, airy, panorama of imaginary houses. Herein the battle-scenes lacked realism; one could not possibly believe that hostile parties were entering one after the other into a room just vacated by their opponents. The flimsy show of pictured buildings was ineffective as a visual accompaniment to the horns of judgement and tragic conclusion. The bright lighting offered no atmospheric help. Sir Laurence's acting was horribly hampered by its impossible context: far better to have used the open heath-set only and left the rest to the poet and the actor. Let the gaunt beauty of the close speak from a setting as cold and elemental as itself.

My criticisms must not be supposed typical of London's response. The production was, and in part rightly, acclaimed. Here is an extract from Mr. Harold Hobson's notice:

When the king himself appears, white-haired, white-bearded, yet swift and eager and active, we recognize him at once for what he is, a humorist, a man of infinite fecundity of wit, choleric maybe, but resilient and alert, ready in sheer intellectual energy and physical well-being for any jest or experimental escapade, whether it be sallying forth at midnight with the Doctor, or for dividing his inheritance according to the whim of a girl's rhetoric.

Before he speaks, he stops to gossip with Cordelia, he eyes one of his soldiers quizzically from top to toe and back again; he is bursting with an overflux of vital forces: from his brain at any moment may spring some plan, some scheme, half joke, half earnest, which, born on the inspiration of a moment, may, in sudden change of mood, have consequences to wreck kingdoms and ruin lives.

Precisely. The difference is that I maintain this to be an untenable reading. More, that the very nature of this reading precludes great acting, while remaining symptomatic of a twentieth-century limitation; for it rules out, from the start, that spiritual intensity, that sense of powers within and beyond man, numinous, Dionysian—call them what you will—whose projection is the one condition in drama of what mankind considers great.

Some of the most important work of our time has been done by Sir Donald Wolfit. The provinces are deeply indebted to his indefatigable labours; his company has a worldwide record, East and West; and one remembers his lunch-hour Shakespeare in blitzed London when theatre-land was dead. Omitting comedy, I have seen, so far, his Ulysses and Iachimo, done at Stratford; and in 1946 his own productions of *Othello*, *Hamlet*, and *Volpone*. The productions are simple, honest and neat, with no nonsense about them; and that in the contemporary Shakespearian theatre is saying a lot. Often today one is expected to accept wide changes in scene before a background whose laborious detail prevents utterly any such acceptances. Here there was no such embarrassment. The semi-permanent setting in *Hamlet* was sensibly devised and did not let one down, as so often happens, in the Graveyard scene, where some well-placed cypresses toned in well. A not dissimilar setting for *Othello* was adequate, though lacking in colour and grandeur. Frederick Valk's Othello showed a massive power alternating with a telling realism. The whole however was certainly a study in mental breakdown rather than poetic tragedy, except for certain moments towards the end. The volcanic bursts, the alternation of quiet and fury, were inappropriate to Othello's flow and swell of passion. Mr. Valk had a great delivery in his fourth-act speech 'Had it pleased Heaven . . .' and his final scene had grand moments. One was pleased to find an actor of such power and breadth, even though the power on occasion lacked control.

Sir Donald Wolfit's Iago, like his Iachimo, was very satisfying, but his Hamlet was, comparatively, weak. His personality scarcely suits the part—it is personality, not face or figure, that matters—at least, according to the conventional reading. Never in recent years have I heard Hamlet's lines spoken with so consistent a truth to Shakespeare, but the performance failed to hold together as a unit. One was tempted to think—wrongly, as his Solness in *The Master Builder* proves—that his abilities are not suited to an introverted type. Certainly where powerful acting was needed, as in the Ghost scenes, Hamlet's interview with the King before leaving for England, and the soliloquy after meeting Fortinbras' army, he was thoroughly at home. His graveyard meditations had vocally the required depth and weight. His use of a long black and purple cloak was effective, but when he appeared in a short Elizabethan cape, a costume having no lines of dignity, his impact was gone; while his less intense scenes lacked assurance. I feel that his interpretation may have been at fault and that, though not an ideal Hamlet, yet by playing less for sympathy and more to give the inwardness, as well as the ghost-ridden agony, the macabre threat, of the part, he might have left us with a striking performance.

Nevertheless, Wolfit's work at times approaches the standard for which I plead. Though his productions at present do not always reflect the curves of the Shakespearian structure as surely as his own speaking follows those of a single speech, yet they do not actually contradict those curves; they do not offend. He himself has grandeur and grace of movement, and a vocal range which is remarkable. Though he possesses a fine sense of the theatre, his speaking is never just stage speaking. Every phrase is given variously and interpretatively; we are not returned continually to the same well-known, favourite, emotional timbre of voice or gesture. His mastery of the long speech, a more difficult art than is usually supposed, involving a projection not merely of its sequences but also of its architectural unity, its structure, was especially vivid in *Volpone*. The wooing scene, with Miss Rosalind Iden as Celia, was outstanding. Faultless speaking, the blend of static position and significant movement, interpretative business (e.g. the mesmerizing effect and the lady's fascinated impotence) in a setting of dignity, simplicity and rich yet simple colour; all contributed superbly to the gathering, growing, unfurling structure of dramatic poetry.

On his return to Leeds in 1947 I saw Sir Donald's *Richard III*, *Macbeth*, *King Lear* and *A Midsummer Night's Dream*.

His Richard III was arresting, though in the earlier scenes the part was perhaps given a too-comic interpretation. The neurotic bitterness defined in Richard's opening soliloquy might have been allowed to counter from the start the almost Jonsonian burlesque in which Shakespeare certainly also indulges. The treatment struck me as not being weighty enough until the Throne scene (IV. ii), when what is a necessary change—and how delightful to find this *gathering* power of the Shakespearian protagonist emphasized—was nevertheless too abrupt: we were faced by almost a different person. There was a sudden unleashing of demonic force, underlined by Richard's heavy red robe and the throne's red drapery into which he sank as into a bed of fire. The scene flamed; for a few minutes, this being one of the most highly charged incidents in Shakespeare, we were confronted by remarkable acting. Sir Donald's favourite trick of infusing dramatic power into his cloak—an art he has probably developed further than any previous actor—was finely in evidence. At the dismissal of Buckingham, Richard's robe was for an instant a live thing, whipping out as a tongue of flame. I could wish that the earlier scenes had done more to prepare for this, but from now onwards the tension of the acting was never relaxed.

I say 'of the acting' since I was less pleased with the production. In bringing the opposing generals' tents on to the stage the Elizabethan dramatist raises an awkward problem. What can be done? In my own experience it seems best to concentrate on Richard's tent and let the ghosts speak into the wings in addressing Richmond. Wolfit elected boldly to use the two tents. They were dangerously realistic—a mistake his productions normally avoid—and, what was yet more dangerous, were directly and equally related to a single back-cloth of greenery and woods which forced a sense of exact locality. Conventional acceptance was accordingly hampered, though had the tents been indicated by plain draperies and set at stage corners rather than central, and with no such realistic background, acceptance would have been easier. The ghost-speeches, done in procession rather than by solid grouping and gesture, lacked weight and power. Throughout the play the choruses of lamenting women might with advantage have been given a more formal and statuesque grouping and a more declamatory manner. Observe again the nature of my demands, involving (i) formal, though never unnatural, artistry as a means to (ii) projection of the super-realistic.

Sir Donald's acting in *Macbeth* was memorable. His speaking was to my ear a trifle slow, but excellent in pointing and luxuriant in vocal colour. His bearing was charged at each instant with visual, almost sculptural, significance. His stage action in movement, poise and gesture in approach to the Ghost in the Banquet scene was artistry of the highest order. His vocal range and control was as usual remarkable, sometimes, as at the second appearance of the Ghost in this scene, on the brink of tears without loss of poetic resonance, and sometimes dragging the last ounce of power from the well-like depths of a single word.

The interpretation of the final scenes diverged strongly from my own. I see Macbeth here on a pinnacle of experience, radiating lines of force, whereas Wolfit followed the more usual and common-sense reading, giving us a broken man drained of strength. Those supreme poetic passages of the close were spoken as wistful, pathetic and nostalgic rather than as expressions of a proud spirituality beyond good and evil. I grant that such an interpretation is usual, though my own could, I think, be defended in terms of criminology; it has poetry, if not ethics and common sense, on its side. Though Sir Donald can revel in portrayal of a straight Jonsonian or Shakespearian villain he here elected to avoid this Nietzschean territory. He certainly has for it as an actor the perfect equipment and his performance at this point appeared as a deliberate curtailment of his natural powers. He wore no cloak; perhaps he felt that it was not ethically safe to do so.

The production was sound and sensible. The acting was throughout virile and the speaking had clarity and vigour. The simple yet rich and weighty settings were telling. As for the supernatural element, it did not annoy but neither was it good. One was glad to get it over. The Weird Women were chattering hags, not elemental forces; the Apparitions and procession of Ghosts were barely adequate. Again, I assert uncompromisingly that there is a technique for making such scenes not merely register but transfix.

We come next to *King Lear*. The long opening action held extraordinary power. Wolfit's exceptional vocal control—he uses a different voice for every part—was strikingly apparent: he played Lear as a carefully composed character study without any loss of poetic force: every accent, every petulant or agonized gesture was an old man's. Yet this Lear was also a figure inspiring fear. There was evil in him. The demonic pleasure with which he suddenly concluded his long curse on Goneril, as though something had been actually accomplished, was magical, Druidical, hideous with an old age, hag-like, malice. His use of the whip, a fine exploitation of the text, in action with Oswald and the Fool was masterly; and yet I have never seen a Lear whose affection for the Fool, excellently played by Mr. Frederick Peisley, was so poignantly given. These grim touches were the necessary contrast to those passages where our sympathies were wrung by Lear's more lovable qualities. Especially fine were certain striking moments of uncanny vocal modulation, where Lear fears approaching madness. His short scene alone with the Fool was almost unbearable in pathos. With all this, Lear was, from first to last, 'every inch a king': we understood Kent's recognition of his authority. One could feel, as the poet means us to feel, that the great earth itself must tremble at his shaking. In all my mature experience I have not been so forced to forget all knowledge of Shakespeare and the theatre and live the action being performed. If this was not great acting, then I do not know where it can be found.

From the Storm scene onwards the tension was relaxed. For this there are many possible reasons. One's attention perhaps tired after the long and so poignantly realized opening. Moreover actual madness, if convincingly played, is by itself and without extraneous support scarcely a theme proper to stage representation. Again, no one can pretend that all the play's action, the loves of Goneril and Regan, the killing of Oswald, Edgar's challenge, is dramatically strong. These are possible reasons, but the production itself cannot be exonerated.

The second half of *King Lear* is a crucial test: after Lear's exit into the storm a change of approach is needed. Unless we are plunged into a *new kind* of action, a new artistic dimension, we not only miss some of Shakespeare's meaning, but, what is perhaps worse, these other contributory elements of weakness in the Shakespearian structure come instantaneously into play. Much hinges on Lear's two addresses to the storm. These were given down-stage from a frontal speech-position beneath a vertical spot, and with a single tree-trunk or monolith behind. I prefer an up-stage central and raised position, the Fool, and later Kent, standing or crouching to solidify the group, all set among gigantic masses of rock, so that Lear can tower as he should. The actor can, for these two speeches, drop his vocal characterization, if, and only if, the setting is right. Sir Donald's speaking seemed, for this once only, to step out of character using a simple rhetorical fling, and in this setting, since the single monolith was quite non-significant, the result was weak; nor did he elect to use one of the weightier of his many stage voices. For the rest, his total performance was, in the manner of the opening, a remarkable study; his prayer 'Poor naked wretches' and his sermon 'When we are born' were fault-less. But something had gone. The surrounding atmosphere, so important from the Storm scenes on, lent no support; it lacked depth, mystery, unity. Some fantastic accompaniment to Lear's madness is needed, since actual madness without any such accom-paniment lacks dramatic relevance. The part of Edgar as mad

Tom was undeveloped. The settings, though weighty and simple, missed the elemental. Something must be done to give visual expression to the Wagnerian quality of the Storm scenes and the gaunt menace of the rest. So a noble performance drooped, standing, except for Rosalind Iden's vivid Cordelia, alone.

To sum up my impressions: in the Throne scene in *Richard III*, the Banquet scene in *Macbeth*, and the whole first movement of *King Lear*, Sir Donald Wolfit's acting touched the quality I am always trying to define; and he is helped by Rosalind Iden, whose exquisite mastery of Shakespearian rhythm in speech and gesture—her Titania was a joy—matches so admirably his own powers.

It seems probable that Stratford productions are to enjoy a new access of power and prestige; the new blood, youth, and vitality of the 1946 Festival promises as much. I saw various plays and shall comment briefly on productions of *Henry V* and *Measure for Measure*.

Miss Dorothy Green's *Henry V* was a straightforward and extremely pleasing production. It was, moreover, interpretatively sound: Shakespeare shone through the performance. The settings, which owed something to the Olivier film, were graceful. The French King as a study in morbid unease was admirably conceived and performed. The reverential pause during the count of British dead and the solemn movement of armed soldiers that followed —and what a treat to see fine armour well-used—at the chanting of the Te Deum; the comedy, especially the quite admirable Fluellen of Mr. Dudley Jones, perhaps as good as that of Mr. Stanley Lathbury before the war—all was in the spirit of Shakespeare's play. I have only two, similar, criticisms. Mr. Robert Harris's Chorus, though an excellent performance, might surely have been given a grand, rousing, fiery manner, a declamatory manner. It was intimate, conversational, almost confidential, following Mr. Leslie Banks' Chorus in the film. There it did not matter, but here one wished that Mr. Harris could have used his fine voice and equally fine stage presence and poise with greater freedom. His failure to do this was the stranger as I remember Miss Dorothy Green herself as a remarkable Chorus in the other manner. My other complaints are similar. Neither the 'Once more unto the breach' nor the Crispin speech was given correctly. Both were spoken intimately, with chatty and haphazard turns to the listeners and no sense of their peculiar structures. The first was well set on a fore-stage with different levels, but these levels were not used. Henry should have maintained a position of greater power, one foot on a step perhaps, his body facing the town but his head turned to his followers: then let it ring out, holding something in reserve for the second wave: all such speeches in Shakespeare gather volume as they proceed. Mr. Paul Scofield, a young actor of considerable promise, has not yet the vocal control for such a speech, but his conception was at fault. So was it too in the more subtle 'Crispin' speech.

This is my reading. The King is hampered by his followers' fears. Can he hold them? He starts weakly, repeating himself, searching for a direction. The start can be colloquial or weakly rhetorical. He is turning over papers—or someone brings him a scroll—his eye catches a word. The Feast of Crispian. The word registers. 'This day is called the feast of Crispian . . .' The word's sound delicately touching, yet just missing, the word 'Christian' neatly corresponds to the chivalric heroism in question. Henry now has the required note; he is newly inspired; quickly the flame spreads, in his words, in his followers' response. He enlists his listeners' deepest selves, awakes their spontaneous desire for heroic renown. Eternity swims into the purview; yet humour is present too; the ring of English names is pure, marvellous, rhetoric. The thing unfolds, gathers height and power, towers up like a cobra. During it the King sees his success; you watch his listeners change; he is working on them, as surely as Antony in the Forum; the victory is enacted. Notice how, laying a basis in a sound realism, in earth, the speech flowers; it unfolds by stages, it accumulates, gathering mass, an organic, structural whole. This is a quality no study will reveal; it is something one must learn, arduously, by many renderings.

Mr. Frank McMullan's *Measure for Measure* moved at a fine pace, brisk and entertaining; the use of small stylized screen sets, central, left the stage free for action, and established a pleasing unity. They all, as it were, belonged. But, and the but is important, we did not have Shakespeare's *Measure for Measure*.

The pace itself, the emphatically light, stepping, movement contradicted that weighty, measured, deliberate motion suggested by the title, fulfilled by the action and reaching crystallization in the Duke's soliloquy:

26. *Othello*, Leeds 1955
(p. 15). At Cyprus: Iago,
Richard Coe; Cassio,
George Smyth; Desde-
mona, Ann Buckle

27. Othello attacking Iago

28. Othello's last speech

29. *King Lear*, Leeds 1951 (p. 15): Goneril, Doreen Harrington; Regan, Diana Holmes; Cordelia, Louie Eickhoff

30. *The Merchant of Venice*, Leeds 1960 (pp. 15, 188): Shylock (the beard thickened in reproduction)

31. *Macbeth*, University of Ein-Shams, Cairo 1963, Devendra P. Varma's production (pp. 18, 295 note): the Weird Sisters

He who the sword of Heaven will bear
Should be as holy as severe.

(III. ii. 283)

Can those rhythms be spoken lightly? No. Duke Vincentio was
misconceived and miscast. He is surely a scholarly recluse, Lucio's
'old fantastical duke of dark corners' (IV. iii. 167; 'fantastical'
means 'imaginative'); a study set between Hamlet and Prospero,
whose depth of psychological insight appears to render the execution of justice repellent.[1] Instead we had a gay young spark with
a perpetual smile, a dandy touching up his face in a mirror, a
practical joker enjoying himself mightily. The performance on
these lines was so good that one temporarily accepted it, but the
play was thrown out of joint. Moreover the Duke was balanced
against an Angelo of depth and dignity; an older man, with a
thoughtful face and a beard. A stage beard has a precise effect;
unless deliberately arranged for a character study, it tends to
suggest a convincing spiritual dignity; whereas for Angelo we
want a pale, precise, would-be ascetic, and a suggestion of weakness. The trick played on Angelo's sexual instincts, if played
by a young man on one many years his senior, is in bad taste; it
jars. This is all wrong. It is inflicted by a man of age, wisdom,
and sanctity—note the Duke's disguise as a monk and Angelo's
reference to 'power divine' (v. i. 370)—on a comparatively weak
tyro in matters spiritual, an amateur. The two parts were miscast: Mr. Robert Harris should clearly have been our protagonist,
the Duke, and Mr. David King-Wood, Angelo. As Angelo, Mr.
Harris' personality was wrong and the beard made it worse.
Moreover his Isabella was not the icy fanatic one expects, but
rather a figure of luxuriant charm. Her brutal denunciation of
Claudio, rising from the depths of her inhibited, repressed soul
—the key to her character and the whole play's thesis—was
shirked, being given through sobs as distracted, meaningless
phrases.[2] Angelo's tragedy is the ironic enthralling of an ascetic
by the charms of an opposite ascetism:

---

[1] I am following my own interpretation as given in *The Wheel of Fire*; but on
these basic matters there is scarcely room for divergence of opinion.

[2] The psychology of my reading here still appears to me sound, provided that we
do not blame Isabella overmuch for a reaction which might be called inevitable.
[1963]

> Oh cunning enemy that, to catch a saint,
> With saints dost bait thy hook.
>
> (II. ii. 180)

To make him, a figure of bearded dignity, fall before a girl of normal feminine appeal is a serious misinterpretation.

As a production, this was technically as good a piece of work as one is likely to see. It failed where others fail, attempting

> To draw with idle spiders' strings
> Most pond'rous and substantial things.
>
> (III. ii. 297)

That is, it failed in the matters of (i) supernatural or semi-supernatural feeling (the Duke as a cowled and ghostly figure), and (ii) psychological understanding, recognition of the Shakespearian depth, the twilit world of unconscious instinct on which this play concentrates.

It seems that our producers and actors do not naturally breathe the Dionysian air of Shakespearian tragedy. It is not that they cannot technically do what is required, but that, in the depths, they do not wish to:

> Look, what I will not, that I cannot do.
>
> (II. ii. 52)

The tendencies I am opposing, which are precisely analogous to those tendencies of Shakespearian scholarship which I have opposed in my more academic studies, remain pervasive, hampering the most sumptuous efforts of our professional stage.

2 [1963]

How far my academic and stage theories have, since their publication in the thirties, affected our professional productions, it would not be easy to say. I have not been able to attend enough of them to make an authoritative comment. Since my 1949 remarks I have, however, had reason to suppose that some influence has been active.

At a Stratford production by Mr. Peter Brook of *Measure for Measure* in 1950, which I unfortunately could not attend, the reading of the Duke's testing of Isabella advanced in *The Wheel of Fire* has, I understand, given us an example of that most rarely ex-

ploited power, the power of the significant pause. I saw Mr.
Brook's *The Winter's Tale* in London in 1951, with Sir John
Gielgud as Leontes. In high comedy or parts asking an electric,
nervous, contemporary contact with his audience Sir John is
adept, but his deeper manner, the gravity I once sensed in his
Shylock, pleases me, as a Shakespearian, more. I thought his
Leontes too reserved during the passionate scenes but admirable
at the end, the beautiful voice tuned to a gravity of wonderful
timbre. The costuming for the final revelation was excellent, the
robes in vertical lines of soft grey and black contrasting with
Hermione's white to form a perfect correlative to the tragic joy
under performance.[1] In Mr. Tony Richardson's *Pericles* at Stratford in 1958, set was cleverly blended into set in a manner suited
to the dream-like sequence of events, the dissolving effects, which
would be dangerous for many Shakespearian plays, proving here
an asset. Lighting and costume gave Marina the right mystic
gleam at her reunion with Pericles. I have reason to think that my
discussions on the integrity and stage-pattern of *Henry VIII*
have had a fairly wide effect; and so, it seems, has my battling for
the Vision of Jupiter in *Cymbeline*, which used regularly to be
rejected by scholars and cut by producers, but today takes its
place, according to recent accounts, as the outstanding incident,
as it should be, of the drama. Mr. Peter Brook deserves our
gratitude for having demonstrated the power of *Titus Andronicus*
in his 1955 production, which I regret having missed. An account
of it has recently appeared in Jan Kott's *Shakespeare notre Contemporain* (Julliard, Paris; reviewed *T.L.S.*, 27 September 1963).

The reputation of Sir Tyrone Guthrie would make me regret
my inability to comment on his Shakespearian work were it not
likely that a certain divergence of viewpoint might have forced
a too animated expression. His contribution to the founding of
the Festival Theatre at Stratford, Ontario, puts all Shakespearians
in his debt. I was gripped by his vigorous *Tamburlaine* at the
Old Vic in 1951, supported by Wolfit's performance (Norman
Marshall, *The Producer and the Play*, 1962 edn., 248); but I have
reason to suppose that Sir Tyrone's *Henry VIII* (Marshall, 191–2)
would have deeply disturbed me. His 1959 modernized *All's Well*

[1] A photograph is given by Professor Moelwyn Merchant in *Shakespeare and the
Artist*, plate 84. Other interesting pictures witnessing to the importance attributed
to this scene in the past appear on plates 78; 79 (Macready); and 81 (Charles Kean).

That Ends Well at Stratford has been highly praised by Mr. Laurence Kitchin in *Mid-Century Drama*. My own judgement would have concentrated less on any modernistic extensions, provided that they did not contradict the *spirit* of the play, than on the King's healing. If Helena's art, in this amazing scene (analysed in my book *The Sovereign Flower*), was given a full dramatic exploitation with far more than a willing suspension of disbelief, then I should have responded with respect.

I was able to see, at Leeds, the Old Vic production of *Macbeth*, produced by Mr. Michael Benthall, which came on tour in 1960 before visiting the Continent. This production differed from that by Mr. Benthall a little earlier. It was, on the whole, strong: certainly it was performed with vigour. Mr. Benthall used a large platform-piece, sometimes with thrones on it, at one side. This was used for Duncan's exit and formal 'good-night' just before the murder; for Macbeth and Lady Macbeth on their thrones; and for the *second* entry of Banquo's Ghost. The scheme was in general conformity with my suggestions (pp. 131–44). There was however no apparent effect of gold, and the setting itself gave less the sense of any solid background construction than of draughty spaces and rafters in an empty darkness. Though this was in a way suitable, yet a better result might have come from something obviously *made* to suggest mystery.

Mr. Paul Rogers' *Macbeth* had one great merit. He showed Macbeth's indomitable courage in face of supernatural horror, rising to his *deliberate* attack on the Ghost at its second appearance by the throne (see p. 136 above). His last scenes had not the *spiritual* power which the poetry suggests—his 'To-morrow' speech was spoken from a weak stage position—but they had the energy we expect. Macbeth ended on an upward course.

The most impressive production, as a production, within my recent experience was that of *King Lear* at Stratford by Mr. George Devine in 1953, with Sir Michael Redgrave as Lear.

Sir Michael is an actor who never fails, perhaps because his work has so firm a foundation in literary perception. His Benedick in Mr. Douglas Seale's Stratford *Much Ado about Nothing* in 1958 was peculiarly fine; I was struck most by its manliness. Benedick in Mr. Douglas Seale's Stratford *Much Ado about Nothing* in 1958 wooing scene; a good soldier un-at-home with refinements and poetry (v. ii. 26–42). Benedick's 'Enough! I am engaged. I will

challenge him' (IV. i. 339) had a telling impact of male responsibility in response to Beatrice's female intuition. Sir Michael's
performance was written into my commentary on *Much Ado about
Nothing* in *The Golden Labyrinth*.

I saw Sir Michael's Lear many years ago when he was a school-
master at Cranleigh, and wrote on it in *The Cranleighan*. It was
strong even then, and has since become impressive. Behind its
every moment was an able actor's keen thought; it could not
strike the blinding force of Wolfit's, but it was memorable.

Mr. Devine's production was outstanding. Recently, in reading
Professor Moelwyn Merchant's *Shakespeare and the Artist* (152–7),
I found my own opinion corroborated. Professor Merchant writes
that it 'combined more qualities of distinguished presentation,
direction, design and music together, than any other Shakespearian production I remember'. It was 'a re-creation of Shakespeare's
play in terms of the modern theatre, without doing violence to
those aspects of it which the direct simplicity of his own stage
demanded'. That was also my impression. Professor Merchant
discusses the highly original centre-piece used in turn for various
purposes, including at one point a phallic suggestion, till 'at the
close it became Lear's couch, gathering up both the regal dignity
of the chair of state with which the play opened and the dereliction
of the third act in which this central structure remained, as the
hovel, the strongest focus of sight'. He also discusses, with printed
quotations, the music, which used variations on a single theme
for sennet, hunting-horns, storm, Lear's awakening and the concluding Dead March. An especial praise is allotted to the inter-
related orchestration of thunder-music, lightning-music and
words. Though I doubt whether music is really preferable to a
correct use of stage thunder, this interplay with the words is, as
I have for long insisted (pp. 57–8, 123), all-important.

I do not say that this *Lear* had all the extensions in acting which
I look for and have tried myself to practise and define (p. 287
below); but it was admirable. Here is a simple test: when Cordelia
entered with her army, though there were only a few soldiers, it
was Cordelia's army, with all that this at this point in the drama
denotes, that entered. That is the kind of detail to which producers are too often insensitive. I do not refer to anything at all
complicated, or even subtle; but what was done was done rightly.

I did not so well like Mr. Devine's *King Lear* done at

Stratford and London in 1955 with Japanese designs by Mr. Isamu Noguchi,[1] despite the presence of Sir John Gielgud, whose Old Vic Lear in 1931 held so striking a promise. I deeply regret having missed his second Lear in 1940 (p. 226, note) and also his recent Benedick, which would have made a fascinating contrast to Sir Michael's. A tribute may be paid to Sir John's growing reputation as one of our most sensitive producers (Marshall, *The Producer and the Play*, 1962 edn., 197).

Stratford under Mr. Peter Hall is a more vital centre of activity than ever before. I was interested in Mr. Michael Langham's *The Merchant of Venice* in 1960, but did not respond so favourably as some to Mr. Peter O'Toole's Shylock. His performance appeared to me disjointed, passing suddenly from quietude to vociferation without warning, external rather than centred. The most piercing performance in voice and bearing was, to my mind, Mr. Paul Hardwick's Morocco. I should like to see him in a leading part.

To come to yet another *King Lear*. Mr. Peter Brook's recent production with the Royal Shakespeare Company first at Stratford and then at the Aldwych Theatre, London, has been widely acclaimed. I found it disturbing.[2]

The setting consisted of plain slanting side-pieces and back-wall, all white or cream-white on a similarly coloured stage which pushed well forward, no proscenium curtain being used. Occasionally dark rectangles were lowered to break the bare side-pieces, and simple objects, such as a formalized fence, were pushed on the stage. The general effect was a non-signifying and non-atmospheric bareness. Lighting was bright, uncoloured and in the main unvaried.

Such an antiseptic setting is not nothing; no setting can avoid saying something, unless we dispense with illusion altogether, and give a simple reading in plain clothes. What this setting *said* bore little relevance to *King Lear*. However, to pass that by, a plain background only throws the greater stress on character-interpretation and acting.

King Lear dramatizes the overthrow of an outward grandeur followed by the protagonist's advance through suffering to a kind

---

[1] A note on this production is given by Professor Moelwyn Merchant in *Shakespeare Survey* 13, 1960; 79.

[2] I am indebted to the kindness of Mr. Peter Hall in helping me to find a seat for this extraordinarily successful production.

of spiritualized royalty. Since we were given no suggestion of
state, no fanfares or regality, at the opening, the lines

> Take physic, pomp:
> Expose thyself to feel what wretches feel . . .
>
> (III. iv. 33)

which are of central import, became meaningless. There had been
no pomp; and there was accordingly no physic.

Lear was presented as a latish middle-aged man soured in
temperament and ill-mannered. His elder daughters' flatteries
were met by the same dour ill-humour as Cordelia's plain-speak-
ing, without discernible difference or climax. His retainers were
a group of scurvy ruffians as ill-mannered, scruffy and coarsely
costumed as the King himself. When Kent in disguise says to
Lear

> . . . you have that in your countenance which I
> would fain call master
>
> (I. iv. 29–32)

and next defines it as 'authority', the words spoken to so visually
mean a figure could only be taken as ironic. Lear's 'Ay, every inch
a king' (IV. vi. 110) sounded remarkably foolish. Such a reading
makes nonsense of Shakespeare's play.

Goneril was not only allowed some justification, which would
be reasonable, but was frankly sentimentalized. One of her cutting
severities had to be gulped by Miss Irene Worth through tears,
and I could sense her stage embarrassment as she came up against
the stone wall of having to say 'Pluck out his eyes' (III. vii. 5)
like a lady. The villainous Cornwall in both make-up and costume
had, like Goneril, a handsome regality which made nonsense
of Kent's laughter-raising 'I have seen better faces in my time . . .'
(II. ii. 99), but the other men, including Albany, were roughly
clothed. The most ill-conceived costume-effect was the Fool's:
ballooning trousers suggesting a circus clown made him the
most physically robust person on the stage, whereas a modern
circus clown bears no relationship to the Shakespearian fool, and
the Fool in *Lear* should, especially after he has been pining away,
be slight, fitting such terms as 'my pretty knave' (I. iv. 107) and
Lear's continual use of 'boy' (I. iv. 119, 146, 163; I. v. 10, 18;
III. ii. 78; III. iv. 26). Had it not been killed by his costume, Mr.
Alec McCowen's performance would have been good.

There was an apparently considered purpose to contradict the lines spoken. In *The Daily Telegraph* (14 January 1963) Mr. W. A. Darlington has suggested that Mr. Brook was trying to make sense of an impossible opening. As we have seen, Olivier went to the extreme of making Lear a lovable old man; Mr. Brook goes to the extreme of an ill-natured middle-aged one. But there is here a fallacy. We meet the same problem in Cressida and Timon's friends (p. 174). People *do* have opposing qualities in them; that is what Shakespeare is writing about. 'This is, and is not, Cressid' (*Troilus and Cressida*, v. ii. 143) may be adapted for use today in most families of the realm. Lear is a full-scale development of Shakespeare's long line of tyrannic fathers; but that such tyranny, which generally derives from a too-possessive love, need not be the final truth, our tragedy exists to demonstrate. It must from the start be the tyranny of a fine man; an autocrat, one born to rule but spoiled by his position as king and father. It should have style and authority. And it must be the tyranny of an *old* man over eighty (iv. vii. 61), who can say

> O heavens
> If you do love old men, if your sweet sway
> Allow obedience, if yourselves are old,
> Make it your cause; send down and take my part!
>
> (ii. iv. 192)

He must be able to talk convincingly of a head 'so old and white as this' (iii. ii. 24): and Cordelia of his 'white flakes', and his 'thin helm' (iv. vii. 30, 36) too weak to be exposed to the elements. Mr. Scofield's Lear had a head of iron ready for anything. He was as tough as he was boorish.

No drama was struck from the approach of madness. Lear's 'I shall go mad' (ii. iv. 289) was given as a plain statement of fact. For his address to the storm he was a solitary figure on an empty stage, the lines spoken in a level voice and without gestures. The incident was in no sense a climax, but just another item in the sequence. Mr. Paul Scofield has a strong voice and his face impressive lines, but the impression remained stolid and the tone of his performance unvaried. Much may be attributed to direction; but his Hamlet a few years ago appeared to me to lack—though I was badly placed in the auditorium—sparkle. Mr. Scofield has power; can he not compass vivacity?

While highly praising the production as 'just short of per-fection' Mr. Darlington writes of Mr. Brook: 'He is nothing if not modern, and is no bardolater. He regards Shakespeare as a dangerous potential bore, and produces him in that spirit'. That was precisely my impression, though how such a treatment could draw near perfection baffles me.[1] What this dangerously in-fluential production seems to be doing is to attempt at the cost of deliberate falsification to *reduce the Shakespearian grandeur to twentieth-century terms*. The costumes with their rough tunics, short boots and loose trousers were modernistic. They were also, the men's anyway—except for the wicked Cornwall—drab. The general result was a mixture of Brecht[2] and Beckett, both admirable in their place, which is not Shakespeare's. Even with this reading Lear could have been accorded eminence, as perhaps an ageing dictator or ruthless capitalist.

What on the other side? It is true that by maintaining a kind of Brechtian level, though the climax of the storm-followed-by-madness was lost, yet we did not suffer from the contrast of what is too often a dull and dragging sequence of less interesting scenes thereafter. For better or worse, all was reduced to one narrative plane. It could conceivably be argued that we have always made too much of these central scenes; but it is probably safer to say that the Shakespearian form, here as sometimes else-where, incurs criticism.

Much depends on the effectiveness of the Gloucester and Edgar scenes, which take over from Lear, assuming centrality. Now, while the Lear-climax was weak or non-existent, it is pleasant to record that this new interest was brilliantly developed.

Edgar's part depends, as we have already (p. 166) argued, very largely on the use of nakedness. This is not a minor theme; it is dramatically basic, since no greater visual power exists than the human form; and it was done well. Edgar's speech

---

[1] I see that Mr. Nigel Dennis in *Encounter* xx. 2 (February 1963) takes a line similar to Mr. Darlington's. Both see the faults which I see, but appear to regard them as minor blemishes on a triumphant production.

[2] Compare Mr. Norman Marshall's account of Brecht's use of ironical effects on a bare stage with his production of *Mother Courage* (*The Producer and the Play*, 1962 edn., 89). It cannot be adduced in defence of Mr. Brook's production—the sugges-tion has been made to me—that Brecht admired Shakespeare. What we want to know is whether Shakespeare admires Brecht.

My face I'll grime with filth,
Blanket my loins, elf all my hair in knots,
And with presented nakedness outface
The winds and persecutions of the sky . . .

(ɪɪ. iii. 9)

was spoken while the clothes were simultaneously, piece by piece, being removed, the actor's hands descriptively sliding over his limbs to live for an instant the poetry of nakedness. As in Timon's disrobing it is important that the underdress first revealed should be such as might be there (p. 168 above); and Edgar's neat loin-dress at this point struck the blend required. When he next appeared he wore a different, wild and ragged, loin-cloth; he was suitably be-grimed and be-slimed; and he slithered about the stage effectively. Here his appearance signified degradation. But in his following scene with blinded Gloucester, his slime was removed and the body clean. Nakedness can have dual pointings: in Timon both are simultaneously present, the higher dominating. Edgar seemed to move from one to the other, from naked-ness-as-degradation to nakedness-as-wisdom. This we may call the wisdom of human purity, the human essence, asserting itself within a world of horror. Here Edgar's physique contrasted with the ugly garments of the rest to state a human hope in harmony with his good words and choric wisdom.

These changes were production of a high interpretative order. The performance did not register as it might have done, since the physical effect was partly destroyed by the unatmospheric lighting on a light background. However in facial as well as bodily expression and in the use of different dialects in a well-modulated voice, Mr. Brian Murray's performance deserves praise. I have not seen a more moving Gloucester than Mr. Alan Webb's.

Why is *King Lear* so popular today? Professor Sadhan Kumar Ghosh has, in a study of tragedy at present being prepared for publication, asserted that it is the only great tragedy wherein the hero repents. Certainly it stands alone in Shakespeare in relating tragic assertion to humility. The Renaissance-Nietzschean powers are blended with Christian valuations. Since that is what we all want, there is little wonder that we so cluster round this grim drama, and it would be a cause for satisfaction that the Aldwych is being filled by audiences if it were not for the fear that success has been bought at the cost of mutilation. The instinctive good-

ness of Cornwall's second and third servants and Edmund's repentance were suppressed (*T.L.S.*, 27 Sept. 1963; 744). In the
process the Shakespearian spirit, which has power to expand the
consciousness beyond an easy acceptance—for drabness and
mannerless deeds are today only too easy to accept—was discounted. The production often seemed like a satire on what
Shakespeare was doing and on the values with which he worked.
King Lear does, we all know, present a dun world; and therein
lies the challenge to the artist. In *A Macbeth Production* (24)
Masefield wrote:

Men will go to see your performance in order to get a heightened
sense of life, to escape from the modern world's horror into an intensity
of feeling. You must strive to delight every eye in your audience with
happy colour and gracious line. Nature gives these with bounty; a
modern city grudges both. Any stinting of colour, any jagging or
blunting of the line is mark of disease, or of a mind at war.

King Lear has its own stark grandeur, which production should
in manifold ways reflect, letting the eye so feed on facial expression, gesture, action, colour and setting, that the theatric imagination is awaked to experience a poetry which has power
to shatter our twentieth-century world-view and lift us to a
different consciousness. That was what Gordon Craig was
envisaging when, writing in 1921, he complained that Shakespeare's ghosts, kings and aristocrats were in our century 'considered a bore', and demanded actors able to measure up to the
Shakespearian stature (pp. 224, 229 above). The danger is today
far greater. The old actor-managers rearranged and cut for their
purposes, but they did not distort; and in their hands the Shakespearian soul-centre remained intact.

Notes on the Filming of Shakespeare

I [1936][1]

Many of the comedies are, I hear, being filmed in Hollywood. The tragedies will sooner or later follow. But if Shakespeare is not to fail there it is necessary that producers should determine to bring out the poetic significances. To rely on the 'story' only will prove fatal: there are many better 'stories'. The problems are different from stage-production. There is not the same play on conventional limits; visually the film has infinite possibilities. These it must rely on; not to give us inessential views of Hamlet leaving Wittenberg but to project the pictorial elements of the poetry itself; and, further, to depict as far as possible the spiritual quality of the action as a whole.

Here are a few suggestions. Othello's speech of farewell to his soldiership could be accompanied by views corresponding to his words; and the earlier account of his wanderings could be excellently done. We could have the dramatic incident first; then the voice speaking lines illustrated by various scenes; then again a return to our first incident. Clarence's Dream would come off gloriously; so would Horatio's 'What if it tempt you toward the flood . . .', and Edgar's description of Dover Cliff. The varied tempest-passages have great possibilities. But Antony's cloud-formations (*Antony and Cleopatra*, IV. xii. 2–8) would be difficult. The more spiritual the suggestions, the harder. Richard's long speeches in *Richard II* would be difficult to illustrate, and Romeo's image of Juliet as an angel or Macbeth's cherubin (*Romeo and Juliet*, II. ii. 26–32; *Macbeth*, I. vii. 22) almost impossible. None of this will finally satisfy unless the quality of the whole

---

[1] This section appeared in the first edition of *Principles of Shakespearian Production* (212–5) but was excluded from the second, Penguin, edition.

is put over. I suggest that the spirit of my general arguments should be followed, but not the letter. The conventions are so different. The first necessity is that the producer should both like and understand the play concerned.

Since writing the above I have seen Max Reinhardt's film-production of *A Midsummer Night's Dream*.

Obvious complaints concerning Hollywood accents are beside the point. It was a Hollywood show. Nor do I feel inclined to complain seriously about the cutting of long speeches, though so severe a pruning seemed a little harsh. The film is primarily a visual medium: we must criticize it as such.

I was impressed by the way the producer brought out, *what is in the poetry*, the nightmarish fearsomeness of the wood and its wild beasts. This was interpretative work with authority in incident and imagery, whereas the average stage-production leaves you with an impression of blue-bells and tinsel. I liked Oberon on his black horse. Compare my recent reference (p. 142 above) to the nightmarish quality and horses of *Macbeth*, which this play atmospherically touches. A reference to my essay on *A Midsummer Night's Dream* in *The Shakespearian Tempest* will make my reasons for approval clearer.

2 [1963]

The name of Sir Laurence Olivier is associated with three distinguished films: *Henry V*, *Hamlet* and *Richard III*. *Henry V* and *Richard III* were highly effective creations. Both gained strength from Olivier's brilliance as a film-actor, and so did the *Hamlet*, though it suffered from a mechanically grunting ghost. On such supernatural matters our modern producers regularly fail. It happened in another sumptuous film, of *Julius Caesar*. Sir John Gielgud's Cassius and James Mason's Brutus were incisive contributions, but there was a lamentable failure to use the almost unlimited resources of the studio to realize those supernatural effects which cannot be more than suggested in the theatre. In place of weird phenomena striking terror along the streets of Rome and 'fierce fiery warriors' contending in its skies, all that I recall was a gust or two of light wind rustling some leaves in a gutter. While such methods continue Shakespearian tragedy will remain stifled.

A worthier attempt at the supernatural characterized the film of *Macbeth* directed by George Schaeffer and starring Maurice Evans and Judith Anderson. The Weird Sisters on their first appearance seemed to grow from a moorland dell swathed in mists. The attempt, though not wholly successful, was in conception sound. Little was made of them afterwards; we had no Apparitions; and the Ghost of Banquo was weak.

The film as a whole deserves praise. Tact and honesty went far towards realization of the drama's primitive world, and on this plane the events were remarkably convincing. The production showed a pleasing honesty and reserve, and Shakespeare's text was allowed to speak for itself without the expected lopping. Lady Macbeth's sleep-walking ranks high among the many successes, for it is comparatively easy to be successful here, achieved by actresses of my experience. Maurice Evans, whose command of Shakespearian rhetoric in *Richard II* electrified New York in the thirties, now as an older man brought a matured artistry to his Macbeth. The result was of a high order, every tint and tone of the poetry receiving an accurate vocalization. This film would be my prize choice among those films of Shakespeare that I have seen; more widely, and including the ordinary stage, I regard it as, despite some weak acting or miscasting in some of the subsidiary roles, one of the few most adequate representations of Shakespearian tragedy in my post-war experience.

Perhaps its effective simplicity was in part due to its having been simultaneously devised for the cinema and for television.

CHAPTER X

Afterthoughts

I

Shakespearian production has for long been in a state of confusion. Now we have also to take into account the recent challenges from the open and arena stages.

My own practice, as opposed to theory, has been simplified by my having been forced to use simple methods. I have tended to rely, as my pictures (e.g., 7, 17, 21) show, on a central platform between two pillars or flats; and even had I had greater resources I should have striven, so far as possible, for a unity of tone. Perhaps the most serious complaint that might be levelled against my approach, both here and in my more academic studies, would be the charge that, by trying to reduce tumult to tidiness, I have been forcing Shakespeare into a classic mould. And yet the will to unity appears inevitable.

William Poel's insistence that the Elizabethan play-house was architecturally stately and its productions sumptuous has been often repeated. Mr. Speaight observes that Miss Tanya Moiseiwitsch's set for the Histories at Stratford-on-Avon in 1951 'had the sovereign merit of being architecture rather than décor' (*William Poel, etc.*, 82–3). But if an 'architecture' is deliberately *made* for the occasion rather than being an accepted part of the building used, it inevitably says something, and must accordingly be devised for the occasion, too; and that means devised for the particular performance and play under consideration; and we are at once involved in some kind of 'décor'. There will certainly be danger in any too elaborated a permanency unless it accords with the whole action, like the blazonings of the two houses for *Romeo and Juliet* or our figure of Apollo for *The Winter's Tale* (pp. 144 above). The trouble is that a Shakespearian play may shift

271

its locality and even vary in tone, as when the poetry of *King Lear* touches the pastoral and idyllic towards the close. On this however we can agree: what we want is a colourful performance without reliance on painted scenery or any too striking changes—unless such seem quite unavoidable, as in *Timon of Athens*—of background. Modern techniques can certainly, by the use of soft blackouts and significant emblems, suggest simple changes with a minimum of elaboration; but too much of it detracts from the permanency, the solids being continually melted before our eyes. One of the most effective examples in my experience of reliance on words and action against a simple and dark, and mainly architectural, background was given by Douglas Seale's production of the three parts of *Henry VI* with the Birmingham Repertory Company at the Old Vic in 1953. The three plays were given in sequence, and at the conclusion of the third night the applause, though I would not suggest that applause is our final criterion, was perhaps the most extravagant that I can recall.

My own breaking of continuity by a fairly frequent use of front curtains might today be called if not out-of-date at least out-of-fashion. Mr. Richard Southern strongly disapproves of such alternations of full set and 'apron', being at pains to distinguish the latter from the true 'open stage' (*The Open Stage*, 65–7). But Masefield accepts a scheme similar to mine (*A Macbeth Production*, 1945; 18–19), and the use of a 'traverse' while properties on the main stage-area are being rearranged has always appeared to me to derive authority of some kind, though of what precise kind I am not sure, from the mechanics of Shakespeare's composition, since the alternations come too regularly for it to be altogether a matter of chance.[1] Many of our short scenes not only lend themselves to a frontal performance against a formal curtain, but actually seem (p. 67) to demand such a projection if their full, often semi-choric, quality is to be brought out. Sometimes, when we have scenes of length which are yet subsidiary to our main background, an intermediate expedient may be used, as in our half-stage use of curtains in *Timon of Athens*. A similar method may be helpful in *Antony and Cleopatra*. Here it is reasonable to use a permanent setting of Egyptian suggestion. Egypt exists in the poetry as a stabilized and enclosing reality overarch-

---

[1] On the Elizabethan 'traverse' see Robert Speaight, *William Poel etc.*, 84, 97, 107–8; also Masefield, as above, 18.

ing the flux of temporal, which here means of Roman, affairs (*The Imperial Theme*, 323–4). But what of the many Roman scenes? If they are done within the main set, this, whatever our theories, does not in practice work, since we cannot accept them as Roman. If we use modern techniques to make one set melt into another, our Egyptian permanence suffers from our watching its solidity being dissolved. It would seem that nothing conceivable—barring the extreme of an open stage technique—attains so satisfying a result as the use of a plain curtain or some equivalent such as the pushing in of a screen; though I myself would prefer a curtain provided that it moves noiselessly, since there *is* a definite break, which needs underlining. The shift from Egyptian realism to conventional formality will be accepted as an honest if unoriginal expedient—it is always better to be unoriginal where possible— and all goes smoothly. Even were we able to use a grand Roman setting it would usurp a disproportionate importance. Naturally these Roman scenes can be built up visually by attendants, standards and other properties: it is wonderful how much can be done by these alone.

Much depends on what play is being done. The Birmingham Repertory Company scored heavily with *Henry VI* by simple means. The trilogy is however made of a sequence of unusually violent scenes: there was more than enough to hold our attention. We must preserve honesty in our approach, and if we find that such a treatment does not do all that is required for *A Midsummer Night's Dream*, *The Tempest*, *Macbeth*, the storm-scenes of *King Lear* or the second half of *Timon of Athens*, we must be ready to admit it. Such plays as *A Midsummer Night's Dream* and *The Tempest* trace their descent from Court entertainments; and that such entertainments, culminating in the Masques of Ben Jonson and Inigo Jones, employed an elaborate machinery, is well known. Shakespeare's imagination could certainly function in such terms. If it were charged against me that in my *Timon of Athens* I departed from my 'principles' by rejecting a permanent setting for a rocky background in the second movement, my defence would be that the play's principle of unity itself changes, demanding a corresponding change of set and style; that the atmosphere of the later action must be preserved and emphasized; and that I was accordingly thinking less of my own principles than of Shakespeare's conception.

Afterthoughts

Though still averse from any primary reliance on lights, especially when coloured, I have since my first productions grown more sympathetic to the electrician, provided that he does not assert himself at the expense of the human figures and the spoken words. Especially when an unclothed body is used, light-variations help to awake the deeper meanings. My Stowe *Macbeth* used them effectively for the second and third Apparitions (pp. 143–4 above). The wild scenes of my *Timon of Athens* relied quite heavily on lighting; a physical effect predominated and the scenes in question, composed on a wave-length more Romantic than Elizabethan, demand an atmospheric treatment. We are concerned less with a community and more with a lonely individual, and for a dramatic movement composed largely of an individual's communing with spiritual or natural forces a play of light is helpful. For *A Midsummer Night's Dream* and *The Tempest* a too ascetic approach might be dangerous. We had light-effects for our figure of Apollo in *The Winter's Tale* (pp. 144–7 above).

We have already discussed Tree's production of *The Tempest*. What we have to ask ourselves is, Can we by our methods do equal justice to the more supernatural or cosmic properties of Shakespearian drama? When in Toronto I wanted to play Caliban it was arranged that another producer, Miss Josephine Koenig, should undertake the production. There were many reasons, some of which I forget; but it certainly looks as though I was not inspired, using the simple methods to which my own principles at that time committed me, to attack *The Tempest*.

Strangely, in view of my own predispositions, one of my main complaints on professional productions today is concerned not with their lack of symbolic or atmospheric profundity, though this may be serious, but with their lack of realism where realism is demanded; 'realism', that is, in the most obvious sense.

I have already (p. 168 above) observed how absurd it would be to show Timon throwing off his grand robes to reveal a rough loin-cloth, as though he had prepared this passionate gesture beforehand; and I have seen this happen, in a production of status. Once in a high-class production of *Richard III* I have seen Richmond go to sleep on the ground in front of a tent which had been carefully pitched before our eyes instead of inside it. Such errors give the impression that Shakespeare is such an abracadabra of nonsense that no sort of convincing reality need be expected.

They derive from a failure to understand what can and what cannot be accepted in terms of theatrical convention. Failure to use an audience's willing suspension of disbelief in the right way will end up by shattering illusion in the wrong. The truth is, we are un-at-home in Shakespeare's world.

2

Our inadequacies derive from a failure to understand Shakespeare's interweaving of human realism and expansive apprehension. The Shakespearian grandeur is always rooted in the soil, and rhetoric related to the colloquial. On the *relation* existent between these two categories his art depends.[1]

My youthful introduction to stage excitement and much of my training in Shakespearian sensibility came from attendances at Tree's productions (pp. 205, 210 above); and when I first started performing the big parts in Toronto, my guide and mentor was the late Leslie Harris, formerly of Tree's company and a life-long disciple of his art.[2] How subtle was his advice on speaking—'Don't *act* it' he would say, countering, at a chosen moment, one of my own ill-placed extravagances. Tree's acting was subtle; his speaking was in general quiet; but he had grandeur, in both speech and gesture. I have already narrated how, when in 1949 I was given a record of Tree's speaking of Antony's lines in *Julius Caesar*—and Tree's *Julius Caesar* was my first experience, in 1911, of professional Shakespearian production—I detected in it both the spiritualized note and structural build-up which I had for long regarded as the most important qualities to be looked for in Shakespearian speaking and to which I then realized that I must have been attuned by Tree's example.

Throughout my own stage adventures it would seem that two strains have been active: the strains of what people call 'grand-style' acting, though I never consciously aimed at it, merely trying despite many incompetences and continual failures to act well; and, second, the acceptance of certain modernistic advances in production, especially the need for solidity, which derived from

---

[1] An interweaving of the colloquial and the rhetorical was found useful when I produced the *Agamemnon* in Louis MacNeice's translation for the Leeds University Un ion Theatre Group in 1946. See Appendix A.

[2] Leslie Harris must have been with Tree about the years 1902 and 1903, perhaps playing under the stage-name 'Eric Leslie', which appears in the programmes.

having witnessed Granville Barker's three productions at the Savoy in 1912 and 1914. In commenting on my *Timon of Athens* at Leeds a critic in the Journal of the National Union of Students Arts Festival (*The Festival Review*, 8 January 1949) remarked that I 'achieved the remarkable duality of producing sensitively in the modern style, but yet acting in the way of the old school'. That may hold some truth, though I was myself unaware of the discrepancy, which was perhaps caused by my directing others to do what pleased myself as a Shakespearian who needed little interpretation, while my own performance was levelled at a non-specialist audience; for we are not normally performing to an audience of specialists.

Both realism and grandeur have their rights; more—in their mutual interaction lies the key to all our problems. In speaking Shakespearian verse failure to get the right vocal artistry for a subtle gradation and interplay of colloquialism and poetic rhapsody will lead sooner or later to displays of raw emotion and rant. What is sometimes called the 'grand style' in speaking is the adoption of a manner which can compass variations without strain. It is not afraid to pause on a glowing phrase; it enjoys a climax, though the climax may on occasion be quiet rather than noisy; it will never shout—unless, of course, a shout is part of the story being enacted—gaining power and intensity instead through an increase of *spoken* volume, whereas a shout is hollow and without significance; and it is as much at home with colloquial accents as with poetic depth. All this it can do because it enjoys a sense of spiritual purpose in the birth of grandeur from realism, and works from that. It is the eternal enemy of rant. All this applies too, *mutatis mutandis*, to gesture.

The easiest way to define my 'key' to Shakespearian acting and production is to repeat once again my old contention regarding the principle of active growth, or unfurling, in Shakespeare's dramatic artistry. This I have already discussed (pp. 31–3, 122); and it is illustrated again and again in my various descriptions. This growth or blossoming may sometimes be seen as a gradual untangling of conflicts and confusions to disclose some simple truth or beauty. Single speeches reveal it. A surface is broken to reveal some splendour.

One such example we have discussed in treating of Henry V's 'Crispin' speech, wherein the King is shown searching for a direction, getting the key-word 'Crispin' and thereafter rising to a victorious rhetoric, where we have a good example of a quiet climax on 'we band of brothers', spoken softly as a crowning thought. Richard III's soliloquy after seeing the ghosts starts with the ego and conscience in baffling self-conflict until the battling gives way to the simple and compelling truth of condemnation. Another fine example is John of Gaunt's speech on England in *Richard II*. It must be spoken with the quavering accents of age which alone justify its repetitions and the involved and drawn-out syntax. The speech should *accumulate* energy, growing with victorious effort from a death-bed struggle to a powerful climax: therein is its structural and dramatic meaning, its conjuring up, through close poetic characterization, of a mysterious power, its soul. It is an indefinable essence, a presence behind, or thrown up by, the lines or events of Shakespearian drama that I am trying to indicate and to which it too often seems that our generation, through its leading exponents, is insensitive.

More subtle is the King's sleep-speech (pp. 31–2 above) in the second part of *Henry IV*, beginning

> How many thousand of my poorest subjects
> Are at this hour asleep.
>
> (III. i. 4)

Its start holds a poignant realism; the King is almost in tears; a catch in the voice may be allowed to suggest them at 'press mine eyelids down' and the cry for 'forgetfulness'. He moves on to a more resonantly poetic realization of kingly state, the generalized thought dominating psychology and character as 'the perfumed chambers of the great' rise before us; and then the speech—it is hardly the King now, but the speech—takes wing as it calls up the image of the ship-boy sleeping at the mast-head in a storm wild enough to awaken 'death'; sleep, already called a 'god', being established as a great cosmic power, twin to death. All this, from tears to thunder, from pathos to apocalypse, must be reflected in the speaking. The conclusion curving down to the final couplet is, in Shakespeare's usual manner, quiet.[1]

In Macbeth's 'If it were done when 'tis done . . .' (I. vii) we move from mental confusion to the disclosure of angels 'trumpet-

---

[1] Many years ago I heard this speech beautifully delivered by Mr. George Skillan in a Stratford production on tour at Cheltenham.

tongued', Pity like a child, and heavenly 'cherubin' horsed in air. When Antony in *Antony and Cleopatra* hears of Cleopatra's supposed death (IV. xii), he is caught between his calling as statesman-soldier and his love.

> Unarm, Eros; the long day's task is done,
> And we must sleep . . .

His following words are disjointed. He speaks in turn to Mardian who brought the message, to Eros, and to his dead love; see-sawing between life and death. As he throws off his armour he is aware of a spiritual 'strength' with which the 'force' of his earthly existence is being 'entangled', until the final revelation springs new-born from these alternations and confusions:

> Stay for me:
> Where souls do couch on flowers, we'll hand in hand,
> And with our sprightly port make the ghosts gaze;
> Dido and her Aeneas shall want troops,
> And all the haunt be ours.

We end for once in excitement at 'Come, Eros! Eros!' The normal procedure is to start quietly, perhaps colloquially, and then, smoothly taking off like an aeroplane, to become poetically airborne, and finally return to earth. The most difficult moments are at the transitions, from earth to air and then back, which if too sudden may ruin the effect. A good example lending itself to a smooth take-off and return is Hamlet's 'Look here, upon this picture and on this . . .' (p. 50 above). Another, embedded before and after in old-man colloquialism, is Prospero's 'cloud-capp'd towers'.[1]

Even were it advisable to speak a long speech in one unvaried gush success would be impossible. I have heard Clarence in a major production of *Richard III* start his long dream-speech like this with the inevitable result. This is an extreme example; but few actors today know quite what is demanded. It is extraordinary that such blunders should be condoned.

Not only speeches but scenes and whole plays show this kind of development and disclosure: we have already (p. 32) discussed

[1] I was privileged to give some illustrative examples of Shakespeare's speech-structure on the Third Programme of the British Broadcasting Corporation on 17 December 1963. Other recordings are in the British Institute of Recorded Sound, and at Birmingham (p. 14). I hope for the support of a gramophone firm.

the Deposition scene in *Richard II* and emphasized the access of power and dignity attained by both Romeo and Othello before their stories close.

These advances are advances in *poetic* stature, and as they assume form they must be accorded a newly expanded emphasis not only in the acting but in the *type of acting* used. I offer a couple of examples easy to describe, both of which have already been touched on (pp. 52-3, 57 above).

The dramatic pivot of Romeo's upward progress is his scene of abandoned emotion with Friar Laurence. Here for the first time he becomes a dramatic *power*, and the acting should become broader, suiting the power. Romeo in distraction speaks to the Friar:

> Wert thou as young as I, Juliet thy love,
> An hour but married, Tybalt murderèd,
> Doting like me, and like me banishèd,
> Then might'st thou speak, then might'st thou tear thy hair,
> And fall upon the ground, as I do now,
> Taking the measure of an unmade grave.
>
> (*Romeo and Juliet*, III. iii. 64)

The voice is at first high and querulous. At 'tear thy hair' the hands clutch the head; at 'fall upon the ground' the body is falling while the vocal note is simultaneously deepening; at the last line, the voice is at its deepest, and the body still. The acting has lived the poetry.

King Lear is, as we have noted (pp. 121-2), at first a realistic character-study in petulant old age, but from Lear's 'No, I'll not weep' onwards the drama becomes air-borne, allowing and demanding new resources of technique in voice, action, and probably setting too. Lear's address to the elements demands care. He should be given a dominating position, raised as on some craggy eminence, one arm up and pointing. We must observe, as does the verse, the correct sequence of wind, lightning and thunder in this order; we must interspace flashes, sounds and speech correctly, sounds dying as the words crest up, in alternate waves;[1] and Lear can act the poetry, his hand for a moment flickering, zig-zagging, for the 'thought-executing fires'; then

---

[1] My methods here can claim an honourable support, since Professor Moelwyn Merchant tells me that Garrick's prompt-book for this scene contains careful directions for the interspacings of thunder.

drawn back as in self-defence, with a salute-like action, at 'vaunt-couriers to oak-cleaving thunderbolts', leaving a perfect position for the back of the hand to be drawn swiftly across the forehead at 'singe my white head'. These expansions should in due course graduate down again to realism and old age pathos; Lear descends; then, at the dictate of the poetry, his actions again up-flower. At

> Close, pent-up guilts,
> Rive your concealing continents, and cry
> These dreadful summoners grace . . .

the hands may be cupped in front for 'close', break apart, palms down, for 'rive', and be raised high for the rest. Though the literary expert may feel no intellectual need for such explanatory gestures, yet for most of the audience, who could not translate 'close', 'rive', 'pent-up' or 'continents' with facility and exactitude, the gestures serve to make the speech live and wing it through the auditorium as a living entity; on an open stage, where the actor might be turned from the spectator, they would help greatly. And yet it is not simply a question of giving expression to the words. Exciting gestures have, during this cosmic movement, rights of their own, however well we know the text. Grand movements or postures may often be regarded as our aim, the text their excuse. 'Drama' means action; 'theatre' means seeing; we want more, in such a scene, than words and reasoning, though words and reasoning may have given us our cue. The poetry is to be expanded and embodied in physical and material terms: that is what staging is for, to embody the poetry.

We shall not, of course, be so excitingly engaged all the time; much of our performance will be on a more pedestrian level. It is too often supposed that there is some single right-and-wrong applicable to every moment of a performance, whereas there should be continual changes of tempo, method and appeal. The intellect is enriched, the eye riveted, the ear delighted, in turn; only rarely should all work together at full pressure; but when such moments occur, we must be prepared for them.

Some disturbing ethical problems face both producer and actor in *Macbeth*. Countering the surface of crime and retribution we have in our tragic hero a steady advance in *poetic* stature. We move from the neurotic stammering of

This supernatural soliciting
Cannot be ill, cannot be good; if ill . . .

(I. iii. 130)

and

If it were done when 'tis done, then 'twere well
It were done quickly . . .

(I. vii. 1)

through the resonance of

Then, prophet-like
They hail'd him father to a line of kings . . .

(III, i. 59)

and all its following reverberations of royalty, to the spiritualized
passages at the close: 'My way of life . . .', 'Can'st thou not
minister to a mind diseas'd . . .', 'Tomorrow and tomorrow and
tomorrow . . .' (V. iii. 22; V. iii. 40; V. v. 19.) The poetry, which is
the soul, of Macbeth has somehow matured, more than fulfilling
the early pointer

Though his bark cannot be lost
Yet it shall be tempest-toss'd.

(I. iii. 24)

Macbeth appears somehow to have gained in stature through the
bravely-borne horrors of crime and guilt. We have already (p. 136)
emphasized Macbeth's bravery in face of the supernatural.

Lady Macbeth shares, differently, in this mysterious assurance.
Directly after the appalling news of the slaughter of Macduff's
family we are, as of set purpose, switched to the sleep-walking
scene where, within the mysterious dimension of sleep, the soul
of Lady Macbeth is felt as overarching her actions in such a
way as to leave her, that is her greater, immortal self, in essence
clean. The mystery is more easily experienced, in this almost fool-
proof scene, than explained. It is, like Ophelia's mad-scene in
Hamlet, 'fool-proof' because, while the actor's normal task is to
make us aware of the soul-reality *through* ordinary speech and
actions, here words and behaviour are merest flotsam and jetsam
whose very inconsequence serves to suggest the otherness which
in the more normal scenes we so arduously labour to establish.
Explanation is difficult, but we are certainly more aware of mystery
than of censure. In his *Defence of Poetry* Shelley, probably thinking
of this scene, has a helpful comment: 'Even crime is disarmed of

281

half its horror and all its contagion by being represented as the fatal consequence of the unfathomable agencies of nature.' The one comment that is not wholly irrelevant is that made by the Doctor: 'God, God, forgive us all.' The soul-reality is not, in such a scene, stated; but its presence is implied. Much the same happens when young Malcolm refers glibly at the play's conclusion to 'this dead butcher and his fiend-like queen'. The line simultaneously serves to preclude any facile sentimentalizing while arousing in us, who have shared in the protagonists' experience, an immediate, if indefinable, reservation.

These considerations react on production and performance. 'Tomorrow and tomorrow and tomorrow' may be spoken in abandoned misery, wistful despair, or fierce rejection. We elect the more dignified and choose the third. *Macbeth* stands near the fountain-head of a long semi-Faustian and semi-Satanic tradition, of which Milton's Satan in *Paradise Lost* and Byron's *Manfred* are outstanding later examplars. In the fifth act Macbeth must be played not 'like a hangman who has taken to drink, but like an angel who has fallen' (Masefield, *A Macbeth Production*, 31). The easiest way to focus what is being done is to note that redemption within the greater works of this tradition subsequent to Marlowe's *Doctor Faustus* comes not through penitence but through recognition; not through self-abasement but through self-condemnation, the centre of consciousness being on the higher level, not in the self but in the soul.[1] It is precisely this recognition that Shakespeare emphasizes, in *Macbeth*, in other tragedies, and most clearly of all in Wolsey's attainment in *Henry VIII* to 'a peace above all earthly dignities' and 'a still and quiet conscience' (III. ii. 380) not through his own penitence but simply through exposure and acceptance. Macbeth attains honesty before the community and before himself; without ceasing to be what he is he yet knows what he is, and what must follow; and he accepts bravely, in terms of combat, his death.[2]

My reading is, in general, supported by Gordon Craig in his essay 'On the Ghosts in the Tragedies of Shakespeare' (*On the Art of the Theatre 1911*, edn. of 1957, 264–80), where, after a plea for

[1] We here draw near to Mr. C. B. Purdom's thesis in *What Happens in Shakespeare* (1963), and in particular to his brilliant commentary on *Macbeth*.

[2] For this reading of *Macbeth* see also my 'Additional Note (1947)' to '*Macbeth* and the Metaphysic of Evil' in *The Wheel of Fire* (enlarged edition); *The Sovereign Flower*, 248–52; and *Christ and Nietzsche*, 85–6.

an adequate realization of the supernatural powers in *Macbeth*, he writes also of the final scenes as follows:

In the last act Macbeth awakes. It almost seems to be a new rôle . . . He is not the man some actors show him to be, the trapped, cowardly villain; nor yet is he to my mind the bold, courageous villain as other actors play him. He is as a doomed man who has been suddenly awakened on the morning of his execution . . .

(269)

This may not be exactly my reading, but we both see the concluding scenes as an advance. Not that Craig regards the ghostly elements as unreal: his whole essay is, as we have seen, a plea, never more needed than today, for a proper atmospheric realization of them, even to the adding of more than Shakespeare explicitly demands.[1]

This, then, is the Shakespearian revelation: a sense of human soul-integrity beneath appearances of good and evil; and in all tragic issues, a sense of some mysterious positive beyond, or within, disaster. The best comment on Shakespeare's total statement is given in Bottom's doggerel lines in *A Midsummer Night's Dream*:

> The raging rocks
> And shivering shocks
> Shall break the locks
> Of prison gates:
> And Phibbus' car
> Shall shine from far
> And make and mar
> The foolish Fates.

(I. ii. 34)

An opacity, a 'prison', is broken, to reveal distant ('far') sun-splendours.

We are here close to the essence of great drama and good acting. A good actor identifies himself with his part, and attuning his own 'I' to that other 'I' accords it to the full that royal worth and dignity which we each attribute to ourselves. The insistent *rise* under tragic stress on which we have laid so great an emphasis is itself but an exploitation of what is in any event a law of good

---

[1] For my opportunity of gaining an acting experience of the part of Macbeth, as also of Macduff, Brutus and Cassius, I am indebted to the various productions of Mr. Brownlow Card of Toronto. See p. 134, note.

stage writing and good performance. I refer to the prime necessity, provided that due place is given also to the cadences and downward curves of voice, for a continual lifting of speech or scene with rising intonations; for without those—though we can of course have too much of them—the most exquisite cadences become soporific. Closely related is the need for an actor in poetic drama to preserve *an upright and firm torso*, which is the location of spiritual power, leaving mental distraction and physical weakness to be reflected by face, hands and legs. Shakespeare's humanism is a humanism drawn directly from his profession.

In writing of *King Lear* (p. 122 above) I used the image of an egg broken to make way for new life. The image is helpful, for without that 'new life' which they exist to bring to birth Shakespearian presentations remain dead. Often have I watched an able actor, or some finely appointed production, labouring throughout the evening to break the Shakespearian egg, and not a crack in it appears; or, worse, an axe is wielded, some mighty crack is made, the shell splits open—and there is nothing inside. On this matter there is no room for compromise since it is precisely this 'new life' felt through tragedy that is Shakespeare's central contribution and the main cause, even when inadequately projected and only semi-consciously received, of his enduring appeal across the globe.

Shakespeare's reading of human affairs is, to this extent, both royal and spiritual; his genius is aware of far more than the superficies of evil and tragedy, instinctively writing from or within a dimension in which their significance is altered. This being so, we must give exact attention to works where fantasy seems to reign; for in such a poet, it is more than fantasy; it is a rendering explicit of what is elsewhere implicit. I am thinking of *A Midsummer Night's Dream*, the more cosmic scenes of the tragedies, of the resurrection of Hermione, of the Vision of Jupiter in *Cymbeline*, and *The Tempest*.

3

We have now to consider the bearing of our discussion on the 'open' stages so much discussed today.

It appears that the new Festival Theatre at Stratford, Ontario, follows a simple lighting scheme of the kind counselled in my text, using whitish lights, as did Granville Barker, and a non-pictorial background. I quote from an article on the methods of Miss

Afterthoughts

Tanya Moiseiwitsch by Mr. Robin Sanborn in the Stratford *Beacon-Herald* (Stratford, Ontario) of 17 June 1961:[1]

Unlike conventional stages no flats or scenic back-drops of any kind are used on Stratford's open platform stage. This, combined with the fact that only white lights are used to illuminate actors playing against a dark, neutral background, makes the use of colour extremely important.

The 'colour' is provided by the design of 'costumes and props'; on these falls the responsibility of making the play's 'mood' visually apparent. The method is in attunement with my own suggestions regarding the power of a darkish background to throw up colourful costumes (p. 66–7 above), though I have never produced on an 'open' stage. Colour is, beyond all question, a necessary constituent, if only as a visual correlative to the colourful emotions being deployed.

I have as yet no wide experience of recent developments on the open stage and what I have to say must remain tentative. There is clearly something unsatisfactory from the actor's standpoint in being placed on a proscenium stage, set apart from the audience and pretending to talk to one's companions while simultaneously striving to project every accent and nuance of facial expression to the gallery. The test is severe, though there is a corresponding thrill to be gained from moments of success. But open stages too have their disadvantages.

The viewing of the actors from so many different angles seems to preclude the kind of reliance on significant grouping that I have hitherto regarded as important, a group, as a group, being essentially pictorial. There is also the danger of the blurring of words. Stage hearing is not merely a mechanical recording of separate words; it is far more the mental reception of phrase and emphasis —good phrasing may be more important for understanding and audibility than good diction—together with the accompaniment of eye and gesture; if this whole is lost through the actor being turned away from the hearer, words may be lost too. According to Gordon Craig the pointing of his words by actions was a main key to Irving's art (p. 235 above). Even if the words are heard, the hearing may have needed a concentrated attention that should never have been demanded, *since for every quantum of psychic power*

---

[1] For my knowledge of this article my thanks are due to Mr. and Mrs. Stafford Johnston of Stratford, Ontario.

given to that concentration there is so much lost from emotional or spiritual experience. Apart from the kind of stage being used, disregard of these simple truths is the cause of much muffled acting among professionals and amateurs alike.[1]

Can our contemporary adventures in open and arena[2] stages solve our problems? They have no strong precedent in the theatres of ancient Greece, where the audience seems to have encircled no more than the chorus, the actors speaking frontally. There was certainly a freer use of the open stage in Medieval and Shakespearian times, though many details remain obscure and we must not forget the indoor stages and the Court masques. In the public theatres we may suppose that by means of a stage projecting into the auditorium there was achieved an intimacy between audience and actors which has since been lost. Even so we must remember that those audiences enjoyed a sense of spirit, royalty and magic in actual persons and events which we do not. Afterwards there was a split; poetry could only survive on a stage demarked firmly from the audience and supported by the visual magic of scene and illumination. Century by century the stage became more and more of a mysterious box of tricks until in the nineteenth the house-lights were gone to make the auditorium an apt symbol of a darkened society while the stage assumed by contrast a yet greater brilliance to fuel through the visual imagination the parched cravings of the spirit.

This split has remained; it is with us still, and even widening. In the theatre we have grown to expect a 'magical' area; with Shakespeare we are never far from the mystique of royalty. May there not be some danger in our return to a stage-conception which presupposes a spirituality and a royalism which we of the twentieth century cannot claim? If actors come too freely within the audience, there is, and it is sometimes claimed, though Mr. Richard Southern avoids the error, as a good too obvious to need

[1] The advantages have been discussed and defended by Mr. Richard Southern in *The Open Stage*, 1953. Some of the dangers, including the threat to facial expression and the actor's eyes, have been surveyed by Mr. Laurence Kitchin with reference to the Chichester stage in *The Listener* of 23 August 1962. An interesting correspondence, to which Mr. C. B. Purdom was a main contributor, lasted until 22 November 1962.

[2] Granville Barker thought that the arena stage would distract attention from the play towards the audience on the other side. Max Reinhardt's production of *The Miracle* was 'largely spoilt by being played under these conditions' (*The Exemplary Theatre*, 217).

defending, a new sense of intimacy. But is there not a danger that in stage-affairs intimacy may be bought, as it has on occasion been bought in other spheres of life, *at the cost of mystery and magic*? For those who love the theatre the thought is terrifying.[1]

The problem converges, more than ever before, on the actor. Of Craig's three dramatic constituents, sight (including lights and colour), sounds (including music and words), and motion (including actions), the first was emphasized by the traditionalists, Irving and Tree; the second by the innovators, Poel and Barker; and the third will be emphasized by the open stage. Much will be lost; facial expression and words *must* often suffer; long set-speeches cannot be spoken effectively for every member of the audience; but the actor's figure will be newly possessed by the eye, as a living statue rather than as a picture, and his physique and *actions* will and must be made to speak from whatever angle we view him.

But action without significance is useless; if the producer moves his actors about simply in order to give his audience varied views, irritation will result. There must *be* action however; and it must be *significant action*. Intimacy and realism will be used; but also there will be needed a new *expansion*, such as I have already described (pp. 279–80), of poetically impregnated poise and gesture. Without scenic support a heavy responsibility will fall on the lighting to provide the atmosphere for what is being done. The acting will, at high moments, have to master the kind of expansion for which Salvini appeared to be asking when of Mounet Sully he said, according to Craig's account:

He and Irving, and most of the foreign actors, while able to *imitate* Nature up to a certain point, can go no further. Beyond that point their imitation ceases to *be Nature* and becomes conventional, with exaggerated gestures and mannerisms.

(Craig, *The Theatre Advancing*, 243)

It is towards that indefinable 'further' already hinted (pp. 219, 224, 226 above) by Craig and Barker, that my own acting has with all its deficiencies and ineffectualities been instinctively aiming; and in the process I have composed a book, as yet unpublished, illustrated with photographs and containing spiritual analyses on the principles laid down by François Delsarte. This new acting

---

[1] For some valuable remarks on the modern theatre's use of visual magic as correlatives to spiritual perception see Aldous Huxley's *Heaven and Hell*, Appendix III.

will not appear 'stylized'; it will mature from an expansion, but never from a distortion, of the human organism and its instinctive expressions. In Salvini's terms it will have 'nature' without the mannerisms of convention. It is not easy. Salvini himself, whom Poel rated as the greatest tragedian of his day (*Monthly Letters*, 1929; 'A Great Tragedian', 1-8), at his best moments appears to have approached the ideal. Of his delivery of one of Othello's speeches George Henry Lewes wrote:

'I remember nothing so musically perfect in its *tempo* and intonation, so emotionally perfect in expression, as his delivery of this passage—the fury visibly growing with every word, his whole being vibrating, his face aflame, the voice becoming more and more terrible, and yet so completely under musical control that it never approached a scream.'

(*On Actors and the Art of Acting*, 1875; 269)

This emphasis on vocal control must be taken to apply similarly to gesture and action so that the 'whole being' of the actor makes one passionate harmony.[1]

Production, given the resources, should hold no insuperable difficulties; speaking can be mastered; but the problems raised by acting, real acting, are endless.[2]

If magic is sacrificed, our open stage and arena theatres will fail; if it can be preserved, then all may be well. It is only because Shakespeare's art is so richly spiritualized that we have to aim so insistently at solidity of projection; for nothing is so easy, and yet nothing wrongs it so much, as to reduce the soul-reality to cloudy abstractions. The quest is difficult; and we may respect both the labours of William Poel and Granville Barker in the causes of solidity and simplicity and also Tree's and Craig's attempts, each after his own fashion, to realize the greater life in terms of scenic art and atmospheric colourings. All are variations of the one drive towards a just revivification of the Shakespearian poetry. But on the open stage a greater responsibility than ever will converge on the actor. A new dimension of *poetic* acting must be awakened. And here it seems that the use of symbolic objects such as I have

[1] For my own attempts in this kind see in my 'Dramatic Papers' (p. 14 above) Mr. Roy Walker's letter of 12 December 1948 (on Timon).

[2] William Poel recounts that his teacher in acting said that he could get his voice right in two years, but that it would take seven for his movements. Poel did not underrate the importance of action, though he wanted it to be sparingly used. He refers to 'notes for an illustrated lecture' (William Poel, *Monthly Letters*, 1929; 11-12; 11, note).

suggested for my 'ideal' production (pp. 144, 147) might make an unsuspected contribution. They would help to give the open stage that dimension of metaphysical meaning which it otherwise lacks.

It is part of Shakespeare's fascination that the problem should be one calling for new, and ever new, solutions, according to time, place, and the particular play, actors and audiences concerned. For a drama written in classic form there are few such problems: do it on a Victorian stage, in a small hall, in a church or garden, through a proscenium frame or on an open stage, the form dominates, its essential nature unaltered and at home. This may be an argument in favour of classic form; 'classic' plays are, apart from the chorus, almost fool-proof for the producer, though not for the actor. But Shakespeare did not write in classic form.

And yet throughout Shakespeare's humanism there is nevertheless a golden thread of unity which may be designated 'spiritual' and 'royal'. Whether in speech, person, scene, or play, that will be our key. If our actors and producers work from this, making us feel the inward spirit-sap and rising power, then it may not so very much matter whether they follow nineteenth century methods at one extreme or work on an open stage at the other; or choose, as most today will, one of the many intermediate methods open to him. Externals may be allowed to vary according to the occasion and the play concerned. For *The Tempest* a style not too far removed from Tree's may have its value; most of the Histories, if rich with royal ensignia and appointments, should do well on an open stage such as that of the Festival Theatre at Stratford, Ontario; and *Timon of Athens* demands such a treatment as we have described. For the rest, if the producer has insight and in-feeling into the spiritual organs of Shakespeare's art, the worst errors will be avoided. The actor-manager or modern producer who adapts Shakespeare for his purpose is to be justified in so far as he remains true to the spirit of what he is handling. The letter can often safely be transgressed; it is too frequent an error to compound for spiritual inadequacy by a meticulous attention to Shakespeare's text, the surface of which asks no deep commitment or creative collaboration. The good production will be one which piles up detail on detail in exact attunement to the play's deeper meanings, which are its soul. Such a production may not super-ficially appear 'original'—it should indeed hope not to—but it will possess the only originality worth having.

What we want is a combination of solidity, grandeur and atmosphere, the last term covering magical and spiritual apprehensions. But to attain such a composite is not easy. Barker touched it at the Savoy, making solidity and buoyancy one (p. 224), the high end of all art, though in terms mainly of pastoral and comedy, of charm rather than grandeur. Were tragedy so mastered we should deserve renown. Meanwhile, might not the Royal Shakespeare Company, or our new National Theatre, do joint honour to our Poet Laureate and to itself by putting its resources to an exact following out of those simple yet masterly instructions which Masefield in *A Macbeth Production* has laid down?

The terms 'magical' and 'spiritual' are apposite, since it is the business of the Shakespearian stage to explore the interpenetration of human affairs and spiritual power. In doing this it is not enough that our productions should remain content with verbal accuracy and an intellectual response; rather they should enlist every legitimate resource of eye and ear and action to awake the imagination and thence expand our consciousness beyond the terms of twentieth century belief. That even half-heartedly or blunderingly aimed at, much of the rest will follow. If advice must be given regarding the outside, the suits and trappings, of production, it will follow Polonius' advice to his son:

> Costly thy habit as thy purse can buy,
> But not express'd in fancy; rich, not gaudy . . .
> *(Hamlet*, I. iii. 70)

That might seem to be our last word. But not quite. It must be completed by Polonius' conclusion:

> This above all: to thine own self be true,
> And it must follow, as the night the day,
> Thou can'st not then be false to any man.
> *(Hamlet*, I. iii. 78)

'True' and 'false' have in Shakespeare wide connotations. So understood they may be applied to both acting and production; for truth to the inner reality or soul, which is one with the Shakespearian royalty, will alone give weight and lustre to the externals.

Postscript, August 1963
The Stratford Ontario Festival, Canada

⟨ornament⟩

Since completing my text I have this summer visited the Stratford Ontario Festival on the invitation of Dr. Berners W. Jackson of McMaster University, Hamilton, to lecture and take part in the Seminar discussions of the courses organized by the University in connexion with the theatre.

The Festival, which started in 1953, has now a world-wide reputation. Originating from a brilliant intuition of Mr. Tom Patterson of Stratford, the venture was supported first by Stratford and afterwards by other Canadian centres; and from abroad. It was given its first impetus, design and direction by Sir Tyrone Guthrie and Miss Tanya Moiseiwitsch; and has now since 1955 been advancing vigorously under the artistic direction of Mr. Michael Langham. Mr. John Hayes, the Caphis—a part which I built up—of my Toronto *Timon of Athens* (Picture 18), is the Festival's Production Manager. Drawing on audiences from great distances in Canada and the United States, as well as from overseas, the Festival packs its 2,200 seats night after night for a period of some fifteen weeks.[1]

Our first interest is the open stage theatre which may be called the 'headquarters' today of open stage Shakespearian presentation, and has become a model, since followed in England and the United States, of theatric design. We may also call it the culmination of the drive for Elizabethan simplicity and freedom inaugurated by William Poel, continued by Granville Baker, and followed, at least in solidity of effects and refusal of elaborate lighting, in my own, and especially my earlier, Hart House Theatre

[1] Authoritative reports of the Festival by Dr. Arnold Edinborough appear regularly in *Shakespeare Survey* (England) and the *Shakespeare Quarterly* (U.S.A.).

productions in the thirties. The use of a neutral, greyish, background fits one of my own demands, as already stated (p. 66 above); the other, and it may seem contradictory, demand (p. 125) for grandeur is not so obviously accommodated. Lighting, confined to white, steel and amber, is directed from lamps circling the auditorium, the main ones high but some, smaller, from the balcony; with the result that, though the stage-area alone receives their concentration, the audience themselves are fairly well lit, and the 'house-lights', in effect, up. At back centre there is a protruding triangular edifice pushing out to a point, supported by small pillars and carrying a small platform approached both from within and by steps on either side leading from the main stage. There are various other entrances, including two down-stage tunnels opening from beneath the audience.

My previous comments on the open stage appear to me in the main sound, though I am now in a position to speak with more authority. I shall next note what I take to be (i) its advantages and (ii) its disadvantages.

So far as the human figures are concerned, there was no loss, as I had feared there might be, of stage magic. Costumes at Stratford are superb and with the help of properties under straight white and amber lighting are our main source of colour. The persons, their robes and bare limbs—provided that not too much of the body is revealed, which tends to demand more subtle illumination—exist in a rounded dimension unachievable on the picture-stage, being possessed by the eye in a new fashion; and even when near, they can be magical. They radiate the power of statuary together with the magic of stage lighting and physical vitality; and all this in close relation to one's self. There is no distancing, as from another world.

Success is also vivid in physical movement. The many entrances allow freedom for every kind of action, and the swirling, jostling, and turning figures are a living display. Any fight, whether in single combat or general warring, comes off splendidly; so much so that, to adopt Bottom's words, one is almost impelled to cry out, 'Let them fight again!' When action is quiescent, the figures, draped as it were around the stage, feed the eye with aesthetic delight.

If we remember Nietzsche's distinction in *The Birth of Tragedy* of his two dramatic principles, 'Apollonian' for sculpture, epic, and visual clarity and 'Dionysian' for music, lyric and mystery, we shall see that the advantages we have noted, being (i) sculptural and (ii) epic are pre-eminently Apollonian. On this stage the 'Dionysian', which covers the elements of sound and mystery in distinction from visual clarity and lively action, appears to be less at home.

The poetry cannot be planned to transfix the whole audience simultaneously as it can on the proscenium stage. Drawing on my own experience and reports from discussion groups, I have provisionally come to the conclusion that if one is near and on the same level, in a 'good' seat but at one side, an actor turned away tends to fail in audibility; but that if one is farther back and higher up and in a 'bad' seat, the actor's position, even from a side or back view, matters less; as though the words first ascend to the bell-shaped roof-structure, devised as a sounding medium for the orchestra (which is set back-stage and invisible), and next splay out and down, fountain-wise; the actor's original speaking position becoming to this extent the less important for those seated high and far. Such is my tentative suggestion; but, since verbal hearing has so much to do with the *simultaneous* reception of the intellectual content, and since that depends in part on facial expression, it would be rash to claim that the words can ever, failing some new kind of mechanical amplification or sound-deflection, have the total impact which is possible on the proscenium stage. Once again, I assert that hearing alone is not enough; one should ideally hear without effort, without active *listening*, since for every modicum of psychic energy given to listening so much is lost of the capacity to experience and enjoy.

It was remarked to me in a seminar discussion that, though the audience's involvement was here undeniable, it was an involvement such as one knows in real life, watching, say, Hamlet as a courtier at Elsinore watches him; but that the mysterious *identification* with Hamlet, the being, as it were, momentarily *inside* his mind or soul, is attained better through the artifice of the proscenium and the greater verbal and visual concentration there attainable. It seems, paradoxically, that the apparently 'distanced' figures on the proscenium (i.e. picture) stage may have an inward meaning more close than physical intimacy corresponding to that deepest self-hood beyond all daylight reason of Nietzsche's *Birth of Tragedy* (v; and see *The Golden Labyrinth*, 7): on the mystic principle, perhaps, adumbrated by T. S. Eliot's words in *Marina*, 'More distant than stars and nearer than the eye'. Nor can an open stage at all easily charge certain areas with particular spiritual or emotional significances, if only because the producer must be allowed freedom to move his actors about to face this way and that in order to satisfy his widely dispersed audience. The open stage disperses; the proscenium concentrates; the one favours externals, the other drives inwards.

We must, moreover, observe a more general lack in spiritual transmission. In so far as human figures are concerned, simple lighting and fine costuming undoubtedly create atmosphere. But if more in the way of scenic effect and atmosphere appears to be needed, as in *Macbeth*, *King Lear* and the latter half of *Timon of Athens*, the problem is severe. Nor can we say that everything may be left to Shakespeare's words, since these, however good the speaking, cannot, as we have seen, have the total effect that is possible on the proscenium stage. Everything on the open stage has to be shown; what is not shown does not exist. On the proscenium stage what is not shown—the thunder-stricken heath in *King Lear*, the sea beyond the rock-line in *Timon of Athens*—may, if accompanied by the mystery of sound—for sound-effects are, if properly done, on the old stages deeply mysterious—open the infinite. The open stage may seem to be buying expanse at the cost of infinitude. Sound effects might conceivably be devised to meet, in part, this charge; but if so, they would probably have to come from all *around the auditorium* (compare pp. 142, 160 above).

Our complaints may be crisply summarized by suggesting that this Stratford theatre can accomplish marvels of Apollonian stagecraft but is less obviously equipped for a more Dionysian task.[1] The only way to make the stage from all angles visually meaningful, and position and grouping within it deeply significant, would be, as I have already suggested, to use certain permanent solids of symbolic content such as those that I have imagined for *Macbeth* and *The Winter's Tale* (pp. 144, 147). These, belonging as they would to the same three-dimensional world as the actors' figures, appear to be the rational expedient.

I add some brief notes on the three Shakespearian productions done this year.

[1] My reaction may be interestingly compared with that of Mr. T. R. Barnes to the Maddermarket Theatre; see p. 79 above, note.

Postscript

The Comedy of Errors, directed by M. Jean Gascon, was done in Commedia dell' Arte style. That such an approach smothers the real comedy under a slap-stick buffoonery of a lower order may, the plan accepted, be forgiven; so too may the masks which when grotesque add nothing to what may be better done by skilful make-up,[1] and when used for a straight part merely obliterate expression. All this was part of the plan, and given the plan the execution was praiseworthy. One strong criticism must nevertheless be registered. The guying of Aegeon's opening and tragic speech was inadmissible. Shakespearian comedy is regularly, as I have shown in *The Shakespearian Tempest*, related to tragic feeling, and no use of a manner drawn from a different type of comedy justifies the distortion of a Shakespearian essence. Besides, the audience cannot follow the drama unless they hear what Aegeon has to say.

Troilus and Cressida, directed by Mr. Langham, was a major success. The subtleties of the drama were responsively projected. The two main parties were well and correctly distinguished, the Greeks drably uniformed and the Trojans beautiful in gold and white, the Troy-filled stage under amber-tinted lights becoming a pool of gold; the only possible complaint being that the parties seemed costumed for different seasons; and perhaps also that Achilles and Patroclus wore light drapes more suggestive of the Trojans than of the Greeks.

The drama's meaning pivots on the characterization of Cressida and Pandarus. If these are satirically and repellently presented, the edifice crashes: make Cressida an obvious minx and Troilus' 'This is, and is not, Cressid' (v. ii. 143) lacks detonation, and we have been agonized for nothing. Miss Martha Henry's Cressida was admirable in its steering of a difficult course, the ambivalence throughout preserved, the 'poor girl' (v. iii. 99) mysteriously convincing, nothing sentimentalized yet the result deeply moving. The conception of Pandarus, played by Mr. William Hutt as the first effeminate old man in my theatre-going experience, corresponded precisely to his peculiar function of enjoying the physical bringing together of the two lovers, whereby he simultaneously recalls the Nurse in *Romeo and Juliet* and embodies the bisexual propensities of all sexual-romantic artistry. When the

---

[1] Note the use of make-up for an effect that might have seemed to require masks in our picture of the Weird Sisters in *Macbeth* (Picture 31).

romance crashes, Pandarus' pathetic distraction, his scattered phrases, snatches of verse, and tears (IV. ii. 83–8; IV. iv. 1–54; V. iii. 97–113), make him a personification of romance in tatters. Here both production and performance showed sensitivity and perception of a high order. Mr. Douglas Rain's speaking and acting were admirably devised to mould Ulysses' long 'order' speech, the repetitive quality of which lends itself well to such a treatment, to the Stratford stage.

Timon of Athens satisfied me less. The use of modern dress was well justified, but its potentialities insufficiently developed. The 'feasts, pomps and vain-glories' (I. ii. 252) exemplified by the first Banquet, at which the chief men of the state are ceremoniously present and which could and surely should have been worked up in full evening dress and flashing orders, was reduced to an ordinary—or so it seemed—business-man's luncheon. Surely too the gold drape thrown from the balcony for the *second* Banquet should have been used not for that ominous occasion, but for the first. Again, since the play opposes Alcibiades' Fascist virility to the effete capitalism and peculiarly *civic* values and legalism of the ruling powers—the conflict in respect to justice at III. v., corresponding to the conflict in Stephen Spender's *Trial of a Judge*—the dressing of the chief senator in *uniform* was disturbing.

Nevertheless, the manipulation of the play's first half was often ingenious. John Colicos' reading of Timon as a young man rendered Timon's foolish generosity not only convincing but charming; and though there is no evidence for youth in Shakespeare's text, the many reworkings of the theme that followed in the eighteenth and nineteenth century had, significantly, young heroes. In these scenes the poise, conviction and charm of Mr. Colicos' acting were superb; and when the change comes, his ironic grace in the second Banquet had a quiet sarcasm of transfixing quality.[1]

The drama's second half lacked atmosphere and weight. Timon, on a bare stage with no properties or visual support, had to carry these long and difficult sequences alone. His costume, tattered trousers and shirt, helped little, and when the shirt was later removed no particular effect of make-up or lights was devised to render his stature Promethean. The rusty earth-soiled caskets for

---

[1] Compare with my comments John Pettigrew, 'Stratford 1963', *Queen's Quarterly* (Canada), LXX, 3; Autumn, 1963.

the treasure, though an improvement on the tinkling coins sometimes used and in their own way effective, were nevertheless
inadequate to the 'yellow, glittering, precious gold' (IV. iii. 26) of
Shakespeare's poetry, which had to be imagined as inside the
caskets and might, especially for so large and encircling an auditorium, have been better embodied by nuggets or ingots, lovely
to hold and address. The supposed locations of city, cave and sea
were not sufficiently clarified. If, as I understand, the sea was supposed to exist down-stage, the audience did not easily receive that
impression. This would moreover mean that the ultimate mystery
of Timon's Nirvana was already among or beneath the audience,
and such an identification is psychologically and theatrically of
dubious relevance, if not impossible. Something might conceivably have been done by the sound of surf coming from the
two down-stage tunnel entrances below the audience; or from
around and behind the audience, as though they were already
within the other dimension; but we had no surf. There was
occasional, very faint, music, but its effect was nugatory. There
was accordingly nothing but the words to suffuse the action with
mystery.

Despite such objections, these appallingly difficult last scenes
held their large and enthusiastic audiences spellbound. The result
was gained by the power of Shakespeare's text and the fine speaking and vivid facial expression of John Colicos, though for one
important sequence at least only a part of the auditorium could
receive what was being offered. In movement Colicos was, to my
mind, too agile; he did not project—and by acting alone on a bare
open stage under a straight lighting perhaps no one could have
projected—the cosmic and prophetic grandeur I myself look for,
and which alone makes Timon, like Sophocles' Oedipus in the
Oedipus Coloneus, a magical power able to redeem his country from
destruction.[1] Even so, the production was a success. Professor
Moelwyn Merchant, who was present at these seminars, directly
after witnessing it said that he regarded it in sweep and power as,

---

[1] I am aware that Timon may not appear to deserve such poetic honours. It can
be argued that his generosity was egocentric and his bitterness unbalanced. That
is probably how we should regard such a person in real life, if he can be imagined
apart from Shakespeare's context. But Shakespeare has laboured hard, in both
parts, to force us to see him differently; there may, if the play is unfinished, be a
discrepancy awaiting the revision that never matured. My own course has always
been to preserve truth to the main structure, fitting in details accordingly.

together with George Devine's *King Lear* (p. 261), one of the most impressive Shakespearian productions in his experience. Mr. Langham had had to take over the production at short notice. The result was an impressive achievement.

The two parts of *Timon of Athens* correspond respectively to Nietzsche's two principles, Apollonian and Dionysian. Now whereas the first indoor scenes lent themselves readily to the Stratford presentation, the *wild* setting of the second part was paradoxically less easily realized on an *open* stage. We have yet another paradox: the long fight starting with Poel and carried on by Barker for respect to Shakespeare's text joined to a rejection of spectacle has culminated in the open stage of today whose chief danger is the dispersal and loss of words and whose chief virtue is, once again, spectacle; for its finest effects are visual, made by human figures, elaborate costume and fine properties in magnificent interplay. The only way to get our focus clear is to admit that the Poel-Barker tradition was, from the first, Apollonian; and so is the open stage; the Dionysian, as yet, appears to need the proscenium. That is the challenge. Can the open stage meet it? If it can, we may suppose that its success would be more valuable than any successes of the past. There is a certain facility about stage effects of the older sort, even when most entrancing, that arouses suspicion, especially when relying overmuch on elaborate lights. To generate power and atmosphere and an aura of spiritual meaning *opening other dimensions of existence* through the simple presence, motion, and speech of human forms on an open stage would be the final triumph. Is this possible?

It seems that in previous years Stratford has had no especial success in tragedy, though in the Histories and the Comedies, and perhaps most notably in *Love's Labour's Lost* in 1961 with Paul Scofield as an exquisite Armado—which I can well believe remembering his Lucio at the English Stratford in 1946—Michael Langham, whose mastery of the open stage is now generally recognized as brilliant, has achieved wonders. *Coriolanus* in 1961, in which Paul Scofield won golden opinions, was reputed a strong success; but *Coriolanus* is a peculiarly unatmospheric tragedy; it is coldly great, and lacks numinous overtones.

Certain improvements might be made in the theatre itself. At present the rather meaningless background edifice lacks dignity, and perhaps that is why I enjoyed *Timon of Athens* more from a seat as far round and behind as possible, where the open stage could be received *as* an open, almost an arena, stage without distraction, than from the front. However, for most of the auditorium the background inevitably exists. For a tragedy the comparatively small and queerly pointed portico and thin pillars are inadequate, diminishing the action. What is needed is mass, some structure more like a Greek palace front or Craig's lifting masses, devised, as he tells us (p. 224), to force the actor to measure up his acting to their height. The Stratford background lacks visual grandeur; some breaking at least of the neutral grey is needed. Authorities from Poel to Merchant never tire of reminding us that the Elizabethan stage was itself gaudy, just as Greek statuary and medieval cathedrals were originally vivid, if not lurid, in colour and the statues' eyes *alive*; whereas we, in a puritanical age, too readily allow our minds to castrate the great periods of art to suit our impoverished imaginations.

My criticisms may seem astringent. But my praise has been equal. Though I have regarded this stage's success as mainly visual, much of theatric art must always be visual, and success there is half the battle. Moreover, the visual success is here a success *in terms of the human form*; and that may be called a great advance, for the human form is the pivot of drama. What I miss is the inwardness and Dionysian essence; and if this cannot be so well projected under open conditions by scene and words and sound-effects as on the old stages, then it must be realized *through the acting*. Where the magical is explicit in stage action, as in *The Tempest*, which was done according to all reports with considerable success in 1962, the open stage may succeed; but in tragedy the numinous is not explicit, but suggested; we have to realize the supernatural in terms of the natural; and here a new responsibility falls on the actor. What appears to be needed is some new kind of Dionysian acting, the kind, as I have already suggested, towards which I myself seem to have been instinctively and often inefficiently aiming (pp. 287–8). It may be called 'old style', over-acting, 'ham'; and it may be called this by those not properly attuned when it is really nothing of the sort. What it is, or should be, is a newly conscious use of the whole man, limb and eye and voice, to express, under a skilful lighting, the inward and the spiritual; showing us, in Nietzschean phrase (*Thus Spake Zarathustra*, II. 13), 'power' becoming 'gracious' and condescending to the 'visible'; and that 'visible' will be, as in Nietzsche, the human form. For Shakespeare, we may, in so far as we use an open stage, have to rely more on action than on the words, the text; together with, whenever relevant, sound effects coming from all *around* the auditorium; and it may be that such stages will finally realize their full potentialities only in terms of some less literary drama than Shakespeare's, such as Craig desired, which can as yet be only dimly apprehended.

For us today there appears to be no exclusive 'right' manner of producing Shakespeare, but rather, in view of his unplumbed depths and manifold radiations, which exist for us as a tangle of riches beyond anything his contemporaries surveyed, we do well to admit that advantages may attend all, provided always that we preserve loyalty to the deepest Shakespearian insights of which we are capable.

Additional Note, 1964

It is excellent news that the Festival Company plans to bring a freshly devised production of *Timon of Athens* to Chichester this spring.

The *Agamemnon* of Aeschylus

M y first production at Leeds was the *Agamemnon* of
Aeschylus, in the translation of Louis MacNeice, done
for the Leeds University Union Theatre Group, then
under the Presidency of Professor Bonamy Dobrée, in 1946.
Since the problems raised by the intermingling of rhetoric and
colloquialism in the long chorus pieces of the drama's first movement may be related to our discussions (pp. 275–7) of this same
intermingling, which T. S. Eliot once observed as a main Elizabethan characteristic ('Seneca in Elizabethan Translation', II),
in Shakespeare, a brief account of the production may be of
interest.

During some preliminary discussion two points were raised
which are worth recording. These were, that the Watchman on
the housetop who speaks first constitutes a difficulty in set-design;
and that the use of masks might be a good idea.

For the first. It is a dangerous but not unusual error to let a
single incident control the design of a permanent set. I have seen
a permanent setting for *Antony and Cleopatra* arranged in such a
way that the quite unimportant hoisting up of Antony at his death
should be effective, though the visual result was of no significance
till then. The Watchman is perfectly well placed on the palace
steps. Picked out by lights, and with no known referentials to
indicate his height, he can deliver his lines to full effect. As for
the masks, such attempts to strike an archaeological note would
be in any case useless without the original Greek surroundings
and climate, the vast open theatre, and so on. Besides, the principle involved is wrong. What is wanted today is a better use of
facial and bodily expression than is usual, not a muffling; faces

are too often muffled as it is by their own mask-like dullness. Moreover, our tendency should be towards a freer use of the physical than is usual, not towards the obscuring of what is normally revealed.

We used a Mycenean setting to tone with the drama's barbaric and Dionysian quality, using two dark pillars widening to the top to give us a palace front of ominous impact. A white or grey edifice would have been less suitable. Classic architecture is so widespread that it holds no overtones of mystery: it is so easy to think oneself in Cheltenham. Besides, the effect is rather Apollonian than Dionysian, and that is not helpful for Aeschylus, though for Sophocles our choice might be different. We had costumes of a more or less Mycenean design using effects of naked shoulders, or for a slave more than that, to build a sense of the barbaric.

The palace door was central between the pillars; steps led down, and the main stage had a central platform and two more levels; there were also *two small fore-stages, on a yet lower level, at either side of the proscenium, so that when they were used the drama widened out.* The auditorium of the Riley Smith Hall at Leeds extends too far on either side of the proscenium for intimacy, and this widening out of our stage did much to remedy the fault. It has two down-stage porticos which made entrances on to the fore-stages easy.

The suggestion of a palace front at one side of the stage was ruled out. The Chorus would lose power. Whether in an ancient or in a modern production its function is to act between audience and actors. When other characters were on the stage it was placed down-stage at the wings and on the fore-stages, widening out on both sides.

Aeschylus' use of the chorus in the *Agamemnon* is unique and presents unique problems in staging. The first third of the play is nearly all chorus, serving as a kind of vast prologue to the trilogy of which the *Agamemnon* is the beginning. These early choric passages constitute probing commentaries of considerable power, but also of considerable obscurity to a modern audience. They discuss the background of mysterious evil impinging on the House of Atreus, and the various rights and wrongs, hereditary, personal, civic and international, from which the action develops. It was necessary that the Chorus should, if only because there is so much of it, be dramatically exciting, even if not fully understood; and that meant working out manifold variations in speech and action to give stage impact to the meanings. The producer must study the text's meanings in detail; the audience is to receive, not these meanings intellectually apprehended, but their stage embodiment. Here we have a peculiarly vivid example of a general principle.

Our chorus was composed of six men and six women. Lines were allotted to separate persons according to their voices and speaking in unison was rare, though much was made of crowd repetitions and crowd murmurs. In MacNeice's translation the speeches divide fairly easily into the colloquial and the formal. The former were given to the men who expressed the communal power of crowd reaction, and the latter to the women who expressed the other, numinous and Sibylline, power of foreboding. The division was in alignment with the nature of poetic, and especially Shakespearian, drama, depending as it did on the interweaving of the colloquial and the formal. We had continual movement. The one group would be central, the other either behind or more usually outfurling down to the side fore-stages, three on either side; and then the men and women would change position, their every movement however appearing to come naturally and being designed not merely to chime with, but also to help interpret, the text. The men, but not the women, carried sticks or staves and acted with burly realism; the women acted in a more stylized fashion. But the former on occasion worked up to a semi-stylized unity of action and voice, and the latter used muted conversation. The men acted freely and individually, and the women sometimes used mime, those of them not speaking miming the speaker's words. Much of the effect for both groups depended on the way speeches were split up among appropriate voices, a single sentence being often made to leap, as it were, from one side to the other of the stage by being divided between two or more speakers at a distance.

This was my arrangement for the early choruses. The six men enter on the main stage, starting 'The tenth year it is . . .' The speeches are at first so divided that each has a few lines. Changes occurred at: 'Their hearts howling', 'But above there is One', 'Many the dog-tired', 'Things are what they are', 'For the marrow', 'While the man'. During this, they move about, variously; any murmurs, laughs, or repetitions that are helpful can be used.

Appendix A

Now the six women enter up-stage of the men who are *grouped towards the wings*, and, half-addressing the palace, speak the words from 'But you, daughter of Tyndareus' to 'eating away our hearts'. Sentences can be split. At 'From here, from there, all sides, all corners', the four pieces can go to different persons, but the supplication 'Of these things tell' is spoken by all, at least down to 'trouble', though the last lines are better with one or two voices only. The women are now looking up-stage, directly addressing the palace.

The men eagerly interrupt, offering answers. They take central positions down-stage and in front of the women. One, my 'No. 4' man, spoke from 'Of the omen' to 'angry birds'. Then followed some rapid-fire interruptions, as follows. I give the men's numbers from my prompt script:

> 5: Kings of the birds to our kings came,
> 6: One with a white rump, the other black,
> 5: Appearing near the palace on the spear-arm side
> 4: Where all could see them,
> 1: Tearing a pregnant hare with the unborn young,
> Men: Foiled of their courses.
> Women: Cry, cry upon Death—1, 2, 3 (Men): but may the good prevail.

Next a long sequence was given to 2, until the second 'Cry, cry upon Death; but may the good prevail', spoken by the six men. The third and last time it was spoken by the whole company.

The men's acting was realistic, as of a crowd of people. The lines were allotted nevertheless with exact care as to their voices, deep or light. A woman speaks the quoted passage 'But though you are so kind, goddess' down to 'forgetting its due'. Then a man speaks. Men shake their heads at 'evil and good together'. These last speeches were given with the women in a line up-stage and the men in two groups of three in front down-stage and widening out a little, but all still on the main stage. In the prayer to Zeus all come close, making a circular group, as round an altar. After it the men stump down to the two small fore-stages far right and left, three to each, muttering, as they move, about the law 'that men must learn by suffering', shaking their heads, speaking in turn, being platitudinously wise.

This leaves the women alone on the main stage for the long passage, starting 'So at that time . . .' After the men's doubtful mumblings the women sound a clearer note, reminding us of wrongs and evils, here the wrong of Iphigenia's sacrifice. Changes of voice occurred at 'For unable to sail', 'But the winds that blew from the Strymon', 'Then the elder king', 'But when he had put on the halter of Necessity', 'Her prayers and her cries of father', 'Then dropping on the ground her saffron dress'. At 'the third libation' the men start to move up from the fore-stages, so leaving free passages for the women to come there during *their* platitudinous, but more formally delivered, lines, divided among them variously, from 'The sequel to this' down to 'the shining of the dawn'. At Clytemnestra's entry the men are on the main stage to meet and talk to her and the women on the two fore-stages. Clytemnestra tells them of Agamemnon's victory. The war is over.

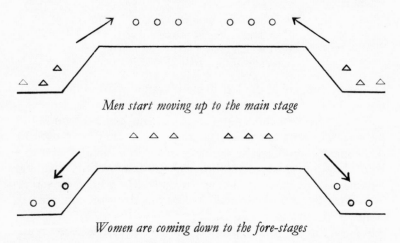

Men start moving up to the main stage

Women are coming down to the fore-stages

Movements of the Chorus following 'The hymn for happiness at the third libation' and leading up to Clytemnestra's entry.

After Clytemnestra's exit we have another long chorus, in which the men show a repellent complacency, attributing the victory to Zeus:

> This at least can be established,
> They have fared according to his ruling.

When one of them observes how foolishly some deny that providence punishes wickedness, a new voice breaks in with 'It is the impious man says this . . .' When someone says 'Measure is the best' there are murmurs of approval, 'Ay, ay'. Great excitement is registered at

> Who makes such things his practice
> The gods destroy him.

Murmurs repeat angrily, 'Yes, destroy him'. The men's talk should arouse a sense of the provisionality and superficiality of their triumph.

Now the women take over. The four lines 'This way came Paris' to 'stealing the wife of his host' were spoken by the men, moving down to the sides, and then repeated by the women, who again take the central position. The women speak allotted sections in separate single voices, down to the lines on the bereavement of women:

> For those they sent to war
> They know, but in place of men
> That which comes home to them
> Is merely an urn and ashes.

Others accompanied the last line with appropriate action, pointing to the earth.

Now comes our third movement, driving home the futility of the war. The men are no longer triumphant. They are caught by the women's mood. At the women's words 'But for another man's wife' they murmur; at 'muffled and muttered words' they are looking half up-stage, and threaten the palace with their staves. They face it more deliberately, repeating the women's phrases 'sons of Atreus' and 'Trojan ground', in anger. All are now moving up to the palace, backs to the audience, in a close group. A man's voice, the figure sideways, half facing up-stage, threatens

> Heavy is the murmur of an angry people
> Performing the purpose of a public curse.

A woman on the palace steps, facing across, cries

> There is something cowled in the night . . .

A woman is still speaking at

> the black
> Furies in time
> When a man prospers in sin

but the whole company, men and women, now come in with terrifying volume, while all turn to the audience, faces flashing out and gestures strong with uplifted arms and staves, for

By erosion of life reduce him to darkness.

That is our climax, 'darkness' being spoken with explosive force. We cut from 'Who, once among the lost can no more be helped', following on with two resounding, but not shouted, concluding sentences, spoken by men. One says, deeply, 'Over-great glory is a sore burden' and the other more resonantly: 'The high peak is blasted by the eyes of Zeus'. This was our curtain line, on a rising note. Aeschylus' long movement, for there is a unity as of a single 'act' running through it all, received in this way a fitting modern exposition. The concentration has been severe and tiring, and an interval is needed.

There has been little speaking in unison. I was asked what I was doing for what the Greeks called their choric 'dance', the word covering formal procession and movement. But there was little need of any specialized technique. The action was made to grow naturally from the living text, and an unspecialized know-ledge of movement and gesture was enough. Reliance was placed on the performers' varied voices in mutual interplay with each other and with stage movement. Speaking in unison was left mainly for repetition of something already said, or for words that could not suffer by it. These choruses are of a peculiar kind, and build a dramatic atmosphere from many precise details and con-trasts which, though their intellectual content may not be fully received by the audience, must be adequately, and that means excitingly, projected. Groups of people chanting together, what-ever they may be saying, convey as a rule no more than a general sense of groups of people chanting together. Instead of that we generated an electrical atmosphere.

The remaining action was easier, being more ordinarily dramatic. The chorus men were grouped on the main stage, sometimes four on one side and two on the other. The women, used for appropriate speeches, entered and left by the down-stage porticos on to the two fore-stages. When the chorus was alone we followed the principles already indicated.

Cassandra is a short part, but difficult. Her every speech is different: trance, clairvoyance, terror, pathos, lyricism, horror, denunciation, bitterness, fury, pride, resignation—never were such changes so compacted. The unique stage power and dramatic inclusiveness of her brief scene may be referred to its occult contacts. A similar power is found in the Ghost scenes of Hamlet: the dramatic essence and the occult are in close relation.

Agamemnon's important entry into his palace over a purple carpet demands care. The drape must first be held up so that everyone can see it, the action being accompanied by doubtful murmurs from the Chorus. His actual ascent cannot be too openly disapproved, or there is no glory; and yet acclamations would be wrong. We used a long fanfare, accompanied by deadly silence from the community. Afterwards Agamemnon's blood-stained body was shown through the doors naked but for the net, making a lurid cameo of horror and beauty.

An interesting problem arose concerning the talk and movements of Clytemnestra. After her crime she is up-stage talking exultantly to the men, drunk with the intoxication of murder. But soon after the chorus of women, on the fore-stages, attribute the deed to the household demon, and as her intoxication wears off Clytemnestra agrees. For her agreement she came down-stage, walking as in a trance, and standing frozen, speaking in a statuesque formality matching that of the women and the nature of the insight being recorded.

It is important to make sure of crowd-work, as when Clytemnestra and Aegisthus are threatened by the crowd at the end; their defence was arranged by the entry of a negro body-guard with bows and arrows. There is a danger in leaving crowds to get right at the last moment; they need as much care as any individual performance, perhaps more, and exact rehearsal. The secret of production consists very largely in giving care to those matters which will not get right by nature and leaving to nature what will.

Since the *Agamemnon* is only the first part of a trilogy its action looks forward. Louis MacNeice composed for us a choric epilogue to round off the performance with some indication of what was to follow. We used only our six women on the main stage. I print the text as given us except for the numerals in brackets which indicate the voices actually used. Only the producer, who knows his people and their vocal qualities, can decide this. Here is the epilogue:

(1)	Omnes:	Milk and wine to the King's tomb.
(3)	First solo voice:	The Queen has dreamed an evil dream.
(1, 2, 3)	Omnes:	Against our will, against our will.
(4)	Second solo voice:	We bear peace-offerings to the dead.
(1, 2, 3)	Omnes:	O gaia Maia, Mother Earth!

(1)	First solo voice:	The Queen has dreamed an evil dream,
(2)	Second solo voice:	The Prophets warned her what it meant,
(6)	Third solo voice:	It meant a muttering in the grave—
(1, 2, 3)	Omnes:	O gaia Maia, Mother Earth—
(4, 5, 6)	Fourth solo voice:	The anger of a murdered man.

(1)	First solo voice:	She is alive and he is dead
(4)	Second solo voice:	But he is calling for his due
(5)	Third solo voice:	And she is hated by the Gods—
(4, 5, 6)	Omnes:	O gaia Maia, Mother Earth!
(1, 2, 3)	Fourth solo voice:	What can atone for fallen blood?

(6)	Omnes:	Milk and wine to the King's tomb—
(5)	First solo voice:	But how can milk or wine atone?
(3)	Omnes:	We bear peace-offerings to the dead—
(1)	Second solo voice:	But Agamemnon wants no peace.
(2)	Third solo voice:	The Queen may offer what she will—
(1, 2, 3)	Omnes:	O gaia Maia, Mother Earth—
(6)	Fourth solo voice:	Earth is stained—
(4, 5, 6)	Omnes:	The stain remains—
(3)	First solo voice:	Blood is shed—
(6)	Omnes:	And blood must flow—
(1)	Second solo voice:	Clytemnestra craves an end,
(4)	Third solo voice:	But milk and wine can bring no end,
(5)	Fourth solo voice:	Only blood can bring an end,
(All)	Omnes:	Only blood—
(5)	First solo voice:	Her own—
(All)	Omnes:	Her own!
(1)	First solo voice:	O gaia Maia, Mother Earth,
(2)	Second solo voice:	Here we pour libations now,
(1, 2, 3)	Omnes:	Milk and wine on the King's tomb,
(5)	Third solo voice:	But well we know,
(4, 5, 6)	Omnes:	Well we know,
(6)	Fourth solo voice:	That this is not the end—
(4, 5, 6)	Omnes:	The end!

It may seem that a single voice was sometimes used where three or more would have been better; but I knew the actual voices and the effect gained was powerful. The withholding of all the voices until near the end had a peculiarly strong impact following our usual principle of *gathering* power, the climax coming on 'Only blood' and 'Her own'. After that the words were more quiet, but firm, and emphatically and deliberately drawn out with pauses at 'Well—we—know'. Throughout vivid tonal contrasts were used, rising for lilting questions and deep for such words as 'The anger of a murdered man'. This brilliantly devised epilogue made a perfect conclusion.

APPENDIX B

John Gabriel Borkman

A recent production of *John Gabriel Borkman* at the Duchess Theatre, which I witnessed on its first performance (4 December 1963), suffered gravely from the contemporary blindness to the positive thrust of high tragedy. In his first scene Sir Donald Wolfit's Borkman was faultless. He, in all potentials our greatest living actor, should have been—he is—the ideal Borkman. But in conception, setting, emphasis and movement the production, directed by Mr. David Ross, showed serious limitations.

Acts I and II are mainly retrospective. Act III concentrates on the present and on *decisions*. Here a new tension must be aroused and maintained. As Erhart and Mrs. Willett face Mr. and Mrs. Borkman, youth's simple life-desires oppose the astringent ideals of Borkman and his wife. The two parties should be positionally and sharply defined, Ella linking them, and the conflict vivid. Ibsen's purpose can be assisted if our natural sympathies with youth are countered by having Erhart look a temporarily assertive, life-inspired, weakling in contrast to the spiritual giants; for they are that. A great issue is at stake: whether the more-than-biological values—for both Borkman's aspiring will to power and his wife's will to ethical and social redemption have this quality—

shall be shouldered or rejected by the new generation. Much is involved in Erhart's only too understandable decision for life as sensuous ease: this 'much' must be driven home, electrically.

Borkman's sudden decision to *go out* is a fearful climax. Ella struggles with him, he hurls her from him, violent: Ibsen's directions are clear. It is a decision to leave the prison of normal existence for an undefined freedom; in effect, death. Borkman is on a Timon quest, and his decision must strike terror.

Act IV concentrates on futurity. The now fierce action is delayed by Foldal's hampering talk; but after its purpose as defining the trivial and half-comic goodness that Borkman transcends is fulfilled, Borkman himself strides on, and up, breasting the elements. Though he is physically failing in the bitter air, a spirit-strength breathes through, rendering him gigantic. I should have him stagger, all but fall, but keep on. The scene grows 'wilder and wilder'. On the heights the Vision opens, of fiord and 'high' ranges in the distance, 'towering one above the other'. This is Borkman's miraculous 'kingdom', seen though not possessed, and it should flood the stage:

> They soar, they tower aloft, one behind the other! That is
> my vast, my infinite, inexhaustible kingdom!

The words resound a triumph. To this cosmic and lifting magnitude Borkman utters his mighty love-song, not to Ella. He and It are right partners and co-equals, Ella subsidiary; though her place as exponent of human love is assured. As I have shown in my *Ibsen* (1962), Borkman dies *happy*, by the hand of the metallic powers which he has loved.

On details I cannot, from memory of a past performance, be sure. But I would ask—How much of all this did we receive? What sense of a steady *increase* in Borkman's stature? He was, in fact, strongest in his first scene, and thereafter declined.

The settings were throughout inadequate. At the start neither the snow without nor the faded splendour within were properly realized. None of the settings supported the action. It is enough to record that *the great mountain ranges to which Borkman is directed by Ibsen to hold out his arms were not there*. Borkman's visionary speech was spoken on a bare stage, inwardly, as by a broken man, to the audience. The vision came across as no more than a subjective delusion.

Ibsen's directions are as much a part of his text as Shakespeare's poetry. They *are* his poetry. So, despite skilled acting by Sir Donald and the supporting cast, the production itself was to Ibsen's central purpose blind. It showed us little more than a series of retrospective dialogues leading to the painful collapse of a deluded dreamer. The visionary conclusion is, paradoxically, central; it is what the whole labouring drama is *for*; and with this understanding must it be acted. Today we fear over-acting. That generally means simply this: that we have not sufficient inward confidence to know at what exact moment to let out all the stops. So, for safety, we muffle the lot.

It is symptomatic of our twi-lit culture that the B.B.C. Critics, while being aware of, and deeply troubled by, a lack, yet showed no insight into what was wrong.

Sometimes, in meditating on our present culture in all its intellectual brilliance and spiritual opacity, and in particular on its approach to tragedy, I am reminded of those deadly words in *The Tempest*:

> Antonio: He misses not much.
> Sebastian: No. He doth but mistake the truth totally.

The riposte is worthy of a wider, and better, context than Shakespeare has given it.

Without vision our theatre perishes.

APPENDIX C

Appreciations

<hr />

From a Notice of
THIS SCEPTRED ISLE
(Westminster Theatre, London)
in *The Times* of 23 July 1941

In the second, and most ambitious, part of his programme Mr. Knight has the assistance of Mr. Henry Ainley, who speaks in that magnificent voice of his the commentaries before and after the scenes.[1]

The competition is indeed severe, and it says much for Mr. Knight's delivery and the persuasion of his acting that he can immediately follow Mr. Ainley and avoid a sense of anti-climax. His methods are simple and illuminating. He appears before the curtain, gives an informal, yet informative, lecture on the speech he is about to deliver and then, rather as if a magic lantern lecturer should turn himself into one of his own slides, launches into the speech itself.

In the opening part Mr. Knight contents himself with putting Richard and Henry into modern uniform and dispensing with scenery and make-up, but in the three scenes from *Timon of Athens* he has the paraphernalia of a full production. In gesture and movement he may not be the complete actor, but he has the voice and the range of one, and there was no trace of the platform manner in his expression of emotion. He shows his scholarship in his attack on character—his Timon and his Hamlet are specially good—as well as in his comments, and, indeed, the whole unusual production firmly establishes his conception of Shakespeare as the poet and prophet of a free and virile people united under a benevolent monarchy and determined to fight in themselves the evils of greed and corruption and to take up arms against tyranny and the lust for power in others.

A facsimile of the programme appears on page 314.

Mr. Roy Walker
on the three productions of
TIMON OF ATHENS
in *New Theatre*, February 1949 (V, 8)[2]

In 1940, when Wilson Knight was Chancellors' Professor of English at Trinity College, Toronto, he produced and acted in

---

[1] Henry Ainley also spoke the introductory lines from *King John* and the concluding prayer (which should have been further to the left in my programme).

My acknowledgment to Miss Margot Davies has already (pp. 14–15) been recorded. I here add the name of Miss Antoinette Pratt-Barlow, who was our stage-manager. Henry Ainley's kindness remains a treasured memory.

A notice by Mr. Ivor Brown, based on a rehearsal, appeared in *The Observer*, 20 July 1941.

[2] See also my reference on p. 288 above, note.

This Sceptred Isle

PART I.—"ST. GEORGE FOR ENGLAND"

Faulconbridge's lines from the conclusion of "King John"

John of Gaunt's speech on England from "Richard II"

Richard III before the battle of Bosworth

Henry V before and during the battle of Agincourt

(INTERVAL OF TEN MINUTES)

PART II.—PATRIOTISM IS NOT ENOUGH

Two Soliloquies from "Hamlet"

Macbeth's vision of Great Britain's expanding royalty

Three scenes from "Timon of Athens," showing Timon's meeting with—

    (1) Alcibiades and his army

    (2) Some bandits

    (3) The Senators of Athens.

(INTERVAL OF FIVE MINUTES)

PART III.—THE ROYAL PHOENIX

From "Henry VIII" :

Buckingham's farewell

Cranmer's prophecy

Queen Elizabeth's Prayer before the Armada

WESTMINSTER THEATRE

PALACE STREET, S.W.I   Near Victoria Station

Licensed by the Lord Chamberlain to   ...   ...   A. B. HORNE

FOR A SHORT SEASON ONLY

THIS SCEPTRED ISLE

Under the distinguished patronage of

The Rt. Hon. LORD QUEENBOROUGH, G.B.E.

(President of the Royal Society of St. George)

and

SIR ARCHIBALD FLOWER

(Chairman of the Council of the Shakespeare Memorial Theatre, Stratford-on-Avon ; and Chairman of the Trustees of the Birthplace of William Shakespeare)

G. WILSON KNIGHT'S

DRAMATISATION OF SHAKESPEARE'S CALL TO GREAT BRITAIN IN TIME OF WAR

WITH

HENRY AINLEY

a performance of *Timon of Athens* that was described by the Canadian critics as 'a phenomenal triumph of scholarship, dramatics, and audacity'. A year later he was back in England where he was already famous, if not notorious, for a series of brilliantly imaginative critical studies of Shakespeare and other poets, beginning with *The Wheel of Fire*. At the Westminster Theatre in July, 1941, he staged his own Shakespearean symposium, *This Sceptred Isle*, and *The Times* noted that 'his Timon and his Hamlet are specially good . . . the whole unusual production firmly establishes his conception'.

A more experimental theatre than ours in London—credit for recent revivals of the rarer Shakespeare plays goes to Stratford, Birmingham, the B.B.C. and Mr. Wolfit's touring repertory, not to the Old Vic or any other London company—might have taken the hint long ago. But *Timon* is generally considered to be a work of divided authorship, and is certainly uneven. On a hasty reading, its theme and treatment seem unlikely to 'take'. A not unfair plot-summary would be: Act I—prodigal good fellowship, Act II—coffers empty, Act III—would-be borrower repulsed, Act IV—he renounces mankind, Act V—death in the wilderness.

What star would see himself in that? What producer would be sanguine about a run, or even reasonable notices? 'All too bitter and gloomy, and we've quite enough of that outside the theatre today. People want to be cheered up'—a view-point that overlooks, as our theatre too often does, that the whole function of serious drama is, as Hamlet defines it, to hold the mirror up to nature, to interpret our condition not run away from it.

Yorkshire was as sceptical beforehand as Toronto or London. 'Is this play good enough for the University?' demanded the *Yorkshire Post*, and took leave to doubt that it was. Wilson Knight, now in the English Department of Leeds University, was repeating his Canadian adventure. With the same result. After his critic's first night report of 'notable success', the Editor came himself, and then reprinted his mournful caption, 'Is this play good enough for the University?' and answered, 'Last night I saw the performance. It changed my mind.' The question now is, 'Is this play good enough for London?' If the Old Vic is going to return to its fine tradition of courageous experiment, there is only one answer. If not, here is opportunity indeed for the Mercury, the Arts Theatre or the Embassy to add to their laurels.

Appendix C

Wilson Knight's strength lies in his being as much a man of the theatre as of the study. There must be times when both scholars and actors fear, despite all good intentions, that never the twain shall meet. The scholar follows literary and historical associations past the bounds of dramatic effect, the actor seizes dramatic opportunities with little regard for underlying meanings and the total poetic design. As Tennyson wrote of Macready, 'Our Shakespeare's bland and universal eye dwells pleased' on the marriage of scholarship and stage as glimpsed at Leeds. Here at last was a theatre for the poets 'who made a nation purer through their art'.

An earlier work, *Principles of Shakespearian Production*, which records some personal experience in acting and producing the major tragedies, is to be republished (Penguins) with a further discussion of the performer's task in poetic drama. Judging by the Leeds production of *Timon*, it should be of first-class importance. When the storm breaks in Stratford and London (as it must sooner or later) over the 'modernized' delivery of great poetry that blunts and obscures the essential imaginative significances in the supposed interests of 'the facts', or of realism, credibility, characterization or pace, such a synthesis of eye and tongue as Wilson Knight offers will be desperately needed.

From Mr. Robin Skelton's
commentary on Wilson Knight's work at Leeds
in *The Yorkshire Post*, 24 May 1962

The grip upon the texture and pattern of each play was sure; the understanding of the characters was subtle; but, above all, the productions and the portrayals[1] were heroically theatrical. Poetry remained poetry and enlarged itself with gesture. Action was always significant. The plays, one felt, had been given their own shapes at last.

Acknowledgment

For permission to reprint the material of this appendix gratitude is expressed to *The Times*, Mr. Roy Walker, Mr. Robin Skelton, and *The Yorkshire Post*.

[1] 'Production' refers to the *Agamemnon*, *Athalie* and *Timon of Athens*; 'portrayals' to Timon, Lear, Othello and Shylock. For these, which had been noted by Mr. Skelton earlier in the article, see p. 15 above.

Index

No distinction is made between references to the main text and those which apply to the notes.

⋙≼≼≼≼≾≽⋙⋙≫≫≫

A. SHAKESPEARIAN WORKS

Index

B. GENERAL

Index

Index

Medwin, Thomas: 100
Merchant, W. Moelwyn: 18, 201, 234, 259, **261-2**, 279, 297-9
Mercury Theatre: 317
Milton, John:
  Samson Agonistes: 170
  Paradise Lost: 170, 192-3, 211, 282
Moiseiwitsch, Tanya: 271, 285, 291
Moszkowski, M.: 174
Monck, Nugent: 23. See also Maddermarket Theatre:
Monsieur Beaucaire: 202
Moore, Dora Mavor: 16
Morris, Sir Charles: 15
Morris, Lady: 15
Morton, Robert A., 205
Moscow Art Theatre: 232
Muir, Kenneth: 15
Murphy, Patricia: 17. *Picture 7 (also the Angel standing before the Queen in 10)*
Murray, Brian: 266
Murray, Gilbert: 231
Murray, John: 198
Murry, J. Middleton: 101, 116
My Fair Lady: 208

Nash, George W.: 18
Nathan, A. J.: 17-18, 200
Nathan, L. & H.: 18
National Film Archive, The: 18
National Theatre, The: 290
National Union of Students, The: 172, 276
Neilson-Terry, Dennis: 22
New Testament, The: 40-1, 155, 157
New Theatre: 243
New Theatre (periodical): 316
Nicoll, Allardyce: 180
Nietzsche, Friedrich: 166, 168, 240, 253, 266, 298
  The Birth of Tragedy: 146, 292-3
  Thus Spake Zarathustra: 299-300
Noguchi, Isamu: 262
Norwood, Gilbert: 47

Observer, The: 16, 314
O'Casey, Sean: *The Plough and the Stars:* 69
Old Testament, The: 192
Old Vic, The: 23, 187, 226, 243, 259, 260, 262, 272, 316-17
Oliver: 208
Olivier, Sir Laurence: **243-9**, 255, 264, **269**
O'Neill, Eugene:
  The Emperor Jones: 103, 169, 171
Orczy, Baroness:
  The Scarlet Pimpernel: 202
O'Toole, Peter: 262
Ottawa Drama League: 85

Parker, Leonard: 14, 79
Parker, Louis N.: 203, 205, 207
Patterson, Tom: 291
Paul, St.: 104, 169
Pearson, Hesketh: 18, 200, 202, 204-8, 217, 231-2, **235-6**, 237
Peisley, Frederick: 253
Petrarch: 103
Pettigrew, John: 296
Phelps, Samuel: 216
Phillips, Stephen: 210
  Nero: 236
  Ulysses: 214
Photo-General, Leeds: 18
Pittar, B. A.: 24
Planché, J. R.: 234
Playfair, Lyon: 14
Playfair, Sir Nigel: 14
Playfair, Lady: 14
Playter, Ruth: 16
Plowman, Max: 128
Poel, William: 22, **120**, 200, 202, **208**, 210, 214, **216-18**, **224-5**, 228, **233-5**, 237, 271, 287-8, 291, 298-9
Pope, Alexander:
  The Rape of the Lock: 101
Potter, Paul M. (adapter of du Maurier's *Trilby*): 202
Powys, John Cowper, 209, 221
Pratt-Barlow, Antoinette: 314
Price, Nancy: 14
Prince of Wales's Theatre: 218
Provençal Troubadours: 103
Purcell, Henry:
  Dido and Aeneas: 219
Purdom, C. B.: 16, 18, 23-4, 200, 224-5, **227, 282**, 286

Queenborough, Lord: 16 (as Patron), 315
Queen's Quarterly: 296

Racine, Jean: 15
  Athalie: 15, 318
  Phèdre: 239
Railton, Roscoe: 23
Rain, Douglas: 296
Redgrave, Sir Michael: 260-2
Reinhardt, Max: 269, 286
Review of English Literature, A: 18, 166, 182
Richardson, Tony: 259
Roberts, Edward: 16, 164. *Picture 7*
Robeson, Paul: 104
Rogers, Paul: 260
Romantic dramatists, The: 172, 180, 186
Rose, Enid: 200, 232
Ross, David: 311
Rostance, Frances: *Picture 10*
Rostance, A. J.: 164
Rotherstein: see Rutherston:

Index

Royal Academy of Dramatic Art: 201, 231
Royal Shakespeare Company:
see Shakespeare Memorial Theatre:
Royal Society of St. George: 315
Rudolf Steiner Hall: 23, 105
Rutherston, Albert: 224

Salvini, Tommaso: 229, 287–8
Sanborn, Robin: 285
Sauerbrei, Revd. Claude: 18
Saul, Patrick: 18
Savoy Theatre, The: 224–5, 227, 237, 276, 290
Schaeffer, George: 270
Scofield, Paul: 256, 264, 298
Scott, Clement: 235
Scrutiny: 79
Seale, Douglas: 260, 272
Seneca: 28
Shakespeare Memorial Library (Birmingham): 14, 15, 278
Shakespeare Memorial Theatre, now The Royal Shakespeare Theatre, Stratford, England: 22–3, 79, 170, 218, 250, 255–67, 271, 277, 290, 298, 315–17
Shakespeare Quarterly (U.S.A.): 291
Shakespeare Society, The British Empire: see British, etc.
Shakespeare Society of Toronto: 13–14, 23, 79
Shakespeare Survey: 262, 291
Sharp, Cecil: 224
Shaw, Bernard: 202–8, 217, **226**, 229, 230–1
Pygmalion: 203, 208
Saint Joan: 15
Shaw, Stuart: *Picture 22*
Sheffield Educational Establishment: 16
Shelden, William: *Picture 7*
Shelley, P. B.: 28
Defence of Poetry: 281–2
Prometheus Unbound: 169–71
The Revolt of Islam: 171
Sherriff, R. C.:
Journey's End: 31, 100
Skelton, Robin, 16, 318
Skillan, George: 277
Smith, W. Lyndon: 17. *Picture 14*
Smyth, George: *Picture 26*
Sophocles: 158, 302
Oedipus Coloneus: 184, 186, 198, 297
Southern, Richard: 272, 286
Speaight, Robert: 19, 22, 120, 200, 216–218, 225, 231, 234, 271–2
Spender, Stephen:
Trial of a Judge: 296
Spurgeon, Caroline: 210
Squire, Sir J. C.: *Berkeley Square:* 74

Stanislavsky, Konstantin S.: 220, 232
Steiner, Rudolf: 238
Still, Colin: 156, 211
Stowe School: 15, 17, 143, 274
Stratford, England:
see Shakespeare Memorial Theatre, etc.
Stratford Festival Theatre:
Stratford Ontario, Canada: 14, 259, 284–5, 289, **291–300**
Sully, Mounet: 287

Tavistock Theatre: 14
Tchehov: see Chekhov:
Tennyson, Lord: 317
The Passing of Arthur: 106
Terry, Fred: 202
Thackeray, W. M.: 202, 204
This Sceptred Isle: **14–15**, 16, 23, 172, 178, **314–16**
Tillott, Peter: 172
Times, The: 16, 215, 220, 314, 318
Times Literary Supplement, The: 213–14, 259, 267
Tolhurst, Frances: 13
Tolstoy, Leo: 201–2
Toronto, The University of: 13–16, 23, 316
Tree, Sir Herbert Beerbohm: 14, 16–19, 21–2, 51, **200–18**, 220, **225**, **227–37**, **240**, **274–5**, 287–9. *Pictures 23, 24, 25*
Nothing Matters: 200–2, 240
Thoughts and After-Thoughts: 200–1, 204, 207–11, 228–9, 232, 234, 237
Tree, Iris: 204, 206, 232
Tree, Lady (Maud): 203, 206, 209
Tree, Viola: 207, 209, 231
Trench, Herbert: 202
Trinity College, Toronto: 15, 23, 313
Tuckwell, C. A. P.: 23
Typhoon: 22

University of Leeds Review, The: 13

Valk, Frederick: 250
Vanbrugh, Violet: 14, 51
Varma, Devendra P.: 18. *Picture 31*
Vedrenne, J. E.: 219
Verdi, Guiseppe: 226
Victoria and Albert Museum: 18, 201

Wagner, Richard: 225, 228, 237, 255
Walker, Roy: 16, 142–3, 288, **316–18**
Waller, Lewis: 202
Walter, Wilfred: 170
Webb, Alan: 266
Webster, John:
The Duchess of Malfi: 104
Welles, Orson: 47
Westminster Theatre: 14, 172, 178, 314–16

322

C. SOME LEADING THEMES